PLATE I

THE WARLOCKS' METAMORPHOSIS
By Goya

THE WEREWOLF
IN LORE AND LEGEND

MONTAGUE SUMMERS

Intrabunt lupi rapaces in uos, non parcentes gregi.
ACTUS APOSTOLORUM, XX, 29.

DOVER PUBLICATIONS, INC.
MINEOLA, NEW YORK

Bibliographical Note

The Werewolf in Lore and Legend, first published in 2003, is an unabridged republication of the work originally published in 1933 by Kegan Paul, Trench, Trubner & Co., Ltd., London, under the title *The Werewolf.*

Library of Congress Cataloging-in-Publication Data

Summers, Montague, 1880-1948.
    [Werewolf]
    The werewolf in lore and legend / Montague Summers.
       p. cm.
    Originally published: The werewolf. London : K. Paul, Trench, Trubner, 1933.
    Includes bibliographical references and index.
    ISBN-13: 978-0-486-43090-4
    ISBN-10: 0-486-43090-1 (pbk.)
    1. Werewolves. I. Title.

GR830.W4S8 2003
398'.45—dc22

2003063519

Manufactured in the United States by LSC Communications
43090110   2020
www.doverpublications.com

CONTENTS

LIST OF ILLUSTRATIONS

INTRODUCTION

SOME three or four years ago when this present book, *The Werewolf*, which had long been planned, definitely began to take shape as a successor to my study, *The Vampire*, it was my original intention to include in the survey the were-tiger and the were-jaguar, the were-lion and were-leopards, the Abyssinian were-hyena, the were-fox and werewolves of China, and many more. I soon realized, however, that owing to the abundance of data it would prove quite impossible in one volume to travel outside Europe, that is to say, if the subject was to be treated in anything like adequate fashion. This led to a slight re-casting, and in some details a curtailment, of the first two chapters.

Owing to various circumstances I was unable to complete this book either as early or as speedily as I hoped, and during the delay, slight though it actually proved, I found notes and references had continued to grow and accumulate in such profusion that it was not merely a question of excluding four continents, but there had now arisen the necessity of making a very limited and by no means easy selection from the material entirely relevant and proper to the inquiry which I was pursuing, and yet difficult to comprise within the boundaries and bournes I had already somewhat rigidly set myself and to whose rules I straitly determined to confine my ambit.

In consequence I cannot but be very well aware that my chapter on France, my final chapter, and my note on the Werewolf in Literature might be and without much labour considerably extended, nor has the temptation to do this often been absent. Indeed, I have constantly been obliged to remind myself pretty sharply *succincti quae sint bona libelli*.

Werewolfery is of itself a vast subject, and when we quite legitimately extend our pervestigation to shape-shifting and animal-metamorphosis in general the field is immense. It would have been only too simple a matter, if I had desired, to farse and bombast my notes with scores upon scores of further references, no mean quota of which might fairly have been argued to be, if unessential, at least not impertinent, but although such a shop-window display will impress the silly crowd, it is justly valued at its true worth by the scholar. πλέον ἥμισυ παντός, quoth Hesiod of old.

Although lycanthropy has incidentally been treated and more or less briefly referred to by many authors, the number of treatises which concentrate upon this important and world-ancient theme is actually very small. Towards the end of the sixteenth century and at the beginning of the seventeenth there may be distinguished four valuable studies, written it is to be noted from different points of view but all directly inspired by Jean Bodin's famous chapter, ii, 6, in the *Démonomanie des Sorciers*, 1580, which has rubric : " De la Lycanthropie & si les esprits peuuent changer les hommes en bestes."

The first, and by far the best, of our mournival is the work of the learned Wolfeshusius, *De Lycanthropia . . . Pro sententia Ioan. Bodini Iurecos. Galli aduersus dissentaneas aliquorum opiniones nouiter assertum*, published at Leipzig, 8vo, 1591. Five years later, in 1596, the Franciscan Claude Prieur published his *Dialogue de la Lycanthropie*, which is full of interest and offers some valuable observations. A slighter thing is the *Discours de la lycanthropie* of the Sieur de Beauvois de Chauvincourt issued at Paris, 8vo, 1599. In 1615 Dr. Jean de Nynauld gave the world his *De la Lycanthropie, transformation, et extase des sorciers*, Paris, 8vo, Nicolas Rousset and Jean Millot. It may be remarked that at the present day these four treatises are pieces of the last rarity.

Throughout the seventeenth century lycanthropy and shape-shifting were the theme of many academic prolusions, such as the thesis maintained at Strasburg by Ambrosius Fabricius on 26th February, 1649, and printed the same year ; and the *De Lycanthropia* of Michael Mei published at Wittenberg, 4to, 1650. In the same category we reckon the *Disputatio contra Opliantriam, Lycantropiam et metempsychosim* of Konrad Ziegra, 4to, Wittenberg, 1650 ; the *De Lycanthropia* of Niphanius, 4to, Wittenberg, 1654 ; the *De Transformatione hominum in brutis* of Joannes Thomasius, Leipzig, 4to, 1667 ; the *De Transmutatione hominum in lupos* of Jakob Friedrich Müller, 4to, Leipzig, 1673 ; the

Therantropismus fictus of Johann Reinhardt, 4to, Wittenberg, 1673 ; the *De Lycanthropia* of Samuel Schelwig, 4to, Danzig, 1679 ; the *De Dubiis hominibus, in quibus forma humana et brutina mista fertur*, of Gottlieb Friedrich Seligmann, 4to, Leipzig, 1679 ; the *Dialogi und Gespräche von der Lycanthropia oder der Menschen in Wölff Verwandlung* of Theophilus Lauben, 12mo, Frankfort, 1686 ; and others of lesser note.

For the most part these monographs are content to refer to the same classical authorities and cite the same examples, traversing ground already sufficiently well trodden. They have not the original value of the pages of Chauvincourt and Claude Prieur, they are argued conventionally and scholastically, without conviction. The dons approached the problems of metamorphosis in dry zetetic mood ; they did not realize that werewolfery was a terrible and enduring fact.

In 1862 Dr. Wilhelm Hertz published his study, *Der Werwolf*, a careful survey which contains much that is of value. *The Book of Were-Wolves, Being an Account of a Terrible Superstition*, by the Rev. Sabine Baring-Gould, London, 1865, is now uncommon, and it is getting difficult to meet with a copy. Mr. Baring-Gould writes graphically and with vigour. I always read his work with pleasure if not with agreement, but I confess that the novelist peeps out of his pages a little too often. Moreover, he has intruded a great deal of extraneous matter. Thus he devotes no less than three chapters, eleven, twelve, and thirteen, to a highly romantic and not very accurate account of Gilles de Rais, who was a Satanist certainly, but not a werewolf. The story of the ghoul from Fra Giraldo (or Fornari) again is impertinent, and there are other irrelevancies as well as omissions. The " Natural Causes of Lycanthropy " and suggested " Mythological Origin " are unacceptable.

Mr. Elliott O'Donnell has brought together in his *Werwolves*, London, 1912, a number of interesting histories of lycanthropy from many quarters, but we approach this vast subject from such different points of view and treat it so variously that I do not think our pages will be found to overlap.

The very readable *Human Animals* of Miss Frank Hamel is widely comprehensive, and indeed touches upon many phenomena which (I feel) hardly fall within my province.

Although not in entire agreement with certain of the theories advanced by this lady, I find some at least of her suggested lines of thought very beautiful and as sincerely expressed. In essaying some explanation of the phenomena of were-wolfery, I approach these problems entirely from the theological and philosophical point of view, where alone the solution can lie. Far be it from me to seem in any way to depreciate or underreckon the valuable work which has been done by the anthropologists in collecting parallels from many countries and tracing significant rites and practice among primitive and distant folks, but they cannot read the riddle, and only too often have their guesses been far away from the truth. It could not be otherwise if they disregard the science of God for the science of man. Anthropology is the humblest handmaid of theology.

It may not be impertinent to remark upon the spelling *Werewolf* which I have adopted and use. Upon this point I think I cannot do better than quote the authority of the great *Oxford English Dictionary*. Both forms, *Werewolf* and *Werwolf*, are admissible without preference. "The first element has usually been identified with O.E. *wer* man . . . but the form *were-* in place of *wer-* (cf., however, *were-* and *wergild* Wergild) and the variants in *war-*, *var-*, makes this somewhat doubtful . . . Until recently the most usual form has been *werewolf*, and occas. *wehrwolf* from German." In the case of a quotation I, of course, retain the form of word employed by the author. Thus Mr. Baring-Gould and Sir James Frazer have *were-wolf*; Mr. Elliott O'Donnell writes *werwolf*; Miss Hamel *wer-wolf*.

The Bibliography does not aim at being a full-dressed bibliography. That is to say, I have designedly not entered into questions of issues, sizes, states, and collation. I felt that all such details were clearly superfluous. In listing classical authors, Petronius, Pliny, Apuleius; or authors of whose works there were many reprints, S. Augustine, Peucer, Jean Bodin; I have given the edition which I myself used, and—in the case of any such existing—an available English translation.

The selection of books to be included in the Bibliography has been quandaried and difficult, and the result must, I am afraid, in some instances seem arbitrary. Here it was wellnigh impossible to adhere to any set rule, and my Bibliography (with its inclusions and its omissions) is open, I make no doubt, to criticism. Regretfully have I passed by the best known of all English wolf stories, *Little Red Riding Hood*, but the enchanted and enchanting domains of the *Cabinet des Fées* with the *Thousand Nights and a Night*, the *Contes Chinois*, and the rest lie outside my scope.

Again, although in many works of fiction there are allusions to werewolfery, I have not included such titles unless the incident seemed some essential part of the tale and not merely episodical, however well done. Thus I omit—to give one only example—Mr. Roy Bridges' first-rate romance *Legion : For We Are Many*, 1928, in Part iii of which ("Black Mass") the Lady Anne Latoner on the ghostly island of Cor trembled as she thought how "A wolf haunted the forest in the night : grey wolf with eyes of fire and bloody mouth : children who strayed into the forest did not return. A wayfarer in the forest had met with the werwolf—Loup-garou—snarling out of the dark, and, on his crying the name of Jesus, a man, in lieu of wolf, had passed him by in silence, hidden in a scarlet mantle, but John of Cor by stature. She had mocked the folly of the tales, finding the origin in the grey wolf on the shield of Cor . . . The old grey wolf of Cor possessed by the spirit of evil ? . . ."

It is plain that the *Metamorphoses* of Apuleius, a work of paramount importance and enduring influence, must have honourable mention, although quite strictly it does not deal with werewolfery but with shape-shifting. Many, however —unless I err—will express surprise at meeting with Samuel Lover's *Handy Andy*. Yet the story of the Irish witch-cat is admirably told and not a little significant.

This furthermore brings us to another consideration. There are many books of some length which, dealing with a number of subjects, give in passing, it may be two or three pages, it may be even one paragraph or a note, to werewolfery. Those few pages or that single note none the less will be found to be more valuable than several chapters or an entire treatise of another writer. In a Bibliography of the Werewolf a student has the right to expect that his attention shall be directed to these sources of information, briefly worded as they are. Accordingly in not a few cases I have indicated exact references to chapter and page.

It is inevitable that in a comprehensive Bibliography the books will be of very varying, and some of very little, value. Indifferent tractates must find their place alongside works of eminent scholarship and supreme authority. To range and distinguish might prove a highly invidious undertaking, so much so, in fact, that even when duty—to say nothing of inclination—seemed to urge have I scrupulously refrained from setting a sea-mark.

I have to thank my friend Dr. H. J. Norman for his most valuable and interesting note upon " Witch Ointments ", those mysterious liniments which throughout the ages have played so large a part in the processes of witchcraft and werewolfery.

MONTAGUE SUMMERS.

IN FESTO PRODIGIORVM B.M.V.
1933.

THE WEREWOLF

CHAPTER I

THE WEREWOLF: LYCANTHROPY

A S old as time and as wide as the world, the belief in the
werewolf by its very antiquity and its universality
affords accumulated evidence that there is at least some
extremely significant and vital element of truth in this dateless
tradition, however disguised and distorted it may have
become in later days by the fantasies and poetry of epic
sagas, roundel, and romance. The ultimate origins of the
werewolf are indeed obscure and lost in the mists of primeval
mythology, and when we endeavour to track the slot too far
we presently find ourselves mused and amazed, driven to
hazard and profitless conjecture, unless we are sensible
enough to recognize and candid enough to acknowledge the
dark and terrible mysteries, both psychic and physical,
which are implicated in and essentially permeate a catena
of evidence past dispute, and which alone can adequately
explain or account for the prominence and the survival
of those cruel narratives which have come down to us throughout the centuries, and the facts of which are being repeated
to-day in the evil-haunted depths of African jungles, and
even in remoter hamlets of Europe, farmy woods and
mountain vales, almost divorced from the ken of man and
wellnigh unvisited by civilization.

The mere somatist; the rationalist, often masquerading
nowadays under Christian credentials; the rationalizing
anthropologist; the totemist; the erratic solarist; " prompt
to impose and fond to dogmatize," each and every, in his
hot-paced eagerness to expiscate and explain the manner
of all mysteries in earth and heaven, will not be slow to
broach and argue his newest superstitions, the fruit of
trivially profound research, vagaries which can neither
interest, instruct, nor yet entertain the true scholar of simpler

vision and clearer thought, since in the end these veaking inquirers commonly arrive at nothing, and like the earth-born sons of Cadmean tilth it has proved in the past that again and again do they painfully destroy themselves by internecine war.

Yet there may be found some in whom the missionary spirit of error is so pertinacious that they will refurbish and seemingly with intenser conviction reiterate sham theories a thousand times discredited and disproved. Thus, with regard to the very subject of the werewolf, which he only touches quite cursorily as he passes by, Sir William Ridgeway in his *Early Age of Greece* was constrained to warn the student that he " must be careful lest whilst he is avoiding the Scylla of solar mythology, he may be swallowed up in the Charybdis of totemism ".[1]

Precisely to define the werewolf is perhaps not altogether easy. We may, however, say that a werewolf is a human being, man, woman or child (more often the first), who either voluntarily or involuntarily changes or is meta-morphosed into the apparent shape of a wolf, and who is then possessed of all the characteristics, the foul appetites, ferocity, cunning, the brute strength, and swiftness of that animal. In by far the greater majority of instances the werewolf to himself as well as to those who behold him seems completely to have assumed the furry lupine form. This shape-shifting is for the most part temporary, of longer or shorter duration, but it is sometimes supposed to be per-manent. The transformation, again, such as it is, if desired, can be effected by certain rites and ceremonies, which in the case of a constitutional werewolf are often of the black goetic kind. The resumption of the original form may also then be wrought at will. Werewolfery is hereditary or acquired ; a horrible pleasure born of the thirst to quaff warm human blood, or an ensorcelling punishment and revenge of the dark Ephesian art.

It should be remarked that in a secondary or derivative sense the word werewolf has been erroneously employed to denote a person suffering from lycanthropy, that mania or disease when the patient imagines himself to be a wolf, and under that savage delusion betrays all the bestial pro-pensities of the wolf, howling in a horrid long-drawn note.

This madness will hardly at all concern us here. Werewolf is also in one place [2] found to specify an exceptionally large and ferocious wolf, and according to Dr. John Jamieson, in the county of Angus, Warwolf, pronounced *warwoof*, was anciently used to designate a puny child, or an ill-grown person of whatever age.[3]

Verstegan, that is to say, Richard Rowlands,[4] in his *A Restitution of Decayed Intelligence*, 4to, 1605, has : " *Were* our ancestors vsed somtyme in steed of *Man* yet should it seeme that *were* was moste commonly taken for a maried man. But the name of *man* is now more knoun and more generally vsed in the whole Teutonic toung then the name of *Were*.

" *Were-wulf*. This name remaineth stil knoun in the Teutonic, & is as much to say as *man-wolf*, the greeks expressing the very lyke, in *Lycanthropos*.

" *Ortelius* [5] not knowing what *were* signified, because in the *Netherlandes* it is now clean out of vse, except thus composed with *wolf*, doth mis-interprete it according to his fancie.

" The *were-wolves* are certaine sorcerers, who hauing annoynted their bodyes, with an oyntment which they make by the instinct of the deuil ; and putting on a certaine in-chanted girdel, do not only vnto the view of others seeme as wolues, but to their oun thinking haue both the shape and nature of wolues, so long as they weare the said girdel. And they do dispose theselues as very wolues, in wurrying and killing, and moste of humaine creatures.

" Of such sundry haue bin taken and executed in sundry partes of *Germanie*, and the *Netherlands*. One *Peeter Stump* [6] for beeing a *were-wolf*, and hauing killed thirteen children, two women, and one man ; was at *Bedbur* [7] not far from *Cullen* in the year 1589 put vnto a very terrible death. The flesh of diuers partes of his body was pulled out with hot iron tongs, his armes thighes & legges broke on a wheel, & his body lastly burnt. He dyed with very great remorce, desyring that his body might not be spared from any torment, so his soule might be saued. The *were-wolf* (so called in *Germanie*) is in *France*, called Loupgarov."

This " etymological explanation ", says Professor Ernest Weekley in his *More Words Ancient and Modern*,[8] " is

substantially correct." This authority remarks that strictly
were " should be *wer*, a word of wider diffusion in the Aryan
languages than *man* or *gome*. It is found in all the Teutonic
languages and is cognate with Lat. *vir*, Gaelic *fear*, Welsh
gŵr, Sanskrit *vīra*. *Were* died out in early Mid. English, but
survives historically in *wergild* ".[9] He also adds : " The
disappearance of the simple *were* led Mid. English writers to
explain the first syllable as *ware*, and, as late as 1576, Turberville tells us, ' Such wolves are called " warwolves ", bicause
a man had neede to be ware of them.' [10] A similar idea
seems to account for archaic Ger. *wehrwolf*, associated with
the cognate *wehren*, to protect, take heed."

As Verstegan notes, the Greek λυκάνθρωπος is a word-
formation exactly corresponding to the Anglo-Saxon *were-
wulf*, which occurs as a synonym for the devil in the laws
of King Cnut, Ecclesiastical Ordinances, xxvi. " Thonne
moton tha hyrdas beon swydhe wacore and geornlice clypi-
gende, the widh thonne theodsceadhan folce sceolan scyldan,
thaet syndon biscopas and maessepreostas, the godcunde
heorda bewarian and bewarian sceolan, mid wislican laran,
thaet se wodfreca werewulf to swidhe ne slyte ne to fela
ne abite of godcundse heorde." " Therefore must be the
shepherds be very watchful and diligently crying out, who
have to shield the people against the spoiler ; such are bishops
and mass-priests, who are to preserve and defend their
spiritual flocks with wise instructions, that the madly
audacious were-wolf do not too widely devastate, nor bite
too many of the spiritual flock." [11]

It is interesting to remark that Werwulf actually occurs
as a proper name, since Asser in his *De Rebus Gestis Ælfredi*
mentions " Æthelstan quoque et Werwulfum, sacerdotes
et capellanos, Mercios genere, eruditos, " who helped that
monarch in his studies, and were duly rewarded by him." [12]
Werwulf, the Mercian priest, was a friend of Bishop Werfrith
of Worcester, and the name is found in various charters,
some of which, however, are by no means altogether above
suspicion. One may compare such names as Ethelwulf,
" the Noble Wolf " ; Berthwulf, " the Illustrious Wolf " ;
Eadwulf, " the Prosperous Wolf " ; Ealdwulf, " the Old
Wolf," and many more.

Bishop Burchard of Worms, who died in August, 1025,

in the nineteenth Book, *De Poenitentia,* of his *Decreta*—
" Liber hic Corrector vocatur et Medicus " [13]—instructs the
priest to ask a penitent the following : " Credidisti quod
quidam credere solent, ut illae quae a vulgo parcae vocantur,
ipsae, vel sint, vel possint hoc facere quod creduntur ;
id est, dum aliquis homo nascitur, et tunc valeant illum
designare ad hoc quod velint ut quandocunque ille homo
voluerit, in lupum transformari possit, quod vulgaris stultitia
weruvolff vocat, aut in aliam aliquam figuram ? Si credidisti,
quod unquam fieret aut esse possit, ut divina imago in aliam
formam aut in speciem transmutari possit ab aliquo, nisi ab
omnipotente Deo, decem dies in pane et aqua debes
poenitere." [14]

It must be here carefully remarked that Burchard's question
does not for a moment imply any doubt as to the reality of
the demon werewolf. In a sense it cuts deeper than that.
The essential point of the priest's query is whether the
person seeking absolution has doubted the omnipotence of
Almighty God, has sinfully allowed himself to wonder
whether the powers of evil may not wellnigh match the
powers of good, and thus be able to perform diabolic miracles
and marvels in despite, as it were, of the Supreme Deity.
This, of course, is the deadly error of the Manichees, the
dualism of good and evil, a divided empire. During the
twelfth century Western Europe, in particular Italy, France,
and Germany, suffered from an extraordinary outburst of
dualism, the adherents of which foul doctrines propagated
their dark creed with tireless zeal until the country began
to swarm with Catharists, Albigenses, Paterini, Publicani,
Bulgari, Tisserands, Bougres, Paulicians, and a thousand
other subversive sectaries.[15] The ultimate principle of these
beliefs, differ as they might in detail, was Satanism. Raoul
Glaber, a monk who died at Cluny about 1050, writing his
contemporary *History,* speaks of their obstinate persistence
in these abominations : " Hos nempe cunctos ita macula-
verat haeretica pravitas, ut ante erat illis crudeli morte
finiri, quam ab illa quoquomodo possent ad saluberrimam
Christi Domini fidem revocari. Colebant enim idola more
paganorum, ac cum Iudaeis inepta sacrificia litare
nitabantur." [16]

Nearly three centuries earlier than Burchard, S. Boniface,

the martyred Archbishop of Mayence, Apostle of Germany, in his sermon *De abrenuntiatione in baptismate*,[17] "concerning those things which a Christian renounceth at his Baptism," speaks of "veneficia, incantationes et sortilegos exquirere, strigas et fictos lupos credere, abortum facere", that is to say, "poisonings, magic spells and the curious seeking out of lots, trusting implicitly in witches and a superstitious fear of werewolves, the procuring of abortion, as among the 'mala opera diaboli', 'the abominable works of the devil.'" The Saint classes these sins with "superbia, idololatria, invidia, homicidium, detractio, . . . fornicatio, adulterium, omnis pollutio, furta, falsum testimonium, rapina, gula, ebrietas . . .", "pride, the worshipping of idols, envy, murder, malice, . . . fornication, adultery, all uncleanness, theft, false witness, despoiling by violence, gluttony, drunkenness, . . .," and other evil deeds. The phrase "strigas et fictos lupos credere" does not mean merely "to believe that witches and werewolves exist", but "to put one's trust in the power of sorcerers and to believe that the devil is able of his own might to transform men into wolves", which is to say one gives the glory to Satan rather than to God, as in truth witches and warlocks use and are wont.

The word werewolf in its first and correcter signification is employed by Gervase of Tilbury, who in his *Otia Imperialia* thus explains the term : "Vidimus enim frequenter in Anglia per lunationes homines in lupos mutari, quod hominum genus *gerulfos* Galli nominant, Anglici vero *werewlf* dicunt : *were* enim Anglice *virum* sonat, *wlf* lupum." [18]

Gervase of Tilbury composed his *Otia* about 1212, and rather more than a century later in the English poem *William of Palerne*, otherwise known as the Romance of "William and the Werwolf", translated from the twelfth century *Roman de Guillaume de Palerne* at the command of Sir Humphrey de Bohun [19] about 1350, we have the word *werwolf*, as in ll. 79–80 :—

> For i wol of þe werwolf· a wile nov speke.
> Whanne þis werwolf was come· to his wolnk denne . . .

and the word is not infrequently repeated throughout the poem.[20]

The following lines occur in *Pierce the Ploughmans Crede* [21] (*c.* 1894) :—

> In vestimentis ouium, but onlie wiþ-inne
> þei ben wilde wer-wolues þat wiln þe folk robben.
> þe fend founded hem first . . .

The Vulgate, secundum Matthæum, vii, 15, has : " Attendite a falsis prophetis, qui veniunt ad vos in vestimentis ovium, intrinsecus autem sunt lupi rapaces." The Douai translation runs : " Beware of false prophets, who come to you in the clothing of sheep, but inwardly they are ravening wolves." The Authorized Version is practically identical : " Beware of false prophets which come to you in sheep's clothing, but inwardly they are ravening wolves." The Revised is the same. The original Greek has λύκοι ἅρπαγες for the words translated " ravening wolves " or in *Pierce the Ploughmans Crede* " wer-wolues ". Here, too, they seem to be regarded as definitely inspired by the demon, although this detail perhaps should not be pressed.

In Sir Thomas Malory's *Le Morte Darthur*, which was completed about 1470, book xix, c. xi, mention is found of " Sir Marrok the good knyghte that was bitrayed with his wyf for she made hym seuen yere a werwolf ".[22]

Among Scottish poets Robert Henryson, who was born about the beginning of the second quarter of the fifteenth century and who died certainly not later than 1508, in his *Morall Fabillis of Esope the Phrygian*, " Compylit in Eloquent, and Ornate Scottis Meter," in " The Trial of the Fox ", writes :—

> The Minotaur, ane Monster meruelous,
> Bellerophont, that beist of Bastardrie,
> The Warwolf, and the Pegase perillous,
> Transformit be assent of sorcerie . . .[23]

In *The Flyting of Dunbar and Kennedie*,[24] the latter poet addresses his rival in the following terms :—

> Dathane deuillis sone, and dragon dispitous,
> Abironis birth, and bred with Beliall;
> Wod werwolf, worme, and scorpion vennemous,
> Lucifers laid, fowll feyindis face infernall;
> Sodomyt, syphareit fra sanctis celestiall, . . .[25]

Alexander Montgomerie in his *Flyting of Montgomerie and Polwart* (1582),[26] has :—

> Ane vairloche, ane woirwolf, ane wowbat of hair,
> Ane devill, and ane dragoun, ane doyed dromodarie, . . . [27]

A little earlier in the same poem he reviles his adversary :—

> With warwoolffs and wild cates thy weird be to wander ; . . .[28]

In the excellent old comedy *Philotus* [29] young Flavius thus conjures and exorcises Emily :—

> Throw power I charge the of the Paip,
> Thow neyther girne, gowl, glowme, nor gaip,
> Lyke Anker saidell, like unsell Aip,
>   Lyke Owle nor Alrische Elfe :
> Lyke fyrie Dragon full of feir,
> Lyke Warwolf, Lyon, Bull nor Beir,
> Bot pas thow hence as thow come heir,
>   In lykenes of thy selfe.[30]

King James VI of Scotland in his *Dæmonologie*, 1597, iii, 1, has " war-woolfes " and " λυκανθρωποι " which signifieth men-woolfes ".

John Sibbald in the Glossary to his *Chronicle of Scottish Poetry* has : " Warwolf, according to an antient vulgar idea, *a person transformed to a wolf.* Teut. *weer wolf,* Swed. *warulf,* lycanthropus ; hoc est, qui ex ridicula vulgi opinione in lupi forma noctu obambulat. Goth. *vair,* vir ; & *ulf,* lupus. It is not unlikely that *Warlock* may be a corruption of this word." [31] This is, of course, a wholly impossible etymology since the first element in *Warlock* is the O.E. *wær* " covenant " ; and the second element is related to O.E. *leogan* " to lie or deny ".[32] Thus the first meaning of Warlock is one who breaks a treaty, the violator of his oath, a man forsworn ; hence in general a false and wicked person, and then a magician, a sorcerer.

In the famous " Discourse of Witchcraft as it was acted in the Family of Mr. Edward Fairfax ", 1621, occurs another form of the word werewolf. " Above all [the transformation of] the Leucanthopoi is most miraculous . . . which Witches that people do call *weary wolves.*"

The modern German is Werwolf, which has a less correct old form Währwolf. There are variants, and also corruptions such as bärwolf, which is given in Johann Georg Wachter's *Glossarium Germanicum*,[33] berwolff in Camerarius,[34] and berwulf.[35] Werwolf, notes Wachter, " componitur a *wer* vir, & *wolf* lupus. Et dicitur etiam *bær-wolf*, quia alia Dialectio *bar* est vir. Galli alio & meliori compositionis ordine vocant *loupgarou*. Nam proprie est homo in lupum mutatus, non lupus homini infestus. De Gallica voce mire nugantur eruditi. *Garou* virum denotare, iam supra demonstravi in *gur* vir. Cæterum homines in lupos transformari, vetustissima fama est . . . Patet . . . hanc transmutationem secundum antiquam credulitatem non fuisse morbum, sed rem liberam & voluntariam." [36]

Eugen Mogk in an article entitled *Der Werwolf*, which he contributed to Hermann Paul's *Grundriss der Germanischen Philologie*, writes : " Die Bedeutung des Wortes ist klar : *wer* = Mann, Werwolf also der Mann in Wolfsgestalt." [37]

Oskar Schrade in his *Altdeutsches Wörterbuch* [38] draws attention to *wërwolf* (*mittelhochdeutsch*) and *werawolf* (*althochdeutsch*). There is a West Frisian *waerûl* and *warûle*, as also a form *waerwulf*, which latter is derived from the Middle Dutch (and Modern) *weerwolf*. Franz Passow in his *Handwirterbuch der Griechischen Spreche*, Leipzig, 1852, under λυκάνθρωπος (ii, p. 89), notes the Dutch *ghierwolf*. The Gothic has *vairavulfs*. The Danish and Norwegian *varulv* and Swedish *varulf* are, it has been suggested, formed on a Romance or German model. *Varulf*, indeed, may be connected with an Old Norman *varulf*.

The Icelandic *vargr* denotes a wolf, and *varg-úlfr*, literally a " worrying wolf ", means a werewolf. Vigfusson quotes from Unger's edition of *Strengleikar* (*Lays of the Britons*),[39] " bisclaret í Bretzku máli en Norðmandingar kallaðu hann vargúlf," and " v. var eitt kvikindi meðan hann býr í vargsham," upon which he comments : " This word [*varg-úlfr*], which occurs nowhere but in the above passage, is perhaps only coined by the translator from the French *loup-garou* qs. *gar-ulf*; *ver-úlfr* [40] would have been the right word, but that word is unknown to the Icelandic or old Norse, the superstition being expressed by *eigi ein-hamr, ham-farir, hamast*, or the like." [41] *Ham-farir* signifies " the ' *faring* ' or *travelling* in the assumed shape of an animal, fowl or deer, fish or serpent, with magical speed over land and sea, the wizard's own body meantime lying lifeless and motionless ".[42]

On the French word *loupgarou* Littré has the following etymological note : " Wallon, *leu-warou, léwarou* ; Hainaut *leuwarou* ; Berry *loup berou, loup brou* ; picard, *leuwarou* ; norm. *varou*, loup garou, *varouage*, course pendant la nuit (*garouage* se dit avec le même sens parmi les paysans des environs de Paris) ; bourguig. *leu-voirou* ; bas-lat. *gerulphus*, loup-garou. Gerulphus a donné *garwall, garou* ; c'est donc *gerulphus* qu'il faut étudier ; il réprésente l'anglo-saxon *vere wolf* ; danois *var-ulv* ; suédois, *var-ulf*, qui étant composé de *ver, vair*, homme, et de *wolf, ulf*, loup, signifie *homme-loup*. La locution *loup-garou* est donc un pléonasme où *loup* se trouve deux fois, l'un sous la forme française, l'autre sous la forme germanique. *Verewolf* est, on le voit, un mot composé semblable à λυκάνθρωπος. Au germanique *ver*, comparez *vir, ἥρως*, en sanscrit *vīra*, homme fort, et en celtique *ver*, homme." [43]

Fréderic Godefroy, *Dictionnaire de l'Ancienne Langue Française*,[44] gives : " Garol, *garwall, guaroul, wareul, varol*, s.m. esprit malin que l'on supposait errer la nuit transformé en loup.

> Quant de lais faire m'entremet
> Ne voil ublier Bisclaveret ;
> Bisclaveret ad nun en Bretan,
> *Garwall* l'apelent li Norman.
> > (Marie, *Lai du Bisclaveret*, 1, Roq.)
> Et si a tant garous et leus.
> > (G. de Coinci, *Mir.*, MS. Soiss., f° 24ª.) [45]
> Que nous deffende, que nous gart
> De ces *guarous* et de ce leus.
> > (Id. *ib.*, f° 24ᵇ.)
> Que n'est lions, *wareus* ne leus.
> > (Id. *ib.*, f° 173ⁿ.)
> Lou *garol*.
> > (Id. *ib.*, MS. Brux., f° 23ᵈ.)
> Et au *guaroul* qui les engine.
> > (G. de Palerme. Ars. 3319, f° 108 v°.)

Haut-Maine, *gairou*. Norm., Guernesey, *varou*." [46]

Godefroy's quotation from the *Lai du Bisclaveret* does not, however, supply the best text which is to be found in the British Museum MS., Harley 978,[47] and which begins as follows :—

Quant de lais faire mentremet
Ne uoil ublier bisclaueret
Bisclaueret ad nun en bretan
Garwaf lapelent li norman.

Garwaf is then the Norman equivalent of the Breton *bisclaveret*. In his *Dictionnaire François-Celtique ou François-Breton*, Rennes, 1732, the learned Capuchin Gregoire de Rostrenen has : " Loup-garou. Bleiz-garv. bleiz-garo. *p.* bleizy-garo (garo, *âpre, cruel.*) den-vleiz. *p.* tud-vleiz. gobylin. *p.* goblinad. (gobilin, *veut dire esprit folet nocturne.*) *Van.* bleidet, un deen bleydet. tud bleydet." [48] In Breton there also exists the term *den-bleiz* ; *den* meaning a man, and *bleiz* signifying wolf.

Bodin in his *Demonomanie des Sorcius*, ii, 6, in his chapter on werewolves writes : " Les Alemans les appellent Vver Vvòlf, & les François loups garous ; les Picards loups varous, comme qui diroit *lupos varios*, car les François mettent g. pour v. Les grecs les appelloyent Lycanthropes, & Mormolycies ; Les Latins les appelloyent *vorios & versipelles*, comme Pline a noté parlant de ce changement de loups en hommes. François Phoebus Conte de Foix, en son luire de la Chasse, dict que ce mot Garoux, veut dire gardez vous, dequoy le President Fauchet m'a aduerty." [49]

Gaston III de Foix (Phébus) was born in 1331 and died 1391. *Le miroyr de Phebus des deduicts de la chasse aux Bestes sauluaiges Et des oyseaulx de proye* is one of the most famous medieval treatises of venery,[50] and the passage to which Bodin refers may be found in chapter x, " Cy devise du loup et de toute sa nature." " Il y a aucuns qui manguët des enfãs et aucüesfois les hommes et ne mãguent nulle autre chair depuis qu'ils sont encharnes aux hommes aincois se laissent mourir et ceux on appelle loups garous : car on fendoit garder."

The learned Capuchin Jacques d'Autun in his *L'Incredulité Sçavante et la Credulité Ignorante*, Lyon, 1678, Troisième Partie, Discours xxx (p. 904), writes : " On voit des Sorciers en forme de Loups se ietter sur les hommes, plustost que sur les bestes ; c'est la raison, dit vn Comte de Foix, pourquoy on les appelle *Loups-garoux*, c'est à dire *gardez vous* : parce que leur rage les porte à esgorger & à courir s'ils peuuent sur les personnes qu'ils rencontrent, & s'ils sont repoussés, on les voit tourner leur furie sur les Troupeaux, où ils font d'estranges rauages."

This curious etymology passed into English, being seriously put forward (as already noted) by Turberville, who derived it from the English treatise *The Booke of huntynge* or *Master of game* (c. 1400), chapter vii, " Of ye Wolf and of his nature." The passage runs : " ther ben some that eten chyldren & men and eteth noon other flesh fro that tyme that thei be a charmed with mannys flesh, ffor rather thei wolde be deed. And thei be cleped Werewolfes for men shulde be war of hem." [51]

Frédéric Mistral, in his *Dictionnaire Provençal-Français*,[52] records many variants of the word *loup-garou* which appears in differing dialects as *loup-garoun, loup-carou, louparou, loup-paumè, loup-berou, loubérou, leberou, garuló*. In Limousin are found *leberoun* and *leberou*. In Dauphiné a werewolf is *lamiaro*. The word *brouch* (sometimes *borouch*) also means a werewolf, although it is more generally employed to denote a wizard, a sorcerer. Cotgrave in his *Dictionarie of the French and English Tongues*, 1611, defines *loup-garou* as " *A mankind Wolfe ; such a one as once being flesht on men, and children will rather starue then feed on any thing else ; also, one that, possesed with an extreame, and strange melancholie, beleuues he is turned Wolfe, and as a Wolfe behaues himselfe* ".

The Italian term for a werwolf is *lupo mannaro* or *mannaro* ; the Portuguese *lobis-homem* or *lycanthropo*.[53] In Spain the word is *lobombre*.[54]

In the Sicilian dialect there are many variants of *lupo mannaro*, among the more common being *lupunàru, lupunàriu, lupuminàru, lupuminariu* (Messina), *lupupunàru* (Franco-fonte), *lupupinàru* (Naso), *lupucumunàriu* (Piazza), *lupiti-minàriu* (Nicosia), *daminàr* (San Fratello), and many more.

Although ancient Greek mythology affords innumerable stories of animal metamorphoses, amongst others it will be readily remembered that Homer describes the witch-queen Circe as surrounded by a strange pack of human animals—

Ἀμφὶ δὲ μιν λύκοι ἦσαν ὀρέστεροι ἠδὲ λέοντες,
Τοὺς αὐτὴ κατέθελξεν, ἐπεὶ κακὰ φάρμακ' ἔδωκεν,[55]

and the story of Lycaon is of dateless antiquity, yet the word λυκάνθρωπος is not of early occurrence, whilst the poem of

Marcellus Sidetes, who lived in the reigns of Hadrian and
Antoninus Pius, A.D. 117–161, Περὶ λυκανθρώπου,[56] deals
with the disease lycanthropy. Paul Ægineta, whose extant
work is conveniently known as De Re Medica Libri Septem,[57]
probably flourished in the latter half of the seventh century.
He employs the term λυκανθρωπία, the disease. Galen
mentions the νόσος κυνάνθρωπος [58] (a cognate formation), in
which malady the patient imagines himself to be a dog, and
the grammarian Joannes Tzetzes in his Chiliades terms the
Minotaur βοάνθρωπος.[59]

E. A. Sophocles in his Greek Lexicon of the Roman and
Byzantine Periods, 146 B.C.–A.D. 1100 (Havard University
Press, 1914), records λυκανθρωπία as " lycanthropy ", and
λυκάνθρωπος as one afflicted with lycanthropy. He does
not appear to recognize the meaning werewolf.[60]

Reginald Scot in his notorious Discouerie of witchcraft, book
v, chapter 1, expresses his agreement with " such physicians,
as saie that Lycanthropia is a disease, and not a transformation ".[61] He has in this passage merely transliterated
the Greek. Nathan Bailey in his Universal Etymological
English Dictionary (8vo, 1721) has : " Werewolf, [Werwolf
or Werewolff, Teut. q.d. A Man-Wolf, or Wolf-Man ;
λυκάνθρωπος, Gr.] a Sorcerer, who by means of an inchanted
Girdle, &c. takes upon hims the Shape and Name of a Wolf."
He also notes : " Lycanthropy. [Lycanthropie, F. lycanthropia.
L. of λυκανθρωπία, Gr.] a madness proceeding from the
Bite of a Mad Wolf, wherein men imitate the Howling of
Wolves." Dr. Johnson does not notice " Werewolf " but
under Lycanthropy [62] he has : " [lycantropie, French ;
λύκαν and ἄνθρωπος.] A kind of madness, in which men
have the qualities of wild beasts.

" He sees like a man in his sleep, and grows as much the
wiser as a man that dreamt of a lycanthropy, and was for
ever after wary not to come near a river.—Taylor."

At some indeterminate period the word λυκάνθρωπος fell
into disuse among the Greeks and its place was taken by
λυκοκάντζαρος. It is quite possible, of course, that even
to-day λυκάνθρωπος may be employed in some obscure and
obsolescent dialect, but the only place where it seems to be
definitely recorded of late is in a tale given by J. G. von
Hahn in his collection Griechische und albanesische Märchen.[63]

The variant of this particular story comes from Attica, and Hahn draws especial attention to λυκάνθρωπος, which in his German version he renders by the unusual " Der Wolfsmann ".

In λυκοκάντζαρος the second element κάντζαρος is the modern form of κένταυρος, and is most commonly known from its combination καλλικάντζαροι.[64] Since the Callicantzari will be described and discussed in the chapter dealing with the werewolf in Greece, it is sufficient here to note that to-day in the few districts (chiefly Cynouria, Messenia, and Crete) where λυκοκάντζαρος is still to be heard, the meaning has changed, and so far from signifying a werewolf, a man transformed to a beast, it almost invariably denotes the καλλικάντζαρος himself, who is generically a grotesque and dangerous demon of no human origin, a bugaboo, sometimes appearing in man's shape and sometimes completely metamorphosed as a hideously fantastic and savage monster.

Antoine Th. Hépitès in his Lexicon Hellenogallicon,[65] Athens, 1909, has : " λυκανθρωπία . . . lycanthropie, n.f. μελαγχολικὴ ἀσθένια καθ' ἣν ὁ ἀσθενὴς περιφέρεται τὴν νύκτα καὶ ὠρύεται ὡς λύκος." Apparently he only recognizes the word λυκανθρωπία as denoting the disease, and not equivalent to werewolfery. Under λυκάνθρωπος, however, he notes : " lycanthrope. n.m. (κυρ. ὁ λαμβάνων τὸ σχῆμα καὶ τὴν φωνήν τοῦ λύκου), ὁ πάσχων ἀπὸ λυκανθρωπίαν [συνεκδ.] ἀγριάνθρωπος, homme-sauvage, n.m. loup-garou, n.m." Ἀγριάνθρωπος, however, conveys little (if anything) more than the English wildman, and under this word Hépitès records[66] : " ὁ μὴ πεπολιτισμένος, homme sauvage ; μισάνθρωπος, ἀκοινώνητος, loup-garou," whilst in the French-Greek section of his work he defines : " Loup-garou. οὐσ. ἀρσ. Μτφ. Ἄνθρωπος περιπλανώμενος τὴν νυκτά ἐν μορφῇ λύκου κατὰ τοὺς δεισιδαίμονας. λυκάνθρωπος, ὁ ἀγριάνθρωπος, καὶ ἐν γένει ὁ μισάνθρωπος." [67] It is clear that the correct and original meaning werewolf is tending to become merely metaphorical and at last to signify nothing more than a misanthrope or a surly fellow.

The ordinary Greek word for a vampire is βρυκόλακας, vrykólakas, and this has a long and interesting history, being derived in the first place from a Slavonic word which in all Slavonic languages save one—the Serbian—is the exact equivalent of werewolf. Franz Miklosich has the following account in his *Etymologisches Wörterbuch der Slavischen Sprachen* [68] : " velkŭ, Old Slav., vlъkъ *wolf* . . . Old Slav., vlъkodlakъ *vulcolaca* : . . . Slovenian, volkdlak, vukodlak, vulkodlak ; Bulgarian, vrъkolak ; Kr., vukodlak ; Serb., vukodlak ; Cz., vlkodlak ; Pol., wilkolak ; Little Russian, volkolak, volkun ; White Russian, volkolak ; Russian, volkulakъ ; Roum., vęlkolak, vęrkolak ; Alb., vurvolak ; Modern Grk., βουλκόλακα, βρουκόλακας ; Lith., vilkakis ; Lett. vilkats. *Man beachte lit.* vilktrasa *werwolf. Der* vlъkodlakъ *ist der Werwolf der Deutschen, woraus mlat.* guerulfus, *mannwolf, der in wolfsgestalt gespenstich umgehende mann : vergl. Neuri in terra Tatarorum, qui mutari possunt in lupos.*"

The second element in the word is perhaps to be identified with *dlaka,* meaning a " hair " (of an animal, generally a cow or horse), a word found in Old Slav., New Slav., and Serbian.

In the Serbian language only does this word, whence is taken the Greek *vrykolakas,* mean rather a vampire than a werewolf. It is probable that this is to be explained by the fact that it is generally held among all Slavonic peoples that the man who has during his life been a werewolf almost necessarily becomes a vampire after his death. None the less a vampire need not once have been a werewolf, and the two must be most carefully distinguished. They are entirely different, separate, and apart.

The Slavonic word for vampire is that which we have taken over in English, *vampirŭ.* I will again quote Miklosich [69] : " Vampirŭ : b. vampir, vapir, vepir, vъpir, *wampir. Davon* vepirêsvam se, vampirêsvam se. *s.* vampir. *p.* upior, upierzyca *neben* wampir. *kh.* vampyr, vepyr, vopyr, opyr, vpyr, opir, *neben* uper. upýr, upyrjaka *für r.* urodъ, urodyšče. *wr.* upir, chodjaščij mertvec, kror čelovêču pъeć. *r.* upirъ (klali trêbu upiremъ), upyrъ, obyrъ *neben* vampirъ *ein gespenst, das den menschen das blut aussaugt. Im s. und r. ist der* vukodlak *werwolf und der wampir in eins verschmolzen. Das wort ist wahrscheinlich türk. : nordtürk,* ubęr *hexe, nsl.* vêdomec, prêmrl (*erstarrt*)."

A vampire, then, is altogether another thing from a werewolf. The former is dead ; the latter is fearfully alive, although there has been much confusion and there is indeed a

connection of a sort between the two. Moreover, Mr. J. C.
Lawson points out that " there is evidence that in the Greek
language itself the word *vrykolakas* does even now locally and
occasionally bear its original significance ".[70] Curiously
enough, an eminent authority denies this, for Bernhard
Schmidt in his discussion of the term βρυκόλακας and its
many variants writes : " Allein das Wort ist unzweifelhaft
slavischen Ursprungs und identisch mit dem slavischen
Namen des Werwolfs, welcher böhmisch vlkodlak, bulgarisch
und slovakisch vrkolak (für vrkodlak), polnisch, vilkolak
oder vilkolek lautet, was wörtlich ' Wolfshaar, Wolfspelz '
heisst, indem serb. dlaka und altböhm. tlak Haare bedeutet.
Nun sind zwar Werwolf und Vampyr im Grunde ganz
verschiedene Wesen, indem man unter jenem einem leben-
digen Menschen versteht, der sich zu Zeiten in einer alles
zerfleischenden Wolf verwandelt, unter diesem dagegen einen
verstorbenen, der aus seinem Grabe wieder kommt und den
Lebenden durch Aussaugen ihres Blutes den Untergang
bereitet ; und der neugriechische βουρκόλακας entspricht
nur dem letzteren. Da indessen doch beide blutgierige, auf
Menschenmord ausgehende Geschöpfe sind, und der Vampyr
auch seinerseits, gleich dem Werwolf, Thiergestalt anzuneh-
men vermag, so konnten sie in der Vorstellung des Volkes
leicht mit einander vermengt werden und demzu folge der
Name des einen auf den Begriff des anderen übergehen
Wirklich lässt sich dieser Vorgang bei slavischen Stämmen
sicher nachweisen, z. B. den Serben, in deren Sprache
vukodlak den Vampyr bezeichnet. Hier durch wird die
Slavicität des Namens βουρκόλακας über jeden Zweifel
gehoben." [71]
Schmidt's somewhat dogmatic pronouncement is, however,
clearly and demonstrably erroneous, nor does he help his
case by seeking to dismiss at least two pieces of in-
controvertible evidence in a footnote.[72] He has, indeed,
fallen into the fatal error of wresting or rather of attempting to
wrest facts to fit his preconceived theories. Hanush [73] was
informed by a Greek of Mytilene that there were two distinct
kinds of *vrykolakes*, the one sort being men already dead
(the vampire), the other living men who were subject to
a weird somnambulism which sent them forth ravening, and
this particularly on moonlight nights. (Cf. Gervase of

Tilbury's " Vidimus enim frequenter in Anglia *per lunationes* homines in lupos mutari ".)[74] Again, Cyprian Robert in his *Les Slaves de Turquie*,[75] thus describes the *vrykolakes* of Thessaly and Epirus : " Ce sont des hommes vivants en proie à une sorte de somnambulisme, qui, saisis par la soif du carnage, sortent la nuit de leurs huttes de bergers, et courent la campagne, déchirant de leurs morsures tout ce qu'ils rencontrent, hommes on bestiaux." Here, too, the connection between shepherds and the werewolves is striking. Amongst other shepherds who were proved to be addicted to werewolfery there is the notorious case of Pierre Burgot and Michel Verdun, a couple of lycanthropic sorcerers who were tried at Besançon in December, 1521, and sentenced to be burned alive by the Inquisitor General, Frère Jean Boin, O.P.[76]

Mr. J. C. Lawson also brings forward new evidence [77] and such as, in spite of Schmidt's contradictions, puts the matter beyond all doubt that the *vrykolakas* is a werewolf. He relates how in Cyprus whilst excavations were being carried out under the auspices of the British Museum during the spring of 1899, the directors heard from their workmen several stories concerning the detection of *vrykolakes*. In one particular village the inhabitants having suffered terribly from the depredations of a nocturnal marauder, armed themselves and kept a strick look out for the evil scourge. Before long in the moonlight watches they espied a *vrykolakas*, and one of the company either with gun or sword succeeded in wounding the monster, who, however, escaped and fled away into the shadows. The next day it was observed that a certain man in the village, who had not been among the picket, was marked with a wound exactly corresponding to the hurt inflicted on the *vrykolakas* the night before. When he was nearly interrogated the varlet at length confessed that he was indeed a *vrykolakas* and the nocturnal visitant of ill.

Mr. Lawson tells how he was informed by peasants on the borders of Aetolia and Acarnania, in the neighbourhood of Agrinion, that the word *vrykolakas* is occasionally applied to living persons in the sense of werewolf, although it is true to say the more common use may be the general " vampire ".

I myself can add a quota of evidence, as during my travels
in Greece I heard the word *vrykolakas* employed by a peasant
to describe a man strongly suspect of sorcery who, as it was
firmly believed, wandered abroad at night for purposes of
rapine and ravishment, and who had woefully assaulted
individuals and torn out the throats of flocks. Whether this
wretch assumed or was seen in the shape of a wolf I could
not exactly learn.

Incidentally it may be remarked that the explanations
given by Hépitès in his *Lexicon* [78] under βρυκόλακας are
a little superficial, not to say incorrect : " βρυκόλακας, ὁ. καὶ
βουρκόλακας. ψυχὴ περιπλανωμένη εἰς τὴν γῆν. ψυχῆς σκινειδὲς
φάντασμα, *revenant*, n.m. brucolaque, n.m. φάντασμα αἱμοδιψές,
vampire, n.f. ἡ ἔμπουσα."
" βρυκολακιάζω, μέλ. ἄσω. ἐπανέρχομαι μετὰ τὸν θάνατον εἰς
τὴν γῆν ὡς βροκόλακας (ὡς πνεῦμα, φάντασμα) *revenir comme
esprit* (ἢ *comme revenant*); ‖ αὐτὸ τὸ σπίτι εἶνε βρυκολακιασμένον,
il revient dans cette maison ; *cette maison est hantée* ;
(στοιχειωμένος, η, ον· ὁ συχναζόμενος ὑπὸ φαντασμάτων)· βλ.
καὶ στοιχειώνω· ‖ λέγουν ὅτι ἐθρυκολάκιασεν ἀφοῦ ἀπέθανε, on
dit qu'il revenait après sa mort." " βρυκόλαξ, ακος. ὁ. βλ.
βρυκόλακας."

The Latin word for a werewolf was *versipellis* (*verto-pellis*),
the original adjective having the meaning " that changes its
skin " and hence in general " that changes its shape or form ".
So in the *Amphitruo* [79] Plautus makes Mercury, who speaks
the Prologue, say of Jupiter, who has turned himself into the
very guise and exact counterpart of Amphitryon—

ita versipellem se facit quando lubet.

Pliny in the *Historia Naturalis*, VIII, xxii, " De lupis,"
drily comments upon the werewolf legends of Greece,
" homines in lupos verti, rursumque restitui sibi, falsum esse
confidenter existimare debemus, aut credere omnia, quae
fabulosa tot saeculis comperimus. Unde tamen ista vulgo
infixa sit fama in tantum, ut in maledictis versipelles habeat,
indicabitur." In the most famous werewolf story of antiquity,
perhaps of all time, told by the freedman Niceros at the table
of Trimalchio, the narrator relates how to his abject horror
he saw the young soldier transform himself into a wolf, and
when the animal was wounded in the neck, later the man was

LYCANTHROPY 19

found to have an ugly gash just in the same spot. " Intellexi
illum versipellem esse, nec postea cum illo panem gustare
potui, non si me occidisses." (" Then I realized that he was
a werewolf in full sooth, and I couldn't have eaten a mouthful
with him, no, not if you had killed me outright.") [80] Apuleius
uses the word *versipellis* of the transformation of witches
into any animal or insect, birds, dogs, mice, flies, " cum
deterrimae versipelles in quodvis animal ore converso
adrepant, ut ipsos etiam oculos Solis et Iustitiae facile
frusterentur." [81]

In the history of *Barlaam and Josaphat*, formerly ascribed
to S. Gregory Nanzianzen, [82] c. xxx, the phrase καὶ γνοὺς τὰ
μηχανήματα τοῦ δολίου Jacques de Billy [83] turns by " intellec-
tisque *uersipellis* hostis technis atque artibus ", [84] and a little
later in the same chapter for ταῦτα συλλαλήσας ὁ δολιόφρων
τοῖς ἑαυτοῦ κυσὶν he has : " haec cum *versipellis* ille ad
socios dixisset." [85] Hence we see *versipellis* aptly applied
as a name for the demon.

Not impertinently then does Julius Briêger in his *Flores
Caluinistici* describe Robert Dudley, Earl of Leicester, as
Versipellis. Relating the efforts of this villain to urge Queen
Elizabeth against the Blessed Thomas Howard, Duke of
Norfolk, he writes : " *Ille vero* (ut Versipellisest) *Reginam in
Ducē concitare hac conatur ratione.*" [86]

Later authors almost invariably express the werewolf
and werewolfery by a periphrasis, as for example, " Credidisti
. . . ut quandocunque ille homo voluerit, in lupum transformari possit, quod teutonice Werewulf vocatur ? " of the
Burchard *Penetential* (c. 1000) ; " homines substantialiter
in lupos non sunt conversi, sed, . . . lupi apparent," of
Peter Mamor, who wrote about 1462, in his *Flagellum
maleficorum* [87] ; and Weyer's " lupi noxii, quos lamias putant,
Germanis *Werwolff* dicti ". [88]

In later medical writers " lycanthropia ", often in Greek
characters, appears signifying the disease, and " lycanthropus " denotes the sufferer. But " lycanthropus " is never
employed to mean a werewolf, in which sense Du Cange
does not recognize this word, although under *lupus* he
has : " *Loup beroux*, idem qui *Loup-garou* vulgatius appellatur, in Lit. remiss. ann. 1415 ex Reg. 169. Charloph. reg.
ch. 204 : *Ribault prestre, champiz, Loup beroux, etc.* Haud

scio an eadem acceptione *Leu wasté* legitur in aliis Lit. ann. 1855. ex Reg. 84. ch. 65 : *Quamplurima verba injuriosa de dictis Johanne et ejus uxore dixit Johannes Cosset, et specialiter dictum Johannem vocarit Leu wasté et ejus uxorem ribaude.*" [89] Thus in the fourteenth century we have " werewolf " used as a term of abuse, and so foul and slanderous in its application that the name was violently resented.

Neither Forcellini [90] nor Maigne d'Arnis [91] include " lycanthropus ", and the term is evidently regarded as wholly Greek. It is uncertain, indeed, whether the word is to be found with the meaning " werewolf " before the seventeenth century, when it occurs in a marginal gloss, " *exemplum de Lycanthropo,*" on part i, question x, of the *Malleus Maleficarum* in the quarto edition of 1669,[92] vol. i, p. 67.

It is amply evident from the etymological history of the word " werewolf " with its many cognates and equivalents in every European language, that the tradition is not only most anciently and universally diffused throughout the whole of this great continent, but that it has further indelibly impressed itself upon the common speech and struck deep into the imagination of the Western peoples. Nor is it merely a grim superstition ; it is a terrible and dangerous truth, and one, moreover, which is by no means confined to Europe alone. A serious belief in some metamorphosis or transformation may be found over the whole wide world. It is not necessarily a change into the wolf, for there are records in other countries of shape-shifting to a very wide variety of animals. In Northern Europe the shape thus assumed was called *hamr* ; the process of changing *at skipta hömum* or *at hamz* ; the travelling in such a form *hamfarir* ; and the supernatural strength acquired by such metamorphosis *hamremmi*. But it must be carefully borne in mind that the soul remains unchanged, and that therefore the eye, which is the mirror of the soul, is also unchanged. In Scandinavian lore no animal is more highly esteemed than the Bear. He is considered rational, and in the Finnbogi saga Finnbogi converses with him, calling him *bessi*. Among the most famous *hamrammir* were the *berserkir*, the bearmen, or were-bears. (Their skin is called *bjarnahamr*, and they have the enormous strength of a bear, which state, however, alternates with extreme lassitude.) Among the

gods and heroes of Norse legend transformations are common.
They are often effected by putting on the skins of beasts
or fur and feather mantles. The goddesses Frigg and Freyja
have their " falcon-cloaks " *valshamr* ; the Valkyries their
alptar hamir " swan-cloaks ", and *krakuhamir* " raven-
cloaks ".[93]

In modern Greece the transformation into a boar, the
were-boar, ἀγριογούρουνο, is believed.[94] The Wallachians
dread the *priccolitsh*, the weredog.[95]

In Abyssinia and in the Egyptian Soudan the wizards are
credited with the power of becoming hyenas at will.[96]
Throughout that vast continent man metamorphoses himself
into many other animals, the leopard, the jaguar, the lion,
the elephant, the crocodile, the alligator, and even into fish
such as the shark.[97]

Throughout India, but more particularly in the northern
Himalayan districts, the weretiger prowls ; in Java, Borneo,
and the Malay States there are wereleopards to boot.[98] The
weretiger is also known in China and Japan, but here the
werefox is both feared and honoured. The werebadger and
the weredog are also sorcerers, sometimes it may be friendly
sorcerers, in animal shape.[99]

The Toradjas of the Central Celebes give their wizards a
yet wider range of metamorphosis which includes cats,
crocodiles, wild pigs, apes, deer, and buffaloes.[100] In the
West Indies we return to the transformation into a hyena.[101]
In North America we meet once more the werewolf as also
the werebuffalo.[102]

Of old in Central America, in Mexico and Peru, men knew
the weretiger, the were-eagle, and the wereserpent.[103] In
South America generally to-day the warlock is generally
credited to shift his shape to the jaguar, but there are also
tales of weretigers, were-eagles, and wereserpents.[104] The
witches of Chili are credited with the power of turning
themselves into a chonchon, a bird resembling a vulture
which flies by night, whilst others assume the appearance
of the calchona, described as a beast with long grey hair,
something between a goat and a prairie dog.[105]

In order then to satisfy his lust for blood, his desire to
hurt, harm, and kill, to terrify and amaze, the witch, the
bond-slave of Satan, by his master's evil power and hellish

craft transforms or seems to transform himself into the shape
of some ravening beast of prey, and naturally enough this
animal will be that most commonly met with in the district
where the varlet inhabits. This explains clearly enough and
logically enough why the werewolf is rare to-day, why
" there can nowhere be a living belief in contemporary metamorphosis into any animal which has ceased to exist in the
particular locality ".[106] For long centuries throughout all
Europe there was no wilder brute, no more dreaded enemy of
man than the savage wolf, whose ferocity was a quick and
lively menace to the countryside such as perhaps we cannot
in these later days by any stretch of imagination even faintly
realize and apprehend. Whilst yet large tracts of every
country, steppes and moorland, sierra and wold, upland,
fell and plain, were utterly deserted and only trodden by
man with peril and mortal danger to himself, the wolf proved
a fearful foe. He dwelt in the heart of those impenetrable
forests which long continued his veritable strongholds,
fortresses whence he could not be dislodged, Riddlesdale and
Bowland, Sherwood and Bere and Irwell in England ; Ettrick,
Braemar, Rothiemurchus, Invercauld in Scotland ; in
Ireland Kilmallock, the wilds of Kerry, the Wicklow
mountains, Shillela ; in France, Fontainebleau, Vincennes,
the thick-hedged slopes of the Jura and Vosges ; in Germany
and central Europe the Schwarzwald, the Böhmerwald,
Wald-Viertel, and many more. Monarchs hunted him, and
legislated and offered rich rewards for his destruction. But
for many a hundred years and hundred years again did the
wolf defy all attempts at extirpation. What better guise,
what better shape of fear and ferocity could the shape-shifting
sorcerer in Europe assume ?

The werewolf is the main object of our study ; the werewolf
who is metamorphosed by black magic, by occult and most
hideous bedevilment.

"Lycanthropy or Wolf-madness, a Variety of Isania
Zoanthropica "[107] is, says a recent authority, " endemic
insanity." [108] *Daemonium lupinum* was the recognized name
for this disease, as Bernard Gordonius testifies.[109]

It is now quite generally recognized that insanity is very
frequently nothing else than diabolical possession. Heurnius
(Jan van Hewin), *De Mania, De Morbis Capitis*, c. xiii, says :

" Prófecto non sine daemone saepe haec calamitas. Permissu summi Dei illi spiritus sensibus incomperti se corporibus insinuant, receptique visceribus valetudinem bonam vastant: somnia terrent, ac formidine animam quatiunt." [110] It were superfluous here once again to demonstrate the facts of possession, " which is one of the most articulately expressed doctrines of both Testaments, and which reigned for seventeen hundred years, hardly challenged, in all the churches." [111] The express witness of Our Divine Lord Himself, both in word and deed, cannot be gainsaid, and is, of course, final and complete.[112] The disease lycanthropy, then, is in the majority of cases, perhaps in all, demoniacal possession.

It is true that the physicians nicely distinguish two kinds of lycanthropy ; the one arising from possession by the Devil, the other natural, as Daniel Sennert [113] says. At which point it is necessary to emphasize very explicitly the difference between lycanthropy and werwolfery, since these are two diverse and heterogeneous things, although both are clearly of a Satanic origin. (An exception may possibly be made if there is adduced so as to convince us an instance of "natural lycanthropy ", although I hold that such can hardly be.) The sufferer, the lycanthrope, may, it is true, be an innocent victim, thus woefully afflicted " that the works of God should be made manifest in him ",[114] as was the man who was blind from his birth, and whom Our Lord healed. Often, again, it is that Satan has betrayed his servant the sorcerer, the werewolf, has plagued him and driven him mad to make him more miserable in life and to involve him even more irretrievably in perdition, for the sorcerer is one who has made a pact with the Devil, and, as Guazzo points out, these pacts " are not only vain and useless ; they are also dangerous and immeasurably pernicious ".[115] Remy also speaks of all who have surrendered themselves to the power of the Demon, as weary of his tyranny and bitterly conscious of their guilt, ever wishing to throw off the yoke of evil, so harsh and unjust a task-master is Satan,[116] who chides and punishes them sorely at each motion towards good, each inspiration of grace.

We have just spoken of those who are innocent victims of evil, and lest there be some misunderstanding or ambiguity with regard to this particular point, one which has already confessedly offered difficulties and (I fear) led some into error, it will accordingly not merely be fitting but also incumbent to inquire how far and in what manner by the aid of the Devil witches are able to torment and torture others, to harm and waste men's goods, to visit their bodies with sickness, even to kill and bring to the grave. The subject has been discussed at ample length and in all its bearings by authorities of the first order, by Kramer and Sprenger in the *Malleus Maleficarum*, by Bishop Binsfeld and Bodin, by Guazzo, Remy, Paulus Grillandus, Delrio, Jacques d'Autun, and many more, but since we are in some sort dealing with it particularly as it regards or may regard lycanthropy we will consider quite briefly the quiddity of the whole question, whether in fact witches and sorcerers can and do afflict others by their spells, charms, and cantrips, their periapts and fascinations, as it is debated by a learned physician, the eminent Daniel Sennert, in the ninth part of his *De Morbis Occultis*,[117] and although we are indeed unable to agree with him on many points he never strays *contra fidem*, and correcting his erroneous propositions from more orthodox and sounder treatises we can profit not a little from the general arguments he advances with such skill and learning.

Born at Breslau on 25th November, 1572, Daniel Sennert was early distinguished by his great parts and his intense application to study. He lectured *summa cum laude* at Wittenburg, and although there were indeed those who said that so vast was his library learning he excelled more in the theoretic rather than in the practic, none the less he was in 1628 appointed body physician to George I, Elector of Saxony. Sennert died of the plague at Wittenburg on 21st July, 1637, being 65 years old. One of his most famous works is the *Practica Medicina*, published 4to 1628.[118]

Much dialectic and controversy, a good deal of misconception and inexactitude, might have been saved had certain writers who took upon themselves to assail the results and reports of experience and reason but borne carefully in mind that these mischiefs cannot be wrought by the Demon at the instigation of his slaves and devotees were they not allowed and permitted by the power of Almighty God—*Deo permittente* is the vital clause. The chief source of error seems to have

lain in some notion that the evidence of the Devil's handiwork
and his interference with the affairs of men to their hurt and
bane seems to impugn the Omnipotence of God. As the
Capuchin Jacques d'Autun lays down : " *Sola permissio
Dei est causa cur Dœmon possideat corpus.*" He adds : " Quoy ?
la diuine Prouidence abandōnera les iustes à la malice & à
la rage d'vn Magicien esclaue du Demon : Et Dieu qui à
donné des Anges Gardiens pour la conseruation des Creatures
rachetées de son Sang, les abandonnera à la furie d'vne
Megere ? Des opinions si mal fondées, ne sont receuës que
du Vulgaire, que ne sçait pas que les Magiciens, ny toutes les
puissances de l'Enfer ne peuuent rien attenter sur vne
personne consacrée à Dieu par le Baptesme, *si Dieu ne le
permet* ; que s'il y a des Possedez (comme il n'y a nul doute)
les malefices des Sorciers n'en font pas la cause, il faut
rapporter vne si rude épreuue en des foibles Creatures, *à la
seule permission Diuine.* Le Concile d'Ephese d'où cette
verité est tirée, ne reconnoit point d'autre cause, & les
Theologiens qui l'ont regardé comme vn phase, pour éuiter
de semblables écueils, ont rapporté la possession des Demons,
non à la malice des Esprits rebelles, ny aux charmes &
Sortileges des Magiciens ou Sorciers, mais à la permission
Diuine." [119] The Fathers continually remind us how the
demons fear and tremble exceedingly before God, as, for
example, S. Cyril of Alexandria, who in his magnificent
Encomium in sanctam Mariam Deiparam, addressing himself
to Nestorius, writes : 'Αλλ' οὐ πιστεύεις προφήταις καὶ
ἀποστόλοις, και εὐαγγελισταῖς καὶ τῷ ἀρχαγγέλῳ Γαβριήλ ; κἄν
τοὺς συν δαίμονὰς σου μίμησαι, τοὺς φρίξαντας αὐτοῦ τὴν δυνάμιν
καὶ φωνήσαντας· " Τί ἡμῖν καὶ σοὶ Ἰησοῦ Υἱὲ τοῦ Θεοῦ ; ἦλθες
ὧδε πρὸ καιροῦ βασανίσαι ἡμᾶς." [120]

As King James has so very pertinently and convincingly
written : " For since by God's permission, he [the Devil]
layed sicknesse vpon IOB, why may he not farre easilier
lay it vpon any other. For as an old practisian, he knows
well inough what humor domines most in anie of vs, and as
a spirite hee can subtillie waeken vp the same, making it
peccant, or to abounde, as he thinkes meete for troubling of
vs, when God will so permit him." [121]

Not only indeed have we in Scripture the example of
holy Job whom God permitted Satan to plague with the loss

of all his possessions, the deaths of his children, and " a very grievous ulcer, from the sole of the foot even to the top of his head ", but we are expressly told : " There are spirits that are created for vengance, and in their fury they lay on grievous torments." [122]

Dr. Daniel Sennert inquires whether diseases can be brought upon a man by means of spells and black magic, so that such a one will wither, consume and decay, peak and pine, and even fall away into death. It is universally agreed that if such an evil charm can prevail it will be wrought in one (or more) of three ways : firstly, by a look, a malign glance, the evil eye ; secondly, by the voice, the mutter of some occult rune, and especially by presumptuously over-praising and in scorn extolling him to be harmed [123]; thirdly, by a touch, a contact, exsufflation or gesture.[124]

Sennert does not, however, discuss a point which we may pause to ask. Have these charms, these cantrips, this abacadabra, and these sigils any evil influence in them-selves, and if not why then are they employed by sorcerers and witches when about their foul businesses ?

Let Jacques d'Autun answer our first question : " Il est vray que les Sorciers par leurs paroles & ceremonies superstitieuses, ne contribuënt pas à l'effet du malefice. I'ay desja dit que leurs mots barbares sont sans vertu, & que de tous les maux qu'il pretendent faire, le Demon en est l'Autheur ; mais il ne le feroit pas, si le Sorcier n'estoit de concert auecque luy, & si non seulement il ne donnoit son consentement, mais encore s'il ne preparoit les sorts & les charmes, auecque les circonstances dont ils ont conuenu. I'auoüe qu'ils sont les instruments du Demon, lequel à la veuë des signes de leur Paction, execute le mal qu'il leur a promis de faire ; mais ce ne sont pas que des Instruments in animez." [125] Accordingly we may be well assured that these mutterings and incantations, these secret songs and signs, have of themselves no power to effect the desired end. That is wrought by the Devil with the co-operation of the will of the witch, who prays and urges him to accomplish the evil act, the blighting of crops, the smiting of cattle with murrain or man with sickness, whatever the intention may be. Yet these words and gestures have a very deep and vital significance not *per se* but *per accidens*. They are the symbols

and witnesses of the unholy pact between Satan and the
sorcerer, and blasphemy moreover possesses of itself a
compelling attraction for evil spirits, so that in a very real
sense the fiend, urged and reminded by these evocations,
performs his part of the contract and will inevitably demand
(although not in right nor in justice) that the other conditions
also be fulfilled at the appointed time. Moreover, Satan
in his boundless pride is always first and foremost desirous
of homage and worship, that adoration due to God alone.
The last, and as it were the climax, of Our Lord's three
temptations was the mysterious view of " all the kingdoms
of the world, and the glory of them "with the Devil's whispered
words : " All these will I give thee, if falling down thou
wilt adore me." [126] Therein Satan put forth the exercise of
all his strength and unveiled his ultimate purpose. Now the
witch by these spells and charms, which are the medial (but
not essential) instrumentality of working evil, definitely pays
that homage to the powers of evil which the demon craves
and demands. Therefore by no means must they be omitted
or forborne.

Having made clear this important circumstance we return
to the treatise of Sennert. Many authors are quoted in the
De Morbis Occultis, historians, physicians, philosophers, and
poets : Vergil, Plato, Ovid, Cicero, Pliny, Plutarch, Vida,
Aristotle, Galen, Livy, Suetonius, Heliodorus, Apuleius,
Hippocrates, Weyer, Boece, Scaliger, Nicolas Jacquerius,
Cardan, Cornelius Gemma, Antonio Beneveni, Bodin, Remy,
Alessandro Benedicti, Gregory Horstius, Battista Codronchi,
John Languis, Zacuto of Lisbon, and other names of lesser
note.

In the first place Sennert is demonstrably in error when he
writes that in his opinion warlocks and evil folk cannot
injure others by a look, and he inclines to reduce any ill
results which follow from overlooking to the effects of
imagination aggravated by terror and alarm, so that those
weak subjects who are prone to an epilepsy or hysterical
affections might indeed fall ill after but not owing to the
malignant glance of some reputed witch. Setting aside the
possibilities and powers of hypnotism, and the horrible
influence of the evil eye which cannot be gainsaid, since there
are the famous cases of the *eye-biting* witches of Ireland [127] ;

and S. Thomas lays down that the eye is able to work evil
on an external object, so that when a soul is vehemently
moved to wickedness, as occurs mostly in little old women,
the countenance becomes venemous and hurtful wherein
spiteful demons co-operate, whilst in the *Malleus Maleficarum* it is definitely stated that there are witches who can
bewitch " by a mere look or glance from their eyes ", so that
as Blessed Angelo says the evil eye is a matter of common
knowledge and daily experience.[128]

Beliefs and practices relating to the evil eye, all extremely
similar in nature, are found the whole world over from the
earliest times.[129]   Thus this fascination is spoken of in the
Vedas,[130] the Zendavesta,[131] whilst allusions are not infrequent
in Greek and Latin literature.[132]   It occurs with the Slavs,[133]
the Scandinavians,[134] and among Celtic peoples.   The
Etruscans and the ancient Egyptians feared the bale of the
evil eye.[135]   In Assyrian incantations it is guarded against,[136]
whilst the Jewish,[137] Phœnician,[138] and Carthaginian traditions
have influenced the creed of Mohammed.[139]   In Scotland [140]
and in modern Greece [141] ;   in England, particularly in the
northern and more westerly counties [142] ;   in Morocco [143]
and North Africa [144] ;   in Central Africa [145] and among the
Zulus [146] ;   among the Bushmen [147] ;   in Asia with the Chinese
and Tibetans [148] ;   in the Malay Archipelago [149] and in
Polynesia [150] ;   among the peoples of America, North, Central,
and Southern [151] ;   everywhere men dread and have always
dreaded the glance of the evil eye.[152]

Bacon said in his essay *Of Envy*, that both Love and Envy
" come easily into the Eye, especially vpon the presence of
the Obiects ;   which are the Points, that conduce to Fascination, if any such thing there be.   We see likewise, the Scripture
calleth *Enuy*, An *Euill Eye* :   And the Astrologers, call the
euill Influences of the Starrs, *Euill Aspects* ;   So that still,
there seemeth to be acknowledged, in the Act of *Enuy*, an
Eiaculation, or Irradiation of the Eye ".   He further remarks :
" the Act of Enuy, had somewhat in it, of *Witchcraft* ;   so
there is no other Cure of *Enuy*, but the Cure of *Witchcraft* :
And that is, to remoue the *Lot* (as they call it) and to lay it
vpon another." [153]   Leonard Vair in his *De Fascino*, speaking
of the eyes as " alter animus ", writes : " Ex ipsis radii
quidam emittuntur, qui veluti iacula quaedam, ac sagittae

ad effascinandorum corda deferuntur, totumque corpus inficiunt, atque ita nulla interposita mora arbores, segetes, bruta animalia, et homines perniciosa qualitate inficiunt, et ad interitum deducunt." It is not without significance that Mr. J. C. Lawson remarked : " The evil eye, it would seem, is a regular attribute both of the Gorgon and of the wolf." Experience indeed will not permit us to doubt that there are to-day no few yelder-eyed witches.

Sennert then catalogues and discusses the various names given to sorcerers and witches : they are *pharmaceutriae, incantatores, veneficae, maleficae, magi, sagae, lamiae, striges,* and their craft is *ars atracia,* " die Schroarkefunst," " non quidem ab atro colore sed ab Atrace in Thessalia."[154] However these several kinds of witches may slightly differ one from another, some using one sort of spoken spell and some another, a philtre or brew, they all have this in common, they have made a pact with the Devil of which the chief article is the renunciation of God, and the chief intent to ensue evil and do it.

Especially do they raise strife in households, they sow discord betwixt man and wife,[155] they procure sterility and abortion, and strike man in his deepest affections, in human love, depriving him of the virile member, " membrum virile veneficio ablatum." [156] These acts are particularly reprobated in the famous Bull of Innocent VIII, *Summis desiderantes affectibus,* 9th December, 1484.[157] Sennert indeed quotes from Condrochi, whose authority he was apparently unaware is the *Malleus Maleficarum.*[158] He also has an interesting history from Zacuto, under whose direct notice the incidents came. A young gallant of Lisbon endeavouring to gain the love of a maiden aged 16, the child of worthy and wealthy parents, had recourse to a witch. This hag moulded a wax image of the girl and used various incantations, with the result that the victim fell into an extraordinary sickness that baffled the physicians, who deemed she was suffering from some affection of the womb. Wellnigh at their wits' end, her parents secretly consulted an astrologer, and eventually the girl was cured by the help of a sorceress. Before she was finally freed she vomited a creature like a mouse.[159]

Sennert controverts and refutes Weyer, whose opinion

was that diseases cannot be induced by spells. He points
out that the Devil is most skilled in poisons, that he instructs
his servants in the art of venefices, and in many cases no
doubt they bring about the illness owing to the subtle
introduction of some toxicant. Some diseases which are
natural they heighten and aggravate; others they induce
by their powders and unguents. The Devil can afflict men
as he afflicted with God's permission Holy Job,[160] but when
he torments men this is not owing to the power of the witch,
although she is deceived and thinks the ill is due to her.
The Devil works on natural causes to produce disease. He
also procures sterility and abortion. He can also hurt and
harm men by sudden violence. He mocks his slaves by
glamour and illusion.

Although the evil is not done by the power of the witches,
they are none the less equally guilty. Upon this point, we
may remark, all authorities are agreed, and it will suffice
to quote Jacques d'Autun, who sums up the matter very
clearly and concisely by emphasizing that the essential
crime of the sorcerer lies in the fact he has worshipped the
Devil, giving Satan that honour and glory which belong to
the Majesty of God alone : " c'est pour cette raison, que
quand mesme le Sorcier n'auroit commis aucun Crime, dont
le prochain auroit esté endommagé, il meriteroit la mort
comme coupable du crime de leze-Majesté Diuine, & Humaine,
commis contre la personne de IESVS-CHRIST, Dieu &
homme." [161]

Sennert reviews the arguments of Weyer, which upon
examination he dismisses as trite and useless. He then
remarks that pacts with Satan are essentially " mendacia
et fallacia ". " Fallit Diabolus." " Licet magna Diaboli
sit potestas nulli tamen etiam ad sagarum voluntatem nocere
potest sine Dei permissione."

The various cures for a disease of diabolic origin are listed
and commented upon,[162] whence rises the point whether
a sufferer may apply to a witch to relieve the sickness which
has been induced by a witch. Sennert replies : No, it is not
lawful. This, however, remains a very difficult and dubious
question,[163] and although Sennert is so definite in his negative,
the conclusion is not quite so easy. The Venerable Duns
Scotus, Blessed Henry of Segusio, Godfrey of Fontaines,

Ubertino of Casale, Francesco Maria Guazzo,[164] and other
authorities not a few argue that it is permissible to remove
witchcraft even by superstitious and vain means, since it is
meritorious to destroy the works of the Devil, which indeed
is hardly to be disputed. On the other hand, S. Thomas,
S. Bonaventura, S. Albertus Magnus, Peter a Palude,
Boguet,[165] and other great names maintain a contrary
opinion.

Fra José Angles, a Franciscan of Valencia, titular bishop
of Posonium, who is regarded as a theologian of moderate
and equable views, in his *Flores Theologicarum Quaestionum
in II. Sent.*, Madriti, 1586, Quaestio unica *De Arte Magica*,[166]
Artic. vi, " An liceat sine peccato opera diaboli uti " ; Secunda
diffic., " Utrum liceat uti opera eius, qui maleficia
exercet ? "[167] asks whether it is permissible to request or
persuade a man to unlock, dissolve, or impede a spell, if there
is none the less good reason to believe such relief cannot be
effected without the mediation of the demon or the confection
of some further spell ? He decides that it is not lawful,
inasmuch as the wizard cannot perform the operation without
recourse to the aid of Satan, which is in itself a heinous sin,
and he who requests or induces another to commit a sin
himself becomes the partaker of and participator in that sin.
Bishop Angles will not even allow a man " bona fide magicis
incantationibus et adjurationibus uti ".[168] But here the
whole point turns on *magicis* and *adjurationibus*. Assuredly
we must not consent to nor yet take part, however remotely,
in any magical practices or casting of spells. But it is the
direct opposite of consenting to a thing if we destroy that
thing. A spell may not then be counter-checked by another
spell, but it may be dissolved by burning the instrument
of evil.

Yet that great and grave theologian Blessed Angelo Carletti
di Chivasso (1411–1495), in his *Summa de Casibus Conscientiæ*
(the *Summa Angelica*),[169] under the title *Superstitio*, 18,
relying upon the *Doctor Facundus*, Pietro Aureoli,[170] whom
John XXII appointed Archbishop of Aix in 1321, and referring
to his *Commentarium in Sententiarum IV* (iv distinctio,
xxxiv, quaest. 2), permits a man in order that a spell may
be removed to have recourse to or consult with one ever
defamed as witch. These two Franciscan theologians base

their judgment upon S. Augustine, who in the matter of an
oath laid down " licitum mihi esse uti ad commodum meum
juramento hominis infidelis quamvis sciam illum juraturum
per Deos suos falsos quos colit ".[171]

It were superfluous to emphasize that neither Pietro Aureoli
nor Blessed Angelo tolerate any dealing with the demon. It
is argued that it does not follow that because a witch has
learned her art from an evil source, every exercise of that
art or every result of that art must necessarily be evil.

Blessed Angelo writes : " Utrum sciens maleficium possit
sine periculo illud solvere. Secundum Petrum Aureolum
[l.c.], aliud maleficium fieri non potest sine peccato infideli-
tatis." He then quotes S. Augustine : " de juramento
infidelis jurantis in nomine dei sui." " Non possit inducere
aliquem ad aliquid maleficium faciendum. Si tunc est
aliquis dispositio actualiter facere aliquid maleficium ut
aliquid destruat possum illo uti ad bonum meum. potest
etiam tolli per destructionem maleficii sui sciens quia eo
destructo demon non amplius fatigaret, quia ex pacto non
assistit nisique diu durat tale signum. [Ven. Dun Scotus is
then cited.] Nedum non est peccatum : immo meritorium
destruere opera diaboli. Nec in hoc est infidelitas aliqua,
quia destructio non ad quies cit operibus diaboli, sed credit
demonem posse vexare et velle fatigare dum tale signum
durat. Et destructio signi talis imponit finem vexationis.
Potest etiam destruere quis maleficia per sacrata :
adjurationes divitias : orationes et hujusmodi meritoria." [172]

Alfonso de Castro in his *De Iusta Haereticorum Punitione*,
Libri iii (Lugduni, 1556), i, 15,[173] lays down that it is not
permissible to dissolve one spell by working another spell.
He terms it justly " malum pessimum " to seem to give
countenance to any operation which may involve the invocation or the reliance upon the help of a familiar. He teaches,
in fine, that " maleficium solicitans, ut maleficium maleficio
solvat, graviter peccat ". But, and here we really have the
important point, he concludes : " Si autem maleficium tale
esset ut sine peccato posset a malefico dissolvi, ut puta, quia
scit ubi laqueus aut imago, aut ligaturae aliquae, aut
characteres cum quibus est jam inceptum maleficium, tunc
sicut ipse potest sine peccato dissolvere maleficium con-
fringendo illa omnia, ita quilibet alius potest sine peccato

petere ab ipso malefico, ut illo modo dissolvat maleficium." [174]

The whole matter is considered at some length by Kramer
and Sprenger, who acknowledge that here we have a most
nice dilemma. They conclude that we must distinguish
the various classes and kinds of remedies. There are, in fine,
three general conditions whereby any remedy is, in ordinary
circumstances, rendered unlawful. First, when the spell is
removed through the agency of another witch, and by further
witchcraft, that is to say, by some evil power. Secondly,
when the spell is removed not by a witch but by an honest
person in such a way, however, that it is placed upon another
individual. Thirdly, when the spell is removed by an honest
person and not even placed upon another, but when some
open or tacit invocation of devils or operation of black
magic is employed in the process. At the same time there
are remedies which, if they do not injure another person,
may be tolerated even should they smack somewhat of
superstitious usage and vanity. Further details can be read
in the *Malleus Maleficarum*, part ii, question 2, introduction,[175]
to which reference should be made.

" Maleficia maleficiis curare non licet," definitely pro-
nounces the Bishop of Benevento, Giovanni Francesco Leone,
in his *Libellus de Sortilegiis*, c. xii ; for he adds : " Mala
enim non sunt facienda, ut eveniant bona : maleficiorum
curatio a Deo est impetranda, qui omnia potest," wise words
of infinite consolation and encouragement.[176]

Further, Sennert asks : *An liceat instrumenta Magica
quaerere et abolere ?* [177] Curiously enough he adopts an
extraordinary position, and now contends at great length
that it is not lawful to seek out, discover, and burn such
instruments or implements of witchdom as are the media
of conveying harm. For, he says, that by destroying such
and looking for a good result as the consequence of their
demolition, one is in some sense acknowledging the Devil's
power. This, however, seems to me to be a mere quibble,
since " Si licet maleficos de medio tollere, ea spe et fine, ne
hominibus amplius noceant per diabolum, ut ejus viva
instrumenta ; licet enim signa maleficii tollere, ne per
diabolum illa amplius noceant, ut ejus fictitia instrumenta,
non operantia quidem, sed eum ad operandum excitantia ".

The whole point is admirably argued by Delrio, *Disquisitionum Magicarum Libri Sex* (Lib. vi, cap. 2, sect. 1, quaestio 3),[178] who decides and indeed proves that one may most certainly seek out and destroy any instrument of witchcraft, any baleful charm, evil amulet, waxen puppet, witches' ladder, and the like, or any property upon which a spell has been cast, so that it has become or may become a conductor, dangerous and infect. I will go further and subscribe to Dominic Soto, who says that it is praiseworthy and meritorious to destroy these things, since thereby the charm is dissolved.[179] Girolamo Menghi, also, most highly approves of, and indeed urges, the destruction of this ensorcelled gear, whatever it may be : " non enim solum licet ; sed etiam est meritorium destruere opera diaboli." [180] He justly terms all such questions as that of Sennert trifling and absurd.

Pietro Piperno, a physician of Benevento, who was also an excellent theologian, has written at length and very learnedly in his *De Magicis Affectibus, horum Dignotione, Prænotione, Curatione, Medica, Stratagemmatica, Divina, plerique Curationibus Electis* (1634) of natural remedies and of superstitious charms and formulas in sickness. In chapter iv, book ii, he discusses : " Ut dæmon nocere desinat estne licitum, signum maleficiis destruere ? " He lays down most emphatically : "Non enim solum licet, sed est meritorium destruere opera diaboli, nec in hoc est aliqua infidelitas, quia destruens non acquiescit operibus malignis, sed credit dæmonem posse, & velle fatigare, dum tale durat signum, ac destructio tali signi finem imponit tali vexationi." He tells us, moreover, that the instruments of witchcraft must be burned, not destroyed in any other way, and " piis ceremoniis ea igne concremari melius est ".[181] He holds that one may even request the witch to remove the spell and pay her money to calcinate and combust the periapts or ladders or figurines, since there will be no invocation of the dark powers whilst the intention is to put an end to and annul the effects of evil.

Piperno argues his case well and is undoubtedly in the right. Any object or instrument of sorcery should be burned, and it is important to get rid of and consign to the flames any articles which have been overlooked.

I have myself known so ordinary and commonplace a thing

as a pair of curtains to which a spell was attached. A woman, afterwards known to have dealt in curious arts, who lived in a certain family, laid some charm upon a pair of blue richly brocaded curtains which usually hung in the drawing-room of the house. The curtains were of themselves costly and fine ; they were handsome and much admired, so that the woman in question judged the family would never consent to replace them or pack them away out of use. When she left the service, which incidentally was in a disagreeable manner, the spell began to work. The family moved from one house to another, and in those years ill-luck always followed. The blue curtains naturally hung in each drawing-room window. At last, owing to various circumstances, suspicion was aroused. The curtains were taken down, and if not destroyed, have been discarded, and are carefully stored out of sight.

It is certain that evil may attach itself to possessions, to jewellery and gems, to objects of value and objects of comparatively no worth, to pictures, to miniatures and photographs, and, almost especially perhaps, to articles of furniture.

It may not be unfitting to give a striking example of this, as I have read and am very well assured is both recent and true. A young couple, who live in a small but ancient coast town in Devonshire, after a courtship unmarred by any cloud, were married. The husband, who was about twenty-five years old, had worked with one firm for seven years, bearing a remarkably steady reputation. They spent a brief honeymoon in London, and then returned to their new home. One night, about a fortnight later, the young fellow came home completely intoxicated. His bride was aghast. The next day he was truly penitent, reproaching himself most bitterly. It was the first time that he had ever drunk to excess and he was usually content with just one glass of beer. About a month later they brought him home one night dead drunk. After this he was miserable and full of remorse. A few weeks later the same thing happened, he again got hopelessly drunk. His wife privately had recourse to a " wise woman " whom she consulted on the case. This sibyl came to the house and at once pointed to a certain piece of furniture, a large old-fashioned arm-chair, which had been given to the young couple as a wedding present, and in which the husband usually sat of an evening. "This is the trouble," said the wise woman. "It is all wrong. If you take my advice you will break it up and burn." The wife forthwith burned the chair, and after that all went well. Her husband never showed the slightest inclination to drink. The history of the chair was traced. It had once belonged to a butcher, who was a hardened drunkard, and who in a delirious fit had killed himself whilst sitting in it.[182] If such ill-luck befell in this case, what may not happen when the evil is directed and propelled of malice prepense and potent ?

Sennert is of opinion that a man may justly resort to threats and blows in order to compel a witch to remove a spell or unlock a charm. It is indeed natural that one who has been harmed either in himself, those dear to him, or his goods, should adopt violent methods, and they are to my mind even praiseworthy, for he is thus showing his detestation of the witch, her master, and his abhorrence of the black art.

Pietro Piperno confirms this and writes : " Licet a malefico petere, imo licet etiam illum minis, & levibus verberibus cogere, ut maleficium tollat, quandocumque probabiliter credo illum sine maleficio modo aliquo licito id facere posse sine quandocumque non sum moraliter certus quod utetur modo illicito." [183]

Benedict XIV, who was among the most learned of all the successors of S. Peter, debates whether a witch, terrified by threats and blows, commits a fresh sin by transferring to an ox (or any brute animal) the deadly spell she has cast upon the son of the man who trounced her. The conclusion is that the hag is guilty of a fresh sin inasmuch as she must have recourse to the demon to convey the spell from the sufferer and lay it elsewhere, whilst the father is in no wise to be held to blame since his only object is to save his child, and he is not bound to know by what methods the woman works.[184]

In January, 1928, a family of Hungarian peasants belonging to a village near Szegedin, were brought to trial at the assizes for causing the death of a witch. A spell was cast upon a farmer named Pittlik, who was seized by a mysterious sickness which in the course of months brought him wellnigh to the grave, and which the doctors were unable to cure. One night he saw a hag who caught him by the throat, and muttered some horrid blasphemy. His relatives resolved to watch for the witch, and accordingly night after night they lay in wait. About a week passed, when there came one midnight a soft tapping and an aged woman crept into the room. The watchers flung themselves on her with sticks and axes, but unfortunately deprived her of life. Nevertheless, from that moment Pittlik was completely cured. The court justly acquitted the accused since the case pointed to the existence of a witch, and they had acted under irresistible compulsion. At a second trial for homicide the family were sentenced to short terms of imprisonment, which were reduced by the supreme court. I understand a third trial was ordered.[185]

Not long ago a Devonshire farmer attacked a woman, reputed as a witch, scratched her with a pin until she bled, and threatened to shoot her, inasmuch as she had ill-wished him and cast a spell on his pig.[186]

The concluding chapters of his work Sennert devotes to the natural remedies which must be tried in cases of sickness through ensorcelling, and the drugs and treatment, which fortunately enough in very many instances are found to be effectual. But it is highly advisable also that, if there be manifest signs of some supernormal malady, strange, irregular, and unusual symptoms, the aid of the Church be required, yet not upon any light cause or occasion. In his final chapter, *De divina curatione*, the doctor writes with a good deal of unction of exorcism.[187]

I have, of course, in this survey only taken up a few points of interest and importance from the *De Morbis Occultis*, and I do not pretend to give a digest or even a conspectus of the whole tract, which in fine I do not consider save in so far as it concerns us here.

Pietro Piperno touches very lightly upon lycanthropy, and seems inclined to suppose that it is not due to demoniacal possession. He has been misled here by Weyer, for he writes : " De lycantropia, seu lupina insania Arabibus Chatrab. unde Avicen. lib. 3. F. 1. T. 4. 15. appellavit quamdam maniam daemoniacam ; Leoninam vel avinam, vel caninam, &c. monstrantem signa fere obsessi Ovid 1. metamorph. sic depingebat . . . qua melancolie refert Forestus lib. 10.

obs. 19. auctoritate Vuierij, multi doctissimi viri Medici decepti sunt ad affirmandum morbum esse daemoniacum."[188] Having established then at least a probable opinion that lycanthropy, *daemonium lupinum*, is for the most part, if indeed not invariably, of the nature of possession, before we proceed to discuss the actual transformation of men into wolves, the methods and possibility of such metamorphosis, it will not be impertinent briefly to consider this disease, which the Greeks termed λυκανθρωπία, which has by more than one writer erroneously been supposed the tradition of the werewolf, and to review the opinions of certain great medical writers from the beginning.

Marcellus Sidetes, a native of Side in Pamphylia, who was born towards the end of the first century, and lived in the reigns of Hadrian and Antoninus Pius, A.D. 117–161,[189] is famous as the author of a long medical poem in Greek hexameter verse, which was so highly esteemed that, as Suidas tells us, the emperors commanded that all public libraries in Rome must be furnished with a copy.[190] Unfortunately only two fragments of this work remain, Περὶ Λυκανθρώπου, *De Lycanthropia*, and Ἰατρικα περὶ Ἰχθύων, *De Remediis ex Piscibus*. The *De Lycanthropia* is preserved, but in a prose version only, by the Greek doctor Aëtius, who compiled an encyclopædic work on medicine from the writings of many authors now no longer extant, for which reason rather than for any original matter the Βιβλία Ἰατρικὰ Ἐκκαίδεκα are valued. Maximilian Schneider writes : " Ex tanta Marcelli Sidetae librorum copia nihil ad nostra tempora servatum est nisi duo vel tria fragmenta . . . Quantum fragmentum Marcelli Περὶ λυκανθρωπίας servatum est in Aetii Iatr. vi, 11 (editum ab J. G. Schneidero, l.c. p. 109 seq. et Kuehnio, l.c. i, p. 7), sed ita ut numeri resoluti sint in orationem pedestrem." [191] Johann Gottlieb Schneider (p. 109) gives : " Marcelli Sidetae Fragmentum Περὶ Λυκανθρώπου quod exstat apud Aëtium S. 6, p. 104 b. περὶ λυκανθρώπου ἤτοι κυνανθρώπου, et apud Paulum Æginet. 8, p. 80 b. qui tacito nomine autoris haec repetiit, περὶ λυκάονος ἢ λυκανθρώπου." [192] Since Schneider thus refers to Paulus Ægineta,[193] who has but conveyed the earlier work of Marcellus Sidetes, we may turn to the later writer, and it will not be amiss to quote the excellent translation by Francis

Adams,[194] who Englished *The Seven Books of Paulus Ægineta* with an ample commentary for the Sydenham Society, three volumes, London, 1844.

The passage in question [195] is the sixteenth section of book iii : " On Lycaon, or Lycanthropia. Those labouring under lycanthropia go out during the night imitating wolves in all things and lingering about sepulchres until morning. You may recognize such persons by these marks : they are pale, their vision feeble, their eyes dry, tongue very dry, and the flow of the saliva stopped ; but they are thirsty, and their legs have incurable ulcerations from frequent falls. Such are the marks of the disease. You must know that lycanthropia is a species of melancholy which you may cure at the time of the attack, by opening a vein and abstracting blood to fainting, and giving the patient a diet of wholesome food. Let him use baths of sweet water, and then milk-whey for three days, and purging with the hiera from colocynth twice or thrice. After the purgings use the theriac of vipers, and administer those things mentioned for the cure of melancholy. [Dodder of thyme, *epithymus* ; aloes ; wormwood after purging ; acrid vinegar as a beverage ; squills, poley, slender birthwort ; phlebotomy and cataplasms. In chronic cases evacuation, by vomiting with hellebore.] When the disease is already formed, use soporific embrocations, and rub the nostrils with opium when going to rest."

Adams comments [196] : " See Aëtius (vi, 11) ; Oribasius (Synops. viii, 10) ; Actuarius (Mett. Med. i, 16) ; Anonymus (de Lycanth. ap. Phys. et Med. Min.) ; Psellus (Carm. de Re Med. ibid.) ; Avicenna (iii, 1, 5, 22) ; Haly Abbas (Theor. ix, 7, Pract. v, 24) ; Alsaharavius (Pract. 1, 2, 28) ; Rhases (Divis. 10, Cont. 1). All the other authorities give much the same account of this species of melancholy as Paulus . . . Avicenna recommends the application of the actual cautery to the sinciput when the other remedies fail. Haly Abbas describes the disease by the name of *melancholia canina*. He says the patient delights to wander among tombs, imitating the cries of dogs ; that his colour is pale ; his eyes misty (tenebricosi), dry, and hollow; his mouth parched ; and that he has marks on his limbs of injuries which he has sustained from falls. He recommends the same treatment as our author : indeed he evidently

merely translates this section of Paulus. Alsaharavius seems
also to allude to this disease by the name of *melancholia
canina.* Rhases' account of it is quite similar to our author's."
Of Aëtius we have just spoken. Oribasius was probably
born about A.D. 325. Suidas and Philostorgius call him a
native of Sardes in Lydia, but Eunapius, who was his friend,
writes that he was born at Pegamus in Mysia, the native
place of Galen. However that may be, Oribasius early
acquired a great professional reputation, and was a particular
favourite with Julian the Apostate, although under the
succeeding emperors he was justly exiled owing to his enmity
against the Christians. He was living at least as late as
A.D. 395, when Eunapius inserted his life in the *Vitae
Philosphorum et Sophistarum.* Of Oribasius three extant works
are considered genuine. Reference is here made to the
Σύνοψις in nine books. It has never been published in the
original Greek, but a Latin version by Joannes Baptista
Rasarius was printed at Venice, 8vo, 1554.

Joannes Actuarius lived at Constantinople towards the end
of the thirteenth century. His *De Methedo Medendi,* in six
books, has only been printed in a Latin translation by
Cornelius H. Mathisius, which first appeared at Venice, 4to,
1554. His works are included in the *Medicae Artis Principes*
of H. Stephens, Paris, folio, 1567.[197]

The *De Lycanthropia,* Περὶ λυκανθρωπίας, is merely a brief
abstract or synopsis of Paulus Ægineta. It will be found
in Julius Ludwig Ideler's *Physici et Medici Graeci Minores,*
Berlin, 1842, vol. ii.[198] In the same collection is included
the *Carmen de Re Medica* of Psellus the Sophist.[199] The
lines in question, 837–841, run :—

Μελάγχολόν τι πρᾶγμα λυκανθρωπία.
Ἔστι γὰρ αὐτόχρημα μισανθρωπία.
Καὶ γνωριεῖς ἄνθρωπον εἰσπεπτωκότα,
Ὁρῶν περιτρέχοντα νυκτὸς τοὺς τάφους,
Ὠχρόν, κατηφῆ, ξηρόν, ἠμελημένον.[200]

Of Avicenna, " un phénomène intellectuel " (980–1036);
Haly Abbas (Ali-ben-el-Abbas) who died 994–5 ; Alsaharavius (Albucasis, Aboul Cassem Khalef ben Abbas
Essahraouy), whose great work is conveniently known as
the *Tesrif (Practice)* ; and Razès (Abou Beer Mohammed
ben Zakarya), who died at a great age in 923 ; full accounts

may be found in Dr. Lucien Leclerc's *Histoire de la Médecine Arabe.*[201]

Of older physicians one may also consult Marcellus Donatus, *De Medica Historia Mirabili,*[202] Liber vi, c. 1, and a writer of later date, Petrus Salius, *De Affectibus Particularibus,* " De Febre Pestilenti Tractatus," c. xix, *De Rabie.*[203]

Robert Burton, speaking of lycanthropia, says : " Some make a doubt whether there be any such disease," which indeed seems a strange thing in the face of history, for not only do very many of the Saints and Fathers and other gravest authors record such terrible happenings, but we also have the testimony of the Sacred Scripture itself. " *This malady,* saith *Avicenna,* troubleth men most in February, and is now-a-days frequent in Bohemia and Hungary, according to Heurnius. Schernitzius will have it common in Livonia." [204]

To Jan van Hewin (Heurne, Heurnius), the celebrated Dutch physician who was born at Utrecht 25th January, 1543, and died at Leyden 11th August, 1601, reference has already been made. He wrote many medical treatises which were accepted as of great authority. The *De Morbis qui in singulis partibus humani capitis incidere consueverunt* was first printed at Leyden 1594, 4to. The rubric of chapter xiii runs : " *De Mania, id est, Insania, aut Furore vel Ecstasi Melancholica,*" and the last paragraph deals with lycanthropy.

" Lycanthropia (λυκάων) qualis sit affectio primum diximus. dicitur Arabibus chatrab, sumpto nomine a bestiola quae sine serie certa super aquas huc & illuc fertur : ita hi etiam stare loco nesciunt. Refert D. Schenckius (*Historia mira*) ex Io. Fincelio, libro 2. Mirac. hanc historiam. Patavii lupus sibi videbatur agricola anno 1541. Multosque in agris insiliit, trucidavitque. Tandem non sine difficultate captus, confidenter se asseveravit verum esse lupum, discrimen solum existere in pelle cum pilis inuersa. Quapropter gladiis feriunt eius tibias & brachia, amputantque, veritatem rei exploraturi. Cognito vero hominis errore, eum chirurgis tradunt curandum, sed post dies non multos exspiravit." Van Hewin then diagnoses the symptoms of lycanthropy, and prescribes the remedies, medicated baths, a light diet with milk, senna, and other drugs. If necessary, the cautery.

The well-known Johann Weyer, in his *De iis, qui Lamiarum Maleficio affecti putantur,* devotes chapter xxiii to lycanthropy:

" *De λυκανθρωπία morbo, quo se in lupos converti credunt homines.*" [205] He is more cautious here than in many passages of this work, and indeed his chapter is largely a paraphrase of the older authorities, especially Paulus Ægineta. Weyer describes the symptoms very exactly, and recommends much the same course of treatment, although he is perhaps a little more detailed in the account of the various remedies. He also quotes William of Brabant, and the famous history given by Job Fincel. We shall have occasion to return to Weyer when dealing with other aspects of lycanthropy.

Weyer is quoted, and indeed largely drawn upon, by Johann Georg Schenck, a celebrated physician of Fribourg, where he was born towards the end of the sixteenth century. The son of Johann Schenck of Graffenberg, he rather grandiloquently describes himself as " a Grafenberg Philiater, Hagenoensium Alsatiae Poliater, Comitisque ab Hanaw Physicus Medicus ". In his *Observationum Medicarum, Rararum, Novarum, Admirabilium, et Monstrosarum Tomus*, Frankfort, 1600, liber i, Observatio cclx, he treats *De Lycanthropia*. " Lycanthropia seu lupinae insaniae exempla horribilia." Actually Schenck only repeats and refers to the former authorities. He cites Altomari, Aëtius, Paulus Ægineta, Job Fincel, and others, including (as we have noted) Weyer. Schenck notes : " Id nostro hoc seculo cuidam Hispano nobili oblatum fuisse edendum traditur, qui per deserta ac montes vagabatur ; se in ursum esse conversum phantasia vitiata ratus."

Joannes Arculanus of Verona in his *Practica* (Venice, Giunta, 1557, folio) in his *In Nonum Librum Almansoris Expositio*, caput xvi, *De melancholia*,[206] treats at length of that species of melancholia which " Avicenna terms cutubutt ". " Mania vero est duplex una lupina, aliter dicta daemonium lupinum, videntur enim non homines sed daemones et lupi, qui patiuntur hanc maniam." This great physician has indeed here put his finger upon the spot, and discerns the whole truth of the matter in a few words, since the patients suffering from this diabolical werewolfery " seem in very truth to be men no longer but incarnate devils and ravening wolves ". He also speaks of the second kind of mania, " mania canina ad canum similitudinem." " Sed causa maniae lupinae est melancholia genita per adustionem

cholerae, aut melancholiae, & est deterior, quia difficilioris
curationis, cum humor genitus per adustionem melancholiae
fit magis crassus, ineptior digestioni & resolutioni &
evacuationi. Et signa ejus sunt agitatio, saltus, inquisitio,
lupinositas, id est mores luporum, & aspectus cui non
assimilatur aspectus hominis, imo est sicut luporum. Differt
etiam ab una specie karabiti quae est cum daemonio,
quoniam cum hac mania non est febris sed karabitus est
cum se."

A little later he continues : " Cutubut . . . nomen sumpsit
a quadam specie araneæ quae movetur super aqua diversis
motibus sine ordine. [The water-spider, *tipula*.] . . .
Cutubut autem est species melancholiae plurimum eveniens
in februario, non exspectans usque ad ver, propter sub-
tilitatem humoris melancholici plurimum . . . haec enim
diligit fugere ab hominibus vivis et approprinquare mortuis
et sepulchris cum malitia furoris repente advenientis ei.
Et est ejus processio nocturna, & occultatio diurna. Et
totum istud facit diligendo solitutidem et elongationem ab
hominibus. Et cum hoc non quiescit in uno loco plus una
hora, imo non cessat discurrere et ambulare incessione
diversa ignorans quo vadit cavendo sibi ab hominibus. . . .
Et citrinus est color faciei. Et lingua sicut sitientis. Et
super crura ipsius sunt ulcera quae non consolidantur. . . .
Et oculi ejus sunt sicci, debiles, submersi, non lachrymantes
propter siccitatem cerebri et oculorum."

Arculanus discusses the remedies for lycanthropy, *De cura
cuthubutt*,[207] at considerable length. In addition to the
usual remedies and courses for melancholia he insists upon
the necessity for sleep and repose, and further advises blood-
letting, " copiosior phlebotomia . . . multa extractio
sanguinis." He concludes : " Quantum [remedium] est
ut verberetur cum hic sit multum inobediens."

It may be remarked that Bernard Gordonius recommends
the same somewhat drastic treatment ; " colaphizetur et
flagilletur " are his words.[208]

Richard Argentine, in his *De Praestigiis et Incantationibus
Daemonum*,[209] emphasizes the use of natural remedies in
cases of possession, that the black bile of the sufferer may be
purged with hellebore : " Nam lunatici ut ait Coelius
Rhodiginus eorum intelligantur nomine qui dicuntur

ἐνεργούμενοι, hoc est obsessi, velut in eos agat μήνυ, hoc est luna, in quibus per atram bilem imaginationi mancipatus animus, facile immundorum spirituum fit conceptaculum, et daemoniacam virtutem nanciscitur, quam Eusebius Paredrum dici affirmat, alii assesorem. Daemoniacos praeterea veteres vocabant a nimia capitis humectatione, Cerebrique humorum exuberantia hygrocephalos, inde a nostris quoque maioribus lymphationis nomen ductum est, ut vicio hoc affecti vocentur Lymphatici etiam pro Nymphatici, quod genus morbi lycaones et lycanthropos facit, cynanthropos et melancholicos feros et immanes. Et exorcistae inquit idem qui spiritus per Orationes sanctorum et aspersione aquae benedictae fugare profitentur, primo euacuant sic laborantes ab atra bile."

Girolamo Mercuriale, in his *Medicina Practica*, lib. i, cap. xii, *De Lykanthropia*, treating of the complaint, says : "Assuredly this is a most terrible disease, and yet not necessarily fatal, not even if it last for months. Indeed I have read that after several years it was completely cured. The treatment is the same as that when dealing with lunacy." The Arab physicians recommend copious blood-letting, moreover they advise castigation and many stripes.

Luigi Celio Ricchieri in his *Lectionum Antiquarum Libri Triginta*,[210] lib. xxvii, c. 12, has but a passing notice of lycanthropy : "Est item melancholica affectio, dicta Graecis λυκανθρωπια, et qui sic officiuntur, Lycanthropi, quoniam lupos imitari prorsum videantur. Exsiliunt quippe noctu, adque diem usque inter sepulchra diversantur. Eorum praepallet facies, καὶ δρῶσιν ἀδρανὲς, oculis arescentibus, praecipue vero lingua. Sunt praeterea διψώδεις, hoc est sitibundi : tibiis ex impactione crebra ἀνιάτως, id est citra medelam ulcerosis. Hosce etiam Lycaonas dici, observavimus."

Pierre van Foreest, the eminent Dutch physician, who was born at Alkmaer in 1552 and died there 1597, in his *Observationum . . . Medicinae Theoricae et Practicae Libri XXVIII*,[211] closely follows Joannes Arculanus. Observatio xxv of the tenth book *De Cerebri Morbis* has for rubric *De lycanthropia seu lupina insania*. It is of especial interest as he gives a case which came under his own notice at Alkmaer. A peasant was noticed in the spring-time to be roving about the streets of the town in a peculiar and indecisive manner. His looks were fierce and frantic. After prowling up and down in the cemetery he entered a church, where van Foreest carefully watched his antics (*ut ipsi spectavimus*). He leaped to and fro over the benches, danced wildly, rushed to and fro in the nave and aisles, and could not remain still for a moment. In one hand he held a great club, which he used to keep off any dog he might see in his path, although he neither approached nor attacked individuals. It was remarked that his bare legs, unwashen and filthy, were scarred with the bites of dogs and old ulcerated sores. His body was gaunt, his limbs squalid and foul with neglect, his face ghastly pale, the eyes deep-sunken, dry, and blazing. From these symptoms van Foreest judged that the man was a lycanthrope, but so far as could be discovered he was under no doctor's care. He avoided, indeed, as far as possible the gaze of men, and fled away secretly by himself.

In his *Scholia* van Foreest discusses the disease and its remedies at length, and gives a careful and interesting account of this malady, although perhaps he does not add anything very vital to the observations of his predecessors. He remarks, indeed, that sufferers often imagine themselves to have assumed other animal forms besides that of a wolf. " Plerosque etiam atra bile vitiatos se leones esse, vel daemones, vel aves imaginari, annotavit Avicenna." [212]

Donato Antonio Altomari, the celebrated Neapolitan physician and philosopher, who was born in the first quarter of the sixteenth century, has a chapter, Περὶ λυκανθρωπίας, *De lupina insania*, in his treatise *De Medendis Humani Corporis Malis*,[213] which he wrote in 1560 and dedicated to Pope Paul IV. Altomari draws chiefly from Aëtius and Paulus Ægineta, to whom he refers the student. He agrees that the disease is at its worst in February and mentions two patients whom he has treated successfully. One of these he encountered on a certain day in the streets. The lycanthropist, who was raving, had been violating a graveyard and was clutching members he had torn from a corpse. " Ipsi quidem ferebat humeris crus integrum, ac tibiam defuncti cuiusdam." Altomari notes : " Qui namque hoc affectu detinentur in Februario mense noctu domo egressi lupos in curatis imitantur, & donec dies illucescat, circa defunctorum monumenta vagantur, eaque maxime aperiunt." He emphasizes as notable symptoms an excessive parching thirst, and a complete loss of memory of the attacks after recovery.

Bartolomeo Castelli, a famous physician of Messina, in his well-known *Lexicon medicum*, writes of lycanthropes as follows : " Aegri noctu domo egressi, urbem circumeunt, quadrupedum more incidentes, lupos imitantur ululantes, donec dies illucescat, defunctorum monumenta quaeritant, adaperiunt, cadauerum frusta arripientes, secumque collo gestantes, fugiuntque die uiuos homines, nocte insequentes mortuos. Sunt autem eorum notae : facies pallida, oculi sicci et caui, uisus hebes, lingua siccissima, saliua in ore nulla, sitis immodica, tibiae perpetuo exulceratae propter frequentes casus. Nonnulli etiam ut canes mordent, ex quo arbitror, morbum ipsum κυνανδρωπίαν uocatum fuisse ueteribus." [214]

Petrus Salius mentions that those who eat the roast flesh of a wolf that happens to be mad will be attacked by the disease.[215] He describes certain of the symptoms of the lycanthrope : " Spuma ad os eis apparet, dentibus alios petunt, ut canes latrant, vel ut lupi ululant, dentibus strident, sudant, et convelluntur." [216] We have here the very symptoms of demoniacal possession as in Holy Writ. When Our Lord came down from the Mount of Transfiguration the man from the crowd thus described the effects of possession in his son : " Lo, a spirit seizeth him, and he suddenly crieth out, and he throweth him down and teareth him, so that he foameth ; and bruising him, he hardly departeth from him." These exact details are, it will be remembered, recorded by S. Luke the physician.

Menghi in his *Complementum Artis Exorcisticae* lists among the " Signa Daemoniaci " : " 14. Stridunt dentibus, spumant, ac signa alia ostendunt tanquam Canes rabidi." [217]

Salius lays especial stress upon the detail that lycanthropes avoid water : " aquam perhorrescunt." It were too curious to inquire how far this unnatural dread of clear water is psychologically connected with the water ordeal to which those suspected of sorcery were so often submitted. The history of the " *judicium aquae frigidae* " is long and interesting, but here we need only touch upon it very briefly. Running water in particular is known to dissolve spells and evil charms ; true and natural water is the matter of the " first sacrament ", " the door of the spiritual life ".[218] Thus the element has of itself a certain quality of holiness. " Living water," the Hebrews of old called it.

Water was appointed as a test in cases of sorcery as early as the laws of Hammurabi, King of Babylon, in the third millennium B.c.,[219] and in England the water ordeal is ancient, a full description of this test being given in the Laws of Aethelstan, 924–940.[220] Other codes mention it, and the test was essayed for theft, adultery, and homicide as well as witchcraft. The Fourth Lateran Council, however, in 1215, under Innocent III, by its nineteenth canon forbade priests to pronounce any benedictions at the ordeals of hot or cold water and of the hot iron. There had been grave abuses, whilst in any case the experiment was not wholly trustworthy.

Nevertheless the ordeal itself persisted, so deep-rooted in the rustic mind was a belief in the completest efficacy of " swimming a witch ". Particularly in England and in Germany did the populace favour the practice. In the sixteenth century King James judged that " their fleeting on the water " was appointed by God " for a super-naturall signe of the monstruous impietie of the Witches, that the water shal refuse to receiue them in her bosom, that haue shaken off them the sacred Water of Baptisme, and wilfullie refused the benefite thereof ".[221]

This, however, was flatly denied by William Perkins (1558–1602) in his *A Discourse of the Damned Art of Witchcraft*, published posthumously in 1608 by Thomas Pickering, minister of Finchingfield in Essex, who writes : " And yet to iustifie the casting of a Witch into the water, it is alledged, that hauing made a couenant with the deuill, shee hath renounced her Baptisme, and hereupon there growes an Antipathie betweene her, and water. *Ans.* This allegation serues to no purpose : for all water is not the water of Baptisme, but that onely which is vsed in the very act of Baptisme, and not before nor after. The element out of the vse of the Sacrament, is no Sacrament, but returnes again to his common vse." [222]

Owing to the activities of the errant and unlicensed witchfinders, swimming even in England presently fell into general

disrepute during the seventeenth century. Even Matthew
Hopkins was obliged to acknowledge that in his high noon
the ordeal is by able divines " condemned for no way, and
therefore of late hath, and for ever shall be left ".[223] None the
less the mobile swum witches in England pretty frequently
throughout the eighteenth century, and not unseldom indeed
during the nineteenth. A particularly notorious case occurred
in 1863, at Castle Headingham in Essex,[224] and the *Daily
Telegraph*, 23rd June, 1880,[225] reports that at Dunmow
Petty Sessions, Charles and Peter Brewster, father and son,
were bound over to keep the peace for six months on a charge
of molesting Susan Sharpe, the wife of an army pensioner,
living at High Easter. The two Brewsters wanted to put
her to the test by throwing her in a pond to see if she would
sink or swim. The young defendant declared that he and his
wife were bewitched. The furniture in their house was
disturbed and moved uneasily ; their domestic animals died
in extraordinary ways ; shadows appeared in their bed-
room, some of which bore an uncanny resemblance to
Mrs. Sharpe. They had consulted several " cunning men
and women " in the neighbourhood, apparently with no
result, save that everything pointed to Mother Susan as the
cause of their troubles. I have no doubt at all that here
was a clear case of witchcraft, and that Mrs. Sharpe was
a sorceress of the tribe of Ursley Kempe, Julian Cox, and
Rose Cullender.

We can hardly be surprised that hag-ridden rustics should
resort to the old—if dishonoured—traditional test for
discovering their tormentor's guilt. That theologians and
physicians looked askance at such rough and ready methods
the vulgar little recked.

Jan van Hewin categorically denied that this fleeting on
the water was any proof of witchcraft. " Nullum esse aquae
innatationem Lamiarum indicium," are his words, and he
proceeds to give his reasons for such a judgment, although
it must be confessed these are not perhaps entirely
convincing.[226] What is far more important with reference
to this ordeal is the pronouncement of Benedict XIV when
he wrote : " In Westphaliae regionibus ea superest corruptela,
ut in sagas, atque veneficos inquireretur, eos dejiciendo in
aquam frigidam, ita manibus pedibusque ligatis, ut, cum

PLATE II

Doctor Keiserßperg von den werwölffen.

A WEREWOLF ATTACKS A MAN

(See p. 252)

[face p. 48

natare non valerent, ei submergerentur, innocentes censeren-
tur, si vero supernaterent, pro reis haberentur. At id ipsum
quoque nunc de medio sublatum, et a Judicibus hujusmodi
experimenta proscripta fuerunt." [227] No contrary opinion
must be maintained in the face of this prelection, but it may
be noted that the Pope speaks of swimming a witch only as
" corruptela " and as an experiment. We are free, perhaps,
to consider it a test, although by no means a satisfactory
test, a mere experiment, and historically it is an essay which
has led to scenes of mob violence that are greatly to be
deplored, on which account, chiefly, the Holy Father
suppresses and forbids any such trial.

King James points out that save " at euery light occasion
. . . dissemblingly " the witch cannot shed tears.[228] Here
we are on safer ground. For from the *Malleus Maleficarum*,
part iii, question 15, we learn that a witch is unable to weep,
and why.[229] Grillandus [230] and Bodin [231] agree with Sprenger
in this particular, but Bishop Binsfeld,[232] Godelmann,[233] and
Delrio [234] more than doubt. The point is a nice one, but
whatever authority we follow it is significant that Joannes
Arculanus particularly draws attention to the fact that the
eyes of the lycanthrope are hot and dry, and that he cannot
shed a tear.[235]

Precisely the same symptom is emphasized by Daniel
Sennert, who in his *Practica Medicina*, lib. i, pars. ii, c. xiv,
distinguishes " Melancholia errabunda, Arabibus Kutubutt
dicta " from lycanthropia.[236]

He notes that " Melancholia errabunda medicis dicta, ea
melancholiae species est, quae plerumque Februario mense
aegros infestare solit; nomenque hoc accipit, quod qui ea
laborant, ne horam in uno loco quiescere possunt, sed hinc
inde continuò vagantur nescientes tamen quò vadunt ",
which are indeed the very features Arculanus, Van Foreest,
and others regard as indicative of lycanthropy. According
to Sennert the appearance of the sufferer is that of the
lycanthropist. " Color corporis est citrinus, lingua sicca, ut
valde sitientis, oculi sicci, concavi, nunquam lacrymantes."
Moreover, " solitulidem amant, noctu magis vagantur,
latebras circa mortuorum sepulchra et alia loca solitaria,
quaerunt. Homines obvios fugiunt." He mentions that
the legs are ulcerated, but assigns a different reason for

this : "cum ob continuum motum melancholia ad crura
descendat."

Lycanthropia, Sennert defines as a kind of madness,
"quando aegri unius bestiae mores in specie referunt, quod
etiam plerumque a veneno et morsu talium bestiarum
rabibadarum communicatur et inducitur, qualis est Lycanthropia, rabies canina, lupina ac felina." [237]

Dr. L.-F. Calmeil, in his well-known work *De La
Folie*, certainly classes lycanthropy among the "folies
démoniaques", which is something. He writes : "La zoanthropie doit aussi prendre rang parmi les espèces de folies
démoniaques . . . les malades qui en ont été affectés en
plus grand nombre prétendaient avoir fait des pactes avec
Lucifer, et avoir obtenu de lui le pouvoir de se transformer
en hiboux, en chats on en loups, pour se gorger plus facile-
ment de sang et de chair. Plusieurs de ces individus
s'imaginaient être couverts de poils, avoir eu pour armes des
griffes et des dents redoutables, avoir déchiré, dans leurs
courses nocturnes, des hommes ou des animaux, avoir sucé
le sang des nourissons au berceau, avoir commis meurtres sur
meurtres. Quelques lycanthropes ont été surpris en pleine
campagne marchant sur leurs mains et sur leurs genoux,
imitant la voix des loups, tout souillés de boue, de sueur,
haletans, emportant des débris de cadavres. On peut donc
présumer que quelques uns d'entre eux ait pu immoler à
leur appétit des êtres vivans ; mais presque tous s'accusaient
de crimes qui n'avaient jamais été en réalité commis,
commes ils se vantaient aussi d'avoir couvert des louves,
d'avoir course certaines nuits sous la forme d'un lièvre.

"Les lycanthropes étaient quelquefois dans un état assez
semblable à l'état extatique lorsque leur cerveau enfantait
les hallucinations et les autres conceptions que nous venons
de relater . . . La zoanthropie a régné successivement dans
beaucoup de contrées ; elle s'y est souvent manifestée sur
un certain nombre de malades à la fois ; les pays déserts
et à demi-sauvages ont été surtout le théâtre de atte espèce
de folie." [238]

We may now pass to a very striking case of lycanthropy
which has been recorded of more recent years, and the details
of which are given by Dr. Daniel Hack Tuke in his *Dictionary
of Psychological Medicine*.[239] The sufferer in question came

under the care of Dr. Morel, who described the case in *Études Cliniques*,[240] 1852. This unfortunate individual was entirely convinced that he had assumed the form of a wolf. " See this mouth," he would exclaim, separating his lips with his fingers, " it is the mouth of a wolf; these are the teeth of a wolf. I have cloven feet; see the long hairs which cover my body; let me run into the woods, and you shall shoot me ! " During his quieter intervals he was sometimes allowed to see children whom he tenderly embraced, and of whom he was very fond. However, after they had gone he cried, " The unfortunates, they have hugged a wolf ! "

He was a victim to the morbid wolfish hunger which is technically known as lycorexia or lycorrhexis. " Give me raw meat," he was wont to yell, " I am a wolf, a wolf ! " When he was supplied with this, he would greedily devour some part, and reject the rest saying that it was not putrid enough.

This lycanthrope endured the most fearful mental agony, accusing himself of and tortured by the guilt of heinous offences which he certainly had not committed. He died at the asylum of Maréville in a state of marasmus, seemingly in the uttermost spiritual dereliction. But this, we may hope, was the climax of his trial, for there appears little doubt from reading the details of the case that here we have a plain case of diabolical possession. It is unfortunate, indeed, that a skilled exorcist was not summoned to deal with the patient.

There can be few histories more melancholy, more terribly sad. But throughout all this darkness we may find comfort in the words of that great pope, Benedict XIV : " Daemones dum homines obsident, in corpora potissimum potestatem habere et exercere, in animas vero non ita multum posse ; et finitam et certam esse eorum potestatem in ipsa corpora obsessorum quia quemadmodum non nisi obtenta a Deo facultate, corpora ingrediuntur, ita eorum corporibus plus damni afferre non possunt quam a Deo Optimo Maximo illis permittatur et praefiniatur." [241]

NOTES TO CHAPTER I

[1] Vol. ii (1931), p. 475.

[2] *The Master of Game, c.* 1400. Bodleian ; Digby MS. 182 ; vi.

[3] Jamieson, *Etymological Dictionary of the Scottish Language,* 1808, vol. ii, *s.v.* Warwolf, Werwouf.

[4] The famous Catholic antiquary, *c.* 1560–1625.

[5] Abraham Ortell or Œrtel, the Flemish scholar and geographer, born 1527, died at Antwerp 1598. " The Ptolemy of the sixteenth century." Verstigan refers to the *Aurei seculi imago sive Germanorum veterun mores.*

[6] Delrio mentions this case of werewolfism in his *Disquisitionum Magicarum Libri Sex,* ii, quaestio xviii (1599). In the edition of 1608 " nunc secundis curis auctior longe ", Moguntiae, folio, the reference will be found on pp. 165–6. There is an allusion to Peter Stump in Samuel Rowlands, *The Knave of Harts. Haile Fellow well met,* 4to, 1612 (p. 47), the *Epigram* preceding the Epilogue. Another reference to " the late accidents in the Netherlands of Stub Peter and others, which Witches that people do call *weary wolves* " occurs in the Fairfax *Discourse of Witchcraft* or *Discourse of Daemonology* (1621), ed. R. M. Milnes, Philobiblon Society, London, 1858–9, vol. v, No. 3, pp. 176–180.

[7] Bedburg on the river Erft near Cologne is at the present day a town of 2,925 inhabitants.

[8] Ed. 1927, pp. 181–4.

[9] Ibid., p. 182, n. 2.

[10] George Turberville, *The Noble Art of Venerie or Hunting.* Printed with the *Booke of Faulconrie, or Hawking,* 4to, 1575 and 4to, 1611. *Art of Venerie,* lxxv, 206 : " Some Wolues . . . kill children and men sometimis : and then they neuer feede nor pray vpon any thing afterwards . . . Such Wolues are called *War-wolues,* bicause a man had neede to beware of them." It has not been recognized that Turberville is merely quoting from the older *Booke of Huntynge* (c. 1400).

[11] *Ancient Laws and Institutes of England,* ed. B. Thorpe, 1840, pp. 160–1. The old Latin version, Quadripartitus, of xxvi (p. 585), runs : " Sane sunt episcopi et sacerdotes qui gregem Domini sapienti doctrina debent custodire et defendere, ne diabolica vesania illum vulneret vel occidat." Felix Liebermann, *Die Gesetze der Angelsachsen,* vol. i, Halle, 1903, p. 307, *Consiliatio Cnuti,* supplies another Latin version which thus turns this passage : " hii sunt episcopi et presbiteri, qui divinam custodiam patrocinari tutarique debent supientibus doctrinis, ne forte ille dementer avidus virlupus supra modum a divina custodia dirripiat et mortificet." Cnut, King of Denmark, became King of all England on the death of Edmund Ironsides 1017, and ruled until his decease in 1035.

[12] Asser's *Life of King Alfred,* ed. W. H. Stevenson, Oxford, 1904, c. 77, pp. 62–8, and notes on that passage, pp. 304–5.

[13] This nineteenth book *Corrector* was frequently circulated as a separate treatise, a manual for confessors. Von Scherer, *Kirchenrecht,* i, 238.

[14] Burchard, *Decretorum libri XX,* Coloniae, 1548, " *opus nunc primum excussum,*" p. 198, verso, *De incredulis.* Migne, *Patr. Lat.,* clx, p. 971. See also H. J. Schmitz, *Die Bussbücher und die Bussdisciplin der Kirche,* Mainz, 1883, pp. 714, 718.

[15] See Montague Summers, *The History of Witchcraft,* 1926, pp. 16–18, 20–8, and *passim.*

[16] *Historiarum Libri Quinque,* Lib. iv, c. 11. " De haeresi in Italia inventa," apud Migne, *Patr. Lat.,* cxlii, p. 672.

[17] Sermo xv. Migne, *Patr. Lat.,* lxxxix, p. 870.

[18] *Otia Imperialia . . .* ed. Felix Liebrecht, Hanover, 1856. xv. De oculis apertis post peccatum, p. 4.

[19] Sixth Earl of Hereford, nephew to Edward II and first cousin to Edward III. Humphrey de Bohun succeeded his brother John as Earl on 20th January, 1336, and died unmarried 15th October, 1361.

[20] *William of Palerne,* ed. W. W. Skeat, Early English Text Society, 1867, p. 9. A plural " werwolfs " occurs in l. 2540 (p. 85).

[21] Ed. Skeat, E.E.T.S., 1867, p. 17, ll. 458–60.

[22] *Morte Darthur*, ed. H. Oskar Sommer, 1889, vol. i, p. 793. Malory's work was first printed by Caxton, folio, 1485.

[23] The earliest known printed text (quoted here) of the *Fabillis* is 4to, 1570. There are various MSS., Harleian, Makculloch, Bannatyne, Asloan-Chalmers. See *Poems of Robert Henryson*, Scottish Text Society, vol. ii, 1906, ed. G. Gregory Smith, who curiously enough does not furnish a note on this passage (vol. ii, p. 66, l. 881), which most certainly requires an ample excursus.

[24] Walter Kennedy (1460 ?–1508 ?). "Flyting" is a literary war of words, which might be more or less serious. Adversaries assuredly did not spare the sharpest invective and coarse abuse.

[25] *Poems of William Dunbar*, S.T.S., part i, 1883–4, ed. Dr. John Small, p. 19, ll. 249–53 : "Syphaerit" means reduced to a cypher, i.e. nothing, and thus having no place among the Saints of Heaven.

[26] Sir Patrick Hume of Polwarth, a favourite of King James VI. Hume died 15th June, 1609. Alexander Montgomerie, *c.* 1545–*c.* 1610.

[27] This is the reading of the Tullibardine MS. ; Harleian MS. has :
Ane warlocke, ane warwoolffe, Ane volbet but hair,
Ane devill, and a dragon, ane deid dromadarrie . . .
See *Poems of Alexander Montgomerie*, S.T.S., ed. George Stevenson, 1910, pp. 174–5, ll. 600–1.

[28] This is the reading of the Harleian MS., the Tullibardine MS. has : "With wolfis and wilcattes." The printed text, 4to, 1629, gives : "With warwolfes and wild cates." *Montgomerie's Poems*, ed. D. Cranstoun, S.T.S., 1887, p. 71.

[29] "Ane verie excellent and delectabill Treatise intitulit Philotus," often ascribed but quite doubtfully to the poet Robert Semple, who is sometimes sought to be identified with Robert, Lord Semple. *Philotus* was printed 4to, 1603, for Robert Charteris, and again 4to, 1612, for Andrew Hart. Both at Edinburgh. The plot is from the story Of Phylotus and Emelia, the eighth tale in Barnaby Rich's *Riche his Farewell to Militarie profession*, 1581. I have used the reprint of *Philotus* for the Bannatyne Club, ed. J. W. Mackenzie, Edinburgh, 1835. When John Pinkerton included *Philotus* in his *Scotish Poems*, 3 vols, 1792 (vol. iii, pp. 1–63), he omitted two lines which he considered obscene. Mackenzie, with some hesitation, printed these, since they were "overshadowed by the decent veil of Gothic characters ".

[30] *Philotus*, E 2, 124.

[31] Sibbald, *Chronicle of Scottish Poetry*, 1802, vol. iv, Glossary, or An Explanation of Ancient Scottish Words, *s.v.* Warwolf.

[32] Cf. tréow-loga, wed-loga.

[33] Folio, Lipsiae, 1737.

[34] *Operae Horarum subcisivarum*, Frankfort, 1615, i, pp. 327 and 328. "Eosque Germani *Berwolff*, Galli autem *Loupe garoux* uocant " ; and " lupi noxi . . . Germanis *Berwolff* ".

[35] Schambach and Müller, *Niederländische Sagen*, Göttingen, 1855, p. 182.

[36] Op. cit., pp. 1880–1.

[37] iii Band 2. Strassburg, 1898, xi, Mythologie, pp. 272–4, sections 81–3. Mogk in a footnote (p. 272, n. 1) has : " Kögel meint dass diese Ableitung falsch sei : ahd. *werwolf*, älter *wariwulf* gehöre zu got. *wasjan*, ' kleiden.' "

[38] Halle, 1872–1882, p. 1130.

[39] Christiana, 1850, p. 30.

[40] *verr* = a man ; *úlfr*, a wolf.

[41] *Icelandic-English Dictionary*, Gudbrand Vigfusson. Oxford, 1874, p. 680.

[42] Ibid., p. 236. *Hamr* = a shape, and is connected with the phrase *skipta hömum* " shape-shifting ". Ham-klepya is a witch travelling in hamfarir. For a vivid description of this see *Yunglinga Saga*, lives of the mythical kings of Sweden from Odin to the monarchs of historical days. The work is by Snorri Sturluson (1178–1241), who drew upon the *Heimskringla*. *Úlfhamr* " Wolf's-skin " becomes the name of a legendary prince.

[43] E. Littré, *Dictionnaire de la Langue Française*, tome ii, Première partie, 1869, p. 350.

[44] T. iv, 1885, p. 236.

[45] A quotation from the *Miracles de Notre Dame* of Gautier de Coinsi (1177–1236), sometime Prior of Saint-Médard de Soissons. This Abbey, originally founded in 557 by Clotaire I to receive the body of S. Médard, was regarded as the chief Benedictine house in France. In 1131 the church, having been partially pulled down and rebuilt, was reconsecrated by Pope Innocent II, who then granted those visiting this sanctuary indulgences known as " S. Médard's pardons ".

[46] Godefroy also draws attention to the word *varol* as used to designate the fish *loup* (*Labrax lupus*), the marine bass. Cotgrave (1611) has : " Lubin: *A Base, or Sea-Wolfe*." For Guernsey, also see Sir Edgar MacCulloch, *Guernsey Folk Lore*, 1903, p. 230.

[47] Vellum ; late thirteenth century, small 4to. Twelve lays are attributed to Marie de France (about 1250), and professedly translated from lays of Brittany. The prologue of 56 lines is addressed to a king, probably Henry III of England. The third lay is *Bisclaveret* in 318 lines, ff. 131b–133b, col. 2.

[48] p. 585. See also Jacques Pelletier, *Dialogue de l'Ortografie e Prononciation Françoese*, Poitiers, 1550, p. 165, p. 197 and *passim*.

[49] Ed. Lyon, 1593, pp. 222–3.

[50] I have used the edition *On les Vend a Paris par Philippe le Noir libraire demourant en la rue sainct Jacques a senseigne de la rose blanche couronee* (no date, *c.* 1515, Bodley ; Douce, pp. 211). There are extant more than forty MSS. of the *Livre de la Chasse*, which was printed by Antoine Vérard *c.* 1507, by Jean Treperel about the same date, and by Philippe le Noir *c.* 1515.

[51] Bodley MS. 546, p. 35, verso (olim Digby MS. 182 ; vi). The book, written at the beginning of the fifteenth century, is dedicated to Henry, Prince of Wales, son of Henry IV.

[52] Aix (no date), s.v. *loup-garou*.

[53] José de Lacerda, *Novo Diccionario*, Lisboa, 1866.

[54] Hertz, *Der Werwolf*, p. 89, incorrectly says that for " werwolf . . . im Spanischen ist kein besonderes Wort vorhanden ". y Pidal, in answer to my inquiry, writes : " La palabra a que usted se refiere, en español debe ser *lobombre*. ' Plinio . . . diz que este que siempre eymos contar en las fabliellas que los omnes se tornan lobos et llaman los lobombres e despues se mudan en omnes, que non lo deuemos creer." *General Estoria*, pág. 559a. " De si los lobos pueden criar un niño, Kunst da dos obras didácticas y dos leyendas sacadas de manuscritos de la Biblioteca de El Escorial.—Bibliófilos españoles, Madrid, 1878, con bibliografía, pag. 136 n.' "

[55] Homer, *Odyssey*, x, 212–13.

[56] Ed. Joh. G. Schneider, 1775, for which see later.

[57] iii, 16. " On Lycaon, or Lycanthropia." See *The Seven Books of Paulus Ægineta*, translated with a Commentary by Francis Adams ; the Sydenham Society, 3 vols, 1844, vol. i, pp. 389–90.

[58] The physician Haly Abbas (*Theor.*, ix, 7 ; *Pract.*, v, 24) designates lycanthropia as *melancholia canina*. Alsaharavius (*Pract.*, i, 2, 28) also seems to allude to the disease as *melancholia canina*. The Arabian term is *cutubut*.

[59] Ioannis Tzetzae, *Historiarum Variarum Chiliades*, ed. Theophilus Kiesslingius, Lipsiae, 1826, Chil. i, Hist. xix, Περὶ Βόος τοῦ Μίνωος, ll. 487–9 (p. 21).

Πασιφαή . . . .
Μινώταυρον γεγέννηκε βοάνθρωπον θηρίον.

[60] λυκανθρωπία appears in a medical writer, Aetius, A.D. 500. *Opera*, Venetiis, 1534 ; 6, 11. Issacius Theophanes, A.D. 817, uses λυκάνθρωπος as an adjective meaning wolfish, savage, cruel. *Opera*, Bonnae, 1839 ; 745, 13.

[61] *The Discouerie of Witchcraft*, edition 1930, " with an introduction by the Rev. Montague Summers," p. 52.

[62] *A Dictionary of the English Language*, folio, 1755, vol. ii.

[63] J. G. von Hahn, *Griechische und albanesische Märchen*, Leipzig, 1864 ; ii, pp. 189–90.

[64] Actually many derivations have been suggested, but we may (I think) take this as certain. Such a theory as that propounded by Oeconomos, who suggested that Callicantzaros might have some connection with the Latin "caligatus" or "calcatura", is frankly impossible. Nor is Bernard Schmidt's reference (p. 144, n. 2) to the Turkish *karakondjolos*, a black scullion slave, a whit more tenable, although it is true that in J. D. Kieffer and T. X. Bianchi's *Dictionnaire Turc-Français*, Paris, 1837, t. ii, p. 469, we have : "*qara qondjolos. Loup-garou ou autre monstre imaginaire, cauchemar.*" The adjective *qara* meaning black also bears the signification "De mauvais augure". See also Hermann Vámbéry, *Etymologisches Wörterbuch der Turko-Tatarischen Sprachen*, Leipzig, 1878 ; pp. 79, 80 (n. 84). Coräes (Ἄτακτα, iv, p. 211) made the word a compound of καλός and κάνθαρος, which, however satisfactory in etymological formation, will not bear anything resembling the sense required. Polites once wrote (in Πανδώρα, 1866, xvi, p. 453) that as καλλικάντζαρος is allied to λυκοκάντζαρος, this latter word may contain two elements, λύκος = "wolf" and κάνθαρος = "beetle". He has, however, abandoned this view, and later inclined to suggest that the obscure dialect form καλιτσάγγαρος, found in some villages on the western shores of the Black Sea, is derived from τσαγγάρης "a boot-make", and for the second element either καλίκι "a hoof" or καλός "fine". It is true that the Callicantzaros is in popular tradition often supposed to have hoofs, the feet of an ass or a goat, but the derivation put forward by Polites appears altogether too far-fetched and unreal.

[65] Vol. ii, p. 434.

[66] Ibid., vol. i, p. 46.

[67] Ibid., vol. ii, p. 101.

[68] Wien, 1886, p. 380.

[69] Ibid., p. 374.

[70] *Modern Greek Folklore and Ancient Greek Religion*, 1910, p. 379.

[71] Bernhard Schmidt, *Das Volksleben der Neugriechen und das Hellenische Alterhum*, Leipzig, 1871, pp. 159–60.

[72] Ibid., p. 159, n. 2.

[73] Mannhardt's *Zeitschrift f. d. Mythol. und Sittenk.*, iv, 195.

[74] *Otia Imperialia*, ed. Felix Liebrecht, Hanover, 1856, p. 4.

[75] Paris, 1844, t. i, p. 69.

[76] See Bodin, *Démonomanie des Sorciers*, ii, 6 ; ed. Lyon, 1593, pp. 219–20. Also Weyer, vi, 13, De Magorum Infamium Poenis. *Opera omnia*, Amstedolami, 1660, pp. 494–7.

[77] Op. cit., pp. 379–80.

[78] Op. cit., Grec. Français, vol. i, 1908, p. 727.

[79] "See how he can change his skin when he likes ! " l. 123.

[80] Petronius. Tertium edidit Buecheler. Berolini, 1895, 62, p. 41.

[81] *Metamorphoseon*, II, xxii. Recensuit J. van der Vlict. Lipsiae, 1887, pp. 38–9. Plautus in the *Persa*, ii, 2, 48, uses versipellus of the hair turning grey ; "Ne ubi capillus versipellis fiat, foede semper servias," says Sophoclidisca to Paegnium. [Another reading has *versicapillus*.] In the *Bacchides*, iv, 4, ll. 658–9, the word is employed with the secondary signification "skilled in dissimulation ", " shifty ".

> vorsipellem frugi convenit esse hominem,
> pectus quoi sapit.

"A chap that's worth anything, a fellow who is smart and knowing, has to be able to change his skin," is the maxim of the slave Chrysalus. Cf. modern Italian, *versipelle*, Prudentius, *Cathemeron*, ix, 91–2, writes :—

> Quid tibi, profane serpens, profiut rebus nouis
> Plasma primum perculisse uersipelli astutia ?

The same poet, *Apotheosis*, Praefatio, 26, has the line : "Hae uersipelli astutiæ ! "

[82] The narrative first occurs in Greek among the works of S. John Damascene. It may be found in the Latin version in the *Vitae Patrum*,

compiled by Héribert Rosweyde, S.J., ed. folio, Lugduni, 1617, pp. 186–259.
See also Migne *P.G.*, xcvi, pp. 857–1246.
[83] 1535–1581. The Latin versions by this great scholar of S. Gregory
Nazianzen, S. John Damascene, S. John Chrysostom, and other doctors are
famous.
[84] Migne *P.G.*, xcvi, pp. 1141–2.
[85] Ibid., pp. 1149–1150.
[86] *Flores Caluinistici*, Neapoli, 1585, p. 23.
[87] First printed at Lyons, no date, *c.* 1490.
[88] *De lamiis*, Basil, 1577, c. xiv.
[89] *Glossarium mediae et infimae Latinitatis*, ed. 1885, vol. v, p. 155.
[90] Lexicon, ed. De Vit., Prato, 1875. Forcellini defines *versipellis* as " che
muta pelle o faccia ". He also draws attention to *versipellis* = a chameleon.
[91] *Lexicon (Recueil de Mots de la Basse Latinité)*, 1866, Migne.
[92] Lyons, *Sumptibus Claudii Bourgeat.*
[93] Konrad Maurer, *Die Bekehrung des Norwegischen Stammes zum Christenthume*, 2 vols, München, 1856, vol. ii, pp. 101–10.
[94] G. F. Abbott, *Macedonian Folklore*, 1903.
[95] H. F. Tozer, *Researches in the Highlands of Turkey*, 2 vols., 1869 (vol. ii,
pp. 80 sqq.). Arthur and Albert Schott, *Walachische Märchen*, Stuttgart and
Tübingen, 1845.
[96] Ernst Marno, *Reisen im Gebeite des blauen und weissen Nil*, Vienna,
1874, pp. 239 sqq. *Life and Adventures of Nathaniel Pearce*, 1831. Ed. by
J. J. Halls, vol. i, p. 288 n. Mansfield Parkyns, *Life in Abyssinia*, 1868,
pp. 300–1, 310–12.
[97] P. B. Chaillu, *Explorations and Adventures in Equatorial Africa*, 1861.
D. and C. Livingstone, *Narrative of an Expedition to the Zambesi and its
Tributaries*, 1865, p. 159. Theophilus Waldmeier, *Autobiography*, 1886.
Basset, *Les Apocryphes Éthiopiens*, iv, 24, 1894. Mary H. Kingsland, *Travels
in West Africa*, 1897, pp. 536–9. T. J. Allridge, *The Sherbro and the Hinter-
land*, 1901. H. J. Beatty, *Human Leopards*, 1915. M. de Lembray, *The
werewolf of the Africans*. Cf. also John Cameron Grant, *The Ethiopian*,
" A Narrative of the Society of Human Leopards," Paris, 1900.
[98] G. A. Wilken, *De Indische Gids*, 1884, pp. 945–50. W. Crooke, *The
Popular Religion and Folklore of Northern India*, 1896, pp. 354–5. W. W.
Skeat, *Malay Magic*, 1900. W. W. Skeat, *Fables and Folklore from an Eastern
Front*, 1901, p. 26. Bezemer, *Volksdichtung aus Indonesien*, 1904, pp. 363–5,
422–3. Bompas, *Folklore of the Santal Parganas*, pp. 229, 256.
[99] Herbert A. Giles, *Strange Stories from a Chinese Studio*, 2 vols., 1880 ;
2nd ed., 1 vol., 1909. The stories are from *Liao chai chih i*, by P'u Sung-ling.
Fox possession in Japan ; Captain F. Brinkley, *Japan*, vol. v (p. 197 sqq.),
Oriental Series, 1902, Boston and Tokyo. J. J. M. de Groot, *The Religious
System of China*, Leyden (1907). Dr. M. W. de Visser, " The Fox and the
Badger in Japanese Folklore," *Transactions of the Asiatic Society in Japan*,
xxxvi, part 3, 1908. E. T. C. Werner, *Myths and Legends of China*, 1922.
G. Willoughby-Meade, *Chinese Ghouls and Goblins*, London, 1928, chap. v,
pp. 102–138.
[100] A. C. Kruyt, " De weerwolf bij de Toradja's van Midden-Celebes."
Tijdschrift voor Indische Taal- Land- en Volkenkunde, xli (1899), pp. 548–551,
557–560.
[101] M. G. Lewis, *Journal of a West India Proprietor*, 1834, p. 295.
[102] Henry R. Schoolcraft, *Indian Tribes of the United States*, Philadelphia,
1853–6, v, p. 683.
[103] Joseph de Acosta, S.J., *Historia Natural y Moral de las Indias*. Libro
septimo, cap. 19. Sevilla, 1590, pp. 499–501. English translation by Edward
Grimston, Hakluyt Society reprint, 1880, vol. ii, pp. 497–9. Also Eusèbe
Salverte, *Des Sciences Occultes*, 3rd ed., 1856, c. xiii, pp. 215–17 (English
translation, *Occult Sciences*, 2 vols., 1846).
[104] *Reise in Brasilien*, von Joh. Bapt. von Spix und Carl. Fredr. Phil. von
Martius. München, 1823–1831, 3 vols. English translation, *Travels in Brazil*,
2 vols., 1824, book iv, c. 2, vol. ii, p. 243. Granada, *Reseña Histórico-
descriptiva de Supersticiones del Rio de la Plata*, 1896, pp. 581–627. Ambrosetti,

La Leyenda del Yaguareté-Abá, Buenos Aires, 1896 ; *Globus, Illustrierte Zeitschrift für Länder- und Völkeŗkunde*, lxx [1896], pp. 272-3.

[105] T. C. Bridges, " Witchcraft To-day," *Occult Review*, xlv, No. 5, May, 1927, p. 330.

[106] *Encyclopædia Britannica*, ed. 1883, vol. xv, " Lycanthropy," p. 89.

[107] Dr. N. Parker, *Journal of Mental Science*, 1854, p. 52.

[108] Dr. Daniel Hach Tuke, *Dictionary of Psychological Medicine*, 1892, vol. ii, pp. 752-5.

[109] " Si ex cholera tunc vocatur proprie mania, et sunt cum saltu et furore et lupinositate, et cum terribili aspectu, et appellatur a quibusdam daemonium lupinum." *De Passionibus Capitis*, Particula ii, xix. *Lilium Medecinae*, Lugduni, 1573 (p. 211). Bernard de Gordon, died about 1320.

[110] *Opera omnia*, 2 vols., folio. Lugduni, 1658, vol. i, p. 377.

[111] *The Nation*, New York, 22nd August, 1895.

[112] S. Matthew, iv, 24 ; viii, 16 ; ix, 32, 33 ; xii, 22 ; xv, 22-8 ; S. Mark, i, 32, 34, 39 ; iii, 11, 12 ; ix, 14-28 ; S. Luke, iv, 41 ; vi, 18 ; vii, 21 ; viii, 27-39 ; xi, 14 ; xiii, 32 ; and elsewhere in the Gospels. See also Montague Summers, *The History of Witchcraft*, 1926, chapter vi, " Diabolic Possession," pp. 198-275.

[113] *Practica Medicina*, Lib. i, pars ii, cap. xvi. *Opera omnia*, Parisiis, 1641, t. i, p. 158.

[114] S. John, ix, 3.

[115] Guazzo, *Compendium Maleficarum*, 1608, i, 6. English translation by E. A. Ashwin, edited by Montague Summers, 1929 (p. 17).

[116] *Daemonolatreia*, folio, 1595, iii, 6. English translation by E. A. Ashwin, edited by Montague Summers, 1930 (pp. 161-3). See also Guazzo, op. cit., ii, xiii.

[117] *Opera omnia*, Parisiis, 1641, folio, t. iii, pp. 1126-1157.

[118] For the life of Sennert (and other physicians of whom mention is made in this chapter) see N. F. J. Eloy, *Dictionnaire Historique de la Médicine*, 4 vols., Mons, 1778, under the several names.

[119] *L'Incredulité Sçavante et la Credulité Ignorante au suiet des Magiciens et des Sorciers*, Lyon, 1678. Seconde Partie ; discours vii, pp. 474-5.

[120] Apud Migne, *Patres Graeci*, vol. x, p. 1338, B.

[121] *Dæmonologie*, 1597, ii, 5 (Bodley ; Douce, i, 230). Reprint ed. G. B. Harrison, 1924.

[122] *Ecclesiasticus*, xxxix, 33.

[123] See Pliny, *Historia Naturalis*, vii, 2 : " In eadem Africa familias quasdam effascinantium, Isigonus et Nymphodorus tradunt, quarum laudatione intereant probata, arescant arbores, emoriantur infantes." Also Aulus Gellius, ix, 4. Cf. R. C. Maclagan, *Evil Eye in the Western Highlands*, 1902, pp. 7-9, 116-18. The danger of over-praising and excessive admiration is common knowledge.

[124] These methods are fully discussed by all the great authorities, and there is a universal consensus of opinion that witches can and do cast spells in these ways, practices which still endure. Boguet, *Discours des Sorciers*, English translation *An Examen of Witches*, by E. A. Ashwin, edited by Montague Summers, 1929, has five chapters : xxv, " Whether Witches kill by their Blowings and their Breath " ; xxvi, " Whether Witches afflict with Words " ; xxvii, " Whether Witches afflict with Looking " ; xxviii, " How Witches afflict with the Hand " ; and xxix, " How Witches afflict with a Wand " (pp. 75-86). Paul Grilland, also, in his *De sortilegiis*, has an important chapter, viii, " Maleficium potest solis verbis perfici," *apud Malleus Maleficarum*, Lyon, 1669, tom. ii, pars. ii, pp. 282-3. Leonard Vair's work, *De Fascino*, Parisiis, 1583, should be consulted, especially c. iii, " De visu qui Fascini diffinitionem impeditur " (pp. 11-16) ; iv, " De tactu Fascinum efficiente " (pp. 17-21), and v, " De vocis natura quae Fascini causa exstitit " (pp. 21-6). The whole subject of *fascinatio*, which he happily defines as *contagio seu infectis* (p. 29), is discussed at length by Delrio, *Disquisitionum Magicarum*, Liber iii, pars. 1, quaestio 3, ed. 1603, t. ii, pp. 26-83, *De Maleficio hostili*.

58   THE WEREWOLF

[125] Op. cit., iii, discours xvi (p. 801).

[126] S. Matthew, iv, 8, 9.

[127] For this phrase see Reginald Scott, *The discouerie of witchcraft*, 1584, iii, 15 ; reprinted with Introduction by Montague Summers, 1930, pp. 36–7. T. Higgins, *Junius' Nomenclator* (1585), has " Fascinus, a bewitching or eyebiting ", and Phillips (1658) notes : " *eyebite* to fascinate or bewitch from a certain evil influence from the eye." T. Ady, *A Candle in the Dark* (1656), ii, 104, derives from Scott. See also Rev. St. John D. Seymour, *Irish Witchcraft and Demonology*, 1913, p. 68.

[128] S. Thomas, *Contra Gentiles*, iii, 103, and *Summa*, i, 117, 3 ; *Malleus* ; Bl. Angelo, *Summa angelica, Superstitio*, 5 ; " multiplex experientia docet " (ed. folio, 1515, Strassburg, fo. ccxxxiii).

[129] The terrible power of the Evil Eye is so general and so potent, that I have thought it well to give ample annotations on this passage so that those who wish to pursue the subject further may be helped in their investigations. For general works see : Leonard Vair, *De Fascino, Libri Tres*, Parisiis, 1583, i, c. 8, pp. 11–16 ; Fromann, *Tractatus de fascinatione novus et singularis*, Norimbergae, 1675 ; Elworthy, *The Evil Eye*, London, 1895 (to be used with caution as to the author's conclusions) ; R. C. Maclagan, *Evil Eye in the Western Highlands*, 1902 ; Seligmann, *Der böse Blick*, Berlin, 1910 ; Westermarck, *Ritual and Belief in Morocco*, 1926, vol. i, pp. 414–478.

[130] Oldenberg, *Die Religion des Vedas*, Berlin, 1894, pp. 482, 502 sqq.

[131] *Vendîdâd*, Oxford, 1895, xix, 6, 45 (141) ; xx, 3 (12).

[132] Arist., *Probl.*, xx, 34. The charm was broken by spitting thrice. Theocritus, vi, 39, a passage quoted by Diogenianus, Prov., iv, 82. Cf. also Theocritus, xx, 12, and Tibullus, I, ii, 100. There is a famous reference in Vergil, *Eclogues*, iii, 103. Aulus Gellius, xvi, 12, 3, has : " Item fascinum appellat [Cloatius Verus], quasi bascanum, et fascinare esse quasi bascinare." Curtius rejects this connection of *fascinare* with βασκαίνειν, but it is accepted by Corssen, ii, p. 257. Professor Robinson Ellis, *Commentary on Catullus*, 1889, vii, 12 (p. 25), suggests that the notion of witchcraft was originally that of the *evil tongue* rather than the *evil eye*. Cf. βάζειν, φάσκειν. Compare *The Witch of Edmonton* by Ford, Dekker, and Rowley, 4to, 1658 (acted 1623), ii, when Mother Sawyer says :—

> Some call me witch . . .
> Urging that my bad tongue—by their bad usage made so—
> Forspeaks their cattle . . .

Cf. Pliny, *Historia Naturalis*, vii, 2, and (of the catoblepas and basilisk) viii, 21. See also Jahn, " Über den Aberglauben des bösen Blicks bei den Alten," in *Berichte über die Verhandlungen der Königlich-Sächsisten Gesellschaft der Wissenschaften zu Leipzig, Philologisch-historische Classe*, xvii. Leipzig, 1855, p. 63 sqq.

[133] Andree, *Ethnographische Parallelen und Vergleiche*, Stuttgart, 1878, pp. 41 sqq.

[134] Feilberg, " Der böse Blick in Nordischen Uberlieferung," in *Zeitschrift des Vereins für Volksunde*, xi (Berlin, 1901), p. 305 sqq.

[135] E. W. Lane, *Manners and Customs of the Modern Egyptians*, 2 vols., 1838, c. xi. Gardiner, " The Evil Eye in Egypt," *Proceedings of the Society of Biblical Archæology*, xxxviii, London, 1916, p. 129 sqq.

[136] Campbell Thompson, *Semitic Magic* (London, 1908), p. 88.

[137] Ludwig Blau, *Das jüdische Zauberwesen*, Strassburg, 1898, p. 153 sqq.

[138] C. R. Conder, *Heth and Moab*, 1883, p. 295.

[139] *Koran*, cxiii, 1, 2, 5 ; *et alibi*. *Mishkât*, xxi, 1, 2. English translation by Matthews, Calcutta, 1810, vol. ii, p. 377.

[140] J. Mactaggart, *Gallovidian Encyclopædia*, 1824, 2nd ed., London, 1876, persons suspected of having " an ill ee ". James Kelly, *Scottish Proverbs*, London, 1721 (and 1818), cites, " God saine your eye, man." R. C. Maclagan, *Evil Eye in the Western Highlands*, 1902.

[141] J. C. Lawson, *Modern Greek Folklore*, 1910, pp. 8–15. Special forms of prayer, commonly known as βασκανισμοί, are provided for those who have been blinked by the evil eye. Margaret Hardie, " The Evil Eye in some

Greek Villages of the Upper Haliakmon Valley in West Macedonia," in *Journal of the Royal Anthropological Institute*, London, 1923, liii, p. 160 sqq. For Albania see George Borrow, *Zincali*, 2 vols., London, 1841, part i, c. 8.

[142] " I do not exaggerate when I affirm, at all events, my own persuasion that two-thirds of the total inhabitants of the Tamar side implicitly believe in the power of the mal' occhio, as the Italians name it, or the evil eye." Rev. Robert Hawker, of Morwenstow, Cornwall, in Mrs. Whitcombe's *Bygone Days in Devon and Cornwall*, 1873, p. 139. See Blakeborough, *Wit, Character, Folk-lore and Customs of the North Riding of Yorkshire*, London, 1898, for northerly beliefs as regards the evil eye. *Word-Lore*, vol. i, 1926, pp. 125–6, has a modern example of overlooking in an English village. Cf. letters in *The Times* from Mr. Andrew Innes of Kendal and Mr. R. Tristram of Witney, 20th and 22nd September, 1930. Also " Spells of the Evil Eye " in Cornwall, Mr. W. H. Paynter, *Daily Express*, 26th September, 1930. In the West Country it is believed that to kiss a corpse renders one immune from being blinked, see *Sunday Dispatch*, 24th April, 1932.

[143] Westermarck, *Ritual and Belief in Morocco*, 1926, vol. i, pp. 414–478. This great authority quotes the current saying : " One half of mankind dies from the evil eye."

[144] Oric Bates, *The Eastern Libyans*, 1914, p. 180 sqq.

[145] R. W. Felkin, " Notes on the Waganda Tribe of Central Africa," in *Proceedings of the Royal Society of Edinburgh*, 1884–6, xiii, p. 760.

[146] Mitford, *Through the Zulu Country*, London, 1883, p. 317.

[147] W. H. I. Bleek, *Brief Account of Bushmen Folklore*, 1875, pp. 10, 14.

[148] Seligmann, op. cit., i, p. 42 sqq. Andree, op. cit., p. 39 sqq.

[149] Seligmann, op. cit., i, p. 43 sqq.

[150] Bullen, *Forty Years in New Zealand*, London, 1876. George Turner, *Samoa, a Hundred Years ago and long before*, London, 1884, p. 23.

[151] Seligmann, op. cit., i, 44 sqq. Andree, op. cit., p. 35.

[152] To deal with Italy and Spain at all adequately would require a veritable chapter of notes alone. The counter-charms against the evil eye and similar fascinations must be familiar to any traveller who has visited these two countries, and indeed to most others beside. The subject in all its bearings is of enormous interest, but demands ample treatment or a mere mention.

[153] *The Essayes . . . Newly enlarged*, 1625. *Of Enuy*, ix, p. 40. " The Act of Enuy," p. 47. Bodley : Arch. Bodl. D. 104 [Glass case, 21].

[154] Sennert derives this from the Commentary on Apuleius of Filippo Beroaldo of Bologna, 1453–1505. The Commentary is printed in the works of Apuleius, Basileae, 3 vols., 8vo, 1620. The phrase in question occurs in book iv, 26, of the *Metamorphoseon* : " sic ad instar Athracidis vel Protesilai dispestae disturbataeque sunt nuptiae," says the captured maiden. [Van der Vlict following the codex Florentinus reads " Attidis ", *Metamorphoseon*, Lipsiae (Teubner), 1887, i, p. 88 with note.] *Atracis* is Hippodamia, the Thessalian woman, Ovid, *Amores*, i, iv, 8 ; *Heroides*, xvii, 248. She is called " Atracia virgo " by Valerius Flaccus, i, 141. *Atracia ars* is the Thessalian art, that is magic, from Atrax (now Sidhiro-peliko), a town in Thessaly on the Peneus. Cf. Statius, *Thebais*, i, 105–6:

> Phoebes
> Atracia rubet arte labor.

" *Athracie* est magica scientia." See Lactantius (who must not be confused with the Christian writer), Bernatius, and others who gloss this passage. Cf. Valerius Flaccus, vi, 447.

[155] Lamb's splendid phrase on *The Witch* of Middleton will be readily remembered : " The witches of Middleton are fine creations. Their power too is in some measure over the mind. They raise jars, jealousies, strifes, *like a thick scurf o'er life*."

[156] Westermarck, op. cit., i, pp. 571–8, speaks of the witchcraft affecting men with sexual impotence, called in Morocco " tᵉqâf ", and much dreaded.

[157] See Montague Summers, *The Geography of Witchcraft*, 1927, ch. vii, pp. 531–7.

[158] *Malleus*, part ii, question i, c. vii : " How [Witches], as it were, . . .

Deprive Man of his Virile Member." English tr. by Montague Summers, 1928, pp. 118–122.

¹⁵⁹ George Giffard, *A Dialogue concerning Witches and Witchcraftes*, 1593, records the popular belief in England : " the witches haue their spirits, . . . some in one likenesse, and some in another, as like cattes, weasils, toads, or mise," B. 4 verso. There are several references to mice as familiars in the statements of Hopkins' assistant, John Sterne, but these examinations are very suspect. E.g. " The impe which the said Joyce Boanes sent was a dund one like a mouse." Howell, *State Trials*, v, 834.

¹⁶⁰ " This example of Job is not fit to prove that a godly man may be bewitched, seeing the deuill is not sayde to deale by witches against him, but it doeth prooue, that not only the godlie, but euen the most godly (as holy Job, who had none like him upon earth) may for their triall be giuen into the handes of Satan to be afflicted and tempted." Giffard, op. cit., D. 4 recto. There is something of a quibble here, for all must agree that *Deo permittente* the Devil is the agent, whether directly or mediately by a witch.

¹⁶¹ Op. cit., partie iii, discours 2, p. 691.

¹⁶² See for a more extended treatment of these details Pietro Piperno, *De Magicis Affectibus*, Benevento, 1634, lib. iii and iv, pp. 79–186.

¹⁶³ " Haec difficultas non est parir momenti." José Angles, *Flores Theologicarum Quaestionum in II Sent.*, Madriti, 1586, p. 877.

¹⁶⁴ Ven. Duns Scotus, *Opus Oxoniense*, In 4 Sent., d. 84. Blessed Henry of Segusio (*Summa aurea*), Godfrey of Fontaines (*XIV Quodlibeta*), Ubertino, are quoted in the *Malleus*, Eng. trans., p. 157. For Guazzo see the *Compendium*, iii, 1, Eng. trans., 1929, pp. 163–4.

¹⁶⁵ S. Thomas (*Summa*, ii, 2, q. 78), S. Bonaventura, Peter a Palude, S. Albertus Magnus, are quoted in the *Malleus*, loc. cit., p. 158. For Boguet see *Examen*, ch. xxxvi, Eng. tr., 1929, pp. 111–14.

¹⁶⁶ Comprising pp. 886–879.

¹⁶⁷ Ibid., p. 377.

¹⁶⁸ Ibid., pp. 378–9. *De Arte magica.* Artic. vi. *Tertia diffic.* " *Licelitne bona fide magicis incantationibus, & adjurationibus uti ?* " Conclusio. " Haud licet."

¹⁶⁹ Father Stephen Donovan, O.F.M., writes in the *Catholic Encyclopædia*, vol. i, s.n. *Angelo Carletti di Chivasso*, that in the *Summa* " one is impressed with the gravity and fairness that characterized [Blessed Angelo's] opinions throughout ". The *Summa* was written, to use the author's own words, " pro utilitate . . . eorum qui cupiunt laudabiliter vivere," and even to-day acclaimed as " a most valuable guide in matters of conscience ".

¹⁷⁰ 1280–1322. (The date of death is also given as 1830, and also 1345.) There is a good edition of the *Commentarium*, Rome, 1596–1605.

¹⁷¹ S. Augustine's exact words are : " Qui utitur fide illius quem constat jurasse per deos falsos, et utitur non ad malum, sed ad licitum et bonum, non peccato ejus se sociat quo per daemonia juravit, sed bono pacto ejus quo fidem servavit." *Epistola xlvii (a) ad Publicolam.* Migne, *P.L.*, t. xxxiii, *S. Augustini Opera*, vol. ii, p. 185 (2).

¹⁷² *Summa Angelica de Casibus conscientie*, folio, 1515. Impensis Joannis Knoblouch. Superstitio, fo. ccxxxiii, 18.

¹⁷³ pp. 138–150.

¹⁷⁴ Ibid., pp. 144–5.

¹⁷⁵ Eng. tr. (1928), pp. 155–164.

¹⁷⁶ *Malleus*, ed. 1669, t. ii, pars. ii, pp. 185–6.

¹⁷⁷ Op. cit., p. 1151.

¹⁷⁸ Ed. Moguntiae, 1603, t. iii, pp. 157–172.

¹⁷⁹ *In IV Sent. libros comment.* (Salamanca, 1555–6), d. 34, q. 1, a. 3.

¹⁸⁰ *Fustis Daemonum*, c. v, ad finem, ed. 1604 (Lugduni), p. 11.

¹⁸¹ *De Magicis Affectibus*, 1634, p. 77.

¹⁸² " Unlucky Possessions," by T. C. Bridges. *Occult Review*, March, 1927, vol. xlv, No. 3, pp. 159–60.

¹⁸³ Remy agrees with this, *Daemonolatreia*, iii, 8. " *That there is nothing which can so quickly and effectively induce Witches to remove an Evil Spell as Threats and Blows and Violence* . . ." Eng. tr., 1930, pp. 148–154.

LYCANTHROPY 61

[184] *Casus Conscientiae Benedicti XIV*, Dec., 1748, Cas. 111, Ferrariae, 1764, p. 155.

[185] *Daily News*, 20th January, 1928 ; *Daily Express*, 26th August, 1930 ; *Sunday Times*, 31st August, 1930.

[186] " Magic—Black and White," by William Hichens. *Contemporary Review*, August, 1931 (No. 788), p. 248.

[187] See *The History of Witchcraft*, Montague Summers, 1926, c. vi, pp. 202–224.

[188] Piperno, op. cit., p. 53.

[189] Suidas, s.v. Μάρκελλος.

[190]   οὗ βίβλους ἀνέθηκεν εὔκτιμένῃ ἐνὶ 'Ρώμῃ
       'Αδριανὸς προτέρων προφερέστερος ἡγεμονήων
       καὶ παῖς 'Αδριανοῖο μέγ' ἔξοχος 'Αντωνῖνος, ...
Anthologia Palatina, caput vii : Epigrammata Sepulcralia, 158, ed. Parisiis, 1864, vol. i, p. 302.

[191] *Marcelli Sidetae Fragmenta*, recognovit Maximilianus Schneider, p. 118. Apud " Commentationes Philologiae quibus Ottoni Ribbeckio . . . congratulantur Discipuli ". Lipsiae, Teubner, 1888.

[192] Πλουτάρχου περὶ τῆς τῶν ἐλευθέρων παιδῶν ἀγωγῆς. Accedunt bina ejusdem Plutarchi et Marcelli Sidetae medici fragmenta Graece recensuit Joh. G. Schneider. Argentorati, [Strassburg], 1775, p. 109.

[193] *Pauli Æginetae Medici Optimi Libreri Septem*. Basileae, 1538, per Hieronymum Gemusaeum. [Bodley, D. 1, 6, Med.]

[194] Physician and classical scholar, 1796–1861, of whom an account may be found in the *D.N.B.*, vol. i, 1885, pp. 95–6.

[195] Op. cit., vol. i, pp. 389–90.

[196] The various Greek authors have been collected in *Physici et Medici Graeci Minores*, ed. Julius Ludovicus Ideler. Berolini, 1841, 2 vols. Nicander's *Theriacs*, Θηριακά, were edited with a useful commentary by J. G. Schneider, Lipsiae, 1816.

[197] See also for the various biographies N. F. J. Eloy, *Dictionnaire Historique de la Medicine*, 4 vols., Mons, 1778, under the several names.

[198] p. 282.

[199] Vol. i, pp. 203–243.

[200] p. 227.

[201] Two vols., Paris, 1876. Avicenna, vol. i, pp. 466–477 ; Haly Abbas, i, pp. 381–8 ; Alsaharavius, i, pp. 437–457 ; and Razis, i, pp. 337–354.

[202] Venice, 1588, pp. 291–7.

[203] Bononiae, 1583, pp. 339–377.

[204] *Anatomy of Melancholy*, part i, sec. 1, mem. 1, subs. 4.

[205] *Opera omnia*, Amstelodami, 1660, pp. 335–7.

[206] pp. 28–33.

[207] p. 32.

[208] *Lilium Medicinae*, Lugduni, 1573, p. 213.

[209] Basilææ, 1568, pp. 142–3.

[210] Francofurti et Lipsiae, folio, 1666, p. 1500.

[211] *Opera omnia*, 4 vols., 1602–6, folio. I have used the ed. Francofurti, 1634, folio.

[212] Ibid., p. 348.

[213] *Omnia opera*, Venetiis, folio, 1574, p. 79, verso ; caput ix, *De lycanthropia*.

[214] Naples, MDCCLXI, tom. ii, pp. 112–13. The *Lexicon Medicum Graeco-Latinum* was first published at Venice, 8vo, 1607. The edition 8vo, Bale, 1628, is esteemed. The work ran into more than fifteen editions when it was edited by Jacques-Pancrace Brum as *Castellus renouatus*, Nuremberg, 4to, 1682, after which date it was again very frequently reprinted in its revised form.

[215] Op. cit., p. 344.

[216] S. Luke, ix, 39.

[217] In the collection, *Malleus Maleficarum*, etc., 4 vols., 1669, vol. iv, p. 13.

[218] For Holy Baptism see the Bull of Eugenius IV, *Exultate Deo*, often

referred to as a decree of the Council of Florence ; and also the Catechism of the Council of Trent, Session vii, " De Baptismo."

[219] Mr. G. L. Kittredge in his *Witchcraft in Old and New England*, 1928 (p. 287), refers to the Laws of Hammurabi, but is not clear (p. 548) as to the purport of the Babylonian statute. For an account of the ordeal of swimming see *The Discovery of Witches*, by Montague Summers, Cayme Press, 1928, pp. 35–40.

[220] Aethelstan, 11, 23, Liebermann, *Die Gesetze des Angelsachsen*, i, 162 ; i, 23 ; Thorpe, *Ancient Laws*, folio, 1840, p. 90 ; cf. also Fuller, *Church History*, 1656, book ii, century x, ch. 9, p. 127.

[221] *Daemonologie*, 1597, third booke, ch. vi (*ad finem*). But see Johann Georg Godelmann, *De Magis, Veneficis et Lamiis*, Francoforti, 1591, lib. iii, v, " De Exploratione per Aquam Frigidam " (iii, pp. 30–45).

[222] Chapter vii, sec. 2, p. 208.

[223] *The Discovery of Witches*, by Matthew Hopkins, 1647, *Querie* 10 (4).

[224] See Montague Summers, *The Geography of Witchcraft*, 1927, c. 11, pp. 178–9.

[225] This case is also noticed in *Folk-Lore Record*, iii, ii, 1881, p. 292 (from the *Telegraph*), and in the *Essex Review*, v, 1896, p. 159.

[226] Op. cit., *De Morbis Ventriculi Liber*, pp. 439–443, Responsum.

[227] *De Synodo Diocesana*, xiii, c. xvii, 6. *Opera omnia*, folio, 1767. In Typographia Bassanensi, tom. xii, p. 162.

[228] Op. cit., iii, vi (*ad finem*).

[229] Part iii, question xv, Eng. tr., p. 227.

[230] *Tractatus de Sortilegiis*, ii, vii. *Malleus*, Lugduni, 1669, ii, pp. 284–5.

[231] *Demonomanie*, iv, 4, ed Lyon, 1593, p. 417.

[232] Commentarius in Tit. Codicis, lib. ix, de Maleficis, ed. Treves (H. Bock), 1605, pp. 720–1.

[233] Godelmann, op. cit., iii, 8 (p. 18) : " Paulus Grillandus, Bodinus & inquisitores, validissimum signum cognoscendi veneficas, & hoc dicunt, quod lachrymas emittere non possunt." Godelmann comments on this and other signs at some length.

[234] Delrio, op. cit., v, iv, 25. Ed. Moguntiae, 1603, t. iii, p. 84.

[235] *Practica*, Venice, Giunta, 1557, folio. *In Nonum Librum Almansoris Expositio*, c. xvi, *De melancholia*, " oculi ejus sunt sicci . . . non lachrymantes," *ut cit. supra.*

[236] *Opera omnia*, Parisiis, 1641, t. ii, p. 150.

[237] *Opera omnia*, t. i, ii, xv, p. 152, where *rabidarum* is misprinted *rapidarum.*

[238] *De la Folie*, 2 ts., Paris, 1845. Tom. i, pp. 87–8. There are other references to lycanthropy in the same volume at pp. 202, 232, 279, 310, 336, and in t. ii at p. 416 ; pp. 310–344, Dr. Calmiel studies the cases of lycanthropy in the Jura and at Angers. He draws his material from Boguet and De Lanere. The case of Gilles Garnier is noted, pp. 279–283. See also for lycanthropy, Böttiger, *Beitr. zur Sprengel's Geschichte der Medezin*, bd. ii, pp. 3–45.

[239] 1892, vol. ii, pp. 752–5. Dr. Tuke notes that lycanthropy is " somewhat obscure and but little discussed in treatises on mental disorders ".

[240] ii, p. 58.

[241] *De Serv. Dei Beatif. et Beat. Canonizatione*, lib. iv, Pars. 1, c. xxix. *Opera omnia*, folio, 1767, pp. 148–152.

CHAPTER II

The Werewolf : His Science and Practice

THE Common Wolf (*Canis lupus*), says St. George Mivart in his monograph *Dogs, Jackals, Wolves, and Foxes*,[1] " is the largest and most dreaded of the Canidae," a family which is one of several others making up the " Order " of " Beasts of Prey " or *Carnivora*. The wild Canidae are distributed over the greater part of the habitable globe, in the Old World from Spitzbergen and Siberia to the Cape of Good Hope and Java, in the New World from Arctic shores to Tierra del Fuego and the Falkland Islands.

The European wolf may be considered as the survivor of a group of ferocious beasts of prey, the cave-bear, the cave-hyena, and others, the fiercest enemies of prehistoric man. Although extinct in Great Britain and Ireland, the wolf still exists in some numbers in the west of the continent of Europe, in the wilder and more mountainous parts of France, Belgium (Forest of Ardennes), Hungary, East Prussia, Austria (Carinthia), and very abundantly in Russia.[2]

The size and proportions of the wolf roughly resemble those of a large mastiff dog, although individuals, particularly from different localities, differ very greatly in size, and the Russian variety especially attains most powerful dimensions. The prevailing colour is a tawny or rufous grey, and the greyness is apt to increase with age. The head, back of the neck, shoulders, loins, and crupper are blackish with yellow tints. There is a very thick and dense underfur of a slate or brown colour, intermixed with whitish and black-tipped hairs. The thighs and outsides of the legs are reddish yellow, varying to a darker brown ; the tail is full, of medium length, dark brown above and lighter below, and tipped with black. The inner side of the limbs is of a dirty yellowish grey. The lower jaw, the margin of the upper jaw, the inside of the ear, and the belly are more or less white. The exterior of the ears is usually dark brown and covered with short velvety fur ; whilst the whiskers are black and few in number.

The teeth are sharp-cutting blades of great strength. This is also noted by Ricchieri, who in his *Lectiones Antiquae*, Liber xxi, c. 24, comments upon a passage in the third *Georgic*, ll. 206-8 :—

> namque ante domandum
> ingentes tollent animos, prensique negabunt
> verbera lenta pati, et duris parere lupatis.

" Quo in loco Servius, et qui abeo mutuati sunt plures, esse lupata tradunt frena asperrima, sic de lupinorum dentium similitudine nuncupata, quos esse inaequales constet, unde et morsus infigatur summi nocumenti." Ulisse Aldrovandi, also, in his *De Quadrupedibus Solidipedibus* has much to say of the " lupata frena ".[3]

" The English wolf," remarks Poland, " was undoubtedly very much of the above description, but of smaller size and darker colour, and was also probably of a fierce disposition." [4]

Wolves frequent both forests and open country, and they are to be encountered by day as well as night, either singly, in pairs, or in packs. In severe and cold winter weather they leave their coverts and assemble in herds for predatory purposes. The packs will thus even penetrate into villages. It has been estimated that in 1875 161 persons fell victims to wolves in Russia, and in 1873 the damage to cattle was estimated at seven and a half millions of roubles. Wolves destroy horses and herds by combined attacks for the most part, but they will singly destroy sheep, goats, and children. They greedily devour birds, and will eat mice, frogs, or almost any small animals. They also feed on carrion, and are said to seek nourishment from buds and lichens.

The voice of the wolf is unmistakable, a long-drawn howl of peculiar and most eerie quality. Wolves in confinement will learn to bark if they hear dogs do so.

The males fight together in January, the successful combatant obtaining a female with whom he remains until the young are advanced in growth. "He goeth to rut in the whole yeere not above twelve daies," says Pliny of the wolf in his *Natural History*, viii, 22.[5]

Throughout the ages, even in the prehistoric world, whilst his howling athwart the stillness of nature and night struck fear into the heart of primaeval man crouching far back in

the dark retreat of some cold rough cave ; further down the
centuries when he was known as the savage plunderer and
swift pitiless marauder of the shepherd's grazing flocks, not
sparing to attack child and maid or even the solitary wayfarer by the wood ; nearer yet, what time the red glare of
his eyes across a drear plain of unflecked snow in the cold
steely moon has paralyzed some lonely leash of travellers,
and the plunging horses mad with terror break into a frenzied
gallop, their unchecked career whirling the heavy sleigh as
a mere straw-weight jerry-jingle behind, whilst the gaunt
shadowy forms muster in a greater company and advance
with fearful rapidity towards their human prey ; all down
the vistas of dateless centuries the wolf has ever been the
inevitable, remorseless enemy of man, and few animals indeed
has the world's fancy, nay, the experience and dearly
purchased knowledge of our forefathers, invested and
surrounded with so many gloomy superstitions and beliefs
that are horribly real and true.

The distinctive features of the wolf are unbridled cruelty,
bestial ferocity, and ravening hunger. His strength, his
cunning, his speed were regarded as abnormal, almost eerie
qualities, he had something of the demon, of hell. He is
the symbol of Night and Winter, of Stress and Storm, the
dark and mysterious harbinger of Death.

In Holy Writ the wolf is ever the emblem of treachery,
savagery, and bloodthirstiness.[6] Our Lord, indeed, in
the New Testament uses words than which nothing
could be darker and more condemnatory. The wolf is
the type of the heretic. " Beware of false prophets,
who come to you in the clothing of sheep, but inwardly
they are ravening wolves," S. Matthew, vii, 15. Again,
to His disciples He said in the solemn moment when
He delivered that great charge and gave them power over
unclean spirits, to cast them out : " Behold I send you as
sheep in the midst of wolves," S. Matthew, x, 16. The
Good Shepherd spoke of the sorrows and tribulations which
were to fall upon His Church : " But the hireling, and he
that is not the shepherd, whose own the sheep are not,
seeth the wolf coming, and leaveth the sheep, and fleeth :
and the wolf catcheth, and scattereth the sheep," S. John,
x, 12. S. Paul also, in his sad farewell, took up Our

Lord's words : " I know that, after my departure, ravening wolves will enter in among you, not sparing the flock," Acts, xx, 29.

The evening wolves, says the learned Cornelius a Lapide, are demons, who verily prowl abroad in the dark hours, and urge man to every kind of lust and murder, and to other infinite crimes.[7] Certes there is in the divine phrase something more than a suggestion of the demoniacal nature of the wolf. He stands not merely for the murderer of the body, that were perhaps a light thing ; but what is infinitely worse, as S. Ambrose tells us,[8] he typifies the heretic, the murderer of the soul.

In Early English use the word Wolf is applied to the Devil (wolf of hell) and his agents, as by Chaucer in the *Persones Tale* (c. 1386) : " As seith seint Augustyn, they been the deueles wolues that stranglen the sheepe of Ihesu crist." In the *Godstow Register*, Kalendar, 18 June, there is an invocation, " Cyryce and Iulytte kepe us fro the wulfe ! " (Satan). Bishop Alcock in his *Mons Perfectionis* (A iij) has : " It putteth from as the wulf the deuyll deuourer of mannes soul " ; whilst as late as 1577 Kendall, in his *Flowers of epigrammes*, speaks of " The feend the woulfe of hell ! "[9]

In classical authors the wolf[10] is the eternal symbol of ferocity and inordinate evil appetite, hard by which rides cruel devouring lust. The desire of blood and the desire of flesh are found to be never far apart. A smock-faced amoroso in Aristaenetus complains of the vampirish lechery of some old unsatisfied dowager who dry-founders him till he has fallen to a mere sapless keck. " Ods my life," he cries, " these men-leeches,[11] hags, love a youngling just like wolves, and in sooth their cravings are the venery of the she-wolf on heat " (λυκοφιλία).[12]

Plato, in the *Phaedrus*,[13] " ὦ παῖ, ξυννοεῖν, καὶ εἰδέναι τὴν ἐραστοῦ φιλέαν, ὅτι οὐ μετ᾽ εὐνοίας γίγνεται, ἀλλὰ σιτίου τρόπον, χάριν πλησομενῆς, ὡς λύκοι ἄρν᾽ ἀγαπῶσ᾽, ὡς παῖδα φιλοῦσιν ἐρασταί."

Remember, my beautiful boy, that a lover's passion is not unselfish, but he thirsts to accomplish his desire. For

The eager lover to the boy aspires,
Just as the wolf the tender lamb desires.[14]

And Strato writes an epigram [15] :—

Νυκτερινὴν ἐπίκωμος ἰὼν μεταδόρπιον ὥρην
ἄρνα λύκος θυρέτροις εὗρον ἐφεσταότα,
υἱὸν 'Αριστοδίκου τοῦ γείτονος· ὃν περιπλεχθεὶς
ἐξεφίλουν ὅρκοις πολλὰ χαριζόμενος.
νῦν δ'αὐτῷ τί φέρων δωρήσομαι ; οὔτ' ἀπάτης γὰρ
ἄξιος 'Εσπερίης οὔτ' ἐπιορκοσύνης.

By night, on pleasure bent, my dinner o'er,
Like to a wolf, I came before the door
Of Aristòcidus, and then I saw
His lamb-like son, and unto him I swore
To give him many gifts, and plighted troth
To him with kisses twain ; now am I loath
To disappoint the boy ; as if my oath
Of wine-bred fancy were indeed the growth.[16]

Thus λύκος was sometimes applied to a homosexual lover. Pollux in his *Onamasticon* [17] lists among the Comic Masks τὸ λυκαίνιον, the wolfish mask. This was worn by the lewd old trot whose face was raddled by wrinkles and ghastly pale, whilst none the less she ogled and was an adept in giving " the languishing Eye, as they call it, that is the Whitings-Eye, of old called the Sheeps-Eye ". In the Orphic Hymns Λύκαινα is an epithet of Aphrodite.[18] It is possible that from this Greek Mask τὸ λυκαίνιον was derived the Latin term *lupa*, literally a she-wolf, but meaning a bulker, a common dirty whore. Pierre Pierrugues, in his *Glossarium Eroticum Linguae Latinae*,[19] gives the derivation of *lupa* from the wolf, since that animal goes prowling abroad after its prey. In the *Truculentus* [20] Strabax has a pun on the original meaning : " Nam oveis illius haud longe absunt a lupis."

Lactantius, *De falsa religione*, i, 20, thus explains the tradition that Romulus and Remus were suckled by a she-wolf (*lupa*). He says that Larentia, the wife of the shepherd Faustulus, who found the babes, and the nurse of Romulus, was commonly named Lupa (whore) because she would shamelessly lie down to any rustic who solicited her. Hence arose the legend that a she-wolf was the foster mother of Rome's founder. " Romuli nutrix Lupa honoribus est affecta divinis. Et ferrem si animal ipsum fuisset, cujus figuram gerit, Auctor est Livius, Larentiae esse simulacrum, et quidem non corporis, sed mentis, ac morum. Fuit enim

Faustuli uxor, et propter vulgati corpore vilitatem, Lupa inter pastores, id est meretrix nuncupata est; unde etiam Lupanar [bawdy-house] dicitur." He then refers to the statue of a lioness erected by the Athenians to Leæna,[21] an Athenian hetaera, who is connected with the story of Harmodius and Aristogeiton. These two lovers killed the brother of the tyrant Hippias, Hipparchus, who offered violence to the young and comely Harmodius. Harmodius was cut down, and Aristogeiton, escaping for a while, when captured expired under tortures. Athens reverenced them as martyrs and the saviours of their country. Their example, moreover, consecrated, as it were, homosexual love, and their two names became eponyms of paiderastia.[22] To do them public honour their statues, cast in bronze by Antenor, were set up in the Agora. Leæna, whose actual part in the history does not seem very clear, was put to the question as being privy to the affair, but she died under her sufferings without making any disclosure, and (as it is said) she bit off her tongue that no secret might be wrung from her. She was honoured by a bronze statue of a lioness (λέαινα) without a tongue, which was set up on the Acropolis between the Propylaea and the temenos of Artemis Brauronia.[23]

The word *lupa* is frequent in Latin authors. The Scholiast on Juvenal, iii, 66, glosses on *picta lupa* " meretrices ",[24] and upon the phrase of Ausonius, Epigram., xxvi, 12, " Et mater est vere lupa," Vinetus comments : " Scortum. Meretricum enim mores, voraci luporum ingenio, haud sunt dissimiles. Alludit autem ad fabulam de Romulo et Remo a lupa lactatis, apud Livium, Plutarchum, Halicarnasseum." [25] Prudentius, *adversus Symmachum*, i,[26] has of Priapus :—

> Scortator nimius, multaque libidine suetus
> Rusticulas vexare lupas, interque salicta
> Et densas sepes obscoena cubilia inire.

In the famous work of Nicolas Chorier, which is generally known under the title *Aloisia Sigæa Toletana De arcanis Amoris et Veneris* (Joannis Meursii, *Elegantiae Latini Sermonis*),[27] Colloquium vi, " Veneres," the erudite Tallia discourses : " Lupae sunt et meretrices, quae, nulla voluptatis habita ratione, pretio merent, aut merere vulgo audiunt, putidae, e misera et jejuna plebecula. Quo cumque protervae se tulerint, lupanaris secum sordes invehent. Ignominiosum ipsae sunt sibi opprobrium . . . Lupa et lupanar inventa sunt vocabula ad ignominiam fortunae, non morum."

From *lupa* we have the cognate words *lupana*, a whore ; *lupatria*, a strumpet ; *lupari*, to fornicate or wimble ; *lupanar*, also *lupanarium*, a brothel-house ; *lupanarius*, a cock-bawd ; and the adjective *lupanaris*, lascivious, lewd.

In Italian *lupo* is sometimes used to designate a lecher, as by Giovanni Rucellai in his tragedy *Rosmunda*,[28] Acto terzo, where the Nurse says :—

> Ma queste nostre misere fanciulle
> Darai in preda ad affamati lupi,
> Ch'insio nel grembo dell'afflitte madri
> Verranno ad isfogar le voglie loro.

Lupa also designates a whore ; for example, Segneri in his *Prediche*, v, 9, has : " Come dunque scialaequar prima la vostra robatra parasiti, tra buffoni, e tra lupe, che darla a Cristo." *Lupanaio*, *lupanario*, and *lupanare* all signify a brothel-house. Segneri, *Prediche*, viii, 6 : " V'invita a feste [il compagno] v'invita a festini, v'invita a balli, v'invita sin tal volta a luoghi infamissimi, a lupercali, a postriboli, a lupanari."

In *Acolastus*, iv, 6, the unhappy prodigal soliloquizes :—

> o dolor, dolor.
> Vt dij uos male perdant lupae obscoenissimae
> Quibus seruiui turpiter.

Upon which John Palsgrave in his interpretation of the comedy writes : " O sorowe, sorowe, i.o. redoubled sorowe, or o sorow upon sorowe that euyl mought the goddes lose you, o you most uggly or abhomynable she wolfes, whom I haue vily serued. i. that I beseche god send you an euyll myschefe, you moste lothesome cutte tayled bytches, whom I haue become slaue unto, thus shamefully. (*Comparatio Lupae i. scorti ad lupam.*) But yet is there a more vehemēce comprysed by the auctour, to lyken myswomen unto she wulfes, as dyuerse latine auctours doo testyfie, and Jehan de Meun, in his frenche Romant of the rose." [29]

Death walked hand in hand with lust, and we may note that in an old Etruscan vase-painting Charon, the ferryman of hell, is wrapped in a wolf's fur.[30] The omen of the wolf was unlucky in the highest degree. He carries disappointment, disaster, and doom.[31]

Lust, then, as well as blood is associated with the wolf.
Giambattista della Porta, physician, philosopher, and
cabbalist, who was born in 1540 and died in 1615, tells us
that in his day the country folk of the kingdom of Naples
still fixed over the door of their huts a wolf's head with wide
gaping jaws to defend from sorcerers and witches; they still
held that the skin from a wolf's neck was a most powerful
periapt.   Moreover, they believed that a man who trenchered
succulently on roast wolf's flesh would be immune from the
frauds and molestations of goblin, evil spirits, bogle, and
incubi.   Wolf's flesh roast and minced with other food was
a sovran remedy for black melancholy.[32]
Thus Mr. Frank Cowper in his stirring and well-told
novel, *Cædwalla, or The Saxons in the Isle of Wight*, just before
the night attack on Cissanceaster, when the warriors are
startled for a moment at the unearthly screech, imagining it
is some foul sorceress yelling to her kind, makes old Ceolwulf
volunteer and say : " Atheling, I will go, I have no fear of
witches ; I have a wolf's snout hung round my neck, and no
witch can hurt me, be her charms never so powerful." [33]
Girolamo Cardano in his *De Subtilitate Libri XXI*, first
published in 1550,[34] writes that a wolf's tail hung up in a
stable or byre, entirely prevents the horses or the oxen from
eating.   Horses treading in a wolf's soreth are mazed and
founder.   They snuff the foe.   The head of a wolf suspended
in a pigeon house has virtue to protect any columbary from
the attack of ferrets or weasels.   He will not, however, vouch
that the chape of a wolf, if buried, keeps off the annoyance
of gnats and flies.   A mash of the intestines, skin and treddles
of the wolf cureth colicky gripes.   But Cardano doubts
whether, as some aver, a wolf's pizzle, dried and minced,
when eaten will prove a potent aphrodisiac.[35]
" It is commonly thought," says Pliny, treating of wolves,
" and verily beleeved, that in the taile of this beast, there is
a little string or haire that is effectuall to procure love, and
that when he is taken at any time, hee casteth it away
from him, for that it is of no force and vertue unless it be
taken from him whiles he is alive." [36]
Leonard Vair, also, in his *De Fascino*, i, 8, remarks : " Lupi
etiam caudae exiguo in villo, amatorium virus inesse credit,
qui si viuenti non detrahatur, vim nullam habere refert." [37]

It is not well even to dream of a wolf, so Artemidorus in his *Oneirocritica*,[38] ii, 12, instructs us : " Λύκος δὲ ἐνιαυτὸν σημαίνει διὰ τὸν λυκάβαντα, τοῦτ᾽ ἐστι, τὸν χρόνον ; ὡς οἱ ποιηταὶ ὀνομάζουσιν ἀπὸ τοῦ περὶ τὰ ζῶα ταῦτα συμβεβηκότος. Ἀεὶ γὰρ ἑπόμενα ἀλλήλους ἐν τάξει δίεισι τὸν ποταμόν, ὥσπερ αἱ τοῦ ἔτους ὧραι ἑπόμεναι ἀλλήλαις τελοῦσι τὸν ἐνιαυτόν. Καὶ ἐχθρὸν δὲ βίαιόν τινα καὶ ἁρπακτικόν, καὶ πανοῦργον, καὶ ἐκ τοῦ φανεροῦ ὁμόσε χωροῦντα."

Seldom, very seldom, is the wolf lucky. Pliny, however, gives us the exception. " In the case of presages and foretokens of things to come, this is observed, that if men see a wolfe abroad, cut his way and turne to their right hand, it is good ; but if his mouth be full when he doth so, there is not a better signe nor more luckie in the world again." [39]

Aristophanes of Byzantium, also, *Historiae Animalium Epitome*,[40] ii, 242, tells us of the virtue of a wolf's tooth : πύκου δ᾽ ὄδοντα τις ἐξαψέμονος τοῦ αὐχένος, ἀδεῶς ἂν τοῖς ὁμοφύλοις ἐντύχῃ θηρίοις. His epithet for the wolf is the significant ἄδικος.

Aubrey, *Remaines of Gentilisme and Judaisme*, remarking upon amulets and corals, says : " The Irish doe use a woolves fang-tooth set in silver for this purpose ; which they hold to be better than coral. And in the very same manner the children in Germany weare about them furnished too with little silver bells." Again, he notes : " Coralls are worne by children still ; but in Ireland they value the fang-tooth (holder) of an wolfe before it : which they set in silver and gold as we doe yᵉ Coralls." [41]

The following is an old Sicilian pastoral wolf-charm : " Per ligari li lupu pignia una strinza di dainu oï capriu e non voi mangiari carni allupata. Santu Silvestru a munte oliveri stava, la sua bistiami pascia e guardava, scisi fera di boscu, quali mangiau, quali pulicau, quali a mmala via li mandau. Santu Silvestru a menzu la via stava e plangia e lacrimava : Jesu Christu et la virgi Maria passava dissi li : Chi ai, Silvestru, chi planzi e llagrimi ? Oï, signuri comu non vognu plangiri e lagrimari ? A munti oliveri stava la mia bistiami, pascia e guardava, scisi fera di boscu quali mangiau, quali pulicau, quali a mmala via li mandau." " Silvestru, per ki non li ligi ? Signuri, chi mi lùgu chi non saggiu, nesci la sira poichi scura, e ddi perchi la stidda una chi luggi piu chi lluna e dal lupu e uligu denti e ad uni animali chi pitterra

strascina ventri chi non faccia mali ala mia bistiami pedi
giaccatu non perdir ritundu per fina chi lu suli non giungi
ala tavul di lu santu Salvaturi. Allaudi di Jesu Christu
eddila virgini Maria dirremu un paternostru ed una avi Maria.
Ariel sichar lormai emanuel sutiel con juru vos spiritus
praenominatus per alpha et o et per principem vestrum
sosolimo ut quam oculus meus viderit, uti conrumpere
faciatis visa ut ineat amorem meum." [42]

There is a seemingly world-wide and most ancient tradition
concerning the wolf, which, since I am unable to decide upon
the truth of the matter, will perhaps best be treated by
reference to a quota of authorities and others noticing
it in their writings. Accordingly I will cite in the first place—
inasmuch as he so concisely in his well-flavoured trenchant
English sums up the point—Dr. George Hakewell, who says
in his *Apologie or Declaration of The Power and Providence of
God in the Government of the World*, book i, chapter i, sect. v, 9
(folio, Oxford, 1627 and again 1635) [43] : " That a *Woolfe* if he
see a man first suddenly strikes him dumb, whence came the
proverbe *Lupus est in fabula*, and that of the poet :—

> *Lupi Mœrim videre priores,*
> The Wolues saw Mœris first.

" Yet *Phillip Camerarius (Meditat.Histor.cap.* 28) professes,
*fabulosam esse quod vulgo creditur, nominem à lupo prœuisum
subitò consternari & vocem amittere*, That it is fabulous which
is commonly beleeued that a man being first seene by the
Woolfe is therevpon astonished and looseth his voyce ;
And that himselfe hath found it by experience to be a vaine
opinion, which *Scaliger (Exercitat.* 844) likewise affirmes vpon
the same ground. *Vtinam tot ferulis castigarentur mendacio-
rum assertores isti quot à Lupis visi sumus sine jactura vocis.*
I wish those Patrons of lies were chastised with so many
blowes as at sundry times I haue beene seene of wooles
without any losse of my voyce."

The most celebrated allusion to this belief is contained in
Vergil's ninth Eclogue, 53–4 :—

> vox quoque Moerim
> iam fugit ipsa ; lupi Moerim videre priores.

which Dryden Englishes thus :—

> My Voice grows hoarse ; I feel the Notes decay,
> As if the Wolves had seen me first to Day." [44]

Servius in his Commentary on this passage of Vergil glosses : " hoc etiam physici confirmant, quod voce deseretur quem prior viderit lupus."

Theocritus, also, xiv, 22, has :—

" οὐ φθεγξῇ ; λύκος εἰδέ σ' ; " ἐπαιξέ τις. " ὡς σοφός " εἶπε, κἠφᾶπτ'.

" Won't you speak ? Has a wolf seen you ? " jested some quiz, " as the wise man said."

Plato, although not precisely mentioning the old belief, refers to it in the First Book of the *Republic*, when Thrasymachus has interrupted the discussion in a loud blustering voice, and Socrates declares : " I was astonied beyond measure, and gazed at the speaker in terror ; and methinks if I had not set eyes on him before he eyed me, I should verily have been struck dumb."

We now approach a very important point in the study of the Werewolf. When a man is metamorphosed into a wolf, or into any other animal form whatsoever it may be, is there an actual, corporeal, and material change, or else is the shape-shifting fantastical, although none the less real and substantially apparent to the man himself and to those who behold him ; and if it be thus simulated and illusory how is the phenomenon accomplished ?

The famous Jean Bodin, who devotes the sixth chapter of the second book of his *De la Demonomanie des Sorciers* (Paris, 1580) to a study of lycanthropy—*De la Lycanthropie et si le Diable peut changer les hommes en bestes* [45]—gives it as his opinion that the demon can really and materially metamorphose the body of a man into that of an animal, only he cannot change and alter the human understanding. Bodin argues for a substantial change, and quotes in his support S. Thomas Aquinas : *Omnes Angeli boni et mali ex uirtute naturali, habent potestatem transmutandi corpora nostra.* [46] " Or si nous confessons que les hommes ont bien la puissance de faire porter des roses à vn cerisier, des pommes à vn chou, & changer le fer en acier, & la forme d'argent enor, & faire mille sortes de pierres artificielles, qui cōbatent les pierres naturelles, doibt on trouuer estrange, si Sathan change la figure d'vn corps en l'autre, veu la puissance grande que Dieu luy donne en ce monde elemētaire."

There are, it is true, other learned and weighty writers who have maintained that (under God) the Devil has power actually to change a human being corporeally into a wolf or some other animal, but it was Bodin who was universally regarded and so violently attacked as the chief exponent of this argument. His chapter is of prime importance in the history of the philosophical conceptions of lycanthropy, and demands a particular examination.

He commences by emphasizing the fact that the transvection of witches to the sabbat, although sometimes fantastical, since the witch lies in a trance whilst psychically she assists at Satan's synagogue, is also oftener material, and she travels thither bodily conveyed. The Devil deludes her so that she imagines she is carried by the power of some muttered words or by the force of the sorcerers' unguent. At these orgies the demon generally appears to the assembly in the form of a huge he-goat. Sometimes he shows himself as a tall dark man.

It is a wonderful thing that the Devil should be able to change a man into a beast. Yet in the *Malleus Maleficarum* we read of a certain leader of witches (part ii, qn. i, ch. 15) [47] named Staufer, who lived in Berne, and whose boast it was that he could change himself into a mouse and thus slip through the hands of his enemies. He left two disciples, Hoppo and Stadlin, who could raise violent hailstorms.

Bodin then rehearses in some detail the case of Gilles Garnier, condemned and executed for lycanthropy at Dole, 18th January, 1583, and refers to the trial of Pierre Burgot and Michel Verdun, two notorious werewolves, in 1521. He also cites the instance of the lycanthrope of Padua, as described by Job Fincel [48]; and the coven of witches who under the form of cats met in the old haunted castle of Vernon. When some of these animals had been wounded, certain old women were found hurt in exactly the same place on their bodies. There is also the example of the wood-chopper who lived in a town not far from Strasburg. Whilst hewing faggots this man was attacked by three fierce cats. These he drove off with great difficulty, beating them back and bastooning them, where there were presently found three women of family and reputation so bruised and injured that they perforce kept their beds. All circumstances agreed beyond any shadow of doubt or incertitude. (*Malleus Maleficarum*, part ii, qn. i, ch. 9.) [49]

Next Bodin appeals to the authority of Pierre Mamor and Ulrich Molitor, a passage which will be found quoted in full below, and therefore need hardly detain us here.

He proceeds to remark that records of this shape-shifting are more commonly to be found in Greece and the East than generally in European countries, as witness the onslaught of werewolves into Constantinople, *anno* 1542, described by Job Fincel.

After a brief consideration of the word *Werwolf* or *loup-garou*, our author returns to his main theme and adduces the testimony of Pietro Pompanazzi, Paracelsus, Gaspar Peucer, Hubert Languet, Archbishop Olaf of Trondhjem, Abbot John Trithemius, and others, including at least one record by an eye-witness of werewolfism.

Next in order are surveyed the traditions and legends of antiquity, Homer, Herodotus, Pomponius Mela, Solinus, Strabo, Dionysius Afer, Varro, Vergil, Ovid, Pliny, and not a few writers more. For although it is freely allowed that the poets were merely reciting for our pleasure romantic fables, it is impossible to suppose that there was not some substratum of truth in a belief that was nothing less than universal both in place and time.

The traveller Pierre Belon [50] in his *Les observations de plusievrs singvlaritez et choses mémorables trouuées en Grèce, Asie, Indée, Egypte, Arabie et autres pays estranges*, Paris, 4to, 1553, relates that whilst at Cairo he saw a young itinerant juggler who possessed an ass which was able to do whatever his master bade him. The animal would, for example, go and kneel down before the fairest lady in the company if so ordered, and this be it noted he only did after he had cast his eyes round the circle, and he would also show that he was capable of such processes of ratiocination as are involved in a disjunctive hypothetical syllogism. It is strongly to be suspected that this ass was a man ensorcelled.

Bodin relates the incident told by Vincent of Beauvais,[51] and draws attention to the striking phrase used by S. Augustine concerning the recital made by Apuleius, " aut indicavit, aut finxit." [52] He also incidentally mentions the change of sex, as when girls seem to become boys, which cases in reality

involve pseudohermaphroditic problems. (For these see
F. L. von Neugebaber's *Hermaphroditismus beim Menschen* ;
Krafft-Ebing, *Psychopathia Sexualis*, English translation by
F. J. Rebman, 1906, pp. 852–864 ; Dr. Havelock Ellis,
Psychology of Sex, vol. ii, *Sexual Inversion*, 3rd edition,
1927, pp. 315–16.)

Bodin stresses the point, which indeed is of first importance,
that if lycanthropes " avoient poil et teste et corps " of the
wolf, or in similar cases of the other animal, but " la raison
ferme, et stable ", the sense of the Canon Episcopi is not in
any way impugned. " Et par ce moyen la Lycanthropie ne
seroit par contraire au canon Episcopi xxvi. q.v. ny à l'opinion
des Theologiens qui tiennent pour la plurpart que Dieu non
seulement a crée toutes choses, ains aussi que les malins
esprits n'ont pas la puissance de changer la forme, attendu
que la forme essentielle de l'homme ne change point, qui
est la raison, ains seulement la figure." Which, theologically
and philosophically is a perfectly sound proposition.

The authority of S. Thomas is accordingly cited, and Bodin
glosses Isaias, xiii, 21, where it is said of the ruins of Babylon,
" and the hairy ones shall dance there." This leads to a
consideration of the magic sleights of Simon Magus before
Nero, and more particularly of the metamorphosis of
Nabuchodonosor to an ox with hairs like the feathers of
eagles and nails like birds' claws.

As Nabuchodonosor was so punished by God, so Heaven
may also well have permitted Gilles Garnier and the sorcerers
of Savoy owing to their vile appetites and their lust for
human flesh to have become wolves, losing human form.

From whatever cause this shape-shifting may arise, it is
very certain by the common consent of all antiquity and all
history, by the testimony of learned men, by experience and
first-hand witness, that werewolfism which involves some
change of form from man to animal is a very real and a very
terrible thing. (It cannot, of course, take place without the
exercise of black magic.) " Mais en quelque sorte que ce
soit, il a pert que les hommes sont quelques fois transmuez
en bestes demeurant la forme et raison humaine. Soit que
cela se face par la puissance de Dieu immediatement,
soit qu'il donne ceste puissance à Satan executeur de sa
volonté."

Such briefly is the tenor of Bodin's famous chapter, and there is assuredly no impossible or unsound doctrine implicated in his theory as it stands, whatever falsity may have been, and indeed actually was, read into his thesis by his enemies.

The erudite Jean de Sponde in his *Commentary upon Homer*, folio, Basileæ, 1583, has a very ample note [53] upon the tenth book of the *Odyssey*, in which he discusses in detail the possibility of the transformation of the human shape to a beast, in reference to the magic of Circe. He says : " The general opinion is that the human frame cannot be metamorphosed into the animal bodies of beasts : but most hold that although there is no real shape-shifting the Devil can so cheat and deceive men's eyes that by his power they take one form, which they seem to see, to be quite another thing from what it actually is." From this he differs. The question is, whether men can be changed into animals, that is whether one body can be substantially transformed into another ? If one considers carefully and weighs the extraordinary and unknown forces of nature, or if one surveys the dark dominion of Satan, such a change is not to be deemed impossible. " I believe," he frankly admits, " that in the wide circuit of this world there are so many unknown and mysterious agents, that there may be some quality which effects this metamorphosis. I am very well aware that many of my readers will deem me impious or trivial." Jean de Sponde then advances the examples of the Arismaspi and Anthropophagi, and he speaks at length of noxious herbs, such as Cohobba, which grows in the isle of Haiti, and which drives men mad. Does not then this herb affect their reason ? Are not those possessed by the Devil wounded, as it were, in their souls ? And if a herb, and the power of evil, can have such control over the higher part of man, his reason and his immortal soul, why cannot a man's body be subject to similar disturbances ? The change, although corporeal and complete, may be considered accidental, not essential. We may well believe that the Devil will employ potions and unguents, having no power in themselves, to effect such metamorphosis.

The question is can men be turned into beasts ? " Possunt, inquam." *I affirm that they can be so changed.*

Jean de Sponde then refers to the authority of Bodin, " uiro eneditissimo & diligentissimo scriptore." He quotes various examples of werewolves, such as Gilles Garnier, Pierre Burgot, Michel Verdun, and others, cases which nobody would think of denying. That these foul warlocks were demoniac lycanthropes admits of no question, the point is how do we explain their lycanthropy.

It is sufficient for de Sponde to safeguard his position by acknowledging that a man cannot be said absolutely to be a wolf unless his soul change into the spirit of a wolf, and that is not possible. " Non posset ergo homo lupus fieri, nisi anima ipsa hominis, in lupi animam uerteretur omnino. Id autem fieri natura non patitur." He also adds : " Notandum est, nos non intelligere formam hominis in hac transfiguratione pensi : quia remanet eadem ratio, quae est uera forma, ex qua suum esse homo accipit." Which is the very position of Bodin, and cannot be said to be unorthodox, even if unusual.

Gaspar Peucer (1525–1602), the physician, son-in-law and friend of Melanchthon, in his *Commentarius De Praecipius Diuinationum Generibus*, 1553, " De Theomanteia," thus explains the shape-shifting of the demon werewolf : " Those who are changed suddenly fall to the ground as if seized with epilepsy, and there they lie without life or motion. Their actual bodies do not move from the spot where they have fallen, nor do their limbs turn to the hairy limbs of a wolf, but the soul or spirit by some fascination quits the inert body and enters the *spectrum* or φάσμα of a wolf, and when they have glutted their foul lupine lusts and cravings, by the Devil's power, the soul re-enters the former human body, whose members are then energized by the return of life." He holds it certain that the individual, the *ego*, becomes enclosed in a wolf's form, with bestial motions and ferocity.

Philippus Camerarius (1537–1624), the jurisconsult, some time Vice-Chancellor of the University of Altorf, in his *Operae Horarum Subcisiuarum Centuria Prima*, c. lxxii,[54] remarks that he has heard of werewolves from Gaspar Peucer and from Languet, but whether the metamorphosis is accomplished by some mysterious force of nature, or whether it is the effect of the divine wrath and a punishment as in the case of Nabuchodonosor he is unable to decide. With regard to the actual change of essential substance in the bodies he is by no means prepared to go so far as Bodin, with whom (he observes) some prudent and scrupulous writers do not entirely agree. Jean Fernel, the physician of Henri II of France, in his weighty treatise *De Abditis Rerum Causis*,[55] lib. ii, cap. xvi : " Et Morbos, et Remedia quaedam trans naturam esse," certainly goes a very long way in support of Bodin. He mentions classical examples of metamorphosis, " de Demancho, quem narrat Plinius degustatis extis pueri immolati in sacrificio in lupum se conuertisse," and others ; adding, " Haec nisi multorum fide comprobata contestataque forent, non tam multas leges Iuris consultorum prudentia in magos tulisset." He amply allows for any glamour, since the demon not unseldom " solas rerum species et spectra quaedam exhibet, quibus hominum mentes quasi praestigiis illudat, et oculorum aciem praestringat."

In his very untrustworthy " Note on Witchcraft " given in the first volume (1886) of *Phantasms of the Living*, chapter iv,[56] Mr. Edmund Gurney says : " To be quite fair, I should add that Bodin says that one Pierre Mamor wrote a little tractate, in which he professed to have actually seen a transformation —this being the only case that I have come across where a man of sufficient education to write something that was printed is ever cited as bearing personal testimony to such marvels." The sneer is cheap and ignorant.

Bodin's actual words are as follows—I quote from the original edition, Paris, 4to, 1580, II, vi, p. 97—" Pierre Mamor en vn petit traicté qu'il a fait des Sorciers, dict auoir veu ce changement d'hommes en loups, luy estant en Sauoye. Et Henry de Coulongne au traicté qu'il a faict, *de Lamijs*, tient cela pour indubitable. Et Vlrich le Meusnier [57] en vn petit liure, qu'il a dedié à l'Empereur Sigismond, escript la dispute qui fut faicti deuant l'Empereur, & dit qu'il fut conclu pas viues raisons, & par l'experience d'infinis exemples, que telle transformation estoit veritable, & dict luy mesme auoir veu vn Lycanthrope à Constance, qui fut accusé, conueincu, condamné, & puis executé à mort apres sa confessiō. Et se trouuēt plusieurs liures publiez en Almaigne, que l'vn des plus grands Roys de la Chrestienté, qui est mort n'a pas long temps, souuēt estoit mué en loup, & qui estoit en reputatiō d'estre l'vn des plus grands Sorciers du monde."

It will be well, then, to see exactly what Mamor wrote, and
to inquire who this "one Pierre Mamor" so scommatically
referred to by Mr. Gurney was. Actually indeed he was a
very distinguished scholar, whose attainments were held in
highest esteem by his contemporaries.

Pierre Mamor was born at Limoges c. 1429–30. Upon
8th August, 1461, he was appointed rector of the Church of
Saint Opportune at Poitiers at the instance of Bishop Louis
Guerinet. It was about this time that the Bishop was
translated to Frejus, but Pierre Mamor was equally honoured
by Dom Jean du Bellay, O.S.B., who next wore the mitre
of Poitiers. Mamor filled the Chair of Theology at Poitiers
with such general applause that later he became the Rector
of the University, a position he resigned upon being elected
a Canon of the Cathedral of S. Peter at Saintes. His *Flagellum
Maleficorum*, which was written 1461–70, and first printed
at Lyons c. 1490, is appropriately dedicated to Louis de
Roché-Chouart, who was Bishop of Saintes from 1460–1492.[58]
It is obvious that the authority of so eminent a theologian
as Canon Pierre Mamor must carry great weight and demands
no small respect.

In his eighth and ninth chapters Mamor discusses at
length the glamour and diabolical illusion, and shows that
men are both objectively and subjectively deceived by the
demon, their senses corrupted, cheated, and tricked ; the
imagination clouded and betrayed. In chapter xi he treats
of fascination and fantastical spells. The question of men
who appear to be transformed into wolves or other animal
forms arises. The classical legends of Circe and the wolves
of Arcady are alluded to ; Apuleius is cited, the testimony
of S. Augustine adduced. "De lupis uero quos ut dictum est
berones siue galones uulgus uocat, uidetur esse dicendum,
quod Daemon homines illos quos mutati in lupos asserunt,
multi aliculi secreto retinent absconsos, et intrans corpus
lupi alicuius, eum educit a siluis quem per uillas et agros
discurrere cogit, et male plurima facit, occidit homines, pueros
comedit, pecora deuorat et fugat, et plurimos homines
terret." Nothing could be plainer. In Mamor's judgment
the werewolf is a wolf possessed by the demon, who has
cast the sorcerer into a deep trance meanwhile and concealed
him in some secret spot. Mamor also points out how fearful

and terrible a monster is the werewolf, a hell-possessed and devil-driven wolf, two fierce relentless enemies of man joined in one body of prey.

Our author then relates a werewolf story. A peasant's wife of Lorraine to her horror saw her husband vomit up a child's arm and hand, which he had devoured when he was in a wolf's form. " I believe," says Mamor, " that this was a demoniacal illusion." None the less, he adds, Pierre de Bressuire, a most learned and pious doctor, deemed that the human body could be metamorphosed to a lupine form corporeally, " but I prefer to go no further than S. Augustine, and I hold that when a werewolf rushed among the flocks and herds, tearing and ravaging, the body of the man was lying entranced in some secret chamber or retreat, whilst his spirit had entered and was energizing the form of a wolf."

Bodin, then, is hardly just in his adduction of Canon Mamor in full support of his especial view.

The *De Pythonicis Mulicribus* (1489), of Molitor, is cast in the form of a dialogue between Sigismund, Archduke of Austria ; Conrad Eschak, a chief magistrate of Constance ; and Ulrich Molitor, who was a Professor of Pavia. In caput iii they argue whether the form of a man may be changed. Sigismund says, No, and quotes the Canon Episcopi. Conrad mentions the crafts of Simon Magus, who so altered the face of Faustinianus that all thought this latter to be the wizard himself. Ulrich argues that men can be metamorphosed into wolves and other animal shapes by the power of the demon, who does not in truth create anything new but only makes something seem to be which actually is not. A proposition denied by nobody. The same points are taken up in caput viii, and Molitor definitely speaks of glamour, " Dæmones perstringendo oculos faciant apparentiam, qua homo iudicat rem alterius formae esse, quam sit, ita ut quis uidens hominem, credat eum esse asinum uel lupum et temen unusquisque retineat formam suam, quanquam oculi nostri decipiantur et ad aliam speciem erroneo iudicio deducantur."

It is not to be denied that in the case of the demoniac werewolf there is a change, both subjective and objective, so that the warlock seems to be a wolf both to himself and also is seen as a wolf by all who observe him.

It must be sufficient to cite only a few of the very many

eminent authorities who discuss the actuality of the metamorphosis of man to a bestial shape.

Although the tractate *De Spiritu et Anima* is certainly not to be assigned to S. Augustine, this work has so often been quoted as by the great doctor that it will not be amiss in passing to cite the famous passage thence to which appeal is found again and again in older writers. " It is very generally believed that by certain witches' spells and the power of the Devil men may be changed into wolves and beasts of burthen, and as pack-animals be made to bear and carry loads, and when their work is done they return to their original shapes, but they do not lose their human reason and understanding, nor are their minds made the intelligence of a mere beast. Now this must be understood in this way, namely that the Devil creates no new nature, but that he is able to make something appear to be which in reality is not. For by no spell nor evil power can the mind, nay, not even the body corporeally, be changed into the material limbs and features of any animal . . . but a man is fantastically and by illusion metamorphosed into an animal, albeit he to himself seems to be a quadruped, and as for the burthens which the beast carries if they be real they are supported and borne by familiars so that all who see the seeming animal may be mocked and deluded by diabolical glamour." [59] But, as we have pointed out, the work is spurious and as such carries no especial weight.

A more important passage is chapter xviii of the Eighteenth Book of the *De Ciuitate Dei*, whose rubric runs : *Of the deuills power in transforming mans shape : what a Christian may beleeue herein.* (I quote the English version of John Healey, folio, 1610.) [60] In chapter xvii, S. Augustine has treated *Of the incredible changes of men that* Varro *beleeued*, namely, the strange tales of that famous witch and excellent herbarist Circe, the metamorphosis into wolves of the Arcadians ; nor does Varro "thinke that *Pan* and *Iupiter* were called *Lycæi* in the Arcadian history for any other reason then for their transforming of men into wolues : for this they held impossible to any but a diuine power : a wolfe is called λύκος in greeke, and hence came their name *Lycæus* ".

What then are we to hold touching this deceit of devils ? *In principio,* " the greater power wee behold in the deceiuer,

the firmer hold must we lay vpon our mediator." It is
ludicrous and trivial to make a sweeping assertion and say
airily that all these legends are lies. " For when I was in
Italy," writes the holy doctor, " I heard such a report there,
how certaine women of one place there, would but giue one
a little drug in cheese, and presently hee became an asse,
and so they made him carry their necessaries whither they
would, and hauing done, they reformed his figure againe :
yet had he his humane reason still, as *Apuleius* had in his
asse-ship, as himselfe writeth in his booke of the golden
asse ; bee it a lie or a truth that hee writeth (*aut indicauit
aut finxit*). Well either these things are false, or incredible,
because vnusuall. But we must firmely hold Gods power to
bee omnipotent in all things : but the deuills can doe nothing
beyond the power of their nature (which is angelicall, although
maleuolent) vnlesse hee whose iudgements are euer secret,
but neuer vniust, permit them. Nor can the deuills create
any thing (what euer shewes of theirs produce these doubts),
but onely cast a changed shape ouer that which God hath
made, altering onely in shew. Nor doe I thinke the deuill
can forme any soule or body into bestiall or brutish members,
and essences : but they haue an vnspeakable way of trans-
porting mans fantasie in a bodily shape (*phantasticum
hominis*) vnto other senses (this running ordinarylie in our
dreams through a thousand seuerall things, and though it
be not corporall, yet seemes to cary it selfe in corporall
formes through all these things) while the bodies of the
men thus affected lie in another place, being aliue, but yet
in an extasie farre more deepe then any sleepe. Now this
phantasie may appeare vnto others sences in a bodily shape,
and a man may seeme to himselfe to bee such a one as hee
often thinketh himselfe to be in his dreame, and to beare
burdens, which if they be true burdens indeed, the deuills
beare them, to delude mens eyes with the apparance of true
burdens, and false shapes. For one *Praestantius* told me that
his father tooke that drug in cheese at his owne house,
wherevpon he lay in such a sleepe that no man could awake
him : and after a few daies hee awaked of himselfe and told
all hee had suffered in his dreames in the meane while, how
hee had beene turned into an horse and carried the souldiours
victualls about in a budget. Which was true as he told,

yet seemed it but a dreame vnto him. . . . So then those
Arcadians, whom the god (nay the deuills rather) turned into
wolues, and those fellowes of *Vlisses* beeing charmed by *Circe*
into Bestiall shapes, had onely their fantasie, occupied in
such formes, if there were any such matter. But for *Diomedes*
birds, seeing there is a generation of them, I hold them not
to be transformed men, but that the men were taken away,
and they brought in their places, as the hinde was in
Iphegenias roome, *Agamemnons* daughter. The deuill can
play such iugling trickes with ease, by Gods permission, but
the Virgin beeing found aliue afterwards, this was a plaine
deceipt of theirs to take away her, and set the hinde there.
But *Diomedes* fellowes, because they were neuer seene (the
euill angells destroying them) were beleeued to bee turned
into those birds that were brought out of their vnknowne
habitations into their places."

Very important in this connection, the power of the Devil
to effect the transformation of men into animals, is the tenor
of the Canon Episcopi.[61]   This Canon is first met with in
the collection of ecclesiastical decrees, *De ecclesiasticis
disciplinis*, ascribed to Abbot Regino of Prüm, A.D. 906.
Actually it is certainly much older than the period of Regino
himself, and even if it be considered as a genuine piece of
legislation enacted by some Council, this was assuredly
not the Synod of Ancyra, A.D. 314, to which it is generally
ascribed as " Ex concilio Anquirensi ".   In any case this
Canon 371 passed into the Collections of Ivo of Chartres
and Gratian.

The rubric runs : " De mulicribus, quae cum daemonibus
se dicunt nocturnis horis equitare."   In the first part are
denounced and condemned " certain wicked women who
turning aside to follow Satan, and being seduced by the
illusions and phantasms of demons, fully believe and openly
profess that in the dead of night they ride upon certain
beasts with the pagan goddess Diana [or with Herodias] and
a countless horde of women, and that in these silent hours
they fly over vast tracts of country and obey her as their
mistress, while on other nights they are summoned to pay
her homage ".

John of Salisbury speaks of this popular belief in a witch-
queen named Herodias,[62] whilst Lorenzo Anania [63] has

PLATE III

THE TRANSVECTION OF WITCHES

[face p. 84

"A maribus pariter ac feminis nonnullis crebro hunc nefandum actum exerceri legimus hunc *Dianæ* ac *Herodiadis* ludum uulgo appellant ". There are many similar allusions, and from these Girolamo Tartarotti in his *Del Congresso Notturno delle Lamie*, published at Rovereto in 1749, evolved the extraordinary idea that witchcraft was a remnant or a continuation of a pagan cult he was pleased to dub the *Società Dianiana*,[64] a foolish maggot taken over (without acknowledgement) and re-presented with singular ill-success in a more modern work, wherein is proclaimed as a wondrous new discovery "this ancient religion the Dianic cult ".

Leaving fantasy and fable it must be remarked that the Canon Episcopi is not at all concerned with witchcraft but with pagan creeds and practice. The transvection of witches by demoniacal agency is a thing amply assured, but their evil flights to the Sabbat are quite another thing from the aerial coursing through the skies led by ethnic goddesses whom they worship and adore.

The point is aptly discussed by Francisco Vittoria, in his *Relectiones undecim*,[65] Salamanca, 1565, *De arte Magica*, where whilst duly insisting upon the transvection of witches by diabolical agency, a thing proved by authority, by the experience of eye-witnesses, and by their own free confession, says that it is false and impossible that they should ride with Diana and Herodias. "Nam Diana nulla est, Herodias autem est in inferno, nec permittitur exire ei, nec est mulier, sed sola anima."

The clause in the Canon which immediately concerns us is the conclusion : "Whosoever therefore believes that anything can be done in this way, or that any creature can be changed for better or for worse or transformed into another species or kind save by God the Creator Himself, Who hath made all things and by Whom all things were made, of a certainty he errs in a matter of faith [and is worse than a very heathen]." This last phrase is very ambiguous, and was bound to cause perplexity and fallacies not a few.

The Dominican Nicolas Jaquerius in his *Flagellum Haereticorum*,[66] cap. ix, "De Consideratione caute habenda circa illud c. Episcopi," very sharply snibs those who misreading the import of the Canon on this account hinder and impede the prosecution of sorcerers, and so in a real sense become fautors of this horrid craft. He shows that the authority of the Canon Episcopi is indeed very slight, and it is most awkwardly worded since as it stands it appears clean contrary to Scripture. He concludes in reference to the last clause : " Qui igitur credit, quod modo praedicto ministerio Daemonum, res aliquae possint de nouo immutari, aut etiam de nouo aliqua corpora formari, hic fidem non perdit, quin potius rectam et catholicam fidem tenet, quicquid dicatur in saepe dicto allegato c. Episcopi."

It were easy, but I think superfluous, to run through a number of writers who have glossed this final clause and set it in its right interpretation. One may well stand for many more. Pierre Mamor in the seventeenth chapter of his *Flagellum Maleficorum* well explains the meaning of the Canon which has been so persistently misunderstood. To resume : There can be no question here of the transvection of witches. That is proved, and approved by immense authority. This clause is directed against those who superstitiously believe that Diana or Herodias are in any sort goddesses possessed of divine or supernatural power, which is assuredly an ethnic creed.

When it is laid down by the Canon that any who hold a creature may be changed not immediately by divine power but by divine permission are in error. We can only say that this clause is awkwardly and badly worded, since S. Paul tells us that Satan can transform himself into an angel of light : " haec omnia informiter et crude dicta sunt, et contra hoc quod prius dictum est, quod sathanas transfigurat se in Angelum lucis." [67]

S. John Chrysostom in his Twenty Eighth (Twenty Ninth) *Homily on S. Matthew*, says that a demon may feign and simulate to be the ghost of one departed. But this is all illusion. The demon cannot essentially change one being to another, no, neither a disembodied nor a corporeal being. He cannot essentially change the body of a man into the body of an ass : καὶ οὐκ ἄν τις ἀνθρώπου σῶμα ὄνου (σῶμα) ἐργάσαιτο. [68]

S. Thomas, *Summa*, pars 1, qu. cxiv, 4 art., says that God alone can work real miracles, but the demons are permitted to perform lying wonders, extraordinary to us, and they employ certain seeds that exist in the elements of the world by which operation they seem to effect transformations. The Devil can from the air compose a body of any form or shape and appear in it ; so he can clothe any corporeal thing with any corporeal form to appear therein. The Seraphic Doctor, S. Bonaventura, in his *Commentarium in Secundum Librum Sententiarum*, Dist. vii, p. 11, art. 11, Quaest. 11,[69] teaches us that demons can by their own power produce artificial forms, but natural forms they cannot produce of their own power, but only by some other force or power. The demon produces forms or changes shapes by some natural force which he knows how to employ, fashioning to his will the secret elemental seeds of things. The same Saint, in Distinctionem viii, *De potestate daemonum respectu hominum*, p. 11, Art. Unicus, Quaest. iii,[70] decides that evil spirits may mock and cheat our senses in three ways : (1) by exhibiting as present what is not really there ; (2) by exhibiting what is there as other than it really is ; (8) by concealing what really is there so that it appears as if it were not.

Alexander of Hales in his *Summa*,[71] Pars secunda, qu. xliii, treats " De praestigiis et miraculis magorum ", and in the First Article of Membrum i discusses those miracles of sorcerers wrought " secundum delusionem et phantasiam ". He concludes that the demon can make things appear other than they really are, a delusion which is subjective as well as objective. This is other than a mere sleight, which is not objective. The delusion may be wrought " per se et per accidens. Et per se dupliciter : proprium et commune ".

In his *Quaestio de Strigibus* [72] Fra Bartolomeo Spina devotes the eighth chapter to a consideration whether witches by diabolical art can turn men and women into brute beasts. He writes that although the demon cannot make material new forms, which is essentially an act of Creation, he can so confuse, commingle, and intermix already existing forms that fantastically he represents to any who behold the human form in a brute shape. Nay more, the subject of such diabolical art and working will steadfastly believe that he is become such or such an animal, and will act according to that brute nature.

So King Nabuchodonosor " was cast away from among men, and as an oxe did he eate grasse, and with the dew of heauen his bodie was imbrued : til his heares grew into the similitude of eagles, & his nailes as it were of birds ".[73]

" It is no matter for wonder that when certain women are deluded and deceived by diabolic and fantastical agencies they exhibit the very nature, the form and likeness, the agility and feline proclivities of cats, and they are persuaded that they are cats, whilst those of their company believe them to be cats, and they in turn believe that those of their society are also cats. This is amply proven by the free confessions of such women."

An explanation of this may very well be that the demon has from certain natural elements formed an aerial body in the shape of a cat, and interposing this fantastical body between the sight of the eyes and the essential human body he thus deceives and deludes one and all.

No thinking person can deny that these witches in the form of cats suck the blood of children and overlook them, and indeed not unseldom kill them by diabolical agency. That many such delusions are wrought cannot be doubted, and the supernatural method in which this is accomplished may be ambiguous. It may be admitted that witches are themselves often mocked and tricked by the demon when they think they are actually cats, and even when they deem they are sucking the blood of some child, for as the demon impresses upon their imagination and vision the form of some animal so may he offer to their sight and taste some fluid of the colour and savour of blood. For as S. Thomas allows, the Devil can entirely bemuse and cheat the senses.

At the same time it is very probable, and indeed it has often been known to happen, that witches do actually and indeed suck children's blood, which they draw either by some sharp needle or by the scratch of their long nails, or else by the aid of the Devil they pierce some vital vein, and scars are left in the tenderest parts of the child's body, whence they have sucked the hot life-blood, and the child becomes anaemic, wastes away, and dies. This cannot be gainsaid since it is proven by irrefragable testimony, and it has been demonstrated that after witches in the form of cats have been seen to attack children, blood is noticed to trickle and trill from wounds, although they may be very small, and accordingly the Devil hath been busy there.

That these cat-witches should find their way most stealthily and silkily into bedchambers, leap walls, run with exceeding nimbleness and speed, and in every way behave as grimalkins wont, is not at all surprising, for they accomplish these actions by the Devil's aid, who assists them lending them excessive fleetness, a swift motion impossible to natural man. Many who have seen these cat-witches have borne witness to these facts, and such circumstances are amply proven and received.

In fine, I doubt whether the whole matter has better been summed up than here. For as the Devil aids the cat-witch, this demon animal that has all the proclivities of a cat, so will he energize the werewolf, who will thus be possessed of all the savagery and fiercest instincts of a ravening wolf.

Sprenger and Kramer, the authors of that great and admirable book, the *Malleus Maleficarum*, therein devote question x of part i to the inquiry *Whether Witches can by some Glamour Change Men into Beasts*.[74] They review the Canon Episcopi and certain arguments of S. Thomas, which must be rightly understood. They then reach the conclusion that " the devil can deceive the human fancy so that a man really seems to be an animal ", with a reference to S. Antoninus, *Summa*, pars i, tit. ii, c. vi.[75] Examples are given, such as will be shown in later chapters. The Canon is more nearly examined, and it appears that " when it says that no creature can be made by the power of the devil, this is manifestly true if Made is understood to mean Created. But if the word Made is taken to refer to natural production, it is certain that devils can make some imperfect creatures ". S. Albert the Great, in his book *On Animals*,[76] says that devils can really make animals, that is to say, " they can, with God's permission, make imperfect animals." Upon this I would remark that many—but not all—authorities hold that the werewolf has no tail. Whence, if such be the case, it is clear the Devil can make a werewolf. The *Malleus* proceeds to debate several points already treated, and therefore not necessary to set out in detail here.[77]

The great demonologists, Remy, Guazzo, and Boguet,[78] have all discussed the problems of werewolfery at length and with much learning, but as their works are easily accessible it were almost superfluous to repeat their arguments

here, the more especially since Remy and Guazzo are agreed
that metamorphosis, true in appearance but not in essential
fact, is caused by the glamour wrought by the demon. Shape-
shifting has the form but not the reality of that which it
presents to the sight. Boguet very wisely says : " There is
much disputing as to whether it is possible for men to be
changed into beasts, some affirming the possibility, whilst
others deny it, and *there are ample grounds for both views.*"

It may not be impertinent to remark that the erudite
Abbot John Trithemius, when relating a case of werewolfism
in his *Chronicon Hirsaugiense*,[79] of Baianus, Prince of
Bulgaria, a most cunning magician who could transform
himself into animal shape, says that we cannot doubt the
metamorphosis was accomplished by black magic and the
Devil's aid, but actually how it took place we do not know,
and it is best not to inquire over curiously therein.

Certain writers, none certainly of the first, nor perhaps yet
of the second, order, incline towards a sceptical view of
lycanthropy. Thus Martin Biermann, in his *De Magicis
Actionibus*,[80] 1590, written directly to controvert the view
of Bodin, is unwilling to allow much more than that the
Devil can stir up depraved appetites and drive men to
imagine themselves in some wild frenzy brute beasts.   If
men do appear as wolves it must be explained as some
objective glamour.

Johann Georg Godelmann has as rubric of the third chapter
of book ii of his *De magis, ueneficis, et lamiis*, 1591, *De
Lamiarum et aliorum hominum in Lupos, feles, aliaue eiuscemodi animantia transformatione*. He argues against a real
and actual metamorphosis, although he admits that demons
appear as wolves, attack and slay men. Generally speaking,
the shape-shifting must be held to be " praestigiosam et
phantasticam ".

Wilhelm Adolph Schreiber, of Marburg, in his *De physiologia
Sagarum*,[81] gives it as his opinion that witches cannot
materially change into cats, dogs, hares, and other animals ;
nor can they transform others by their spells.   " Apparens
ista et phantastica omnis fuit uisio, fucataque, et umbratilis
tantum imago, ut homines quidem maneant, sed brutorum
animantium specie · extrinsecus apparantes solummodo
uideantur.   Imago scilicet uel ab ipso Cacodæmone, eiusue

auxilio, uel ex mera illorum, quos hoc modo mutatos esse dicimus, imaginatione orta. Facilimum enim est dæmone Sagarum corpora alterius cuiusdam bestiæ siue rei cuiuslibet figura aut imagine superinducta tegere, ne quales sint homines agnoscentur."

The Minim Pierre Nodé, in his *Declamation contre l'Erreur Execrable des Maleficiers Sorciers, Enchanteurs, Magiciens, Deuins, & semblables obseruateurs des superstitions*,[82] only touches on lycanthropy in passing, and paraphrases S. Thomas with allusions to S. Augustine and the Canon Episcopi.

Bishop Binsfeld, in his learned *De Confessionibus Maleficorum*,[83] points out that the Devil cannot work true miracles, and hence he denies that witches and enchanters can by their evil power essentially change them to wolves, cats, or any other animal; there is no *transmutatio totius in totum*. The metamorphosis then is *secundum apparentiam*.

In his *De Spirituum Apparitionibus*,[84] Peter Thyraeus, S.J., sometime Professor of Theology at Trèves, Mayence, and Würzburg, gives very ample consideration to lycanthropy, to which indeed he devotes chapters fifteen to twenty-five of his Second Book.

Since he covers—although, be it remarked, with a learning and clarity that rank him with the foremost—much the same ground as other writers with whom we have already dealt in ample detail—whilst paying fit tribute to his erudition, the elegance of his style and vigour of exposition, it is hardly necessary to do more than take a comparatively brief survey of this important piece. He first marshals the various instances of metamorphosis from legend, from tradition, from history, from contemporary records and trials. Upon these he builds a thesis which is seemingly so firm and logical as not to be traversed and rebutted. He does not spare to emphasize the cogency of these arguments, the force of these examples, and he expressly says : " We must not venture too rashly to accuse and reprehend those authors who have deemed that a shape-shifting to the form of wolves, asses, or cats may be actual and real." Yet he proceeds to search out the flaw in his former indagation, so carefully and so nicely planned, and after much subtle philosophical inquiry and theological argument he not without difficulty arrives at the conclusion that a man cannot be transformed by another nor transform himself essentially and absolutely into the body of a beast.

When it is asked how is this metamorphosis then effected, Thyraeus sums up various opinions. Some hold that this shape-shifting results from mere hallucination. This may be waived, as it certainly will not hold good in the vast majority of cases. Others consider that the form of an animal is superimposed in some way upon the human form. Others again believe that persons are cast in a deep slumber or trance by the demon's power, and that then the astral body is clothed with an animal form.

Thyraeus favours an explanation on the lines that by the power and agency of the fiend both the man himself and all who espy him are fully persuaded and convinced that he is metamorphosed to the shape of some animal, wolf, cat, or another, what it may be, whereas actually he is not so transformed. For the demon, be it observed, can energize with superhuman agility, gigantic strength, and a tenuous pliancy almost amounting to volatility the bodies of demoniacs and the possessed.

It is disappointing to find that the genius of Martin Delrio, in his masterpiece, *Disquisitionum Magicarum Libri Sex*,[85] deals with werewolfism in a somewhat summary and condensed chapter. It is not improbable, of course, that he intended to handle so difficult a subject in a separate treatise. Be that as it may, Delrio in his Second Book, Quaestio xviii, inquires : *An corpora ex una in aliam speciem Magi queant transformare ?* He had already mentioned the subject in his notes upon Seneca's Tragedies, *In L. Annæi Senecæ . . . Tragœdias decem*, Antwerp, Plantin, 4to, 1576 ; *Agamemnon*, v. 690, and he at once refers to S. Augustine and the Canon Episcopi. This latter he stresses, as I venture to think, unduly. To the disease lycanthropia he gives a few lines, directing us for details to the physicians. He then relates a history from Bartolomeo Spina and an instance of werewolfism at Dixmude which came under his own notice, as will be detailed later. He refers to the case of Peter Stump, and also draws attention to Binsfeld, Remy, Lorenzo Anania, and Claude Prieur's *Dialogue*. Delrio would offer as his explanation of werewolfism a fantastical body formed by the demon from the elements and obtruded or superimposed upon the lycanthrope, which he supposes to have happened in the case of Gilles Garnier of Dôle. I may be wrong, but in reading Delrio upon lycanthropy I cannot divest myself of the impression that he has given us a meagre selection from his notes upon this subject ; and, as I suggest above, I conceive that in view of a fuller dissertation he refrained from but touching upon it somewhat superficially here.

Pierre le Loyer in his *Discours et Histoires des Spectres, Visions, et Apparitions des Esprits,*[86] Livre ii, ch. 7, writes *de la transmutation des Sorciers et sorcieres.* His explanation of any metamorphosis of witches attributes shape-shifting to diabolical glamour, the demon imposing a lupine or feline form upon his slave. Le Loyer, who snibs Bodin at every turn, seems to misunderstand that great writer very grossly, and his unwonted animus betrays him into some errors which go far to vitiate this section, the weakest undoubtedly in his whole vast work.

Dr. Tobias Tandler, who held the Chair of Mathematics at Wittenberg at the beginning of the sixteenth century, in his *Dissertatio de Fascino,* a public disputation held in the University on 24th October, 1606, and printed that same year,[87] busied himself in controverting propositions nobody ever thought of maintaining in regard to animal transformations, and finally involved himself in a muss of words, misconceptions, and inexactitudes.

Strozzi Cicogna, in his *Pelagio degli Incanti,* Vincenza, 1605, translated into Latin by Gaspar Ens as *Magiae Omnifariae Theatrum,* Coloniae, 1606, part i, lib. iv, cap. 5,[88] has a very ample treatment of the question *An daemones corpora hominum in alias species transformare, ac sexum mutare queant ?* He posits at the outset that neither by the utmost power of the demon nor by any natural force can the body of a man be organically changed into the animal species. For God created the various species of living things, as we are told in the first chapter of Genesis, and the handiwork of God cannot be altered. (That is to say, it cannot be essentially altered. For it might be argued that the body of Job was altered when by the Devil's action it was covered with a loathly ulcer, as God permitted.)

With regard to reincarnation Cicogna has much to say, and he is at some pains to disprove these theories, but his

arguments hardly concern us directly here. Nor need we
feel ourselves detained in this place by the example of
Nabuchodonosor, and it will suffice to note that our author
considers a species of madness to have fallen upon the King
of Babylon, who had incurred the wrath of God, and therefore
he wandered forth lunatic into the fields living as a wild
animal, but in no way transformed to a beast.

The disease of lycanthropy is next dealt with, after which
Cicogna reviews at some length the various well-known
instances of shape-shifting and werewolfism. These, as he
remarks, being reported by solid authors cannot be disputed
or denied. He regards, then, werewolves as demon-wolves,
not the witch in that shape, but a devil who assumed the
form of a wolf. The witch meanwhile is held in an evil
trance, what time the Devil impresses on the imagination
of the sleeper those acts of destruction he himself has
accomplished in lupine shape.

A curious dissertation upon changes effected in sex
concludes this chapter. Many examples are proferred, and
he rather fantastically adds : " Neroni quidem in emascu-
lando atque in feminam transformando Sporo conatus irritus
fuit. Idem quum Heliogabalus conuocatis medicis in se ipso
tentasset, ut Uenerem utramque experiretur, sic ab eis
tractus fuit, ut nec mas amplius nec femina esset, dignam
scilicet tam turpi ac diabolico conatu mercedem consequutus."

It were barely possible to review all the particular tracts
concerning lycanthropy which were written throughout the
sixteenth and seventeenth centuries, and indeed so prolonged
a task were superfluous since of necessity we find a certain
repetition both in the expository and in the arguments,
whilst from the multiplicity of varied examples the most
important (if not all) will be given in their due place in
later chapters here. A couple of examples then may suffice
for all.

The *Dialogue de la Lycanthropie ou Transformation
d'Hommes en Loups vulgairement dits Loups-garou et si telle
se peut faire*, written in 1595 by an observant Franciscan
of the Louvain house, Frère Claude Prieur, was published
early in 1596,[89] " Chez Iehan Maes, et Philippe Zangre," at
Louvain. The work was examined and approved by Heinrich
de Cuyek, Bishop of Ruremonde, whilom Chancellor of the

Theological Faculty of Louvain, and Gilles Cheheré, Professor of Theology at Louvain, as also by Frère Gerard Jacé, the provincial, and Frère Arnold Ysch, the Guardian of the Louvain house, so it comes from the Press with full weight of authority. After a lengthy preface the *Dialogue*, wherein the interlocutors are Eleion, Scipion, and Proteron, commences on p. 13 B and occupies 120 well-filled pages.

The " forme of a Dialogue " was no doubt adopted "*for to make this treatise the more pleasaunt and facill* ", as King James once wrote of his own *Dæmonologie*.

The speakers commence by bewailing the misfortunes of their time, whilst they acknowledge the justice of divine chastisement. Never, they cry, did Satan rage up and down more furiously. Men in their wickedness have become worse than the very beasts of the field and are as ravening wolves. Hence the question, poised by Eleion, easily arises, can a man actually shift his shape and transform himself into a wolf ? Scipion and Eleion maintain that such a corporeal and essential metamorphosis is possible, and Proteron (who stands for the author) proceeds to enlighten them. It is hardly needful to follow him through all his intricate theological and philosophical debate, in the course of which he takes occasion to controvert many Platonic and Pythagorean ideas, in particular the theory of reincarnation. The true sense of Our Lord's words concerning the Baptist : he is Elias that is to come, S. Matthew, xi, 14, is insisted upon and expounded. There had been some suggestion, it appears, bruited among the vulgar that the souls of men returned and were reincarnated in wolves.

Proteron, or Claude Prieur, declares that wolves are the natural agents of God's wrath, and he tells how in the year 1587, when he was preaching in Perigord and for several months was living in a little Minorite convent at Rions, about five leagues from Bordeaux, it so happened that on S. John's day, 27th December, he was sent by the Guardian to say Mass at a remote village some little way distant. On his return, passing near a hamlet, he met a poor woman all in tears, who told him that only half an hour before a huge wolf had snatched up a little girl who was playing at the door of her hut, and in spite of all that she or her neighbours could do the child was carried off into the forest.

The Guardian, Père de Roca, informed Claude Prieur that the ravages of wolves in that district had reached such a height that men could only go to work armed and together in numbers.

Some three or four years later, when Prieur was stationed at Rodes, the cloisters one night about ten o'clock rang and re-echoed with most horrible howling. The whole company were greatly alarmed as the sound had an unearthly note. The porter of the convent, all trembling, informed the religious that he had seen in the pale moonlight a pack of eighteen or twenty wolves who swept resistlessly through the streets at hurricane speed. Their teeth gleamed sharp and white; their red tongues hung from their hot panting jaws; their eyes glinted horribly; and the grey fur bristled as they ran. It seemed as though it were a hunt of demons who passed in headlong course.

Prieur remarks that after All Saints Day the villagers expect wolves to invade the very houses, coming down in packs from the mountains of Auvergne, driven by hunger from their lair. The good father himself met a wolf in the environs of Villefranche, and only drove off the animal with great difficulty.

It is hardly to be doubted that the Devil often possesses the bodies of wolves and drives them to madness, then urging and lancing this furious host against men.

A very great many examples are debated of cannibalism, of sorcerers who rifle cemeteries and cook young children. Amongst others Gilles de Rais is mentioned. There are also the lycanthropes, who have been brought to trial and executed for this crime, Pierre Burgout, Michel Verdun; those of whom Olaus Magnus tells; the cases related by Peucer; Peter Stump of Bebur, near Cologne, and very many more. How can one explain this mass of evidence? "Il ne semble plus qu'on puisse doubter," says Scipion.

However, Proteron commences to examine the proposition at considerable length according to the scholastic method, and with references to S. Augustine, S. Thomas, S. Bonaventura, Richard Petrus de Aquila, Dionysius the Carthusian, Durandus, Alexander of Hales, Bartolomeo Spina, Binsfeld, Petrus Thyraeus, Alfonso a Castro, and other doctors, he demonstrates that according to these authorities there cannot be a corporeal transformation, whether wrought by an enchanted girdle or unguents or by any means whatsoever. None the less, lycanthropy is a fact not to be denied. Where then shall we seek an explanation ? What do we see when we espy a werewolf ? Sometimes we behold a real body, not created indeed but newly formed from existing elements by Satan ; sometimes it is a fantastical shape.

There next arises the question of King Nabuchodonosor,[90] and the glosses of the great Biblical exegetes are passed in review.

The virtue of the Sign of the Cross is lauded, and Prieur has a very striking pronouncement : " L'heresie et magic sont fort parens, depuis que tout Magicien est heretique."

The hideous abuse of the Most Holy Sacrament by sorcerers is spoken of, and the prevalence of necromancy deplored. God is praised in the deliverance from possession of Nicole Aubry, a celebrated case, who was deluded by a demon feigning to be the shade of her grandfather, but at last unmasked as Beelzebub.[91]

After an eloquent peroration the treatise concludes with six resolutions : (1) Animals and brute beasts are sometimes made the instruments of Heaven's wrath ; hence (2) wolves may be energized by unusual savagery in their mission, or they may be veritably possessed by demons ; (3) there are not lacking examples of men, some of whom were sorcerers, and some who perchance were not, that have given themselves over to cannibalism ; (4) an essential transformation, the which involves creation, is not according to Catholic teaching, since neither unguents, nor haunted streams, nor incantations, nor magic girdle, nor Satan himself can effect such transformation. Wherefore lycanthropy must be explained in some other way as has been duly expounded. (5) Sorcerers by diabolical aid, or demons, can assume some other shape or form, and this appears to be real, both subjectively and objectively, but is in the strictest and narrow sense fantastical. (6) Let us use the methods Holy Church has provided, the Sign of the Cross, the Rosary, Sacramentals, and other pious practices to arm ourselves against the Devil, who if we are so fortified cannot harm or hurt us. Above all, let us frequently sign ourselves with the healthful and life-giving Sign of Salvation which dispels all enchantments, and as Jacob with his staff only passed over Jordan, so let us by the Cross pass through this world to everlasting felicity and eternal glory. Amen.

A gentleman of Angers, Sieur de Beauvoys de Chauvincourt, in his *Discours de la lycanthropie ou de la transmutation des hommes en loups*, Paris, 1599, after a review of the various histories of werewolves, both ancient and more recent cases, concludes that the fittest explanation lies in the power of the Devil who by his craft produces a glamour that is both subjective and objective, deceiving both the sorcerer and those who behold him. This change is wrought by means of unguents, powders, potions, and noxious herbs, which are able to dazzle all who come under their baleful and magic effluence. This opuscule is slight and, I venture to think, adds little to the solution of these dark and vexed problems.

A direct and particular answer to Bodin, *De la Lycanthropie, Transformation, et Extase des Sorciers*, by Sieur Jean de Nynauld, Docteur en Medecine, was written in 1614, and published at Paris in the summer of the following year.[92] A tractate of 109 pages, it was approved, 6th April, 1615, by two Doctors of the Sorbonne, Colin and Forgemont, as being orthodox and containing no proposition contrary to the Catholic Faith. It is dedicated to the Primate of France, Cardinal Jacques du Perron, Archbishop of Sens.

The work is divided into seven chapters, the several rubrics of which will serve adequately to show its scope. Chapter i, *That the Devil cannot in any way transform men into beasts. Moreover, the Devil cannot separate the soul of a sorcerer from the body, in such fashion that after a while the soul returns to the body and the sorcerer is alive.* It would not require much to qualify these propositions as heretical. The first posit is clearly contrary to S. Augustine's teaching, which we have shown. Chapter ii, *Of the Simples which enter into the composition of the witch's ointment, and what particular virtue each has.* Nynauld lists : " la racin de la belladonna, morelle furieuse, sang de chauue sourris, d'huppe, l'Aconit, la berle, la morelle endormante, l'ache, la saye, le pentaphilon, l'acorum vulgaire, le persil, fueilles du peuplier, l'opium, l'hyoscyame, cyguë, les especes de pauot, l'hyuroye, le *Synochytides*, qui fait voir les ombres des Enfers, c.d., les mauuais esprits, comme au contraire, *l'Anachitides* faict apparoit les images des saincts Anges."

Chapter iii, *Of the Composition and use of the first Ointment which Sorcerers confect.* Chapter iv, *Of the Composition and use of the second Ointment which Sorcerers confect.* Chapter v, *Of the Composition and use of the third Ointment which Sorcerers confect.* In the course of this last chapter Nynauld remarks : " Regarding the reality of this metamorphosis of men into beasts I have already proved that it cannot be achieved by any natural means, nor even by the Devil even if he strain to the utmost of his power, for he cannot even make a fly. God alone is the Creator and Preserver of all things." There is flat heresy here. It is a solemn truth which nobody would think of denying to say that God alone can create. In the eighth chapter of Exodus it is written that " Aaron stretched forth his hand upon the waters of Ægypt", and the frogges came up, and covered the Land of Ægypt. And the enchanters also by the enchantments did in like manner, and they brought forth frogges upon the Land of Ægypt ".[98] It was the power of Satan by God's permission which brought forth these frogs. Therefore Nynauld plainly contradicts the sense of Scripture.

Chapter vi, *Of Lycanthropy,* the disease.

Chapter vii, *Of those natural things which have the quality of presenting to the imagination things which are not present in reality but only in effect.* Such for example are strong potions, and drugs as hasheesh, strychnos, and preparations of belladonna. The vapour and incense of violent perfumes will also dazzle and cheat the senses. Nynauld concludes that all shape-shifting is mere hallucination, and he ends up this chapter with a fling at miracles, which he declares to look for to-day would be a sign of infidelity and weak faith. Here he plainly shows the cloven hoof, and one can only remark that it is surprising such a passage should have been permitted by the censors.

As an Epilogue he adds a *Refutation of the Opinions and Arguments which Bodin sets forth in the Sixth Chapter of his Demonomania to attest the reality of Lycanthropy.* This is a piece without value, and only remarkable for the fact that when he has contradicted Scripture and the Fathers, denied tradition and experience, in a fine roulade at the end Nynauld congratulates himself upon having vindicated the Bible, the Doctors and Fathers of the Church, the Theologians and Philosophers, nay even the very Pagans and ethnic writers themselves.

I have designedly left until this point a consideration of the *Oratio pro Lycanthropia* of the learned and judicious Wolfeshusius, a celebrated Professor of Leipzig. This was delivered at Leipzig on the 4th of February, 1591, and printed at that town, quarto, shortly after in the same year. Wolfeshusius poises the question : Fierine queat, ut homo per Magiam seu Daemonis artem lupi aut alterius bestiae formam uerè assumat induatque, aut an omnia λυκομανία illa, quae de gente potissimum Arctoa scriptis autorum memoratur phantasticè sit et ex iudicii Dei prauatione existat. " Is it possible that a man may by magic spells or the power and craft of the Devil verily and indeed assume, and transform himself into the shape of a wolf or some other animal, or are all those histories and accounts which we read of lycanthropy in particular as detailed in authors who have written of the peoples of far Northern climes, merely fantastical, and if we accept them do we in any way seem to impugn the omnipotence of Almighty God ? " The mention of the Arctic writers seems especially to refer to Olaus Magnus.

Wolfeshusius in the course of an erudite and acutely argued disquisition sums up various theories which have been advanced to explain lycanthropy. Some hold it is " morbum ex praua humorum corporis dispositione ortum uel merum diaboli hominis salua corporis figura demendantis praestigium ", that is to say a disease, or maybe a diabolic hallucination. Others again prefer to think that " per Satanae praestigiis glaucoma quasi quoddam animo hominis per · fascinatos inter et extra sensus obiciatur, quò feram aliquam bestiam se esse credat, eiusque mores imitando exprimet ", that the Devil casts both a subjective and objective glamour upon the werewolf, who not only believes himself to be a very wolf and acts as such, but also when seen by others is taken to be a fierce howling wolf.

Yet a third explanation is that the Devil casts the sorcerer into a trance, " stuporem arte diabolica immissum in lupos aliqui se falsè credant transformatos." The evil one " mirifica somnia excitet iisque confudat imaginibus ", whilst the actual witch is drenched and overtaken with sleep, " corpora collapsa atque sopita."

Some endeavour to sustain a trivial argument : " friuolam alteram de Lycanthropia opinionem qui solum illusione quadam Satanae aspicientium oculos perstringi aiunt." Werewolfism resolves itself into a mere jugglery : the Devil cheats the eyes of those who see the werewolf.

Wolfeshusius refers to the following lines from Book IV, *Aprilis*, of the *Fasti*,[94] a well-known poem by Blessed Baptista Mantuan, the Carmelite, who speaking of various perils says :—

Adde lupos, qui tartareis agitantibus ambris
In furias acti, ne dum iumenta per agros,
Audebant laniare homines, et in urbibus ipsis,
Casibus hic perculsi omnes diuina coacti
Quærere subsidia, et Diuos excire precando.

These occur in the *De Litanea Minore*, ll. 13–17, a description of the gang-days.

After citing two or three more authors, Wolfeshusius sums up by saying that " uiri undequaque celebres et docti " support Bodin in his explanation of lycanthropy, and concludes : " conati sumus efficere ut ueritas patefieret mirandae illius immutationis, qua hominum Magica ac diabolica arte in brutum uerti posse, tum ueterum saeculis creditum esse, tum hoc tempore communi rumore peruulgatum."

It is incidentally worth noting that he has a reference to the transvections by the black art of Faust : " Et patrum aetate Faustus, qui pallio securi insidentem ad longinquas terras baiulasse fertur."

It will here be interesting to consider one or two of the more modern views of lycanthropy. Adolphe d'Assier, in his *Posthumous Humanity* [95]—I quote from the English translation made by Henry S. Olcote and expressly sanctioned by the author of the *Essai sur l'Humanité Posthume et le Spiritisme, par un Positiviste*—chapter xi, writes : " I will finish this study of the mesmeric personality with some views upon lycanthropy. This feature, perhaps the most obscure of the manifestations of the fluidic being, long seemed to me so utterly unreasonable that I did as with questions of posthumous vampire and the incubus—I turned over without reading the pages that treated of this theme, and I gave but a very inattentive hearing to what was told me about these singular metamorphoses. If I decide to speak of it now, it is because it would not be wise to oppose a systematic denial to a multitude of facts reputed authentic which corroborate each other."

Two recent and very striking cases of werewolfism are then related, and d'Assier sums up with the utmost frankness, a candour which wins our respect and which we should be glad to see more widely imitated. He writes : " I shall not attempt to give an explanation of these prodigies, which are, in fact, an insoluble problem for myself. The fluidic and, consequently, elastic nature of the mesmeric personality permits of its adapting itself to lycanthropic forms ; but where shall we place the efficient cause of these meta-morphoses ? Must we fall back upon atavism ; in other words, upon the most delicate and least-known chapter of biology ? I prefer to confess my incompetency, and to leave to those who are more skilled than myself the task of expounding the enigma."

In *The Mysteries of Magic* [96] Éliphas Lévi writes : " We must here speak of lycanthropy, or the nocturnal transforma-tion of men into wolves, histories so well substantiated that sceptical science has had recourse to furious manias, and to masquerading as animals for explanations. But such hypotheses are puerile, and explain nothing."

This author gives it as his opinion that werewolfery is due to the " sidereal body, which is the mediator between the soul and the material organism ", and largely influenced by a man's habitual thought being attached by strong sympathetic links to the heart and brain. Thus in the case of a man whose instinct is savage and sanguinary, his phantom will wander abroad in lupine form, whilst he sleeps painfully at home, dreaming he is a veritable wolf. The body being subject to nervous and magnetic influences will receive the blows and cuts dealt at the fantastical shape.

C. W. Leadbeater, in his *The Astral Plane, its Scenery, Inhabitants and Phenomena*, [97] offers a theosophical explana-tion of the many problems concerning vampires and were-wolves. His view is that certain astral entities are able to materialize the " astral body " of a perfectly brutal and cruel man who has gained some knowledge of magic, and these fiends drive on this " astral body ", which they mould into " the form of some wild animal, usually the wolf ", to blood and maraud.

In his monograph, *The Book of Were-Wolves*,[98] Baring-Gould is inclined to attribute werewolfery, the terrible truth of which he does not for a moment evade, to a species of madness, during the accesses of which the person afflicted believes himself to be a wild beast and acts like a wild beast. "In some cases this madness amounts apparently to positive possession."

Mr. Elliott O'Donnell, in his *Werwolves*,[99] remarks that "the actual process of the metamorphosis savours of the superphysical". The werewolf is sometimes in outward form a wolf, sometimes partly wolf and partly human. This may be the result of the fact that he is "a hybrid of the material and immaterial". The opinions of those whose views of the werewolf postulate a complete denial of the supernatural need not, I think, detain us here, and are in themselves unworthy of record.[100]

We may now proceed to inquire how this change, the shape-shifting, was effected. In the case of those who were metamorphosed involuntarily, the transformation was, of course, caused by some spell cast over them through the malignant power of a witch.[101]

With regard to the voluntary werewolf, under whom for this consideration we may include any kind of shape-shifting. In the first place, an essential circumstance and condition is a pact, formal or tacit, with the demon. Such metamorphosis can only be wrought by black magic. This is in itself a mortal sin, for, as S. Bonaventura instructs us (*In II Sent.*, Dist. vii, p. 11, art. ii, quaest. iii),[102] it is sinful to seek either counsel or aid from the demon. Again, the werewolf is a sorcerer well versed and of long continuance in the Devil's service, no mere journeyman of evil. For Guazzo tells us [103] : "this seems particularly worth noting : that just as Emperors reserve certain rewards for their veteran soldiers only, so the demon grants this power of changing themselves into different shapes, as the witches believe, only to those who have proved their loyalty by many years of faithful service in witchcraft ; and this is as it were a reward for their long service and loyalty. This was amply proved by Henry Carmut in the year 1583 by his own particular confession, coming after that of many others of his sort."

In the first place, the sorcerer strips himself mother-naked. In certain obscure magical rites nudity was required. The witch of whom Giovanni Battista Porta speaks [104] cast aside all her clothes before she smeared her limbs with fatty grease as a preparation for her journey to the sabbat. The Four Witches, as portrayed by Dürer, are naked for the sabbat orgy, as also are the witches in the celebrated pictures by Hans Baldung, who depicts the confection of the witches' salve, the anointing of the brooms, and the horrid crew in full flight to their Satanic synagogue. Jaspar Isaac, in his *L'Abomination des Sorciers*, portrays these abandoned ministers and slaves of the demon divesting themselves of their garments in hot haste to repair to a nocturnal rendezvous. Equally elaborate is the detail in Frans Francken's *An Assembly of Witches*, where the women are undressing for their dark revels, and one naked witch is already being anointed. A woodcut in Keisersberg's *Die Emeis*, ed. 1516, 36ᵇ, depicts three naked *unholden* raising a storm. Teniers and Queverdo, in their several pictures *Le Départ pour le Sabat*, have drawn nude witches at the moment they commence their diabolic transvection, whilst Goya's *La Transformation des Sorciers* shows us four hideous naked warlocks, one of whom, already metamorphosed to a wolf, is about to take his flight by the chimney, through whose yawning aperture is fast disappearing yet another of the foul fraternity. It will be remembered that the soldier in Petronius divested himself of his clothes before the lupine metamorphosis.[105] In one of the most famous of the werewolf trials, that of Pierre Bourgot and Michel Verdun in December, 1521, by Frère Jean Boin, O.P., Prior of the house of Poligny and General Inquisitor for the diocese of Besançon, Pierre Bourgot confessed that in order to effect the shape-shifting into a wolf's form, he cast off his clothes and anointed his naked body with the mysterious salve. Michel Verdun was changed into a wolf whilst he was yet clad, which is noted by Weyer [106] as altogether exceptional.

The unguent used by the werewolf was, according to Weyer, that employed by witches in their transvection. De Lancre justly sees in this unction a mockery of the Holy Chrism at Baptism : " Satan est le singe de Dieu : il void qu'au Baptesme les Chrestiens sont oincts du sainct Chresme

comme athletes, pour entrer au combat contre les vices et
Esprits immondes . . . Le Diable graisse les siens et mesme
les loups-garoux comme ses athletes en tous ses malefices." [107]
Ulisse Aldrovandi, in his *De Quadrupedibus Digitatis
Uiuiparis*, observes : " olei . . . Lupi sunt amantissimi." [108]
There are constant references to the use of this ointment by
the demoniac lycanthropes. As we have just seen, it was
employed by Pierre Bourgot and Michel Verdun. Guazzo
in the first chapter of his Second Book says : " The ointment
they use is either given them by the demon or brewed by
themselves with devilish art." [109] Boguet in his forty-seventh
chapter speaks of lycanthropes rubbing themselves with the
ointment before the metamorphosis. In his twenty-fourth
chapter he even more precisely says, when treating of their
unguent : " The witches anoint themselves with it when
they go to the Sabbat, or when they change into wolves." [110]
De Lancre notes that the werewolf Jean Grenier, who was
tried in 1608, smeared himself with this liniment of hell :
" Il rapporte auoir esté graislé et parle du pot de graisse que
le malin Esprit luy gardoit." [111] Delrio in the second book,
Disquisitionum Magicarum, quaestio xviii, speaks of certain
anointings and spells the werewolf employs : " ad hoc
inunctionibus certis (ut Dolani ille Lycanthropi, de quibus
Acta iudicaria sunt edita) uel solis uerbis utuntur." [112] Elich,
in his *Daemonomagia*, quaestio xii, repeats this when treating
of werewolves : " inunctionibus certis . . . uel solis uerbis
conceptis utuntur." [113] Claude Prieur, also, in his *Lycanthropie*, draws attention to the baleful unguent of the werewolf,
and De Lancre in his *Tableau de l'Inconstance des Demons*,
livre iv, discours 4, [114] notes how the Demon impresses a
lupine shape on the sorcerers " quand les loups-garoux se
sont graissez de certaine graisse ".
It will readily be remembered that Vergil, in the Eighth
Eclogue, the *Pharmaceutria*, has a reference to these witch
ointments, lines 96–100, a passage which Dryden turns
thus :—[115]

> These poys'nous Plants, for Magick use design'd,
> (The noblest and the best of all the baneful Kind),
> Old Mœris brought me from the Pontick Strand ;
> And cull'd the Mischief of a bounteous Land.
> Smear'd with these pow'rful Juices, on the Plain,
> He howls a Wolf among the hungry Train :

And oft the mighty Negromancer boasts,
With these to call from Tombs the stalking Ghosts :
And from the roots to tear the standing Corn ;
Which, whirld aloft, to distant Fields is born.

In his *De Miraculis Rerum Naturalium Libri IIII*,
Antverpiae, Ex Officina Christophori Plantini, 1560, lib. ii,
cap. xxvi,[116] Giovanni Battista Porta has a section *Lamiarum
unguenta*, which is as follows : " Quae quanquam ipsae
superstitionis plurimum admiscent, naturali tamen ui euenire
patet intuenti ; quaeque ab eis acceperim referam. Puerorum
pinguedinem ahaeno uase decoquendo ex aqua capiunt,
inspissando quod ex elixatione ultimum, nouissimumque
subsidet, inde condunt, continuoque inseruiunt usui : cum
hac immiscent eleoselinum, aconitum, frondes populneas, et
fuliginem. Uel *aliter* sic : Sium, acorum uulgare, pentaphyllon, uespertilionis sanguinem, solanum somniferum, et
oleum, et si diuersa commiscent, ab iis non parum dissidebunt,
simul conficiunt, partes omnes perungunt, eas antea per-
fricando, ut rubescant, et reuocetur calor, rarumque fiat,
quod erat frigore concretum : Ut relaxetur caro, aperiantur
pori, adipem adiungunt, uel oleum ipsius uicem subiens, ut
succorum uis intro descendat, et fiat potior uegetiorque :
id esse in causam non dubium reor. Sic non illuni nocte per
aera deferri uidentur, conuiuia, sonos, tripudia, et formosorum
iuuenum concubitus, quos maxime exoptant : tanta est
imaginationis uis, impressionum habitus, ut fere cerebri pars
ea, quae memoratiua dicitur, huiusmodi sit plena : cumque
ualde sint ipsae ad credendum naturae pronitate faciles, sic
impressiones capessunt, ut spiritus immutentur, nil noctu
diuque aliud cogitantes, et ad hoc adiuuantur, cum non
uescantur nisi betis, radicibus, castaneis, et leguminibus.
Dum haec pensiculatius perquirendo operam nauarem :
ancipiti enim immorabar iudicio, incidit mihi in manus
uetula quaedam, quas a strigis auis nocturnae similitudine
striges uocant, quaeque noctu puerulorum sanguinem e
cunis absorbent, sponte pollicita breuis mihi temporis spatio
allaturam responsa : iubet omnes foras egredi, qui mecum
erant acciti testes, spoliis nudata tota se unguento quodam
ualde perfricuit, nobis e portae rimulis conspicua : sic
soperiferorum ui succorum cecidit, profundoque occubuit
somno, foris ipsi patefacimus, multum uapulat, tantaque uis

soporis fuit, ut sensum eriperet, ad locum foras redimus, iam medelae uires fatiscunt, flaccescuntque, a somno seuocata, multa incipit fari deliria, se maria, montesque transmeasse, falsaque depromens responsa, negamus, instat, liuorem ostendimus, pertinaciter resistit magis. Sed quid de eis sentiam ? dabitur alias narrandi locus, ad institutum nostra redeat oratio : satis enim prolixiusculi fuimus. Hoc praeterea praemonendum censeo, ne facile experientes dilabantur, non haec aeque omnibus euentura : sed inter caeteros melancholicis, cum natura praealgida, algiosaque sint, eorumque uaporatis multa non sit : recte enim quae uident percipiunt, et referre possunt."

In 1562 was printed at Cologne, 12°, *Magiae Naturalis, siue de Miraculis Rerum Naturalium Libri IIII*, and the above passage duly appears, II, xxvii, pp. 197 and 198.

However, in the edition *Io. Bapt. Portae Neapolitani Magiae Naturalis Libri XX*, " ab ipso authore expurgati," Naples, folio, 1589, which was approved and licensed by the Dominican Fra Tommaso de Capua, 9th August, 1588, this passage is not included. Indeed, the work has been most thoroughly revised, and the four books of the original are now divided into twenty, with additional matter, excisions, and variations. The only cognate passage seems to be in the second chapter of the eighth book, *De Medicis Experimentis*, pp. 150–2, *Of Physical Experiments.* (I quote from the English translation of Porta, *Natural Magick in XX Bookes*,[117] London, folio, 1658.) In the preface Porta complains :
" *A certain Frenchman in his Book called* Daemonomania, *Tearms me a Magician, a Conjurer, and thinks this Book of mine, long since Printed, worthy to be burnt,*[118] *because I have written the Fairies Oyntment, which I set forth onely in detestation of the frauds of Divels and Witches ; That which comes by Nature is abused by their superstition, which I borrowed from the Books of the most commendable Divines. . . . I pass over other men of the same temper, who affirm that I am a Witch and a Conjurer, whereas I never writ here nor elsewhere, what is not contain'd within the bounds of Nature.*"

Nevertheless Porta merely mentions *Medicines which cause sleep.* He describes *How to make men mad with Mandrake* ; and how " To make a man believe he was changed into a Bird or Beast ", which is done by infusing mandrake, stramonium or solanum manicum, belladonna, and henbane, into a cup of wine. Porta says that he has known those who on drinking this menstruum imagined themselves to be fish, endeavouring to swim ; or geese, hissing and trying to peck grass, and similar idle fancies. " These, and many other most pleasant things, the curious Enquirer may finde out : it is enough for me only to have hinted at the manner of doing them."

Weyer gives the condiment of these unguents in his *De Lamiis*, iii, 17,[119] exactly following, and indeed reproducing Porta's own phrase. The first liniment, then, is composed of the fat of young children seethed in a brazen vessel until it becomes thick and slab, and then scummed. With this are mixed *eleoselinum*, hemlock ; *aconitum*, aconite ; *frondes populeae*, poplar leaves ; and *fuligo*, soot.

The second formula is : *sium*, cowbane ; *acorum uulgare*, sweet flag ; *pentaphyllon*, cinquefoil ; *uespertilioris sanguis*, bat's blood ; *solanum somniferum*, deadly nightshade ; and *oleum*, oil.

In the eighteenth book, " De Mirabilibus " of his *De Subtilitate*,[120] Girolamo Cardano gives a recipe for the confection of the witch-ointment. He mentions the lamiae, " quae apio, castaneis, fabis, cepis, caulibus, phaselisque uictitantes, uidentur per somnum ferri in diuersas regiones, atque ibi diuersis modis affici, prout uniuscuiusque fuerit temperies. Iuuantur ergo ad haec unguento, quo se totas perungunt. Constat ut creditur puerorum pinguedine e sepulchris eruta, succisque apii aconitique tum pentaphylli siligineque. Incredibile dictu quanta sibi uidere persuadeant : modo laeta, theatra, uiridaria, piscationes, uestes, ornatus, saltationes, formosos iuuenes, concubitusque eius generis quales maxime optant : reges quoque et magistratus cum satellitibus, gloriamque omnem et pompam humani generis, multaque alia praeclara, uelut in somniis et picturis quae maiora sunt quam quae natura praestare possit. Uelut et contraria ratione tristia, coruos, carceres, solitudinem, tormenta. Neque id mirum, quanquam ueneficum, ad naturales enim causas traduci debet."

Cardano goes on to describe various unguents, which (he says) not only induce sleep but cause dreams of certain kinds, glad or sorry. He mentions that he has himself made trial of " uulgatum unguentum quod Populeon a frondibus populi dicitur ".

Here then we have for the witch-ointment, the fat of children, whose bodies have been dug from the grave; henbane; aconite and cinquefoil. I presume the fine wheaten flour was added to make a thick paste.

Dr. Jean de Nynauld discusses the composition of these unguents in his *Les ruses et tromperies du Diable descouvertes*, Paris, 1611, and again in his *De la Lycanthropie*, 1615, where the rubric of the second chapter runs : " Des Simples qui entrent en la Composition des Onguents des Sorciers & de leur vertu en generale." Chapters three to five enlarge upon the uses of these witches' ointments.

Dr. J. B. Holzinger, who, however, does not mention Nynauld, has devoted a detailed monograph to the subject, *Zur Naturgeschichte der Hexen*, Graz, 1888.

Dr. H. J. Norman informs me that these witches' concoctions could of themselves have no effect.

The spells recited by the sorcerer about to shift his shape to a werewolf are profane and horrible in the last degree. To inquire into these were impious ; they were accursed to know. Unfortunately some such mantras have been preserved in ancient grimoires and evangels of Satan, which I will not specify too nearly. As Boguet [121] tells us, witches can indeed cause injury by mere words and uttered spells, for barbaric jingle and meaningless though the phrases be, they are none the less a potent and energetic symbol of the pact between the witch and Satan. Yet, be it remarked, the sounds and syllables have not of themselves, when spoken by another, the power to hurt and kill, neither has the mere spell (as Leonard Vair and Bodin also write) [122] a malign quality of itself to shift the human shape into bestial form.

Merely as a piece of folk-lore, interesting and sufficiently curious, there can be no harm in giving here the *zagovór* " to be employed by a wizard who desires to turn into a werewolf ", as supplied by W. R. S. Ralston in his *Songs of the Russian People* [123] : " In the ocean sea, on the island Buyán, in the open plain, shines the moon upon an aspen stump, into the green wood, into the spreading vale. Around the stump goes a shaggy wolf ; under his teeth are all the horned cattle ; but into the wood the wolf goes not, into the

vale the wolf does not roam. Moon, moon ! golden horns !
Melt the bullet, blunt the knife, rot the cudgel, strike fear
into man, beast, and reptile, so that they may not seize the
grey wolf, nor tear from him his warm hide. My word is
firm, firmer than sleep or the strength of heroes."

Ralston comments : " In this spell, says Buslaef (*Istor.
Ocherki*, i, 86), the aspen stump is mentioned because a buried
werewolf or vampire has to be pierced with an aspen stake.
The expression that the wolf has all the horned cattle in or
under his teeth resembles the proverb now applied to
St. George, ' What the wolf has in his teeth, that Yugory
gave '—St. George, or Yegory the Brave, having taken the
place which was once filled by the heathen god of flocks,
the Old Slavonic Volos. And the warm hide of the werewolf
is in keeping with his designation *Volkodlak*, from *dlaka*, a
shaggy fell."

Peter Thyraeus, S.J., *De Spirituum Apparitionibus*, liber ii,
cap. xxxiv, 826, speaks of these metamorphoses being
seemingly accomplished by " unctiones corporibus adhibitas,
incantationes et carmina, baptismata, siue in aquas im-
mersiones, caseum, uel alium aliquem cibum, poculum denique
certis uerbis incantatum ".[124]

Olaus Magnus, *A Compendious History of the Goths, Swedes,
and Vandals*,[125] book xviii, chapter 82, *Of the Fiercenesse of
men who by Charms are turned into Wolves*, writes : " The
reason of this metamorphosis, that is exceeding contrary to
nature, is given by one skilled in this witchcraft, by drinking
to one in a cup of Ale, and by mumbling certain words at
the same time, so that he who is to be admitted into that
unlawful Society do accept it. (Liber xviii, cap. xlvi :
per poculum ceruisiae propinando, dummodo is, qui huic
illicito consortio applicatur, illud acceptat, certis uerbis
adhibitis consequitur.) Then when he pleaseth he may
change his humane form, into the form of a Wolf entirely,
going into some private Cellar, or secret Wood. Again, he
can after some time put off the same shape he took upon
him, and resume the form he had before at his pleasure."
Here then a ritual draught was drunk whilst the spell was
muttered o'er by unhallowed and fearful lips.

The transformation was sometimes effected by donning
a girdle made of the pelt of the animal whose shape was to

be assumed, or else made of human skin, which must be that of a murderer or some criminal gibbeted or broken on the wheel for his offences. The girth was three fingers wide. It will be borne in mind that formerly the girdle was an essential part of a man's attire. Again, the demon presented the sorcerer with such a girdle in hideous mockery of the Cincture of S. Augustine, the Black Leather Belt of S. Monica, S. Augustine, and S. Nicolas of Tolentino. This Belt, which forms a distinctive feature of the habit of Augustinian Eremites, originated in a vision of S. Monica, who received a black leather belt from Our Lady. Such a belt is worn by members of the Archconfraternity of Our Lady of Consolation.[126] Guazzo particularly informs us that the witch upon her solemn profession of witchcraft is required to cast away this holy girdle should she be wont to wear it.[127]

Peter Stump, who was condemned for werewolfism in 1590, confessed that the demon has bestowed a girdle upon him, with which he girt himself when the lust came upon him to shift his shape to a wolf. Elich calls particular attention to this, and speaks of the Succubus who gave the wizard lycanthrope this belt : " ille ab hac donatus fuerat zona, qua cum cingebatur, et sibi et aliis in lupum uerti credebatur." [128] Claude Prieur also notes that Stump possessed " une telle ceinture laquelle auoit telle force que de la transmuer et lycanthropier quand bon luy sembloit ".[129] Delrio, also, does not forget to mention Stump, executed only some ten years before, " eo quod cum dæmone succuba plus quatuor lustris consuesset ; ab hac donatus fuit lata quadam Zona, qua cum cingebatur, et sibi et aliis in lupum uerti uidebatur." [130]

It will be remembered in this connection that Richard Rowlands—from whom there has been occasion to quote before—in his *Restitution of Decayed Intelligence*, 1605, wrote how the " *were-wolves* are certaine sorcerers, who hauing annoynted their bodyes, with an oyntment which they make by the instinct of the deuil ; and putting on a certain inchanted girdel, do not only vnto the view of others seeme as wolues, but to their own thinking haue both the shape and the nature of wolues, so long as they weare the said girdel. And they do dispose theselues as uery wolues, in wurrying and killing, and moste of humaine creatures " [131]

The wolf-girdle passed into common tradition, and was in the opinion of the vulgar perhaps the most usual way (after the magical ointment) of shape-shifting.

Sometimes the demon assigned a complete hide or wolf-skin to the sorcerer, as is duly noted by Delrio : " Aliquando uero hominibus ipsis ferarum exuuias huiusmodi ueras aptissime circumdat : quod fit quando illis dat lupinam pellem in trunco quopiam cauae arboris occulendam, ut ex quorundam confessionibus constat." [132] Elich closely follows this : " dat [dæmon] pellem lupinam in trunco quodam cauae arboris occultandum, ut ex quorumdam confessionibus in confesso fuit." [133]

The werewolf Jean Grenier [134] told De Lancre of his wolf's skin. " Ce ieune garçon m'accorda qu'il auoit vne peau que Monsieur De la forest luy auoit donnee en la forest de Droilha, qui est près la parroisse de sainct Anthoine de Pison, dans le Marquisat de Fronsac, laquelle il cachoit sur le toict d'vne grange en son païs, non pas qu'il la luy portast toutes les fois qu'il le vouloit faire courir." He also confessed that " ce Mōsieur (le demon) se trouua deuant luy, et luy bailla aussi tost vne robbe de peau de loup qu'il vestit, puis en forme de loup il se jetta sur le plus petit des trois enfans ".

Boguet, that great and erudite judge, tells us that during the trials of the lycanthropes, " The confessions of Jacques Bocquet, Françoise Secretain, Clauda Jamguillaume, Clauda Jamprost, Thievenne Paget, Pierre Gandillon, and George Gandillon are very relevant to our argument ; for they said that, in order to turn themselves into wolves, they first rubbed themselves with an ointment, and then Satan clothed them in a wolf's skin which completely covered them, and that they then went on all-fours and ran about the country chasing now a person and now an animal according to the guidance of their appetites." [135]

We must remind ourselves that, under God's permission, all these transformations are wrought by diabolic power.

A werewolf of whom Gervase of Tilbury speaks assumed the form of a wolf by rolling naked for a long while in the sand.[136]

Other methods of transformation, such as the drinking of water out of the footprint of a savage wolf ; eating the brains or flesh of the animal ; drinking from haunted streams or pools ; plucking and wearing, or smelling to the lycanthropic flower ; the chawing of some herb ; however interesting, and indeed significant, in themselves, all seem to belong to the domain of folk-lore, and hardly concern us here.[137]

It may be remarked, however, that Pliny, in his *Natural History*, liber viii, cap. 36,[138] says that the Spaniards believe there is a certain poison in a bear's head, and if this be distilled and a man drink thereof he will imagine himself a bear. This is noted by Weyer,[139] who says that he knew of a certain Spanish grandee who having eaten of bruin's brain rushed forth out of the city to the lonely hills and deserts, prowling up and down, and imagining that he had been transformed into a bear.

It may now be asked how the removal of the shape was effected and the return to the human form duly accomplished. By divesting himself of the wolf's skin or the girdle the sorcerer was able to recover his man's body, and the glamour dispersed. The lycanthropes whom Bodin tried said " that when they wished to resume their former shape, they rolled in the dew or washed themselves with water ".[140] This agrees with Sprenger's statement that a man who has been changed into a beast loses that shape when he is bathed in running water.[141] Again, the man mentioned by Vincent of Beauvais, who was changed into an ass, resumed his human shape when he was dipped in the water.[142]

Gervase of Tilbury writes that according to many authorities the werewolf recovers his shape if he be maimed and a member be lopped off his lupine body.[143]

In some parts of France, as for example la Creuse, it is believed that those who wander in the skin of the loup-garou are suffering souls, and that the wolf thanks the man who is brave enough to withstand and wound him, thus securing his deliverance. " Chaque nuit, ils sont forcés d'aller chercher la maudite peau à un endroit convenu et ils courent ainsi jusqu'à ce qu'ils rencontrent une âme charitable et courageuse qui les délivre en les blessant." [144] " Lous loups-garous soun gens coumo nous autes ; mès an heyt un countrat dab lou diable, e cado sé soun fourçatz de se cambia en bestios per ana au sabbat e courre touto la neyt. Ya per aco un mouyén de lous goari. Lous cau tira sang pendent qu'an perdut la forme de l'home, e asta leu la reprengon per toutjour." [145]

That there is some truth at any rate in these relations
seems certain, and thus they have been preserved in French
tradition. A writer of Périgord tells how at the beginning
of the nineteenth century it was believed in this district
that at each full moon certain lads, particularly the sons
of priests, are compelled to become werewolves. They go
forth at night when the impulse is upon them, strip off their
clothes and plunge naked into a certain pool. As they
emerge they find a number of wolf-pelts, furnished by the
demon, which they don and thus scour the countryside.
Before dawn they return to the same pool, cast off their
skins, and plunge into the water again, whence emerging in
human form they make their way home.[146]
The werewolves of the Montagne Noire at the beginning
and end of their metamorphosis also dived deep into certain
pools.[147]
At Guéret (la Creuse) a haunted stream called La Piquerelle
was long reputed to be the spot where the wizard werewolf
lurked waiting for his prey. The foul beast would suddenly
leap out on passers-by, but if the stranger wounded him so
that his blood flowed, he fled howling.[148]
Exorcism and, above all, the Blessed Sacrament of the
Altar will disperse all glamour and objectively restore to
human shape those upon whom an evil spell of fascination
and metamorphosis has been cast. In which connection the
history related by the authors of the *Malleus Maleficarum* [149]
is very memorable, and must not be omitted here.
The events took place in the city of Salamis about the
year 1450, or a little earlier. A trading-vessel having put
in at that port there went on shore one of the company
a likely enough young man, who during his view of the town
came to a little house on the sea-shore at the door of which was
standing a woman. He asked her if she had any eggs to
sell, and the woman after some delay brought out some eggs,
bidding him haste back to his ship ere it set sail. When the
young merchant arrived at the vessel, which was still hulling
and showed no signs of weighing anchor, being hungry he
determined to eat the eggs, and presently he found himself
dumb, without the power of speech. Amazed and sick at
heart he wished to go on board, but the mariners drove him
off with sticks, bawling out : " Look what this ass is doing !

Curse the beast, you are not coming on board." When he persisted they redoubled their blows, and he was obliged to take to flight. Wandering sadly hither and thither he found that everyone saw and regarded him as a donkey, and at length he took his way to the woman's house to beg relief. This witch, however, kept him for three years, compelling him as a beast of burden to carry loads and serve her businesses. His only consolation was that although everybody else took him for an ass, the witches themselves, severally and in company, who frequented the house, recognized him as a man and he could talk to them in human accents. At length in the fourth year the youth was driven to the city by the woman, and it chanced she followed some way behind. Passing by a church, the door of which was open, he heard the sacring-bell ring at Holy Mass—for it was the Latin rite—and he saw the Body of the Lord lifted up by the priest. Whereupon he kneeled in the street, bending his hind legs, and lifting his forelegs, his hands, over his head in adoration of his God. It so happened that some Genoese merchants observed this, and swiftly came the witch to belabour the ass with her stick. The merchants, however, seized her, and caused both her and the ass to be taken before a judge, where presently she confessed her crimes and was compelled to restore the young man to his proper form. He then returned, giving thanks to God, to his own country, and the evil woman paid the penalty her sorceries most justly deserved.

We may well believe, and indeed are very well assured, that by this signal instance of God's mercy, devotion to the Blessed Sacrament was wonderfully increased in those parts.

Here then we have a notable example of diabolical glamour dissolved by the might of the Blessed Sacrament.

Such ensorcellments may also be put an end to by exorcism, for as S. Cyprian says in his Letter to Magnus, " by the power of the exorcist whose words are energized in the sovranty of Almighty God the Devil is exceedingly chastised, yea, and burned as with fire and sore tormented." [150] Again, in his *Liber Apologeticus*, addressed to Demetrianus, proconsul of Africa, the same Saint writes : " If you could but hear and see how what time the possessed and demoniacs are exorcized and smitten, as it were, with spiritual blows, the demons screeching and yowling, are compelled to abandon the bodies they have so foully invaded, and release the afflicted from their travail and pain." [151] Some very ancient forms of exorcism, traditionally ascribed to S. Basil the Great and doubtless written or used by that father, may be found in Migne, *Patres Graeci*, vol. xxxi (1678–1684). In Migne, *Patres Latini*, vol. lxxxvii (929–954), are given some very valuable *Formulae Ueteres Exorcismorum et Excommunicationum*,[152] of which number x is clearly applicable to werewolfism.

To the domain of folk-lore of a very ancient tradition would seem to belong such beliefs as that which tells us the shape of the werewolf will be removed if he be reproached by name as a werewolf, or if again he be thrice addressed by his Christian name, or struck three blows on the forehead with a knife, or that three drops of blood should be drawn. That he should be saluted with the Sign of the Cross is, of course, natural to any Christian. Some say that the werewolf may recover his human form by shifting the buckle of his strap (*ûlf-heðnar*) to the ninth hole.[153]

It may be asked if a person who has the fearful power of shape-shifting can be in any way recognized. It is almost certain that a mysterious and unnatural horror must lower about these bond-slaves of Satan, and the animal will devour the human as when their ears become pointed and they lope stealthily in their walk. Boguet notes that the werewolves who came before him to be tried, owing to their nocturnal coursings through briars and brambles over the countryside, " were all scratched on the face and hands and legs ; and that Pierre Gandillon was so much disfigured in this way that he bore hardly any resemblance to a man, and struck with horror those who looked at him." [154]

De Lancre describes the werewolves as follows : " Ceux qui ont figure de loups comme ce ieune garçon ont les yeux affreux et estincelans comme loups, font les rauages & cruautez des loups, estranglent chiens, couppent la gorge auec les dents aux ieunes enfans, prennent goust à la chair humaine comme les loups :

> Eadem feritatis imago
> Colligit os rabiem et fuso iam sanguine gaudet : [155]

ont l'addresse et resolution à la face des hommes d'executer tels actes, leur dents et leur ongles sont fortes et aigusees cōme celles des loups, ils trouuent goust à la chair crue comme loups, ils courent à quatre pates, et quand ils courent ensemble ils ont accoustumé de departir de leur chasse les vns aux autres, et s'ils sont saouls ils heurlent pour appeller les autres : s'il n'en vient point ils enseuelissent ce qu'il leur reste pour le garder : dans Albert le Grand li. 22. De animali."

When De Lancre visited the werewolf Jean Grenier (who was then aged about twenty) at the Franciscan house at Bordeaux, he gives a very full account of the wretched creature : " Il auoit les dents fort longues, claires, larges plus que le cōmun, et aucunement en dehors, gastees, et à demi noires, à force de se ruer sur les animaux, et sur les personnes : et les ongles aussi, longs, et aucuns tous noirs depuis la racine iusqu'au bout, mesme celuy du poulce de la main gauche, que le Diable luy auoit prohibé de rogner : et ceux qui estoiēt ainsi noirs, on eust dict qu'ils estoient à demy vsez et plus enfoncez que les autres, et plus hors leur naturel parce qu'il s'en seruoit plus que de ses pieds. Qui monstre clairement qu'il a faict le mestier de loup-garou, et qu'il vsoit de ses mains, et pour courir, et pour prēdre les enfans et les chiens à la gorge."

De Lancre justly considers the command of the demon to the effect that the werewolf must not cut the nail of his left thumb which grew long, horny, and hard as the talon of a beast, to be merely a piece of foul superstition, harmful in itself, as indicating a certain obedience to the Devil's tyranny even in small details. " Il monstre l'ongle du poulce gauche fort espoix et fort lōg, que le Diable luy a defendu de coupper, qui est vne pure folic en foy, mais marque de creance et obeissance au mauuais Demon, qui tient les couers bandez par telles superstitiōs." [156]

The signs upon which our author, than whom nobody perhaps, save the great Boguet, was more qualified to pronounce and had better opportunity of judging, insists upon most emphatically are the horrible eyes of the werewolf, " les yeux hagands, petits, enfoncez et noirs, tout esgarez," the mirrors of the bestial soul ; and also that the werewolf even in human form is unmistakably animal, " ayant tousiours gardé du bestial." [157]

This werewolf walked more easily on all fours than upright as a human being, and his agility in clambering and leaping limberly was almost supernatural. " Il auoit vne merueilleuse aptitude à aller à quatre pattes . . . et à sauter de forrez comme fort les animaux de quatre pieds." [158]

He was marked on the buttock with the Devil's mark, which spot upon his being first taken was altogether callous and insensible, though very plain to see; but afterwards when he was reclaimed from his sorceries it gradually grew tender and soft, almost fading away and indiscernible. All werewolves—I do not speak of the involuntary ensorcelled transformation—are witches, and therefore all werewolves will be found to be branded with the Devil's mark.[159]

Among the Danes it was said that if the eyebrows met so as to form a bar across the brow this signified the man was a werewolf, which would seem to be an old wives' saw.[160] However, Professor Westermarck, in his *Ritual and Belief in Morocco*,[161] when speaking of the evil eye mentions that " Persons with deep-set eyes and those whose eyebrows are united over the bridge of the nose are considered particularly dangerous ".

The " rangen *wolfs-zagel* " or *wolfs-zagelchan* of which Grimm speaks belongs to the realm of nursery lore.[162]

De Lancre tells us that the reason why the Devil is more ready to change the sorcerer into a wolf rather than any other animal is owing to the ferocity of the natural wolf, who ravages and devours, who does more harm to man than any other marauder beast in his kind. Moreover, the wolf typifies the eternal enemy of the lamb, and by the Lamb is symbolized Our Lord and Saviour Jesus Christ.[163]

We are now in a position briefly to sum up the results of our inquiry, and to ask what it is permitted to believe concerning werewolfism or shape-shifting, the metamorphosis of men into animals.

In the first place, we say that all such transformations are effected by diabolical power. S. Lorenzo Guistiniani tells us in his *De spirituali et casto Uerbi et Animæ connubio* [164] that by black magic and the craft of Satan extraordinary wonders are wrought, although not true miracles, for true miracles are of God alone, and if He will He works by His Angels or through His Saints. In the history of holy Job

we read that God permitted the Devil to have power over
His servant : " And the Lord said to Satan, Behold he is in
thy hand, but yet save his life." [165]
It must, however, always be remembered that there can
be no metamorphosis, no transformation, which implies or
involves any act of creation. Master Conrad Koellin, a
famous Dominican professor of Ulon, writes in all reverence
that Creation is the greatest act of God : *Maximum opus
est creationis, in quo ex nihilo fit aliquid.*[166]
Creation belongs to God alone. But we may distinguish,
as Bodin says in his refutation of Weyer : " Mais VViers
s'est bien abusé de prēdre la creation pour la generation, &
la generation pour la transmutation : la premiere est *de
nihilo,* qui est propre au createur, la seconde est ex eo quod
subsistit, qui s'appelle γένεσις, *in informarum generatione :*
& la troisieme n'est pas *motus,* c'est à dire κίνησις, ains
seulement vn changement, & alteration accidentale, c'est à
dire ἀχλοίωσις & μεταβολή, demeurāt forme essentielle.
Et par ainsi ce que le createur a vne fois creé, les creatures
engendrent par succession & transformēt par la proprieté
& puissance que Dieu leur a donnees, que Thomas d'Aquin
appelle Vertu naturelle, parlant des esprits en c'este sorte,
*Omnes angeli boni & mali habent ex uirtute naturali potestatem
transformandi corpora nostra.* Or tous les anciēs depuis
Homere, & tous ceux qui ont faict les procès aux Sorciers,
qui ont souffert tel changemēt, sont d'accord que la raison,
& forme essentielle demeure immuable comme nous auons
dict en son lieu. C'est donc vne simple alteration de
la forme accidentale & corporelle, & non pas vne vraye
transformation." [167]
In fine, shape-shifting may be accomplished in three ways.
The first method is by a glamour caused by the demon,
so that the man changed (either voluntarily or under the
influence of a spell) will seem both to himself and to all who
behold him to be metamorphosed into the shape of a certain
animal, and although, if it be a spell which has been cast
upon him, he retains his human reason he cannot exercise
the power of speech. The authors of the *Malleus Maleficarum*
tell us that such transmutations are " proved by authority,
by reason, and by experience ".[168] It was this metamorphosis
which the father of Praestantius suffered when he thought

he was a pack-horse and carried corn, whose story
S. Augustine relates in the *De Ciuitate Dei*, xviii, 18. And the
young merchant who was ensorcelled by the witch of Salamis
and seemingly became an ass endured the same glamorous
transformation. There are many other similar examples
recorded, and to this demoniacal hallucination Remy [169]
would refer most, if not all, cases of werewolfism ; as I think,
wrongly. The authors of the *Malleus Maleficarum* are of
opinion that this matter of shape-shifting was Nabuchodonosor's case. As for the luggage and bales, which were
loaded upon the sumpter-horse and the metamorphosed ass,
they explain " that devils invisibly bore those burdens up
when they were too heavy to be carried ".[170]

Henri Boguet allows another mode, for he writes : " My
own opinion is that Satan sometimes leaves the witch asleep
behind a bush, and himself goes and performs that which
the witch has in mind to do, giving himself the appearance
of a wolf ; but that he so confuses the wolf's imagination that
he believes he has really been a wolf and has run about and
killed men and beasts . . . And when it happens that they
find themselves wounded, it is Satan who immediately
transfers to them the blow which he has received in his
assumed body." [171] " When the witch is not bodily present
at all," says Guazzo,[172] " then the Devil wounds her in that
part of her absent body corresponding to the wound which
he knows to have been received by the beast's body." We
have here then a complete explanation of the phenomenon
of repercussion, namely, that if the werewolf be wounded or
maimed the witch will be found to be instantaneously
wounded in numerically the same spot or maimed of the
identical corresponsive limb, a piece of evidence which occurs
again and again in the trials of lycanthropes. Guazzo tells
us that on these occasions the demon " assumes the body
of a wolf formed from the air and wrapped about him ",[173]
whilst other authorities rather hold that the demon actually
possesses some wolf. But whichever it be, this detail skills
not. Moreover, as the learned Capuchin, Jacques d'Autun,
teaches us,[174] even if this method be employed in shape-
shifting, and the sorcerer is thrown into a mesmeric trance,
whilst the familiar prowls abroad, the consenting witch is
none the less guilty of the murders and ravages wrought by

the demon in lupine form, and by very force of his evil pact with hell he cannot in any whit disculpate himself from the shedding of blood and bestial savagery.

This method of werewolfism and metamorphosis, although infrequent, is amply proven. It does not, however, account for the immense weariness felt by the sorcerer after his animal expeditions and courses of the night. When treating of a similar matter, Remy, in his *Demonolatry*, book i, chapter xxiv,[175] explains how *The Transvection of Men through the Air by Good Angels, of which we read in Time past, was calm and free from Labour ; but that by which Witches are now transported by Demons is full of Pain and Weariness.* By the very confessions of the witches themselves it was acknowledged that when the demon " carries his disciples through the air in this manner, he leaves them far more heavily overcome with weariness than if they had completed a rough journey afoot with the greatest urgency ". Father Jacques d'Autun points out that the cases when the sorcerer is thrown into a coma, and the ravages of lycanthropy are impressed upon his imaginative faculty by the demon, so that he supposes himself as a wolf actually to have been galloping tantivy over hill and dale, through forest and bosky dingle, are very rare ; and to attribute the decrepit lassitude of the werewolf merely to the sick fantasy of a nightmare cannot but be regarded as inconsequential and vain.[176]

The third method by which shape-shifting may be accomplished, and that which from accumulated evidence would seem to be immeasurably the more general mode of werewolfism and other devilish transformation, cannot be better described than in the words of Guazzo : " Sometimes, in accordance with his pact, the demon surrounds a witch with an aerial effigy of a beast, each part of which fits on to the correspondent part of the witch's body, head to head, mouth to mouth, belly to belly, foot to foot, and arm to arm ; but this only happens when they use certain ointments and words. . . . In this last case it is no matter for wonder if they are afterwards found with an actual wound in those parts of their human body where they were wounded when in the appearance of a beast ; for the enveloping air easily yields, and the true body receives the wound." [177]

" I maintain," says Boguet, " that for the most part it is the witch himself who runs about slaying : not that he is metamorphosed into a wolf, but that it appears to him that he is so." A little later he adds, after having reviewed the confessions of the lycanthropes at their trial : " Who now can doubt but that these witches themselves ran about and committed the acts and murders of which we have spoken ? For what was the cause of the fatigue they experienced ? If they had been sleeping behind some bush, how did they become fatigued ? What caused the scratches on their persons, if it was not the thorns and bushes through which they ran in their pursuit of man and animals ? " " They confessed also that they tired themselves with running." Clauda Jamprost, a horrible hag, old and lame, when asked how it happened that she was able to clamber over rocks and boulders in the swift midnight venery, answered that she was borne along by Satan. " But this in no way renders them immune from fatigue."

On one occasion Benoist Bidel, a lad of fifteen or sixteen, had climbed a tree to pluck some fruit, leaving his younger sister at the foot. The girl was attacked by a wolf, who suddenly darted from the bushes, whereupon her brother quickly descending endeavoured to protect her. The wolf, turning to the boy, with a fierce blow of its paw drove into his neck a knife he was carrying. By this time a number of people had rushed to the assistance of the children and beat off the animal, maiming and hurting it. The lad was carried into his father's house, where he died of his wounds in a few days. But before he died he declared that the wolf which had torn him had its two forefeet like a man's hands covered on the top with hair. There expired, maimed and injured (although nobody exactly knew how) precisely as the wolf had been hurt, a woman in the village, who was a notorious witch, Perrenette Gandillon. They then realized that it was she who had killed the boy.

Similarly, when Jeanne Perrin was going through a wood with Clauda Gaillard, Clauda, grumbling that she had received so few alms, darted into the bushes and there came out a huge wolf. Jeanne Perrin, crossing herself and letting fall the alms she had collected, ran away in terror, for she swore that this wolf had toes on its hind feet like a human being.

There is a strong presumption that this wolf was no other than Clauda Gaillard, for she afterwards told Jeanne that the wolf which attacked her would not have done her any harm.[178]

These then are instances when the human figure was hideously breaking through the animal envelope. Precisely the same thing happened in the case of Gilles Garnier, who was condemned at Dôle in January, 1573,[179] a circumstance attested by many creditable witnesses.

In some instances the demon supplied the sorcerer with an envelope of wolf-skins, but the effect was the same. As we have already seen, the werewolf Jean Grenier possessed a pelt of this description.

Not without reason did the werewolf in past centuries appear as one of the most terrible and depraved of all bond-slaves of Satan. He was even whilst in human form a creature within whom the beast—and not without prevailing—struggled with the man. Masqued and clad in the shape of the most dreaded and fiercest denizen of the forest the witch came forth under cover of darkness, prowling in lonely places, to seek his prey. By the force of his diabolic pact he was enabled, owing to a ritual of horrid ointments and impious spells, to assume so cunningly the swift shaggy brute that save by his demoniac ferocity and superhuman strength none could distinguish him from the natural wolf. The werewolf loved to tear raw human flesh. He lapped the blood of his mangled victims, and with gorged reeking belly he bore the warm offal of their palpitating entrails to the sabbat to present in homage and foul sacrifice to the Monstrous Goat who sat upon the throne of worship and adoration. His appetites were depraved beyond humanity. In bestial rut he covered the fierce she-wolves amid their bosky lairs. If he were attacked and sore wounded, if a limb, a paw or ear were lopped, perforce he must regain his human shape, and he fled to some cover to conceal these fearful transformations, where man broke through the shell of beast in horrid confusion. The human body was maimed or wounded in that numerical place where the beast had been hurt. By this were his bedevilments not unseldom betrayed, he was recognized and brought to justice. Hateful to God and loathed of man, what other end, what other reward could he look for than the stake, where they burned him quick, and scattered his ashes to the wind, to be swept away to nothingness and oblivion on the keen wings of the tramontane and the nightly storm.

NOTES TO CHAPTER II

[1] *A Monograph of the Canidae*, 1890, by St. George Mivart, F.R.S., pp. 3–33. This book gives nine exceedingly fine hand-coloured plates of different varieties of wolves. See also *Fur-Bearing Animals*, by Henry Poland, F.Z.S., 1892, pp. 65–76. St. George Mivart is my principal authority for the natural history of the wolf.

[2] *Zoologische Garten*, xxiv, Jahrgang (1883), p. 91. See further, *Archives Cosmologiques*, Bruxelles, 1868, p. 78, plate 5. (A black wolf killed near Dinant, Belgium, in 1868.) Also É. Griffith, F.S.A., *Animal Kingdom* (Cuvier's *Le règne animal*), 15 vols., 1827–1832 ; vol. ii, p. 348.

[3] *Coelii Rhodogini Lectiones Antiquae*, folio, 1666, p. 1185. Ulisse Aldrovandi, *De Quadrupedibus Solidipedibus*, folio, Bononiae, 1616, pp. 118–19. Vergil, *Georgics*, iii, 206–8, speaking of horses.

[4] Poland, op. cit., p. 67.

[5] Holland's translation, folio, 1601, vol. i, p. 207.

[6] *Genesis*, xlix, 27, "Benjamin, a ravenous wolf," whom Cornelius à Lapide, *In Pentateuchum*, Antverpiae, folio, 1616, p. 299, compares to "Romulum rapacem . . . eo quod lacte lupae esset nutritus ". *Ecclesiasticus*, xiii, 12 ; *Jeremias*, v, 6 ; *Ezechiel*, xxii, 27 ; *Sophonias*, iii, 3.

[7] "*Lupus quis* ? Lupus primo est haereticus. Secundo, quiuis sceleratus, qui fideles uerbo, uel exemplo rapere et peruertere studet [ut puta modernista]. Tertio, lupus est diabolus." A Lapide, *In Ioannem*, x, 12. *In IV Euangelia*, Lugduni, folio, 1638, ii, p. 402.

[8] "Nonne lupis istis haeretici comparandi sunt ? " *Expositio Euangel. sec. Lucam*, lib. VII, c. x, 3. Migne, *Patres Lat.*, xv, col. 1711 (49).

[9] Chaucer, *Complete Works*, ed. Skeat. One vol., Oxford, n.d., p. 703 (*Sequitur de Auaricia*, 67). *English Register of Godstow Nunnery*, ed. A. Clarke, 1905, part i. (The holy martyrs Cyriac and Julitta, his mother, under Diocletian, *Roman Martyrology*, 16th June.) John Alcock, Bishop of Rochester, 1430–1500. The Hill of Perfection was printed 1491, 1497, and 1501. Kendall, *Epigrammes*, 8vo, 1577, 43.

[10] *Iliad* iv, 471–2 ; xi, 70–3 ; xvi, 351–7. Among Homeric epithets of wolves are πολίοι, grisly ; ὠμοφάγοι, devourers of raw red meat ; κρατερώνυχες, with strong sharp claws ; ὀρέστεροι, brood of the mountains. Æschylus, *Septem*, 1035, terms them κοιλογάστορες, with void ravening bellies. Cf. the English "hungry as a wolf ", as in John Palgrave's *Acolastus*, 1540, iii, 3, when the parasite Pamphagus says : "Nam uel lupo esurientior Sum," and Palgrave has, "I am more hungry thā any wolfe is " (sig. L). Cf. again, "to keep the wolf from the door," as "he maye the wolf werre from the gate ", Hardyng's *Chronicon* (c. 1470), and in *Institutions of a Gentleman*, 1555, sig. G. i, "keping yᵉ wulf from the doore (as they cal it)." Also John Goodman, *The Penitent Pardoned* (1679), seventh ed., 1713, i, 11, p. 31. The word wolf is applied to a ravenous appetite, as in Gesner's *Jewell of Health*.

For the Latin phrase *Lupus in fabula* (or *sermone*), an adage used when such a one who had been recently spoken of arrived abruptly on the scene, see Plautus, *Stichus*, iv, 1, 71, also the *Adelphi*, iv, 1, 21, with the gloss of Donatus who gives rather a different turn to the phrase. Also see Thomas Wilson, *The Art of Rhetorique*, ed. 1580, p. 202 : "We saie Whiste, the Woulfe is at hande, when the same man cometh in the meane season, of whom we spake before."

For a dilemma, "lupum auribus tenere," *Phormio*, iii, 11, 21, and the gloss of Donatus. Marlowe, *Edward II* (1594), 2115–17, Mortimer to Isabel :—
For now we hould an old Wolfe by the eares,
That if he slip will seaze vpon vs both,
And gripe the sorer, being gript himselfe.
Quarles, *Samson*, xi, 63 (1631). For a difficult job, " lupo agnum eripere," *Poenulus*, iii, 5, 81. Cf. " To be in the wolf's mouth," " à la gueule du loup," for deadly peril. " There was Eilred in the wolfes mouth," Robert Mannyng of Brunne, *Chronicle*, ed. 1810, p. 42. Erasmus in his *Adagia* has noted several interesting and important proverbial references to the wolf. Ælian says the wolf is the fiercest and most malevolent of all animals, *De Nat. Animal.*, ed. Hercher, Paris, Didot, 1858, vii, 20. He is a harpy, unclean. Ibid., *Fragmentum 354*, p. 470. He is baleful, accursed, something wholly evil, Aristophanes of Byzantium, *Historiae Animalium Epitome*, ii, 285–244, ed. Spyridion P. Lambros, vol. i, par. 1. *Supplementum Aristotelicum*, Berolini, 1885, pp. 89–90.

[11] Beaumont and Fletcher, *The Custome of the Countrey*, folio, 1647, iv, where Rutilio speaks of " these unsatisfied Men-leeches, women ".

[12] Aristaenetus, Ep., ii, 20. " ὡς γὰρ λύκοι τοὺς ἄρνας ἀγαπῶσιν, οὕτω τὰ γύναια ποθοῦσιν οἱ νέοι, καὶ λυκοφιλία τούτων ὁ πόθος." *Epistolographi Graeci*, ed. W. Hercher, Didot, Paris, 1873, p. 170.

[13] 241 D.

[14] The couplet is from Taylor's translation of the *Phaedrus*, 1792 (anon.), p. 42.

[15] *Anthologia Graeca*, xi (Musa Puerilis), 250, ed. Didot, Parisiis, 1872, vol. ii, p. 429.

[16] *The Greek Anthology, Epigrams from Anthologia Palatina XII.* Translated into English verse by Sydney Oswald. Privately issued, 1914, p. 21, " Drunken Vows."

[17] iv, 19. Frankfort, 1608, p. 209. See also the edition by Dindorf, Lipsiae, 1834, 5 vols., vol. iv, p. 822. " τὰ δὲ γυναικῶν πρόσωπα εἴη τοιαῦτα. γρᾳδίον ἰσχνὸν ἢ λυκαίνιον . . . τὸ μὲν λυκαίνιον ὑπόμηκες· ῥυτίδες λεπταὶ και πυκναί. λευκόν, ὑπωχρον, στρεβλὸν τὸ ὄμμα." *Pollucis Onamasticon*, ed. Eric Bethe, Lipsiae (Teubner), мсм, p. 245.

[18] 55 (54), 11.

[19] Auctore P.P., Parisiis, 1826, p. 295. See also *Supplementum et Index Lexicorum Eroticorum Linguae Latinae*, Paris, 1911, pp. 176–7.

[20] iii, 1, 12.

[21] Lugd. Bat. Apud Franciscum Hackium et Petrum Lessen, 1660 ; pp. 101–2.

[22] " The most famous of all (homosexual romances) remains to be recorded. This is the story of Harmodius and Aristegeiton, who freed Athens from the tyrant Hipparchus. There is not a speech, a poem, or essay, a panegyrical oration in praise of either Athenian liberty or Greek love which does not tell the tale of this heroic friendship. Herodotus and Thucydides treat the event as a matter of serious history. Plato refers to it as the beginning of freedom for the Athenians. The drinking-song in honour of these lovers is one of the most precious fragments of popular Greek poetry which we possess. . . . Harmodius and Aristegeiton were reverenced as martyrs and saviours of their country. Their names gave consecration to the love which made them bold against the despot, and they became at Athens eponyms of paiderastia." J. A. Symonds, *A Problem in Greek Ethics*, p. 179, *Sexual Inversion*, by Havelock Ellis and John Addington Symonds, 1897.

[23] Pausanias, i, 23, 2 ; Plutarch, *De Ganulitate*, 8 ; Polynaeus, viii, 45. Pliny, *Nat. H.*, xxxiv, 72 ; Clement of Alexandria, *Stromata*, iv, 19, 122, ed. Potter. p. 618 ; Athenaeus, xiii ; Lactantius, i, 20. Athenaeus represents Leaena as the mistress of Harmodius ; Pausanias and Polynaeus name her as the mistress of Aristegeiton. These accounts are incorrect. She was mistress of neither of the lovers.

[24] Ed. Amstelædami, Apud Henricum Wetstenium, 1684, p. 69.

[25] The Commentary on Ausonius of the great French Scholar Élie Vinet

(1509-1587) is much esteemed. His Ausonius was first printed 8° 1575, and again 8° 1590, 8° 1604, etc. I have used the Amsterdam Ausonius, 1671, "Apud Ioannem Blaev," p. 23.

[26] ll. 107-8. Migne, *P.L.*, lx, p. 126. The old gloss on l. 107 has Lupas, *meretrices*. Barthius cites an old codex for a reading " ruricolas " and suggests (quite needlessly) " lustricolas " in this passage.

[27] The author of this work was Nicolas Chorier, who was born at Vienna in 1609, and died in 1692, highly honoured for his scholarship and literary genius. He ascribed his erotic masterpiece, first published in 1649, to Luisa Sigea, an erudite Spanish lady, who was born about 1530 and died at Burgos in 1560. She was often termed in compliment the Minerva of her age.

The *Satyra sotadica* is represented as having been translated into Latin by Jean Meursius, the celebrated antiquary, 1623-1653, son of the more famous Jean Meursius.

It is said that M. Rochas possessed a key to the interlocutors of the Satire. " La *Satire* de Chorier est un chef-d'œuvre et l'on ne saurait trop louer . . . cet art suprême de varier merveilleusement un sujet limité."

[28] Acted before Pope Leo X in the Rucellai Gardens on the occasion of a Papal visit to Florence.

[29] *Joannis Palegravi Londoniensis Ecphrasis Anglica in Comoediam Acolasti*, 1540. Lond. in aedibus Tho. Berthel (sig. x).

[30] Schwenck, *Sinn bilden der alten Völker*, p. 524.

[31] A few references in Greek and Latin literature to the wolf as an omen of ill may serve for many. Pausanias, ix, 13, 4 (Battle of Leuctra) ; i, 19, 6 ; i, 41, 3 ; v, 15, 8 ; vii, 26, 3 and 11 ; viii, 82, 4. Livy, iii, 29, 9 ; xxi, 46, 1-2 ; xxi, 62, 5 ; xxii, 1, 12 ; xxvii, 37, 3 (sentinel at Capua killed by midnight wolf) ; xxxii, 29 ; xxxiii, 26, 8-9 ; xli, 9, 6 ; see also Julius Obsequens, *De Prodigiis*, ed. C. H. Hase, Parisiis, 1823, xvii (p. 44) ; xxv (p. 47) ; ciii (p. 184) ; and cix (p. 48). F. B. Krauss, *An Interpretation of the Omens, Portents, and Prodigies recorded by Livy, Tacitus, and Suetonius*, Philadelphia, 1930, attempts a rationalistic explanation of the phenomena, and is singularly inconclusive and unsatisfactory. See also Zonaras for Mark Antony at Brundisium, *Annales* ex recensione Mauricii Pinderi, Bonnae, 1844, ii, pp. 876-7 (*Corpus Scriptorum Historiae Byzantinae*). Also Horace, *Carm.* III, xxvii, 1-4. Also Aratus, *Geoponika*, i, 3, and xv, 1 (Eng. tr. T. Owen, 1805, vol. ii, p. 190). For curious wolf lore one may consult Antoine Mizauld, *Centuriae IX Memora-bilium*, 1566 ; ed. 1592, Cent. i, 24 (p. 7) ; Cent. viii, 5 (p. 164) ; et alibi. See also Pliny, *Hist. Nat.*, xxviii, 10 and 20.

[32] Phytognomonica, iii, 13 ; Neapoli, 1588, p. 113.

[33] *Cædwalla*, London, Seeley and Co., 1888, ch. iv, p. 55.

[34] *Norimbergae apud J. Petreium*, folio. Also the same year (1550) Lugduni.

[35] Basiliae, folio, 1557, pp. 498-9.

[36] *Naturall Historie*, Holland, folio, 1601. The first tome, p. 207, viii, 22.

[37] Parisiis, 1583, p. 41.

[38] Ed. J. G. Reiff, 2 vols., Lipsiae, 1805. Vol. i, p. 159. See also Ulisse Aldrovandi, *De Quadrupedibus Digitatis Uiuiparis*, Bologna, folio, 1637, i, pp. 164-5.

[39] For further wolf lore see Philip Camerarius, *Operae Horarum Subcisiuarum*, Centuria altera, cap. 90 ; Alessandro Alessandri, *Geniales Dies*, v, xiii ; Giampietro Valeriano of Belluno, *Hieroglyphica*, Basle, 1566, xi (ed. Basileæ, 1575, pp. 79-82). Camerarius has the story of Gelon of Syracuse and the kindly wolf. Antigonus of Carystus in his *Historiae Mirabiles* tells how wolves guard the tackle of fishermen living on the shores of Lake Maeotis (Azor), and how the animals are fed as a reward for their pains.

[40] Ed. Spyridion P. Lambros, *Supplementum Aristotelicum*, vol. i, Berolini, 1885, p. 90.

[41] Ed. James Britton, Folk-Lore Soc., London, 1881, p. 115 and p. 204.

[42] *Zeitschrift fur Romanische Philologie*, xxxii (1908) : " Sizilianische Gebete, Beschwörungen und Rezepte in griechischer Umschrift," Heinrich Schneeguns, pp. 571-594.

[43] I quote from folio, 1635, as a fuller text, pp. 13–14. Of 1629 Bodley has a fine—perhaps a unique—copy, formerly in the library of that great bibliophile James Crossley (Antiq. c. E. $\frac{1627}{1}$).

[44] *The Works of Virgil*, folio, 1697 ; Pastoral ix, 74–5 ; p. 43. There are constant references to this belief. Plato, *Laws*, x, 906, says that dogs may be charmed to silence by the wolf's gaze. See Pliny, viii, 22 ; S. Ambrose, *Expos. Euang. sec. Lucam*, vii, 48 (Migne, *P.L.*, xiv, col. 1711) ; Themistus, Oratio XXI, ed. Petavius, Parisiis, fol., 1684, p. 253 ; *Geoponika*, xv, 1 ; Vincent of Beauvais, *Speculum Doctrinale*, Lib. xvii, cap. 92 (fol. Venice, 1591, tom. ii, p. 270) ; William of Auvergne, *De Uniuerso*, ii, i, cap. 32 (*Opera Omnia*, Venetiis, 1591, p. 786) ; S. Isidore, *Etymologies*, xii (*P.L.*, lxxxii, col. 438) ; Le Loyer, *Des Spectres*, i, viii (Angers, 1586, pp. 206–7), where he derives *Coqueluche* from κακά λύκου. Cotgrave (1611) defines Coqueluche as a " *new disease, which troubled the French about the yeares* 1550, *and* 1557 ; *and us but a while ago* ". See also Vair, *De Fascino*, i, 1 and i, 3 (ed. 1583, p. 5 and p. 14) ; Thomas of Cantimpre, *De Apibus*, ii, cap. 57 ; Cardano, *De Subtilitate*, lib. xviii (ed. Basileæ, 1557, pp. 498–9) ; Delrio, *Disquisit. Mag.*, i, cap. iii, q. 4. Sennert, *De Morbis Occultis* (Opera om. 1641, t. i, p. 1180), derides the tradition. Robert de Triez, *Ruses, Finesses et Impostures des Esprits Maleris*, Cambrai, 1563, p. 28 *uerso*, upholds the belief " si le loup descouure de preme veue l'h̄ōme, il le rēd enroué et le priue de voix et de parolle ". See also Basile, Pentamerone, Jorn. i, tratt. viii, ed. 1788, tom. i, p. 84 ; Tasso, *Aminta*, i, 2 ; and Marino, *L'Adone*, xii, 75.

[45] In later editions *si le Diable peut* became *si les esprits peuuent*.

[46] For the teaching of S. Thomas see particularly *Supra IV Libros Sententiarum*, liber ii, Distinct. septima et Distinct. octaua, ed. Parisiis, 1574, pp. 212–19.

[47] *Malleus Maleficarum*, tr. Montague Summers, folio, 1928, p. 148.

[48] *Wunderzeichen, Warhafftige Beschreibung und gründlich verzeicnus schrecklicker Wunderzeichen und Geschichten, die von . . . MDXVII bis auff . . . MDLVI geschehn und ergangen sind, noch der Jarzal . . .* Jhena, 8vo, 1556.

[49] *Malleus*, ut sup., pp. 126–7.

[50] *c.* 1517–1564. Belon in chapter lii (ed. Paris, 4to, 1554, pp. 120–1) writes *Des Basteleries qu'on Faict au Caire.*

[51] *Speculum Naturale*, lib. ii, cap. cix. The incident, which I relate at length in Chapter III, occurred under Pope S. Leo IX, 1049–1054.

[52] *De Ciu. Dei*, xviii, xviii.

[53] pp. 137–140.

[54] Ed. Francofurti, 1602, p. 328.

[55] First ed., Paris, folio, 1548. I have used the Æditio Secunda, Paris, fol., 1551, pp. 159–161. Jean Fernel, " the modern Galen," 1497–1558.

[56] pp. 172–185.

[57] Binsfeld, *De Confessionibus Maleficorum*, 3 Conclusio, ed. Aug. Treu. 1605, pp. 194–5, mentions Ulrich Molitor, and adds " male eum Bodinus pro se allegat ".

[58] Dom Paul Piolin, *Gallia Christiana*, tom. ii (Paris, 1873), 1200–1. Ibid., 1080. Bishop Louis Guerinet was translated to Fréjus about 1462, see *Gallia Christiana*, tom. i (Paris, 1870), 489–40.

[59] Cap. xxvi. Migne, *P.L.*, xl, col. 798.

[60] pp. 694–5.

[61] Regino of Prüm, *Libri Duo de Synodalibus Causis et Disciplinis Ecclesiasticis*, ii, 371, ed. Wasserschleben, 1840, pp. 354–6. The text is conveniently given by Hansen, *Geschichte des Hexenwahns*, Bonn, 1894, pp. 38–9.

[62] Policraticus, ii, 17, ed. Webb, i, 100–1.

[63] *De Natura Daemonum*, Venice, 8vo, 1581, iv, 4.

[64] Libro Primo, capitolo ix. " Si mostra l'identità della Società Dianiana colla moderna Streghiera, e si esamina il *Can. Episcopi* 26. q. 5," pp. 50–63.

[65] pp. 380–1.

[66] Francofurti, 1581, " summo studio Fr. Joan. Myntrenberg Carmeliti," pp. 61–72.

[67] Malleus Maleficarum ; Daemonastrix ; 1669, t. iii, p. 183.

[68] Migne, Patres Graeci, lvii, col. 353.

[69] *Opera omnia*, ed. by the Quaracchi Fathers, tom. ii (1885, pp. 200–4).

[70] Ibid., pp. 227–230.

[71] Folio, Cologne, 1622, tom. ii, pp. 147–151. See further, *Relationes Undecim* of Fra Francisco Vittoria, O.P., Salamantiae, 1565, " De Arte Magica," pp. 350–385 ; and François Garassus, S.J., *Somme Théologique*, folio, Paris, 1625, pp. 915–18, for a discussion of *Signum, Prodigium, Monstrum, Miraculum*.

[72] Venice, 1523. I have used the ed., Coloniae, 1581, pp. 54–9.

[73] *Holie Bible*. Doway, 1610. Vol. ii, p. 784. Daniel, iv, 30. Lambert Daneau in *Les Sorciers* translated as *A Dialogue of Witches* by Thomas Taylor, 1575, in his discussion of shape-shifting, chapter iii (sig. F. i), says that " it is thus to be understoode of *Nabucadnezer*, that we must not thinke that his humane nature was conuerted into the essencil or being of a brute beast. But his conuersation was chaunged, and his mynde and affection ". Daneau has nothing new to offer in his consideration of metamorphosis but is trivial to a degree with his easy prattle of " meere tryfles and oulde wyues tales ".

[74] Eng. tr. by Montague Summers, folio, London, 1928, pp. 61–5.

[75] *De fantasia, capitulum sextum*. " Operatur etiam angelus malus, id est diabolus circa fantasiam hominis ad decipiendum." S. Antoninus cites the examples of S. Macharius and Simon Magus. He also examines the Canon Episcopi. He teaches that the Devil effects these wonders " alterando fantasias hominum. Cum autem potentia fantastica siue imaginatiua sit corporalis id est affixa organo corporeo, naturaliter est subdita angelis malis ut possint ea transmutare ". Of the *Summa* of S. Antoninus I have used the Venice folio, 1487.

[76] *Albertus Magnus : De Animalibus Libri XXVI*, ed. Hermann Stadler, Band i, Münster, 1916 ; Band ii, Münster, 1921. (*Beitrage zur Geschichte der Philosophie des Mittelalters*, Band xv, Band xvi.)

[77] Part ii, question 1, chapter 8 deals with *the Manner whereby (Witches) Change Men into the Shape of Beasts*. Eng. tr., pp. 122–4.

[78] Remy, *Demonolatry*, book ii, ch. 5, Eng. tr., London, 1929, pp. 108–114 ; Guazzo, *Compendium Maleficarum*, book i, ch. 13, Eng. tr., 1929, pp. 50–3 ; Boguet, *Examen of Witches*, chap. 47, Eng. tr., 1929, pp. 136–155.

In his *Daemonomagia*, Frankfort, 1607, quaestio xii, pp. 153–4, Philip Ludwig Elich has some valuable remarks upon werewolfery. He refers to " quodam λυκανθρώπῳ, cui nomen Peter *Stumpff* ", and he mentions the terms " *Beer-Wolff*, nobis uerius atque magis proprie *Teuffelswolff*, Graecis λυκανθρώπους et μυρμολυκίας, siue ἀρκτολύκους ".

[79] Typis . . . Monasterii S. Galli, Anno MDCXC, 2 vols., folio. Vol. i, p. 112. Sub anno 1470. Baianus is spoken of as one who " in arte Magica peritissimus omnium suo tempore mortalium habebatur ", cf. p. 120. " Daemonum cooperatione mutauisse non dubium a nescientibus praestigiorum eius rationem occultam putabatur." All such wonders are termed " daemonum ludibria ".

[80] Fourth ed., Leucoreis Athenis (Wittenberg), 1613, pp. 263–4.

[81] *De Sagarum Natura et Potestate, Deq.; His Recte Cognoscendis Et Puniendis Physiologia Gulielmi Adolphi Scribonii Marpurgensis. Ubi De Purgatione Earum per aquam frigidam*. Marpurgi, 1588. " De Sagarum in catos, feles, aliaue eiuscemodi animantia transformatione," pp. 66–77. For Scribonius see N. F. J. Eloy, *Dictionnaire Historique de la Médicine*, t. iv (1778), p. 236.

[82] Paris, 1578, ch. xiv, pp. 26–7.

[83] Trèves, 8vo, 1591. (Ed. Trèves, 8vo, 1605, pp. 193–204.)

[84] Col. Agrippinae, 1594, pp. 111–136. " De Prodigiosis Uiuorum Apparitionibus sub Peregrina et Bestiarum Forma."

[85] Folio, Moguntiae, 1603, pp. 163–6.

[86] Paris, 1605, pp. 134–145.

HIS SCIENCE AND PRACTICE 129

[87] Wittenberg, 1606, pp. 22–6.

[88] pp. 496–517.

[89] Privilège, 1 Dec., 1595.

[90] Nabuchodonosor, King of Babylon ; Daniel, iv, 23–84. For a discussion of the lycanthropy of Nabuchodonosor see Dr. Pusey's lectures, *Daniel the Prophet*, 1864, pp. 425–487 ; also M. l'abbé Henri Lesètre, curé of Saint-Etienne-du-Mont, Paris, article *Folie* in the *Dictionnaire de la Bible*, F. Vigouroux, Paris, 1899, fasc. xv, 2801–2 ; Brière de Boismont, *Des hallucinations*, Paris, 1852, p. 383 ; Petrus Archidiaconus, *Quaestiones in Danielem*, Migne, *P.L.*, xcvi, coll. 1549–50 ; Nicolas de Lyra, *Bibliorum Sacrorum . . . Postilla Nicolai Lyrani*, folio, Lugduni, 1589, tom. iv, 1553–6 ; Michael Medina, *De Fide*, ii, 7 ; Cornelius à Lapide, *Comm. in Danielem*, Antverpiae, folio, 1621, pp. 45–7 ; Girolamo Mercuriale, *Medicina Practica*, I, xii, *De Lykanthropia*, fol., Francofurti, 1601, pp. 56–7 ; Dom Augustin Calmet, *Dissertation sur la Metamorphose de Nabuchodonosor*, in his *Commentaire Littéral sur tous les Livres de l'Ancien et de Nouveau Testament*, Paris, 25 vols., 1709–1716, vol. xiv (1715), pp. 542–555. The Danish Archbishop, Joannes Suaningius, in his *Commentarium in Danielem*, 2 vols., folio, Hanniae, 1564, vol. i, pp. 508–4, is frankly rationalistic, and Dr. Richard Mead in his *Medica Sacra*, 1749, cap. vii, is of the same temper. For the Rabbinical traditions concerning Nabuchodonosor, which are very curious, see S. Jerome, Migne, *P.L.*, xxv, col. 1300–2 ; *Biblia Sacra Lyrani*, Lugd., 1589, vol. iv, 2058–9 ; Cornelius à Lapide, *In XII Prophetas Minores*, Lugd., 1625, *In Habacuc*, cap. ii, 15, 16, pp. 61–2.

[91] *Le manuel de l'admirable victoire du corps du Dieu sur l'esprit maling Beelzebub obtenue à Laon* 1566, by Iehan Boulæse, Paris, 16mo, 1575.

[92] Privilège, 9 Avril, 1615.

[93] *Holie Bible*, Doway, 1609, i, p. 177. Exodus, viii, 6, 7.

[94] F. Baptistae Mantuani Carm. Theo. *Fastorum Libri XII*. Argentorati, 1518.

[95] London, Redway, 1887, pp.258–263.

[96] *A Digest of the Writings of Éliphas Lévi*, by A. E. Waite ; London, 1886, pp. 218–220.

[97] *Theosophical Manuals*, No. 3. Third ed. (revised). London, Theo. Pub. Soc., 1900, pp. 58–61.

[98] London, 1865.

[99] London, 1912. Chapter i, pp. 14–15.

[100] A few names may perhaps be briefly mentioned in a note. Voltaire in the *Dictionnaire philosophique* (under *Enchantement*) thought a young shepherd dressed in a wolf's skin settled the whole question. J. G. Keysler in his *Antiquates Selectae Septentrionales et Celticae*, Hanover, 1720, pp. 494–7, has no better suggestion to offer than Crusaders' tales from the East. J. G. Wachter, *Glossarium Germanicum*, Lipsiae, 1737, under *Werwolf* (pp. 1880–2), appears to attribute the belief in werewolfism to some ritual dressing in pelts and furs. Dunlop in his *History of Fiction*, 1814 (new ed., H. Wilson, 1888, Bohn, vol. ii, pp. 542–3), thought that werewolfery " had its foundation in the imposition of pretended sorcerers ", a hint which was eagerly seized upon by Sir E. B. Tylor in his *Primitive Culture* (fourth ed., London, 1903, vol. i, p. 312), who wrote airily enough, as anthropologists wont, of " the tricks of magicians ". De Gubernatis (*Zoological Mythology*, Eng. tr., 2 vols., 1872 ; vol. ii, p. 145) saw in lycanthropy " the zoological transformations of the solar hero ", whatever that may mean. Canon MacCulloch in his *Mediaeval Faith and Fable*, London, 1932 (chapter v, Shape-Shifting), regards " werewolves as lunatics who imagined that they were wolves ". If I read him aright he denies any " diabolic influence in the mental delusion ". This is not surprising since this study, most painful in its frank scepticism, seems throughout almost entirely to reject the supernatural. Canon MacCulloch has a lengthy article, " Lycanthropy," in the *Encyclopædia of Religion and Ethics* (Hastings), vol. viii, 216. The writers in the *Encyclopædia Britannica*, eleventh ed., 1911 (article " Lycanthropy " by N. W. Thomas,

130 THE WEREWOLF

vol. xvii, pp. 149–50, and article " Werwolf ", vol. xxviii, pp. 524–6, N. W. Thomas and J. F. M'Lennan), do not arrive at any definite conclusions concerning these dark problems. Ritual anthropophagy, arising and developed from some forgotten totemic belief, is the fanciful postulate of Mr. Lewis Spence, who seems to be misled by the whimsey that witchcraft was a survival of a so-called " Dianic cult ", " The Cult of the Werwolf in Europe," *Occult Review,* Oct., 1921, vol. xxxiv, No. 4, pp. 221–6.

101 For instances see : *Malleus Maleficarum,* part ii, qn. 1, ch. 8 (Eng. tr., pp. 122–4) ; Remy, ii, 5 (Eng. tr., pp. 108–14) ; Binsfeld, *De Confessionibus Maleficarum,* 3 Conclusio (ed. 1605, pp. 193–204) ; Vincent of Beauvais, *Speculum naturale,* ii, cix (Venice, fo., 1591, tom. i, p. 26) ; Baptista Fulgosi, *Dictorum Factorumque Mirabilium,* viii, xi, " Recentiora " (folio, Basle, 1555, p. 989) ; Prierias, *De strigimagibus,* ii, viii, Ed. 1521, Romae, pp. 105 (uerso)–109, actually the pages are not numbered, Sigs. cc ii–dd ii ; Pico de Mirandola, *Strix . . . Dialogi tres,* ed. Argentorati, 1612, pp. 81, 135–9, 156–9 ; Simone Maiolo, *Dies Caniculares,* coll. ii, ed. 1691, pp. 28–9.

102 *Opera,* Quaracchi, tom. ii (1885), pp. 204–5. " Daemonum consilium uel auxilium non potest requiri absque peccato."

103 *Compendium Mal.,* ii, i, Eng. tr., p. 84.

104 " Nudata tota." *De Miraculis Rerum Naturalium,* Antuerpiae, 1560, lib. ii, xxvi.

105 Ed. Buecheler, Berolini, 1895 (Iterato), 61 and 62, pp. 40–1.

106 " Michael in lupum transfigurabatur uestitus, Petrus uero exutus." De. Mag. Poenis. vi, xiv. *Opera Omnia,* Amstedolami, 1660, p. 497.

107 *Tableau de l'Inconstance,* Paris, 1613, livre iv, p. 290.

108 Folio, Bononiae, 1637, lib. i, cap. vi, p. 149.

109 Eng. tr., p. 84.

110 Eng. tr., pp. 146, 150–1, and 69.

111 *Inconstance,* u.s., p. 295.

112 Ed. folio, Moguntiae, 1603, p. 164.

113 Francofurti, 1607, p. 154.

114 p. 322.

115 Virgil, folio, 1697, pp. 39–40, ll. 135–144.

116 p. 85.

117 viii, 2, pp. 219–20.

118 In the " Refutation des Opinions de Iean Wier ", which forms an appendix to the *Demonomanie,* Bodin snibs Weyer for following " l'opinion de *Baptiste Porta* Italien, le louant bien fort ", and describing at length the witch-ointment. He speaks chidingly of " l'Italien Baptiste " and " son liure de la Magie, c'est à dire Sorcellerie ", ed. 1580, pp. 231–2. In livre iv, ch. 5, Bodin calls upon the magistrates " de brusler sur le champ tous liures de magie " (p. 208).

119 *Opera,* Amstedolami, 1660, pp. 222–5.

120 Folio, Basileæ, 1557, p. 500.

121 *Examen,* Eng. tr., ch. xxvi, pp. 77–80 : *Whether Witches Afflict with Words.*

122 Vair, *De Fascino,* Paris, 1583, lib. ii, cap. xi, pp. 137–160. Bodin, *Demonomanie,* ed. 1580, livre ii, ii, pp. 60–2. Speaking of muttered spells he justly says : " Et ne se peut faire par la vertu des paroles . . . mais le Diable est le seul autheur, & ministre de telles fascinations."

123 1872, p. 406.

124 Col. Agrippinae, 1594, p. 282.

125 *Historia Septentrionalis,* Romae, 1555, xviii, cxlv, p. 643. But in the English translation which I quote in the text, folio, 1658, book xviii, chapter xxxii (p. 193). The English version is an abridgement (in parts) of the original, and when citing this for the flavour of the phrase sake, I have compared the translation with the original, and amended or added as necessary.

126 See Montague Summers, *History of Witchcraft,* London, 1926, ch. iii, pp. 82–8.

127 *Compendium,* Eng. tr., book i, ch. vi, pp. 13–19. Also Sinistrari,

Demoniality, Eng. tr. by Montague Summers, 1927, pp. 8–9, with notes pp. 104–5.

[128] *Dœmonomagia,* 1607, p. 155.

[129] *Dialogue de la Lycanthropie,* 1596, p. 38.

[130] Ed. ut cit. sup., folio, 1608, lib. ii, q. xviii, p. 165.

[131] *Restitution,* p. 237.

[132] Ut cit. sup., p. 164.

[133] *Dœmonomagia,* 1607, p. 153.

[134] *Tableau de l'Inconstance,* livre iv, p. 310, and pp. 260–1.

[135] Eng. tr., chapter xlvii, p. 150.

[136] *Otia Imperialia,* ed. Felix Liebricht, Hanover, 1886. Tertia Decisio, cxx, pp. 51–2.

[137] Various legends concerning the wolf will be found in De Gubernatis, *Zoological Mythology,* 1872, vol. ii, ch. xi, pp. 141–152.

[138] " Potum in ursinam rabiem agat." *Naturalis Historia,* apud Hackios, 1669, t. i, p. 536.

[139] *De Maleficio Affectis,* iv, cap. xxiii, 6. *Opera Omnia,* Amstedolami, 1660, p. 836.

[140] English tr., ut cit., p. 154.

[141] *Malleus,* part ii, qn. 2, ch. 4.

[142] *Speculum Naturale,* ii, cap. cix. Folio, Venice, 1591, tom. i, p. 26.

[143] Ut cit. sup., pp. 51–2.

[144] J. Bonnafoux, *Legendes et Croyances Superstitieuses de la Creuse,* Guéret, 1867, p. 27.

[145] J. F. Bladé, *Contes et Proverbes Populaires recueillis en Armagnac,* Paris, 1867, p. 51.

[146] Paul Sebillot, *Le Folk-lore de France,* Paris 1904–7, t. ii, p. 205 ; Wigrin de Taillefer, *Antiquités de Vésone,* i, p. 250 ; J. L. M. Noguès, *Les Moeurs d'autrefois en Saintonge et en Aunis,* Saintes, 1891, p. 233 ; Americ-Jean-Marie Gautier, *Statistique du département de la Charente-Inférieure,* La Rochelle, 1839, p. 235.

[147] A. de Chesnil, *Usages de la Montagne-Noir,* p. 374.

[148] J. Bonnafoux, *Legendes* . . . ut cit., p. 28.

[149] Part ii, qn. 2, ch. 4, Eng. tr., pp. 173–5.

[150] Migne, *Patres Latini,* tom. iii, 1198.

[151] Ibid., tom. iv, 574–5.

[152] " Stephanus Baluzius Tutelensis in unum collegit, magnam partem nunc primum [anno 1677] edidit, reliquas emendauit."

[153] For other similar details and traditions see Jacob Grimm, *Teutonic Mythology,* tr. from the 4th edition by J. S. Stallybrass, 4 vols. : vol. iii (1883), pp. 1093–9 ; and also for further notes, vol. iv (1886), pp. 1629–30.

[154] *Examen,* xlvii, Eng. tr., p. 151.

[155] This is a conflation of three lines from Ovid, *Metamorphoseon,* i, l. 239, l. 234, and l. 235. In the last line, " et nunc quoque sanguine gaudet " has been changed to " et fuso iam sanguine gaudet ".

[156] *Tableau de l'Inconstance,* livre iv, p. 296.

[157] Ibid., p. 309.

[158] Ibid., p. 309.

[159] See Montague Summers, *The History of Witchcraft,* 1926, pp. 70–5 and p. 89.

[160] " A man whose eyebrows meet . . . may be marked by this sign either as a werewolf or a vampire." Tylor, *Primitive Culture,* 4th ed., 1903, vol. ii, p. 198. Jacob Grimm (ut sup.) quotes Thiele, i, 133, to the effect that if a man's eyebrows meet over his nose, although retaining a human shape by day, at night he will become a wolf. See also C. G. Seligmann, *Der böse Blick,* Berlin, 1910, i, 75 ; and Blaer, *Das Altjüdische Zauberwesen,* Strassburg, 1898, p. 153.

[161] 1926, vol. i, chapter 8, p. 419.

[162] Grimm, op. cit., vol. iv, p. 1630.

[163] *Tableau de l'Inconstance,* livre iv, p. 323.

[164] *Opera Omnia,* folio, Venice, 1606, p. 117. " Nam quamuis magica

arte fiant multa signa, uel per medium naturae, quod possunt angeli, sed
etiam daemones, sola tamen illa miracula dicenda sunt quae operatur Uerbum
per ministeria angelorum, quibus hoc in priuilegium praestari dignatur,
aut per Sanctos, in quibus Idem."

[165] Job, ii, 6.

[166] *In Primam Secundae S.*, *Romae*, folio, Venice, 1589, p. 962. Art.
Decimus, Quaest. 113 ; v ; *De iustificatione impii.* For Conrad Koellin see
Quétif and Echard, *Scriptores Ordinis Praedicatorum*, folio, Paris, 1721,
tom. ii, p. 100.

[167] *Demonomanie*, 1580, p. 241.

[168] Eng. tr., p. 123.

[169] *Demonolatry*, book ii, ch. 5. Eng. tr., 1930, pp. 108–114.

[170] Part ii, qn. ch. 8, Eng. tr., p. 123.

[171] *Examen*, c. xlvii, Eng. tr., p. 146.

[172] *Compendium*, book i, ch. xiii, Eng. tr., p. 51.

[173] Ibid.

[174] *L'Incredulite Sçavante*, Lyon, 1678. Discours xxx and Discours xxxi,
pp. 890–908.

[175] Eng. tr., p. 73.

[176] *L'Incredulite Sçavante*, Lyon, 1678, p. 900.

[177] *Compendium*, book i, ch. xiii, Eng. tr., p. 51.

[178] *Examen*, ch. xlvii, Eng. tr., pp. 146–151.

[179] Bodin, *Demonomanie*, ii, vi.

CHAPTER III

GREECE, ITALY, SPAIN, AND PORTUGAL

FAR to the north of Europe, as the ancients knew it, in the centre of the region which now comprises Poland and Lithuania, about the river-basin of the Bug, dwelt the nomad Neuri, a mysterious and wellnigh unknown folk who were reputed enchanters of mickle might (γόητες), as, indeed, are the Shamans among Siberian vagroms of to-day. Concerning the Neuri, the Father of History, Herodotus of Halicarnassus (484–c. 404), writes in his Fourth Book, *Melpomene* [1]: " The Neuri have the same customs as the Scythians. In the generation before that land was invaded by Darius the whole nation was forced to migrate on account of the plague of serpents, since not only did their own territory produce very many, but even vaster numbers thrust in on them from the deserts of the north. Being thus tormented they abandoned their native soil and took refuge with the Budini. It appears that the Neuri are sorcerers, and such they are confidently held to be both by the Scythians and by the Greek settlers in Scythia, who relate that once every year each Neurian becomes a wolf for a few days, and then again resumes his original form. This, however, they will never persuade me to believe, although they assert it roundly and confirm their statement by a solemn oath."

Pomponius Mela, in his *De Situ Orbis, Of the Situation of the World*, II, i, follows Herodotus : " The Neures haue a certaine time to euerie of them limitted, wherein they may (if they wil) be chaunged into Woolues, and returne to their former shape againe." [2]

Herman Hirt, *Die Indogermanen*, I, i, 18, " Das Baltisch-Slavische," remarks : " Wir können die Neuren nicht einmal mit Sicherheit für einen slavischen Volksstamm halten. Man sieht in ihnen eigentlich nur deshalb Slaven, weil von den Neuren berichtet wird, dass sich jeder einmal in einen Wolf verwandle, worin offenbar die Sage vom Werwolf verleigt. Abu wenn diese Sage auch bei den Slaven weit

133

verbreitet ist, so ist sie doch nicht auf diesen Volksstamm
beschränkt. Ausserdem hat man den Namen *Neuren* mit
dem slavischen Worte *nurija* ' territorium ' zusammer
gebracht, aber dies ist sicher aus dem Griechischen ἐνορία
entlehnt." [3]

The attempted explanation of Adolf Erman,[4] who ascribes
the metamorphosis of the Neuri into wolves as a legend due
to their appearance in the winter months wrapped in thick
furs, is trivial to the last degree. It is very plain that werewolfism was rampant among this boreal tribe of witches.

Pausanias, in the Eighth Book of his *Description of Greece*,
a section which must have been written after A.D. 166, and
was indeed probably composed at least a decade later,[5]
when dealing with Arcadia, speaks of the werewolfism still
prevailing in those districts. So important is his testimony
to these magical rites that the pertinent passages must be
quoted in full : " The Arcadians say that Pelasgus was the
first man who lived in this land . . . Pelasgus' son Lycaon
outdid his father in the ingenuity of the schemes he projected.
For he built a city Lycosura on Mount Lycaeus, he gave to
Zeus the surname of Lycaean, and he founded the Lucaean
games. . . . In my opinion Lycaon was contemporary with
Cecrops, king of Athens. . . . Cecrops was the first who
gave to Zeus the surname of Supreme,[6] and he refused to
sacrifice anything that had life. . . . Whereas Lycaon
brought a human babe to the altar of Lycaean Zeus, and
sacrificed it, and poured out the blood on the altar ; and
they say that immediately after the sacrifice he was turned
into a wolf. For my own part I believe the tale : it has been
handed down among the Arcadians from antiquity, and
probability is in its favour. . . . They say that from the
time of Lycaon downwards a man has always been turned
into a wolf at the sacrifice of Lycaean Zeus, but that the
transformation is not for life ; for if, while he is a wolf, he
abstains from human flesh, in the ninth year afterwards he
changes back into a man, but if he has tasted human flesh
he remains a beast for ever." [7]

In chapter xxxviii of the same book Pausanias describes
Lycosura, which he deems the oldest of all cities on earth.
To the left is Mount Lycaeus, the Sacred Peak of Arcady.
Actually Lycosura, which was excavated 1889–1895, is

about five miles from Mount Lycaeus, of which I made the ascent from the little village of Karyaes or Isioma. The journey occupies three-quarters of an hour to an hour, the traveller passing through a most attractive country. To-day Mount Lycaeus is known as Diaphorti or Mount S. Elias, from a chapel dedicated to that Saint,[8] which is built near the summit. There are two peaks, the higher being Stephani; whilst the lower, Mount S. Elias, is the ancient Lycaeus. Here is an artificial platform strewn with blocks of stone and other fragments plainly marking the site of the temple of Zeus Lycaeus, which must (I suppose) be one of the most terribly haunted places in the world. The summit is about a quarter of an hour from the simple shrine of the Saint, to whose protection those ascending as far as the top will do well to commend themselves in all sincerity.

The panorama spread out beneath as one gazes from the crest of the mountain is indeed magnificent, a landscape extending over the broad plains of Megapolis, Elis, and Messenia, whilst to the west the sea is visible as far as Zakynthos.

Extremely significant is the reserve of Pausanias as he goes on to speak concerning the worship on that Mount : " Of the wonders of Mount Lycaeus the greatest is this. There is a precinct of Lycaean Zeus on the mountain and people are not allowed to enter it ; but if any one disregards the rule and enters, he cannot possibly live more than a year. It is also said that inside the precinct all creatures, whether man or beast, cast no shadows [9] ; and, therefore, if his quarry takes refuge in the precinct, the huntsman will not follow it, but waits outside, and looking at the beast he sees that it casts no shadow . . .

" On the topmost peak of the mountain there is an altar of Lycaean Zeus in the shape of a mound of earth, and most of Peloponnese is visible from it. In front of the altar, on the east, stand two pillars, on which there used formerly to be gilded eagles. On this altar they offer secret sacrifices to Lycaean Zeus, but I do not care to pry into the details of the sacrifice. Be it as it is and has been from the beginning."[10]

" Very evil was the beginning," justly comments Sir William Ridgeway,[11] for Lycaon, son of Pelasgos, sacrificed a human babe to the demon there. Not without reason has it been suggested that the Zeus who was secretly worshipped with ritual bloody and obscene upon the mountain heights of Arcady may well have been some Semitic Baal imported by Phœnicians from the Syrian groves and hills.[12]

Arcadia itself was the cradle of the human family, primitive tradition aversed. The people who dwelled there were the oldest of all races, elder brothers of the sun and moon.[13] Their land was enclosed on all sides by great ranges, Cyllene and Erymanthus, Artemisius, Parthenius, and dread Maenalus, the sanctuary of Pan.[14] Fabled Alpheus, that stream which in his course sank beneath the earth, rose at Phylace. The story of Lycaon takes us back to remotest antiquity, to the days before a flood covered the world, the age of the Giants and the Titans, for Lycaon was the son of Pelasgos, who was the son of Mother Earth. And it was when Nyktimos, the son of Lycaon, ruled in his father's room that the deluge of Deucalion overswept the continents.

We have seen what Pausanias has to say of the sacrifice of Lycaon, but other authors give different stories. Apollodorus in his *Bibliotheca*[15] relates that Lycaon, the son of Pelasgos, was by many wives the father of fifty sons,[16] whose names he duly chronicles.[17] Now these sons were impious and proud above all other men. In order to prove them, under the guise of a wayfarer weary and seeking hospitality Father Zeus visited their palaces, and in mockery they slew a child at the hest of cruel Maenalus, commingling his warm entrails with the savoury mess they served up to the guest. But then in wrath the god arose, and overturning the table—whence the place is called Trapezus (Τραπεζοῦς) to this day—he blasted King Lycaon and his son with the red levin bolt. Nuktimos, the youngest, alone was spared, for old Mother Earth stayed the hand of the angry god.

Hyginus, in his *Fabulae*,[18] says that Zeus sought hospitality with Lycaon, the son of Pelasgos, being fired with love for the king's daughter Callisto, whom he presently enjoyed, and Arcas was born. In the *Poeticon Astronomicon*[19] the same author has it that Arcas was sacrificed by Lycaon, as also Eratosthenes tells in the *Catasterismoi*.[20] Lycaon was turned into a wolf, his sons struck by the thunderbolt.

In the *Alexandra*[21] of Lycophron are two lines :

χερσαῖος αὐτόδαιτος ἐγγόνων δρυὸς
λυκαινομόρφων Νυκτίμου κρεανόμων,

upon which the old scholiast, whose work was so ably used
by Isaac and John Tzetzes, glosses allowing two versions
of the tale, either that when Lycaon and his sons had mingled
the boiled flesh of Nuktimos with the fare set before Zeus
the outraged deity turned them all into wolves, or that he
destroyed them with thunder and Mother Earth alone
prevented him from ravaging all Arcady.[22]

Nicolaus Damascenus,[23] the friend of Augustus Caesar
and Herod the Great, knows yet another version of the
story. In his *History* he tells that Lycaon himself was
righteous, but that his sons were impious and profane.
Sleeveless was his warning that Zeus in the form of a stranger
every day assisted at the solemn sacrifice. In evil jest they
slew a child and mingled his members with the meat offered
upon the altar, saying, " Let the god discern ! " Whereupon
consuming fire fell upon them from heaven.

Ovid in the *Metamorphoses*, book i,[24] makes Jupiter speak
thus to the synod of Olympus :—

> The Clamours of this vile degenerate Age,
> The Cries of Orphans, and th' Oppressor's Rage
> Had reach'd the Stars ; I will descend, said I,
> In hope to prove this loud Complaint a Lye.
> Disguis'd in Humane Shape, I Travell'd round
> The World, and more than what I hear'd, I found.
> O're *Mœnalus* I took my steepy way,
> By Caverns infamous for Beasts of Prey :
> Then cross'd *Cyllenè*, and the piny shade
> More infamous, by Curst *Lycaon* made.
> Dark Night had cover'd Heav'n and Earth, before
> I enter'd his Unhospitable Door.
> Just at my entrance, I display'd the Sign
> That somewhat was approaching of Divine.
> The prostrate People pray ; the Tyrant grins ;
> And, adding Prophanation to his Sins,
> I'll try, said he, and if a God appear
> To prove his Deity, shall cost him dear.
> Twas late ; the Graceless Wretch, my Death prepares,
> When I shou'd soundly Sleep, opprest with Cares :
> This dire Experiment, he chose, to prove
> If I were Mortal, or undoubted *Jove* :
> But first he had resolv'd to taste my Pow'r ;
> Not long before, but in a luckless hour
> Some Legates, sent from the *Molossian* State,
> Were on a peaceful Errant come to Treat :

Of these he Murders one, he boils the Flesh ;
And lays the mangl'd Morsels in a Dish :
Some part he Roasts ; then serves it up, so drest,
And bids me welcome to this Humane Feast.
Mov'd with disdain, the Table I o're-turn'd ;
And with avenging Flames, the Palace burn'd.
The Tyrant in a fright, for shelter, gains
The Neighb'ring Fields, and scours along the plains.
Howling he fled, and fain he wou'd have spoke ;
But Humane Voice, his Brutal Tongue forsook.
About his lips, the gather'd foam he churns,
And, breathing slaughters, still with rage he burns,
But on the bleating Flock, his fury turns.
His Mantle, now his Hide, with rugged hairs
Cleaves to his back, a famish'd face he bears.
His arms descend, his shoulders sink away,
To multiply his legs for chace of Prey.
He grows a Wolf, his hoariness remains,
And the same rage in other Members reigns.
His eyes still sparkle in a narr'wer space :
His jaws retain the grin, and violence of face.

According to Ovid, then, the tyrant Lycaon in order to test the power of his visitor places before him at a banquet the flesh of a Molossian whom he has foully slain, mingled with the baked meats of the day. The outraged deity destroys his palace in flames and transforms him to a howling wolf. Crime upon crime are heaped upon the head of Lycaon, who in Ovid's poem outrages every law human and divine. We do not know how far Ovid modified or altered the incidents of his story, nor indeed from what author he may have derived it nor under what form.

We are on surer ground with Pliny, who in his *Naturall Historie*, book viii, chapter xxii, adds further important details. The passage in question is as follows : " That men may be transformed into wolves, and restored againe to their former shape, we must confidently believe to be a lowd lie, or else give credit to all those tales which wee have for so many ages found to be meere fabulous untruths. But how this opinion grew first, and is come to be so firmly setled, that when wee would give men the most opprobrious words of defiance that we can, wee tearme them *Versipelles* (i.e. Turn-coats), I thinke it not much amisse in a word to shew. *Euanthes* (a writer among the Greekes, of good account and authoritie) reporteth, that hee found among the records of the Arcadians, That in Arcadia there was a certain house

and race of the *Antæi*, out of which one evermore must of
necessitie be transformed into a wolfe : and when they of
that familie have cast lots who it shall be, they use to
accompanie the partie upon whome the lot is falne, to
a certaine meere or poole in that countrey : when he is
thither come, they turne him naked out of all his clothes,
which they hang upon an oke thereby : then he swimmeth
over the said lake to the other side, and being entred into
the wildernesse, is presently transfigured and turned into a
wolfe, and so keepeth companie with his like of that kind
for nine yeeres space : during which time, (if he forbeare
all the while to eat mans flesh) he returneth againe to the
same poole or pond, and being swomme over it, receiveth
his former shape againe of a man, save onely that hee shall
looke nine yeeres elder than before. *Fabius* addeth one
thing more and saith, That he findeth againe the same apparele
that was hung up in the oke aforesaid. A wonder it is to see,
to what passe these Greekes are come in their credulitie :
there is not so shamelesse a lye, but it findeth one or other
of them to uphold and maintaine it. And therefore *Agriopas*,
who wrote the Olympionicæ, telleth a tale of one *Dæmœtus
Parrhasius*, That he upon a time at a certain solemne sacrifice
(which the Arcadians celebrated in honour of *Iupiter Lycœus*)
tasted of the inwards of a child that was killed for a sacrifice,
according to the manner of the Arcadians (which even was
to shed mans blood in their divine service) and so was turned
into a wolfe : and the same man ten yeeres after became a
man againe, was present at the exercise of publicke games,
wrestled, did his devoir, and went away with victorie home
againe from Olympia. Over and besides, it is commonly
thought and verily beleeved, that in the taile of this beast,
there is a little string or haire that is effectuall to procure
love, and that when he is taken at any time, hee casteth it
away from him, for that it is of no force and vertue unlesse
it be taken from him whiles he is alive. He goeth to rut in
the whole yeere not above twelve daies."

For the sake of the flavour and the vigour of his phrase
I quote old Philemon Holland's translation of Pliny,[25] but
there are one or two points which call for amendment. In
the first place it must be noted that the name *Fabius* [26]
is due to following a corruption in the MS., and the passage

should more correctly run : "He addeth one thing more."
There are several variants of the name *Agriopas* ; Kalkmann
and Mayhoff both prefer Apollas ; Gelenius has Agriopas ;
Jahn and Detlefsen conjecture Copas or Scopas.

Unfortunately it is impossible to identify the authors
whom Pliny quotes. Evanthes may be the historian of
Miletus who is mentioned by Diogenes Laertius [27] ; or
Evanthes of Samos to whom there is a single reference in
Plutarch [28] ; or yet again Evanthes, the author of μυθικά,
who is spoken of by the Scholiast on Apollonius Rhodius.[29]
He may even be another Evanthes concerning whom nothing
is known. Owing to the corruption of the MSS. as noted
above it were idle to attempt to guess the date of Agriopas
or Apollas or Scopas, whichever name it is selected to read.

M. Terentius Varro Reatinus, "Romanorum doctissimus," [30] in the *Antiquitates Rerum Diuinarum*, which was
the second part of his great work *Antiquitatum Libri*, than
the loss of which there have been few more serious misfortunes
to scholarship, dealt in some detail with shape-shifting and
is quoted by S. Augustine in the *De Ciuitate Dei*, xviii, xvii,
where the holy Doctor speaks of "Pan Lycaeus" and
"Iuppiter Lycaeus", both of whom were worshipped in
Arcadia, and whose cults had some mysterious connection
with the metamorphosis of men into wolves, a transformation
"which could only be wrought by some supernatural power ".

S. Isidore also mentions the "sacrifice which the Arcadian
offered to their god Lycaeus, and of which whosoever partook
was changed into beastial shape ".[31]

Solinus, it may be remarked, who echoes Varro in his
account of Arcadia, writes briefly "in qua montes Cyllene
et Lycaeus, Maenalus etiam diis alumnis inclaruerunt ", but
curiously enough he does not refer to the wolf-cult or to any
shape-shifting.[32]

Professor Robertson Smith thought that the worship of
this god on Mount Lycaeus was the cult of a wolf-clan, and
that Zeus Λύκειος was the god of the clan. Thus Lycaon,
who sacrifices his son and is changed into a wolf, "may
darkly figure the god himself." [33] This theory is provisionally
allowed as possible by Dr. Farnell and Sir William Ridgeway,
both of whom, however, justly show a marked reluctance to
press it too far. Dr. Farnell writes [34] : "The strangest, and

in some respects, most savage was the Arcadian worship of
Zeus on Mount Lycaeum, a worship that belonged to the
pre-historic period, and continued at least till the time of
Pausanias without losing its dark and repellent aspect . . .
it was chiefly as a god who demanded and received human
sacrifice that Zeus Lyceius was known and dreaded . . .
The human sacrifice is a noteworthy fact of very rare
occurrence in the worship of Zeus . . . The rite of human
sacrifice on Mount Lycaeum, and at Alus, whatever its
original significance may have been, seems to have become
connected with a sense of sin and the necessity for expiation,
that is, with the germ of a moral idea. We might perhaps
be able to say how far this conception of Zeus Lycaeus, as
a god who demanded atonement for sin, advanced to any
spiritual expression, if the ode of Alcman that commemorated
this worship had been preserved."

Sir William Ridgeway writes of the sacrifices to Zeus
Lycaeus [35] : " It is possible that the story of the transformation of some one of those present into a wolf may have arisen
from the circumstance that as the medicine-men of modern
totem clans often get themselves up like their totem animal,
so the priest who officiated at the Lycaean rite may have
arrayed himself in a wolf-skin."

H. D. Müller [36] suggested that the belief in Arcadian
lycanthropy may have arisen from dramatic representations
and dancers dressed in wolf-skin about the altar of the god.
This theory is wholly untenable.

Mons. G. Fourgères sums up a very ample study *Lykaia* [37]
(τα Λύκαια) by setting forth three explanations which have
been advanced concerning the cult of Zeus Lycaeus :—

(1) The worship is that of a sun-god, originally from
Egypt or Phœnicia, where the wolf is a symbol of light. Or
the deity is a god of the underworld, the name being derived
from a root *vl'g*, to rend or tear (cf. *lupus*, *luperci*, and the
Etruscan *lupu* which is *dilacerator*).

(2) The cult is that of a god who was worshipped on high
places, and is of Semitic origin, imported by a Phœnician
race, to which the human sacrifice pretty clearly points.
The sanctuary then is of the Syrian Maabeds, and Zeus
Lycaeus is the same as Baal-Louki, a Moloch cult such as
Baal-Libau, Baal-Hasios, and Baal-Hermon.

(3) The cult is that of a totem. The wolf-god was the primitive deity of the aborigines of Arcadia, in which case the human sacrifices were the cannibalistic feasts of a tribe of wolf-men whose totem was the wolf.

Although I will not attempt to decide definitely between these three suggested origins, and it is indeed an inquiry unessential to the point in view, it seems more probable that Zeus Lykaios may indeed be regarded as a Baal of the Moloch cult, such a god as was worshipped " upon high mountains, and hills " [38] (super montes excelsos et colles) with bloody and obscene rites, a deity who was in truth a demon of hell.

There is an allusion in Plato's *Republic*, book viii, to the Arcadian cult as follows : " What are the first steps in the transformation of the champion into a tyrant ? Can we doubt that the change dates from the time when the champion has begun to act like the man in that legend which is current in reference to the temple of Lykaean Zeus in Arcadia ?

" What legend ?

" According to it, the worshipper who tasted the one human entrail, which was mixed up with the other entrails of other victims, was inevitably metamorphosed into a wolf. Have you never heard the story ?

" Yes, I have.

" In like manner, should the people's champion find the mobile so very compliant that he need make no scruple of shedding kindred blood, should he . . . render himself blood-guilty, making away with human life, and tasting the blood of his fellows with unholy tongue and lips defiled . . . is it not thenceforth the inevitable destiny of such a man either to be destroyed by his enemies, or to become a tyrant, and so to be transformed from a man into a very wolf ? "

Strabo in his *Geographica*, viii, 388,[39] notes that in his day, the reign of Augustus Cæsar, the sanctuary of Zeus Lykaios was wellnigh deserted.

It should be mentioned, moreover, in connection with the rites of Mount Lycaeus that Zeus was under one aspect regarded as an elemental power, a rain god, for in times of drought the Arcadian wizard ascended to the summit of the mountain and propitiated the god by certain sacrifices and ceremonies thus ensuring the rain.[40] The authors of the

PLATE IV

FIGURE *de la Bête feroce que l'on nomme l'hyenne, qui devore plus que 80 personnes dans le Gevaudan.*

A — F.
R. Mangin 1765

J. Lepy sculp.

A Representation of the Wild Beast of the Gevaudan, who is said to have devoured upwards of 80 Persons. From a drawing now in p. 1765 in the hands of Mompton in Normandy.

THE WILD BEAST OF THE GEVAUDAN
(See p. 235)

[face p. 142

Malleus Maleficarum, part ii, question 1, chapter 15,[41] tell
how devils and their disciples can cause rain and storm,
disturb the air and raise up winds, and give us many examples
of the same. Remy in his *Demonolatry*, book i, chapter xxv,[42]
explains that witches have the power of raising the clouds
and shaking them down in rain on the earth. Guazzo, also,
in his *Compendium Maleficarum*,[43] book 1, chapter vii,
shows that " It is most clearly proved by experience that
witches can control not only the rain and the hail and the
wind, but even the lightning when God permits ". Very
many other authorities might be cited to the same effect,
for there is a profusion of evidence. The Arcadian priests,
then, were deeply versed in black magic.

The cult of Zeus Lykaios, the human sacrifice, the killing
of babes,[44] the werewolfism, and in fact every detail may be
exactly paralleled in the worship of the Satanists, and there
can be no doubt that among the Arcadians sorcery and
witchcraft were rife, the synagogue of the witches being
Mount Lycaeus.

The wolf is very closely and very mysteriously connected
with yet another Panhellenic deity, the god Apollo, to
whom it may at the outset be noted that human sacrifice
was offered at Leukas and in Cyprus.[45] In the Dorian
epoch the Argives worshipped Apollo Lykaios, Λύκειος.[46]
Dr. Farnell even ventures to say that the wolf is far more
intimately at home in the legend and ritual of Apollo Λύκειος
than in the legend and ritual of the Arcadian Zeus Λυκαῖος.[47]
Be that as it may, and whatever the real derivation of the
epithet Λυκαῖος, it is clear enough that werewolfism even
if not an original circumstance of the worship of Arcadian
Zeus on Mount Lycaeus, was at any rate soon grafted into
that horrid liturgy. When Leto was in her pains the wolves
led her, who was in the form of a she-wolf,[48] from the Hyper-
boreans of the north to the isle of Delos [49]—some say to the
river Xanthos [50] in Lycia—and then she gave birth, whence
Pandaros in the *Iliad* [51] calls Apollo " Son of the She-
Wolf ", Λυκηγενής.[52] The wolf shape was on occasion assumed
by the god. As a wolf he destroyed the wizard Telchiries [53];
as a wolf he covered Kyrene, who bare him Aristaios.[54] The
Wolf was sacrificed to Apollo at Argos,[55] and " being then
the familiar animal, and at times the sacrificial victim, it is

probable that the wolf was in some way regarded as 'the double' or the incarnation of the deity ".[56]

Ælian states that the people of Delphi worshipped the wolf,[57] Clement of Alexandria mentions that divine honours were paid to the wolf by the Lycopolites, and according to the Scholiast on Apollonius Rhodius,[58] " the wolf was a beast held in honour by the Athenians, and whosoever slays a wolf collects what is needful for its burial."

It seems probable that it was as Λύκειος, the wolf, that the god first pronounced his oracles and assumed his mantic character.[59]

Various later legends were invented to explain the term Wolf-god, such as that which said that when Apollo served Admetus it was his task to kill the wolves who molested his flocks,[60] or that when Athens was infested by wolves he bade the citizens sacrifice on the site of the Lyceum, and there they dedicated a temple to the god since the smell of the holocaust had driven the animals from the spot.[61] At Sikyon, too, there was a shrine of Apollo Lykaios, who had counselled the Sikyonians to mingle the bark of a certain tree with meat and set it out for the marauding wolves. They did so, and the beasts were poisoned by the bark. The tree they laid up in the sanctuary of the Wolfish God, but no man knew of what wood it was.[62]

Dr. Farnell hints that it is not impossible that the Attic hero Λύκος, whose statue as a wolf stood near the law-courts, was merely a degenerate form of the god. In the *Heroicus* [63] of Philostratus Apollo Lykaios is named Φύξιος, but this perhaps can hardly be pressed to mean that the wolf-god protected the exile, although if such were the case we find an interesting parallel in the laws of the Franks and Normans, among the Anglo-Saxons and in later England,[64] and it is certain that the connection between the wolf and outlawry is of very ancient date.

That werewolfism was practised in the worship of Apollo as in the cult of Arcadian Zeus can hardly be doubted. It was an old temple of Apollo, surrounded with a grove in which certain sorcerers and idolators continued their abominable rites on the summit of Monte Cassino, that S. Benedict destroyed in 529 to build two fair chapels there under the invocation of S. Martin and S. John. Round about

the ancient pagan oratory " upon all sides there were woods
for the service of devils, in which, even to that very time,
the mad multitudes of infidels did offer most wicked
sacrifice ".[65] Although not expressly stated, it seems more
than probable that werewolfism was practised here amid the
foul mysteries of the demon.

Driven underground or lurking only in the darkest and
dustiest corners, werewolfism yet persisted, and now and
again we catch a curious half-glimpse of these abominations.
Such a one is afforded accidentally enough in the Byzantine
tale which finds a place among the *Fabulae Aesopicae.*[66]
This collection was made in the fourteenth century by the
Basilian Maximus Planudes, one of the most learned of the
Constantinopolitan monks of the last age of the Greek
empire under Andronicus II and III Palaeologi. It is
impossible even to guess at the date or locality of the original
story. A cunning thief put up at a certain wayside hostelry
in the hope that he might be able to spring a partridge or two.
After some shiftless days he noticed that mine host in a
tearing-fine cloak (for it was a festa) had sat him down on
a bench by the inn door. The road was empty, and so
Prince Prig sits him down too and begins a comfortable
gossip. After a bit slyboots yawns horribly and utters a
dismal howl. Mine host soon inquires what a pox the matter
may be. " I' faith, cummer," answers his companion, " you
shall know. First, however, I am going to ask you to keep
a sharp eye on my clothes for me. I protest I cannot tell
why I should be seized with these sudden gapings and
yawns, for my sins I shouldn't wonder, or on some other
old account, I can't imagine what. But after I have yawned
thrice, just like that, hey presto ! I turn into a huge wolf—
one of those beasts that gobble men in a trice, bones and all."
At this up jumps mine host in a very great hurry, and is
rubbing off fast enough. But the thief clutched tight of his
cloak, bawling out, " Pray, good sir, wait a bit until I give
you my clothes, for I don't want to miss 'em." As he spoke,
he nearly cracked his jaws with gaping a third time. Whereon
mine host, little minded to be made a meal of, in a sad fright
bolted rous through the door, which he took good care to
double lock and bar behind him, leaving his cloak to shift
for itself. So the budge nims the togeman, and Prince Prig

is off on his way to see more of the world. Moral : We must not believe everything we hear.

From the frank simplicity of this little tale we can judge how constant was the belief in shape-shifting and what a very real and present danger the werewolf was conceived to be.

In the year 1542 Constantinople was so plagued by were-wolves that Solyman II, " the Magnificent," at the head of his Janizaries, led an attack against them and destroyed no less than 150 of these monsters who were prowling the streets and lanes of the city. Nor is this at all strange if we consider the terrible doom of Constantinople less than a century before, when amid unspeakable cruelty and carnage an Imperial City of the Christians became the capital of the Ottoman Empire, the monasteries were violated, the churches turned into mosques, and incontinently under the rule of the turban the rank weeds of magic flourished and grew most luxuriantly. Our authority for this incident is Job Fincel, a German physician of the sixteenth century.[67] Born at Weimar, he studied philosophy at Wittemberg, and medicine at Jena, where he proceeded Doctor in 1552. At this University he occupied the Chair of Philosophy, and was afterwards aggregated to the Faculty of Medicine. However, he soon returned to Weimar, where he practised as a consulting physician until 1568, after which he resided at Zwichau in the same capacity. He died at this town, but the date is uncertain. He wrote a *De Peste*, Wittemberg, 8vo, 1598, and his elegant Epithalamium *In Nuptiis Dauidis Chytrœi* may be found in the *Delitiae Poetarum Germanorum*.[68] His most important work is the *Wunderzeichen, Warhafftige, Beschreibung und gründlich verzeicnus schrecklicher Wunderzeichen und Geschichten, die von . . . MDXVII. bisauff . . . MDLVI. geschechen und ergangen sind, noch der Jarzal . . ,* Jhena, 1556.

Throughout the centuries lycanthropy has been known to the Greeks, and it is terribly prevalent in Eastern Europe to-day, a horrid legacy from Arcadia of old, so difficult is it to eradicate the foul arts of sorcery, so sleepless is Satan in his craft.

The Rev. H. F. Tozer, in his *Researches in the Highlands of Turkey*,[69] writing upon " The Vrykolaka, or Eastern

Vampire ", remarks : " Mr. Baring Gould in his ' Book of Were-Wolves' has spoken of the *Vrykolaka* as if it was identical with the were-wolf, and says that those who are believed to be lycanthropists during life become vampires after death. This, however, is, I think, a mistake. In the great majority of cases the were-wolf superstition is wholly independent of this belief ; so much so, that one writer, who has carefully collected the authorities on the subject, expresses his opinion that the nature of the were-wolf is no longer to be recognized in the modern Greek *Vrykolaka*.[70] Among the Wallachians, however, there is a kind of *murony* that corresponds to the belief in kynanthropy, which is one of the forms of the same superstition. This is described as ' a real living man, who has the peculiarity of roaming by night as a dog over heaths, pastures, and even villages, killing with his touch horses, cows, sheep, swine, goats, and other animals in his passage, and appropriating to himself their vital forces, by means of which he has the appearance of being in continual health and vigour '.[71] The name of this being, the *priccolitsch*, is evidently another form of *vrykolaka* ; from which it is probable that the modern Greek belief was once connected with the same notion, more especially as the idea of lycanthropy was well established among the Greeks in classical times. Indeed, if we may believe M. Cyprien Robert,[72] this same belief is also found as a form of vampirism in Thessaly and Eperus ; but his authority is hardly sufficiently trustworthy to be received on such a subject. Another proof of the connection of the two ideas is found in the notion, that one of the causes which convert men into vampires after death is the eating the flesh of a lamb that has been killed by a wolf. . . . Without entering further on the question of lycanthropy, we may notice how easy the transition is from the one superstition to the other ; for at a very early period in the history of the Indo-European race the wolf, partly as being the great enemy of shepherds and partly, no doubt, from its sinister appearance and habits, came to be regarded as a representative of the evil powers. Hence the Germans and Slavs have always attributed to the wolf a demon nature ; and M. Wachsmuth tells us that he was informed (though I cannot say that this is confirmed by my own observation)

that the modern Greeks are in such fear of this animal
that they shrink from even pronouncing its name."

I do not know why Mr. Tozer should speak so slightingly
of the authority of M. Cyprien Robert, who was the Professor
of Slavonic Letters and Litterature at the College de France,
a distinguished name and a writer who is held in marked
esteem by all other scholars. In his *Les Slaves de Turquie*,
vol. i, Introduction,[73] M. Robert writes : " The people of
Servia and Herzogivina have preserved more than one dark
tradition of unhappy souls who after death are condemned
to wander hither and thither over the earth to expiate their
sins, or who live a horrid life in death in the tomb as *voukodlaks*
or vampires. The *voukodlak* (literally *loup-garou*, werewolf)
sleeps in his grave with open staring eyes ; his nails and
his hair grow to an excessive length, the warm blood pulses
in his veins. When the moon is at her full he issues forth
to run his course, to suck the blood of living men by biting
deep into their dorsal vein. When a dead man is suspected
of leaving his place of sepulture thus, the corpse is solemnly
exhumed ; if it be in a state of putrefaction and decay
sufficient for the priest to sprinkle it with holy water ; if it
be ruddy and fresh-complexioned it is exorcized, and placed
in the earth again, where before it is covered a sharp stake
is thrust through and through the carcass lest it stir forth
once more. Not long since it was customary among the
Serbians to riddle the head of the corpse with their bullets
and then to burn it entire. This is seldom done now, but
they firmly believe that even the carrion crow will shun
the living corpse, and wing fast away from such ill-omened
flesh. In Thessaly, in Epirus, and among the *Vlachi* of the
Pindus district the country-folk believe in another kind of
vampire, one which their fathers also well knew in days of
old. These *vampires* are living men who in a kind of somnam-
bulistic trance are seized by a thirst for blood and prowl forth
at night from their poor shepherd's huts to scour the whole
countryside, biting and fiercely tearing with their teeth all
whom they meet, man or beast. These *voukodlaks*, who are
especially eager to quaff the hot blood of young girls, go to
rut—the peasants say—with the *viechtitsa*, a succubus with
wings of flame who swoops down in the dark hours upon any
fine and gallant fellow as he lies asleep, wellnigh throttling

him in their avid caresses and firing him with unbridled lusts. Sometimes, too, the *viechtitsa* in the shape of a hyaena will carry off children into the depths of some fearsome wood."

In his *Macedonian Folklore* [74] Mr. G. F. Abbott writes : "The 'were-wolf' of English and the 'loup-garou' of French folklore find in the Macedonian 'wild-boar' (ἀγριο-γούρουνο) a not unworthy cousin. The belief, though not quite so general at present as it used to be, cannot be considered extinct yet. According to it, Turks, who have led a particularly wicked life, when at the point of death, turn into wild boars, and the ring worn by the man on his finger is retained on one of the boar's forefeet. The meta-morphosis takes place as follows : the sinner first begins to grunt like a pig (ἀρχινάει νὰ μουγκρίζῃ), he then falls on all fours (τετραποδίζει), and finally rushes out of the house grunting wildly and leaping over hedges, ditches, and rivers until he has reached the open country. At night he visits the houses of his friends, and more especially those of his foes, and knocks at their doors for admittance. He chases with evil intent all those whom he meets in the way, and generally makes himself disagreeable. This he continues doing for forty days, and at the end of that period he betakes himself to the mountains where he abides as a wild beast. . . .

" The Bulgarians hold that Turks who have never eaten pork in life will become wild boars at death. . . . The Bulgarian superstition is practically the same as that of the Melenikiote peasantry, but the latter presents the curious point that the transformation of the Turk into a boar is supposed to occur *before* death and to be gradual. That peculiarity seems to identify it rather with a process of metamorphosis than of metempsychosis, especially as the doctrine of transmigration is so rarely found in Christian countries. . . The Albanians believe in some strange beings which they call *liougat* or *liouvgat*, defined by Hahn [75] as 'Dead Turks, with huge nails, who wrapped up in their winding sheets devour whatever they find and throttle men '.

" Akin both to the above superstition and to [the vampire] is the Wallachian belief in a being called *priccolitsch*."

Mr. J. C. Lawson, in his admirable study *Modern Greek*

Folklore and Ancient Greek Religion,[76] devotes nearly seventy pages to an account of " the most monstrous of all the creatures of the popular imagination " in the Greek-speaking world, the Callicantzaros (καλλικάντζαρος). The diversities of their outward form are almost endless, but their activities have one feature in common—mischief, although this ranges from dirty practical jokes and boisterous pranks to violent assaults, ravishments, and even blood and murder. The Callicantzaros may be a giant, a mere pigmy, or of the stature of a man, yet all are grotesquely and hideously deformed, in spite of which, as Leone Allacci wrote, " they devour a road at the pace of Pegasus," [77] and they are terrible in strength. Gaunt and lean, with fierce red tongues slobbering from great yawning mouths, set with sharp white fangs, often furnished with thin ropy tails, the bestial form here predominates the human.

The Callicantzari are only active in the night hours and appear but during one set period of the year, the δωδεκαήμερον, the twelve days between Christmas and Epiphany. Leone Allacci, even, assigns them a week, Christmas and the octave.

Local tradition differs as to their exact nature, and Mr. Lawson sums up the matter by saying : " On the mainland they are most commonly demons ; in the islands of the Aegean, more usually human." [78] Professor Polites, the great Greek scholar, tells us that in Oenoë it is said " they are really evil demons ", whilst in Tenos they declare " The Callicantzari are not demons ; they are men ; as New Year's Day approaches they are stricken with a fit of madness and leave their house and wander to and fro ".[79]

The tradition of Tenos is distinctly supported by Leone Allacci, who says that in the isle of Chios children born in the octave of Christmas are seized with a madness, during which they range up and down the highways. If they meet a wayfarer they ask him " Tow or lead ? " If he answer the former he passes on unhurt ; if he replies " lead " they attack him and leave him half-dead, lacerating him with their nails which grow long and sharp like claws. He adds that children born at this time had the soles of their feet scorched until the nails were singed so they could not become Callicantzari. This cruel custom is exceedingly significant, for a human being who is disposed to scratch will presumably use his hands, whilst a beast will tear with paws and hind-feet as well.

That werewolfism has been mixed up in popular tradition with the ideas of the Callicantzari is very clear, and this becomes even more certain when we find that in Messenia, in Cynouria (east Laconia), and in districts of Crete the Callicantzari are also known as Λυκοκάντζαροι, of which word the first compound is actually λύκος, wolf. Moreover, in parts of Macedonia Callicantzari are often dubbed plain λύκοι, wolves. In Mykonos, too, they have been described as " savage quadrupeds ".[80]

The Callicantzari are not, indeed, werewolves, but in certain districts the idea of werewolfism is a not unimportant factor in the tradition concerning these monstrous beasts.

Even more closely is werewolfism interwoven with the Greek tradition of the vampire. There must, however, in the first place be made a very clear distinction between the vampire and the werewolf. The vampire is a dead body which continues to live in the grave, whence it issues by night for the purpose of sucking the blood of living persons, and thereby indefinitely preserving its vitality and securing the carcass from decomposition. The werewolf is a sorcerer, a living man, who by his pact with hell and demoniacal charms is able to assume the form of a wolf, in which shape he roams abroad giving himself to all the bestial propensities and horrid appetites of that animal.

Nevertheless, as we shall have yet further occasion to remark, the two are not infrequently something confused in tradition and grannam lore.

The history and signification of the word *vrykolakas* have already been dealt with, and it were superfluous to recapitulate these points here. Mr. Lawson writes : " The Slavs brought with them into Greece two superstitions, the one concerning werewolves and the other concerning vampires. The old Hellenic belief in lycanthropy was apparently at that time weak—confined perhaps to a few districts only—for the Greeks borrowed from their invaders their word *vrykolakas* in the place of the old λυκάνθρωπος, by which to express the idea of a ' werewolf '." [81] To this I would only add that even if at one time the old belief in lycanthropy was obscured, such is far from being the case to-day.

Werewolfism in modern Greece is a very real and hideous thing.

By its very nature this most debased form of sorcery must in modern times be rare, but it would indeed be a mistake to argue that it does not exist, and it is to be found in the remoter districts of Italy as well as in Greece.

Sufficient has, I conceive, already been said with regard to the wolf legends of ancient Rome,[82] more especially as these, deeply interesting as they are, lie something outside our present scope, and need not then detain us here.

At the foot of Mount Soracte in Etruria, in the territory of the Falisci, some six and twenty miles from Rome, there stood of old a sanctuary dedicated to the goddess Feronia, who was probably a deity president over vegetation and the fruits of the earth. Here once a year they held a great fair and festival, to which flocked the whole countryside, aristocrats from the City itself as well as rustics and villagers numberless. In the presence of vast throngs the men of certain families walked barefoot, but without scathe or harm, over the hot glowing embers of a huge fire of pine-wood. These sorcerers, who performed the feat, were known as *Hirpi Sorani*,[83] or Soranian Wolves, and Pliny tells us that in consequence of this function they were exempted by a special decree of the senate from military service, taxation, and any sort of public service or duty. Strabo remarks that they were supposed to be inspired by the goddess Feronia, and the ceremony unquestionably took place at her shrine, in a spot especially dedicated under her name, but according to Vergil and Pliny this ritual was not conducted in her honour, but as an act of worship towards the god of the mountain, whose native name was Soranus, but whom they call by the Greek name Apollo, a detail which is extremely significant as linking up the wolf-men of Soracte with the cult of Apollo Λύκειος—the Wolf.[84] Silius Italicus in the *Punica*, v,[85] speaks of men passing thrice through the fire and carrying in their hands the entrails of the sacrificial victims, a truly wizard touch, since in primitive days these were probably human holocausts. This fire-walking at Soracte was a magic *signum*, or surpassing wonder wrought by the demon's aid. Varro, as cited by Servius, informs us that these fire-walkers anointed the soles of their feet with a

certain drug before they trod the furnace, so we have here
again an instance of the witches' ointment used in lycanthropic
practices.

One of the best-told werewolf tales of all time was related
by the freedman Niceros at the splendidly spectacular banquet
of his old chum Trimalchio.[86] Thus runs his story : " Some
while since, when I was still but a slave we used to live in
Small Street, in the house which now belongs to Gavilla.
And there, as luck would have it, I fell head over heels in
love with the wife of Terentius the inn-keeper ; you all used
to know Melissa—she came from Tarentum originally—and
a lovely bussing-bit [87] she was too ! Not that I cared for
her just for the sake of mutton-mongering and a ride, i'vads ;
no, no, I liked her because she was a good honest wench,
frank and free. If one ever asked her for anything one
never got No for an answer ; if she made a spanker, half of
it was mine ; and as far as I was concerned too, every penny
that came my way she had the handling of, nor even once
did she chouse me of a doit.

" Well, her husband—good man !—died at a little country-
house they had, and there I was casting about how to get
to her by hook or by crook, for I needn't tell you that you
learn who are your real friends when you are in a bit of a
fix like that. It so happened that just then my master
had gone off to Capua to dispatch some business he was
concerned in there, and I of course took advantage of such
a fine opportunity. I had no difficulty in prevailing upon
a young man who was staying in the house to bear me
company for a good bit of the way.[88] He was a soldier,
and as lusty a lad as the very deil.[89] Off we set about cock-
crow, and the moon was shining as bright as midday. We
were on the high road with the grave-stones on either side,[90]
when my man turned apart to do his jobs (as I thought)
among the monuments, so I sat me down singing away to
myself and counting the stars overhead. After a while I
looked round to see what my companion was up to, and
ecod ! my heart jumped into my very mouth. He had
taken off all his clothes and laid them in a heap by the
road's edge. I tell you I was as dumped as a dead man,
for I saw him piss in a circle all around his clothes, and then
hey presto ! he turned into a wolf. Please don't think I'm

joking ; I wouldn't tell a lie, no, not for a mint of money.
But as I was just saying, in a trice he turned into a wolf,
and thereupon he began to howl horribly and rubbed off
full tilt into the woods. I didn't know whether I was standing
on my head or my heels, and when I went to gather up his
clothes, why they had all been changed into stone !
Frightened ! phew ! I was half-dead with fear. None the less
I lugged out my porker, and as I made way along I kept
thrusting at the haunted shadows, until at last I came to
my pretty leman's house. There I tottered in looking like
a ghost ; every second I thought I was going to breathe
my last ; my eyes were set and staring ; the sweat was
pouring down my fork in streams ; it was all I could do to
gather my wits. Nobody could be more astonished than
Melissa to see me out so late on a night jaunt ; and, ' If you
had only been a little earlier,' she said, ' your help would
have come in very pudding time. A huge wolf has just
broken into the place, and made sad havoc among our sheep
and kine. You might think a flesher had been at work with
his knife from the blood. Master Wolf didn't get off scot
free all the same, for our man gave him a good jab across
the neck with a pike.' When I heard all this I couldn't so
much as close an eye, but no sooner was it broad daylight
than I beat the hoof back to my master's, Gaius, and I
hurried (I can tell you) as fast as mine host scours after a
bilking cheat. When I got to the place where the younker's
rigging had been turned into stone I could see nothing but
a horrid pool of blood ! At last I reached home, and there
I found my soldier abed, bleeding like an ox in the shambles,
whilst the doctor was busy dressing a deep gash in his neck.
Then I knew that he was a werewolf,[91] and after that I
could neither bite nor sup with him ; no, not if you had
killed me for it. Yes ; you can all think what you like
of my tale, but Heaven help me never ! if I've told a word
of a lie."

There are several points of great interest in this werewolf
story, which we may take to be a typical yarn of its day,
and which shows how prevalent and rooted the belief in
shape-shifting was in Italy during the first century of our
era, a belief, moreover, founded on fact. To discuss it at
length in all its bearings would require a separate monograph,

and I must be content to draw attention to but a few of the most salient details.

In the first place the transformation is effected in the moonlight, which, as we shall see later, in modern Portugal also is considered to play a vital part in such metamorphosis. No magic belt is employed, and no ointment or salve is rubbed over the skin. An essential condition preliminary to the shape-shifting is that the man should strip himself stark naked, whilst his return to the human form appears to be accomplished by his repossession of the clothes he had doffed. That the apparel which he has thrown off should be safeguarded during his appearance as a wolf is a matter of the first importance, and he secures this by a magic rite, by urination in a conjurer's circle around the garments as they lie on the ground.

In very many countries ensorcelling properties are ascribed to urine, and (under certain conditions) to the act of urination. Thus we have a similar phrase in Petronius, *Si circumminxero illum, nesciet qua fugiat* [92] (if I were to piss round him in a circle he would be unable to stir). In Hindostan, as in Italy, urinating in a circle was supposed to be a charm binding one fast, and Richard Pischel quotes an Indian formula of great antiquity (*utûlaparimêhah*), " Das Umharnen des Knechtes."[93] One may compare as a mystic function the Urine Dance of the Mexican Zunis, performed by one of their secret Medicine Orders, the *Nehue-Cue*, a dramatic representation of some half-forgotten wizard rite.[94] The Shamans of Siberia brew and drink a magic potion in which human urine is the chief ingredient.[95] The urine of cows is used for sacred lustrations and worship among certain hill-tribes at the foot of the Himalayas, and holy images are even sprinkled with the magic stream.[96] In Coromandel it is supposed to have supernatural healing properties so that the sick are often laved therewith.[97] Similar beliefs and practices are found among the Huron Indians.[98] Thiers, in his *Traité des Superstitions*,[99] records an old tradition that those who first thing in the morning dip their hand in urine cannot be ensorcelled or harmed by any spell of witches during the day. Thus in some parts of Ireland [100] urine was sprinkled on children suffering from convulsions to rescue them from the clutches of their fairy persecutors. "American boys urinate upon their legs to prevent cramp while swimming." [101] Torquemada says that the ancient Romans had a feast to the mother of the gods, Berecinthia, whose idol the matrons in secret ceremony solemnly sprinkled with their urine.[102]

It may be remarked that in Petronius the werewolf does not turn upon his comrade on the lonely road, but rushes off to a homestead to attack the cattle and sheep. The effects of repercussion are emphasized ; the soldier is bleeding copiously from the neck, exactly in the same spot where the farm-hand had wounded the marauding wolf.

No classical author is more frequently quoted by mediaeval— and indeed later—writers on werewolfism than Lucius Apuleius, and by some the *Metamorphoses* or *Asinus Aureus* was even considered to be in every detail an exact record of actual happenings. This, of course, is pressing the point too far, but there can be no question that a very great deal of plain fact is presented by Apuleius in a romantic dress. "Aut indicauit, aut finxit," shrewdly comments S. Augustine [103] with reference to the *Metamorphoses*, implying that there is something more than a substratum of truth under the most extraordinary adventures.

As I have already dealt at considerable length with the *Metamorphoses* twice before in connection with the supernatural, important as this work is, I may be excused if I pass it over rather briefly here.[104]

Born about the year 125, Apuleius was of African origin ; *semi-Numida* and *semi-Gœtulus* he calls himself. The *Metamorphoses*, his greatest work, was probably written at Rome before he was thirty, soon after he had completed his course of study at Athens. The thread of the main story is, no doubt, borrowed from that Greek tale whence also Lucian took his version Λούκιος, ἢ "Ονος (*Lucius, siue Asinus*), rewriting the original in his own limpid and racy style with all the wit and wickedness of Voltaire. For him the supernatural was no more true and could be no more true than were the pretty adventures of *La Chatte Blanche* or *Babiole* to the graceful Comtesse d'Aubroy. Apuleius, however, was evidently attracted, one might justly say, absorbed by that very quality a sceptic Lucian despised ; the occult element with its infinite possibilities would appeal to him as a professed mystic and something more than a dabbler in necromancy and the astral sciences. " In the *Metamorphoses*," it has been admirably said, " a brooding spirit of magic is over the whole narrative."

The main incidents of the transformation will be readily remembered. Lucius, a traveller in Thessaly, the home and cradle of all magic, is the guest at Hypata of an old usurer named Milo, whose wife Pamphile is a notorious witch. The lickerish young gallant intrigues with the wanton Fotis, the serving-maid, who allows him to see her mistress change herself into a bird. In order to accomplish this shape-shifting Pamphile strips naked and carefully anoints herself with a mysterious ointment, smearing her body from head to foot that she may fly off through the air. Burning with curiosity Lucius entreats Fotis to allow him to essay the same experiment. But the wrong unguent is used, and Lucius laments : " After that I had wel rubbed euerie part and member of my bodie, I houered with mine armes, and mooued my selfe, looking still when I should be changed into a bird as Pamphiles was, and behold neither feathers nor appearance of feathers did burgen out, but verely my haire did turne in ruggednesse, and my tender skinne waxed tough and hard, my fingers and toes loosing the number of five, changed into hoofes, and out of mine arse grew a great taile, nowe my face became monstrous, my nosethrils wide, my lips hanging downe, and mine eares rugged with haire : neither could I see any comfort of my transformation, for my member encreased likewise, and without al helpe (vewing euerie part of my poore bodie) I perceiued that I was no bird, but a plaine Ass." [105] This form he can only lose if he eat roses, since this flower alone has virtue to dissolve the magic. During that night the house is burgled, and the thieves loading the ass with their prey drive him to their mountain cave. Adventure follows adventure and episode episode as the picaresque panorama unfolds before our eyes. Some are of the most exquisite beauty ; some are grossly obscene ; some are mere thumb-nail sketches ; some are of consider-able length ; some arise directly out of the main narrative ; some are introduced accidentally ; all are of such sur-passing interest we would not lose a page, no not a line anywhere.

Finally, owing to a vision of the goddess, during a solemn
festival and procession of Isis the ass Lucius is enabled to
approach one of the priests, who holds a chaplet of roses, and
grasp with his teeth the fragrant garland.   Immediately
the unsightly and brutal figure leaves him.   " For my
deforme and Assie face abated, and first the rugged haire of
my body fel off, my thick skin waxed soft and tender, the
hooves of my feete changed into toes, my hands returned
againe, my neck grew short, my head and mouth became
round, my long eares were made little, my great and stonie
teeth, waxed lesse like the teeth of men, and my taile, which
combred me most, appeared no where : then the people
began to marvaile, and the religious honoured the goddesse,
for so evident a miracle." [106]   In humblest gratitude he
dedicates his life to the service of the deity, and is initiated
among the hierophants of her Egyptian temple.   The
conclusion, the whole of the eleventh book, rises to a strain
of rapturous mysticism, where the words often melt in an
ecstasy of Platonic loveliness.   " In the *Metamorphoses* of
Apuleius the syncretistic cult of the Egyptian goddess
expresses itself in terms of tenderness and majesty that
would fit the highest worship, and in the concluding prayer
of the Apuleian Hermes, an ecstatic adoration of God is
manifested in language and thought never equalled, still
less surpassed, save in the inspired writers of the Church." [107]

The *Metamorphoses* of Apuleius has a fascination, perverse
and baroque as it may often be, which is equalled by few
books of any literature.   Unbroken is the spell which that
decadent mystic has cast upon the ages.

It is quite impossible to believe that any work, which at
its close rises to the heights of mystic exaltation and rapture
achieved in the eleventh book of the *Metamorphoses*, should
be in any part a mere romance.   Indeed it is not so ; a
profound and mysterious truth throbs through every page,
is felt even in the most untoward incidents, in the lightest
and most wanton novella.[108]

From the very neighbourhood of Rome itself there is
recorded a very striking history of shape-shifting and sorcery,
incidents which took place in 1050, during the reign of
Pope S. Leo IX. We have this account from William of
Malmesbury, who when a boy heard it from an old monk

of Acquitaine, a member of the same house,[109] Malmesbury
Abbey.   Now William, who was born about 1090, was
educated and professed in the Benedictine family, and he
had certainly completed his *Gesta Regum Anglorum* before
1125.   There is no question that the French monk was
himself an eye-witness of the strange events which he related
to the ardent young English scholar.   The history with
rubric *De aniculis quae iuuenem asinum uideri fecerunt* is
given in liber ii of the *Gesta Regum*, cap. 171.[110]

At the beginning of the reign of Pope S. Leo IX, who
ascended the Chair of Peter on 12th February, 1049, there
were two old women, hard-drinkers and very lecherous,
who kept an inn on the high road to Rome, and if it so
chanced that any solitary passenger took his halt there for
the night they would change him by their evil craft into a
horse, a pig, or some other animal, and so sell him at a price
to the next buyer.   On a day there came to this house a
certain young strolling player, a likely lad, whom they transformed into an ass, and since he was skilled in many tricks
they gained much money in this way by exhibiting the
wonderful animal, who obeyed their every beck and nod,
for so they compelled him by force of their magic.   Now
the youth had not lost his human reason and intelligence,
although he was unable to speak.   The rumour spread abroad
and many came to see the ass out of curiosity, bringing
much traffic to the place.   A certain wealthy nobleman
who lived not far off was resolved to possess this beast,
and he paid a great sum of gold to the old women, who straitly
enjoined upon him never to allow the ass to enter the water.
Accordingly the animal was consigned to the care of a most
watchful and keen-eyed servant, and often at a merry-
making or feast, when the wine flowed red, he would be
summoned to the banqueting hall to show his tricks.   Howbeit
after some time, taking advantage of a momentary negligence,
the youth, eluding his keeper, was able to plunge into a lake,
and the form of the ass in a moment disappeared as he
regained his human shape, revealing what had happened
to his whilom keeper, who in his turn reported the matter
to his lord.   The old women were seized, and upon interroga-
tion confessed their manifold sorceries.   The facts were
reported to Pope Leo, who could at first scarce believe them

to be true.   S. Peter Damian, however, investigated the whole case and was soon able to convince the Pontiff.[111]

Many grave and accepted authorities relate this history,[112] and Baptista Fulgosi, in his *Dicta Factaque Memorabilia*, lib. viii, cap. xi,[113] " Recentiora de quibusdam Italicis magis," among the more recent examples mentions this case of enchantment as proven beyond all doubt : " iuuenis ille, qui per magas fœminas, in Asinam conuersus uidebatur, de quo coram Leone pontifice, Petrus Damianus accurate cum disputasset, magicae artis effectum, et non figmentum esse asseruit."

The Blessed Torello of Poppi, a solitary and one of the glories of the Vallumbrosan Order, which habit he took at Avanelleto, was eminent for his power over savage beasts. On one occasion when a wolf had carried off the little son of a poor woman of Poppi, the blessed hermit by his word compelled the wolf to bring the child unharmed to his anchorage where he restored him to the weeping mother. The beast fled into the woods.   The Bollandists write : " lupus, quem uulgo Moninum uocant, hoc est humana carne uescentem," " a wolf, commonly called *Moninus*, which is to say a feeder upon human flesh."   It may very well be, however, that *Moninus* signifies a Werewolf.   Blessed Torello died in 1282, and it is most certain that when the district was plagued by warlocks and werewolves he kept his Poppi free and secure from the onslaughts of these abominations.   His feast is upon 16th March, under which day he is noticed by the Bollandists, *Acta Sanctorum*, xvi Martii (tomus ii).

There are few better known examples of lycanthropy than that of the peasant, who dwelt near Pavia, an incident which happened in the year 1541, and which is recorded by Job Fincel.[114]

This unhappy lycanthrope was firmly convinced that he appeared in the shape of a wolf to all who beheld him, and indeed that he was actually a wolf with bestial cravings and appetites.   Thus he attacked and killed several persons in the fields, tearing their flesh with his strong teeth.   When at last he was captured, although this was not effected without very great difficulty, he maintained stoutly that he was a very wolf, only whereas wolves were hairy outside, his fur grew within his body. Some of the bystanders, showing themselves to be more cruel wolves than he, actually made deep wounds in his arms and legs to test the truth of his frantic imaginings. The poor wretch was consigned to the care of skilled physicians, but he died a few days afterwards.

Writers upon lycanthropy never fail to draw attention to this case, which is indeed sufficiently striking, and became a stock instance, so to speak. Our great English poet John Webster, in that supreme masterpiece, *The Tragedy of the Dutchesse of Malfy*, Act V, 2, 4to, 1623, has thus finely utilized the circumstance. The Marquess of Pescara is inquiring of the Doctor concerning Ferdinand, who is sick :—

> *Pesc.* 'Pray-thee, what's his disease ?
> *Doc.* A very pestilent disease (my Lord)
> They call *Licanthropia*. *Pesc.* What's that ?
> I need a Dictionary to 't. *Doc.* I'll tell you :
> In those that are possess'd with 't there ore-flowes
> Such mellencholy humour, they imagine
> Themselues to be transformed into Woolues,
> Steale forth to Church-yards in the dead of night
> And dig dead bodies vp : as two nights since
> One met the Duke, 'bout midnight in a lane
> Behind St. *Markes* Church, with the leg of a man
> Vpon his shoulder ; and he howl'd fearefully :
> Said he was a Woolffe : onely the difference
> Was, a Woolffes skinne was hairy on the out-side ;
> His on the In-side : bad them take their swords,
> Rip vp his flesh, and trie : straight I was sent for,
> And hauing ministerd to him, found his Grace
> Very well recouered.

Lycanthropy is several times alluded to by the Elizabethan and Jacobean dramatists, and one or two instances, which may stand for many, will perhaps be not altogether impertinent here.

In Ford's *The Lovers Melancholy*, 4to, 1629, Act III, " the Maske of Melancholy " (borrowed from old Burton) is presented before Prince Pallador of Famagosta, and we have (p. 66) : *Florish. Enter Rhetias, his face whited, blacke shag haire, long nailes, a piece of raw meate.*

Rhetias. Bow, Bow, wow, wow ; the Moone's eclipsed, Ile to the Church-yard and sup : Since I turn'd Wolfe, I bark and howle, and digge vp graues, I will neuer haue the Sunne shine againe, tis midnight, deepe darke midnight, get a prey, and fall too, I haue catcht thee now. *Arre.*

Corax. This kind is called, *Lycanthropia*, Sir,
When men conceiue themselues Wolues.

In the same author's *The Chronicle Historie of Perkin Warbeck*, 4to, 1634, Act V, the last scene, Urswicke, King Henry's chaplain, has the following allusion :—

Thus Witches,
Possest, even their deaths deluded, say
They haue beene wolues, and dogs, and sayld in Eggshells
Over the Sea, and rid on fierie Dragons ;
Past in the ayre more then a thousand miles,
All in a night ; the enemie of mankinde
Is powerfull, but false ; and falshood confident.

A belief in werewolfism prevailed in Italy throughout the seventeenth and eighteenth centuries, and to come down to yet more recent times, Signora Angela Nardo Cibele in her *Zoologia Popolare Veneta* [115] (Palermo, 1887, Curiosità Popolari Tradizionali, Pitre, vol. iv, pp. 92–3, xlii, Lòvo, Lupo) says that to-day in Venice and the district the belief in the *lupo mannaro* is almost vanished, although the older Venetian nursery tales often speak of the hideous werewolf who devours children and flocks. The tradition still lingered, however, in Belluno and the neighbouring hamlets, where I have myself met peasants who firmly believed in and dread the *lupo mannaro*. The local saw has it that a wolf must kill a hundred sheep to slake his thirst in their blood. A Venetian proverb, " La morte del lovo xè la salute dela piégora," implies that the death of a tyrant frees his country.

Curiously enough in the Monferrato district the shadow of an old belief in the werewolf seems to survive in a children's game at Pontelagoscuro, where one player represents the wolf who has to catch one of the other players who stand in file protected by " la direttrice ". The one who is first caught then becomes *lupo*.[116] (Superstitioni Usi et Proverbi Monferrini, Palermo, 1886. *Cur. Pop. Trad.*, vol. iii, pp. 41–2. Giuseppe Ferraro.)

Among the Italians of the Alpine provinces it is believed that the demon can transform himself into a wolf, and the *Fontana del Nobiet* near Cimapiasole is locally regarded as a lycanthropous stream. In Campania old folk say that those who are born on Christmas night, which is seemingly held to savour of irreverence, are compelled to be werewolves throughout their lives during the Octave of the Natale.[117]

Lu Lópe menare (il Lupo mannaro) is greatly feared among the Abruzzi.[118] About Christmastide he may be met with on lonely country roads. He utters the most discordant howls, and in his voice there is something hellish and infinitely horrible as it strikes the ear. It is the custom on Ascension Day, which is kept with especial solemnity, to bless a number of waxen crosses, *capecróce*, and these are regarded as most safe preservatives against witchcraft. They are often affixed to wayside shrines and Calvaries. Should the werewolf as he wanders abroad at night come in sight of one of these his power fails him and he slinks away into the darkness.

In Sicily the belief in the *lupo mannaro* [119] is still quite general. A vast number of ancient superstitions are connected with the animal himself. His howl is known as *rùcculu* or *rùzulu,* and a common proverb says : Master wolf is known by his note, *Lu lupu si conusci a lu rùcculu.* It is still held that a man seen by a wolf is struck dumb, and the phrase *Lu vitti lu lupu* can often be heard. A wolf's skin has extraordinary virtues, and the man who wears one will be full of zest and courage even to audacity. A wolf's foot is a potent charm for colic and other pains. In the Salaparuta district any animal bitten by a wolf is known as *allupatu,* and is henceforward inured to pain. In Nicosia *ulupa* is used of a man who has tasted wolf's flesh, which induces an eternal hunger, *allupamentu* or *lupa. Fami di lupu,* a wolf's hunger, is said of a large appetite, and if a man eats heartily he is often asked, *E chi manciasti carni di lupu* ? Have you been devouring a wolf ? In fable, nursery tale, and local proverb the wolf makes a constant appearance. Thus a crafty slyboots is said to be *lupu vecchiu* ; of two mortal enemies it is remarked, *si sparanu pri lupi. Sà cusu è lu Megghiu ! dicia Silivestru a lu lupu,* A rogue and a worse rogue, is an old phrase the exact reference of which is lost in antiquity.

According to the Sicilian tradition a child conceived at the new moon will become a werewolf, as also will the man who on a certain Wednesday or Friday in summer sleeps at night in the open with the moon shining full on his face. In Palermo they say that as the moon waxes to her round the werewolf begins to feel the craving ; his eyes sink deep and are glazed (*si cci'nvitrìanu*), he falls to the earth wallowing in the dust or mud, and is seized with fearful writhings and pangs, after which his limbs quiver and contract horribly,[120] he howls and rushes off on all fours, shunning the light, especially (they say at Menfi) torches, candles, or lanthorns. The lycanthrope dashes to and fro, and will bite anyone whom he may meet in his wild courses. His hideous cries may, however, be heard from afar and all hasten to avoid the wolf-man.

When he first feels the horrid desire he sometimes warns his family or his friends to shut fast the door and windows, and not to open to him however instantly he may call and summon them. There is a belief in Francoforte that if a *lupo mannaro* knocks thrice at his door, the third time it is quite safe to admit him as the access will then be over. It is generally supposed throughout Sicily that by some instinct the werewolf first seeks his own home, and in San Fratello they say that with his long sharp prensile nails he can clamber up a wall or a balcony with horrible agility.

The sight of the wayside shrines fills him with fear and trembling, and before the Crucifix or the Madonna he falls impotent to the ground, which shows that he is in truth possessed of the demon, and that werewolfism is clearly diabolical.

No blow with a stick will injure him, but if he be struck with a knife, especially on the forehead or the scalp, and blood drawn, he will be cured. Some say that if the backs of his front paws or hands are pierced the spell is broken. The blood which flows is black and thick, welling in great clotted gouts, *sangue pazzo*.

In Messina there is a curious tradition that the *lupo mannaro* can be cured if he be struck with a key of a certain shape. In Chiaramonte and Modica, however, they say once a werewolf always a werewolf.

A story is told of an incident which is said to have happened at Palermo, or, as some writers prefer, at Salaparuta. The fact is that two happenings have commingled in one narrative, the setting of which is accordingly placed in different localities. A certain wealthy man, the scion of a noble house, at the full of the moon was seized with lycanthropy, a horrid circumstance only known to one trusted attendant, who was wont during the wild height of his fury to let him rush out abroad, as the fit constrained him, by a secret angiport of the palace into a narrow lane, whence he prowled up and down the piazze of the city, filling all with terror and amaze, for not a man but wondered who this dread werewolf might be, seeing that my lord's face and features were so convulsed and hideously lupine as to be unrecognized even by those of his intimacy and own household. It so chanced that at one plenilune when the werewolf was scouring the midnight streets, there encountered him in his hot chase a young gallant, who perchance flown with wine, or it may be of a natural hardihood, by no means gave the wall but drew his toledo and slashed the foul grinning monster, whose white fangs had already snapped to bite, criss-cross over the slanting forehead. There gushed out great drops of black blood, thick like very pitch, the *lupo mannaro* uttered a long discordant howl of agony, his limbs convulsed, and there broke through the animal the man, whom the juvenal recognized as one of his near and most honoured friends. Since that happy encounter, and owing to the courage of the youth, the whilom lycanthrope was never again attacked by his lupine frenzy, but was thenceforth freed from the evil spell.

In the sestiere del Borgo of Palermo there lived a religious lady of honour and unspotted fame. One night, whilst at her devotions, she heard beneath her window the ominous howling of a wolf. Peeping through the heavy close-drawn curtains she saw in the moonlit court not far below a hideous monster. Gaunt and huge it paced ; from the gaping muzzle set with keen white teeth all arow to rend and tear lolled the great slobbering tongue ; the snout was lifted snuffling the wind with eager appetite. It paused, and then loped forward stealthily, when in a moment by a horrid bound and clambering with demoniac agility it had scaled the loggia itself. Full of courage, and commending herself to Our Lady and S. Rosalie, she took a sharp poniard in her hand and boldly stepped out on to the balcony. With a snarl and a snap the thing leaped up at her, its eyes blazing with hellish fury, its hot fetid breath panting horribly, the foam dripping from its champing jaws. Inspired by Heaven she struck out with all her force, and as the steel cut deep and true into the hairy forehead whence oozed the cruddling

black blood, the wolf seemed to shrivel as it fell back and
limped swiftly away into the shadows. The next morning
there came to her house a majordomo followed by two
servants bearing costly gifts of silks and jewelry, rare wines,
and a sumptuous regalia. These he prayed the lady to
accept on behalf of his master, a Prince of the reigning
family, whom by her brave and pious deed she had delivered
from his hideous lycanthropy when in his madness he beset
her the night before.

To-day one often hears in Sicily of such and such a place
that *c'è lu lupundriu*, the haunt of werewolves, although in
a secondary sense the phrase may be used merely to describe
any dangerous or unfrequented spot.[121]

Domenico Tempio, a celebrated poet of Catania of the
eighteenth century, speaking of a lycanthrope has the
following lines in his *La Caristia* [122] :—

> Chistu stranu fenominu,
> Critti lu vulgu ignaru,
> Chi sia un 'atroci bestia
> Chiamata, *Lupinaru*.
>   Li picciriddi in sèntirlu
> Fra cupi notti ed atri
> Pri scantu si stringevanu
> In senu a li soi matri,
>   E li padri medesimi
> Pri lu spaventu immenzu,
> Lu santu matrimoniu
> Lasciavanu in suspenzu.

As has been previously observed, the Spanish word for
werewolf, *lobombre*, is of such rare occurrence that Hertz [123]
(although quite erroneously) denied the existence of this
term. It is probable that the saving influence of the Church
for the most part repressed this bestial and most degraded
pravity of the witch. Indeed, although werewolfism is not
unknown in Spain, tradition speaks very seldom of this
metamorphosis.[124] One of the most remarkable of Goya's
pictures,[125] however, shows us four sorcerers, old and hideous,
confecting their loathly charms in some mysterious hovel.
A fifth warlock, mounted on a besom, is just disappearing
by the huge chimney. All four lean atomics are stripped
naked, and he who is next to be transvected to the sabbat
is already transformed into a wolf, albeit he yet stands erect
upon his feet. One of this foul crew stales in a corner. Upon

PLATE V

THE WEREWOLVES

[face p. 166

the earthen floor are two carious skulls and a dish of unguent. From the roof-tree hang noxious herbs and rotting bones.

As might be supposed, werewolfism lingers in the remoter Pyrenees, in the Cantabrian Mountains of the north, and in the Sierra Morena. Mr. Elliott O'Donnell writes : " Though they are extremely rare, both flowers and streams possessing the power of transmitting the property of werewolfery are to be found in the Cantabrian mountains and the Pyrenees." [126]

A very ancient and widespread tradition concerns itself in Portugal [127] with the *lobis-homem*, who are for the most part believed to be ensorcelled by some stroke of fate, *fado*, or slaved by a spell, *sina*. The Portuguese *lobis-homem* of the southern province differs in many respects from the were-wolf, for he is a clandestine and even a timid creature. The man (or woman) who is under the charm of the wolf goes out by night to some lonely spot, generally where four cross-roads meet. After having turned round five times with giddy speed, he falls upon the earth grovelling and howling. (If by chance some wild animal has previously lain upon the spot he will assume the shape of that animal.) He then rises transformed to a wolf. But unlike the northern werewolf and the loup-garou the *lobis-homems* seek to harm none. They run about country lanes, but at the least glimmer of a light they gallop off at full tilt into the kindly darkness. If they prowl near a cottage they utter long howls and a kind of sobbing noise, which is taken to be an entreaty for the candle or lamp to be promptly dowsed. M. Ferdinand Denis [128] says that werewolfism seems to have been most prevalent in Portugal in the fifteenth century, but if a belated peasant chanced to meet one of these hapless wretches he had only to strike a flint or show the glim of the lanthorn he was carrying and the *lobis-homem* fled.

A curious point is that the *lobis-homem* was generally supposed to have a short tail, which was covered with yellow fur.

There was, however, quite another and most evil kind of *lobis-homem*, who seems to have been closely connected with the *bruxa*, the Portuguese witch, a Satanist of the vilest and most deadly courses.

Writing in 1870, Oswald Frederick Crawfurd [129] says that

in Portugal " the superstitions have the peculiar gloomy
stamp of the legendary mysteries of ancient Italy. . . . The
type of Latin legend to which I refer, is that well-known
and most grisly and hideous of all ghost stories, the tale of
the soldier in Petronius Arbiter. Now the belief in the
' *Lupus-homem* ' is very prevalent in parts of Northern
Portugal . . . [and] nowhere is this belief invested with so
many peculiar and gloomy circumstances as in Portugal ".

He relates a werewolf history which was told him by a
farmer at whose manor he received the generous hospitality
of the country. When a young man this farmer was working
at a farm, near Cabrasam, among the mountains of Estrica,
one of the wildest districts of Portugal. The master of the
farm had recently married a young wife, and as the time
drew near for their first child to be born it became necessary
to engage a woman to help in the many household duties.
Accordingly the young hand was dispatched to the nearest
town, Ponte de Lima, with orders to hire the first strong
young serving-wench he should meet. As he jogged along
the road it so chanced he saw sitting by the wayside a likely
girl wrapped in a brown cloak with whom he entered into
conversation. She gave her name as Joana, and said that
she was from Tarouca in the mountains of Beira. Her
object was to look for a good situation as a servant in the
district. It seemed exactly to jump with the young fellow's
mission, and accordingly he suggested that she should
present herself to his master. This she did, and although
the farm-folk thought that there was a strange look about
her, inasmuch as she seemed sturdy and willing she was
engaged, and took the mistress' place for a while, undertaking
the cooking and housework.

In due time the child was born, a fine healthy boy, made
much of and lavishly admired by all the neighbours with
the single exception of one old lady, a wise woman, who looked
askew when she saw the babe, but on being pressed, in a few
moments said plainly that the child was under a spell. All
laughed, but the old lady maintained the Devil's mark could
be found on the babe, and sure enough between the shoulder
blades there was a tiny crescent or half-moon, which looked
as though it had somehow been tatooed there and appeared
indelible. Now the mirth changed to consternation, but the

wise woman cheered the wondering parents kindly enough,
only she straitly counselled them to watch the cradle carefully
during the time of the new moon, since (said she) there was
no cause for anxiety at any other season. This accordingly
was done, and as two or three months went by nothing
happened.

It was casually remarked that from the first the serving-
wench, Joana, exhibited the greatest animosity toward the
old lady, and whenever she visited the house the new maid
was sure to be abroad or else sat in a dark corner nursing
the sullens with her big brown cloak pulled right over her
face. Nothing was said since the lass was known to be
extremely hot-tempered, and when in a fury her eyes, which
were curiously narrow and slanting, would literally blaze fire
as she snarled out angry words. To her master and mistress
she was always respectful, and not unnaturally before long
she became the complete confidante of the latter.

One morning the mistress even entrusted her with the secret
the wise woman had disclosed, to her vast surprise, and the
girl replied : " Alas, indeed, it is only too true, I have known
it a long while, only I feared to tell you. Children with that
mark grow into *lupis-homems* unless it is prevented before
they reach sixteen."

" Can anything be done then ? " eagerly inquired the
mistress. " Why, yes, there is a way. You must cover the
mark with the blood of a white pigeon, strip the child naked,
and lay him on a soft blanket on the mountain-side the very
first time the new moon rises in the heavens after midnight.
Then the moon will draw the mark up through the blood,
just as she draws the waves of the sea, and the spell will
be broken."

In order to save their boy from the fearful doom of the
lobis-homem the farmer and his wife, after some talk, decided
to follow this advice. There happened to be a new moon
some few days later, and accordingly, accompanied by the
servants whom they apprised of their plan, they laid the babe
sleeping in his blanket in the warm summer night on the slope
of a hill near the house, whilst the thin silver sickle of the
moon yet tarried below the horizon. This done, they returned
indoors, for no eye must see the working of the magic charm.

The farmer, it is true, had expressed himself uneasy lest

there should be wolves near, but his men reassured him, since for many a long year no trace of a wolf had been seen in the whole neighbourhood for many miles around. Nevertheless, he got down his old blunderbuss and rammed it with rusty nails for lack of other ammunition. Hardly had he loaded when piteous cries were heard from the spot where the child was lying. All rushed out of the house to see in the light of the new moon just riding above the mountain crest a huge brown wolf, gaunt and lean, standing over the body of the babe. The animal's hot fangs dripped with blood, and the narrow eyes were lit with the fires of hell.

The distracted father fired as the beast was silently slinking away, and it fell, rolling over with a long-drawn howl, just before it could gain the shelter of the wood. The farmer's lad, who wielded a stout club, ran forward to finish it, but only succeeded in dealing the beast a heavy blow on the foreleg as it shuffled yowling and limping into the darkness beyond.

The child was dead, its throat hideously mangled, and the blanket soaked with blood.

When the tiny body had been borne sadly back to the house it was remarked that Joana was not with the company, and indeed had not been seen for some little time. Then the horrible truth flashed upon all—the girl was an accursed witch, a whore of Satan, and as a wolf had killed the child for some black purpose of her own. At earliest dawn the men followed the track of the wounded wolf into the wood, and not ten paces from the place where the animal had dragged itself away was Joana lying on the ground covered with blood. She immediately declared that she had hidden behind the trees to watch the child, fearing some harm, that she heard its piteous cries and ran out as the moon rose, only to see the wolf bounding forward from the covert. At the sound of the gun it had turned and fled unscathed in the confusion, whilst she received the full discharge, and fell wounded. These, of course, were lies suggested by the Devil. She could not explain how her right arm was bruised and wellnigh broken where the lad had struck the blow with his stick, moreover did he not (as he himself swore) see Joana's own eyes glaring in the wolf as the animal wheeled in fury ?

In charity they sent for the priest, but she died ere he could reach the spot, and they buried her where she lay. Before the earth was thrown on her body the wise woman who came to see it pointed out that the girl had the mark of the *lobis-homem* on her breast quite plainly, and was evidently one of Satan's wolf-pack, a witch of long continuance. She added that if she could have seen the girl's eyes she would have known at once what the evil wench was, for all *lobis-homems* acquire the long narrow eyes and savage look of the wolf. She further explained that if a *lobis-homem* can kill a newly-born child and drink the warm blood, the charm is broken and they are *lobis-homems* no more.

The priest, who had not till then been apprised whence the new servant came, declared that the farm-folk were fools and worse to have anything to do with a woman from Tarouca, for it was just a foul nest of warlocks and witches.

NOTES TO CHAPTER III

[1] 105. Teubner, Lipsiae, 1894, ed. Dietsch and Kallenberg, p. 368.

[2] *De Chorographia*, recognovit Carolus Frick, Teubner, 1880, p. 31. I quote the translation by Arthur Golding, *The Rare and Singuler worke of Pomponius Mela*, London, *Anno* 1590, p. 39. Solinus, also, merely echoes the older authorities, and has nothing to add. He writes, xv, 7 : " The Neuri indeed, as we are told, at certain seasons are transformed into wolves, and then after a given time, assigned by lot, they recover their original form. *C. Iulii Solini Collectanea Rerum Mirabilium*, Iterum Recensuit Th. Mommsen, Berolini, 1895, p. 82.

[3] *Die Indogermanen, Ihre Verbreitung, Ihre Urheimat, und Ihre Kultur*, 2 vols., Strassburg, 1905 ; vol. i, p. 120.

[4] *Reise um die Erde durch Nord-Asien und die beiden Oceane in den Jahren 1828, 1829 und 1830*, Berlin, 1833, i, p. 232 : " Es scheint nämlich kaum zu bezweifeln, dass die bei Herodot, nicht nach eigner Ansicht sondern nach indirekter Überlieferung, ausbewahrte Erzählung : ' die Neuren werden alljährlich während einiger Zeit in Wölfe verwandelt ' (Herod. iv, 105) ganz einsach auf winterliche Bekleidung mit Thierfellen sich beziche."

[5] Pausanias's *Description of Greece*, tr. by Sir J. G. Frazer, six vols., London, 1898 ; vol. i, Introduction, p. xvii.

[6] Eusebius, *Praepartio Euangelica*, x, 9 : " Πρῶτος δε Κέκροψ λέγεται Ζῆνα κεκληκέναι τὸν Θέον, μὴ πρότερον οὕτω παρ' ἀνθρώποις ὠνομασμένον." Migne, *Patres Graeci*, xxi, 809.

[7] viii, i, 4 ; ii, 1, 2, 3. Frazer, vol. i, pp. 373–5.

[8] For the cult (both in East and West) of S. Elias the Prophet, the Father of the Carmelites, see the Bollandists, *Acta Sanctorum*, under 20th July, the Feast of the Prophet. *Iulii Tomus V*, folio, Antwerp, 1727, *De S. Elia Propheta*, i, ii, and iii, pp. 4–10. G. F. Abbott, *Macedonian Folklore*, 1903,

pp. 240–1, remarks that the highest summits of mountains are generally dedicated to S. Elias and are often chosen for his shrines. Mr. J. C. Lawson, *Modern Greek Folklore*, 1910, p. 44, speaks of " S. Elias whose chapels crown countless hilltops ", and adds in a note, " I am unable to determine whether this Saint is the prophet Elijah of the Old Testament, or a Christian hermit of the fourth century. The Greeks themselves differ in their accounts." An error has crept into popular belief in some places. It is the Prophet S. Elias (not the holy hermit), to whom the shrines on the hills are dedicated.

⁹ By many primitive folk the shadow is conceived of as being the soul, or at least a vital part, of a man. For various modern Greek superstitions connected with the shadow see Bernhard Schmidt, *Das Volksleben der Neugriechen*, Leipzig, 1871, pp. 196 sqq., also more generally Frazer, *The Golden Bough*, vol. iii (*Taboo*, 1927), pp. 77–96.

¹⁰ Frazer's *Pausanias*, op. cit., vol. i, pp. 423–4.

¹¹ *The Early Age of Greece*, vol. ii (1931), p. 474.

¹² V. Bérard, *De l'origine des cultes Arcadiens*, pp. 49 sqq. Philippe Berger, *Revue des Deux Mondes*, 1896, cxxxviii, p. 886. See also Immerwahr, *Die arkadischen Kulte*, p. 14 sqq.

¹³ Thus Statius, *Thebaidos*, iv, 275 :

Arcades huic ueteres astris lunaque priores.

Cf. Pliny, *Nat. Hist.*, vii, 48 and 49 ; also Ovid, *Fasti*, i, 469–70 ; ii, 289–90, " Arcades, et luna gens prior illa fuit " ; also the Scholiast on Apollonius Rhodius, iv, 264 ; upon Aristophanes, *Nubes*, 398.

¹⁴ Thus Ausonius, *Technopœgnion*, De Deis, l. 8, has : " Mænalide Pan." Ovid, *Fasti*, iv, 649–50 : " Silua uetus . . . Stabat, Mænalio sacra relicta Deo." On which Burmann glosses : " *Maenalius Deus*, Faunus, quem passim poetae Latini cum Pane, Deo Arcadum, confundunt."

¹⁵ III, viii, 1. *Bibliotheca*, ed. E. Clavier, Paris, 2 vols., 1805 ; vol. i, pp. 317–321.

¹⁶ Dionysius of Halicarnassus, i, 13, says Lycaon had twenty-two sons ; Pausanias, viii, 3, counts the tale as twenty-seven.

¹⁷ He gives the name of Maenalus twice over. Delete the repetition and supply Melaneus, also add Oenotnes.

¹⁸ Ed. Mauricius Schmidt, Jenae, 1872, p. 30. Fabula clxxvi.

¹⁹ l. ii, c. iv.

²⁰ 8.

²¹ Ed. Kinkel, Teubner, 1880, p. 21. For the notes see pp. 113 and 114.

²² Nonnus in his *Dionysiaca*, xviii, 20 sqq., and Arnobius, *Contra Gentes*, iv, 24, both say that Nyktimos was sacrificed. So also Clement of Alexandria, *Protrepticon* (*Cohortatio ad Gentes*), cap. ii : Λυκαων ὁ 'Ἀρκὰς, ὁ ἑστιάτωρ αὑτοῦ, τὸν παῖδα κατασφάξας τὸν αὑτοῦ (Νύκτιμος ὄνομα αὑτοῦ) παραθείη ὄψον τῷ Διί. Migne, *Patres Graeci*, t. viii, 113–16.

²³ Orelli, *Hist. Excerpt.*, Leipzig, 1804, pp. 41 sqq.

²⁴ ll. 211–239. I quote Dryden's translation. " *Examen Poeticum* : Being The Third Part of Miscellany Poems," London, 1693, pp. 18–21, from "The First Book of *Ovid*'s Metamorphoses, Translated into English Verse by Mr. *Dryden* ".

²⁵ *The History of the World*, two tomes, folio, London, 1601, " Translated into English by Philemon Holland," tome i, p. 207. For the original text of this particular passage I have used *C. Plinii Secundi Naturalis Historiae, Libri XXXVII*, ed. Carolus Mayhoff, Teubner, 1904 ; vol. ii, pp. 105–6.

²⁶ The edition of Pliny " Apud Hackios, A° 1669 ", vol. i, p. 516, has " Fabius " in the text without comment.

²⁷ i, 29.

²⁸ *Solon*, xi.

²⁹ i, 1063–5.

³⁰ Quintilian, *Instit. Orat.*, x, 95. See also S. Augustine, *De Ciuitate Dei*, vi, 2, where the Saint quotes Cicero in praise of Varro's learning, also a line from Terentianus Maurus :

Uir doctissimus undecumque Uarro.

In the *De Ciu. Dei*, iii, 4, Varro is spoken of as " uir doctissimus eorum (i.e. paganorum) ".

[31] *Etymologia*, VIII, ix, 5.

[32] C. *Iulii Solini Collectanea Rerum Memorabilium*, vii, 21. Iterum recensuit Th. Mommsen. Berolini, 1895, p. 57.

[33] " Sacrifice " in *Encyclopædia Britannica*, ninth edition, vol. xxi, 1886.

[34] *The Cults of the Greek States*, Oxford, vol. i (1896), p. 41.

[35] *The Early Age of Greece*, vol. ii (1931), p. 475.

[36] *Über den Zeus Lykaios*, Progr. des Gymnasiums zu Göttingen, 1851, pp. 33 sqq.

[37] *Dictionnaire des Antiquités* ; Daremberg, Saglio, and Pottier. Paris, 1904. Tom. iii, deuxième partie, fascicule 81, pp. 1432–7.

[38] Deuteronomy, xii, 2. For the consecration of mountain tops to Zeus (Ὕπατος) see Dr. Farnell, op. cit., 1896, pp. 50–1, and the notes p. 152 with illustrative quotations. The lewd cult of these Baals is described by J.-A. Dulaure, *Des Divinités Génératrices*, Paris, 1805, ch. iv (new ed., Paris, 1905, pp. 55–62) ; Julius Rosenbaum, *Geschichte der Lustseuche im Alterhume*, English translation, Paris, 1901, vol. i, pp. 49–64.

[39] *Geographica*, ed. Aug. Meineke, Teubner, 1895, vol. ii, pp. 549–50. C. J. Groskurd in the introduction to his edition of Strabo, 8 vols., 8vo, Berlin and Stettin, 1831–3, judges that Strabo died about A.D. 24. It should be remarked that the temple of Zeus Lykaios had neither statue nor treasury.

[40] Pausanias, VIII, xxxviii, 3.

[41] Eng. tr., ut sup., p. 147.

[42] Eng. tr., ut sup., pp. 74 and 75.

[43] Eng. tr., ut sup., pp. 19–22.

[44] See the *Malleus Maleficarum*, part ii, qn. i, ch. 13 : *How Witch Midwives commit most Horrid Crimes when they either Kill Children or Offer them to Devils in most Accursed Wise*. Eng. tr., pp. 140–4. Also Guazzo, *Compendium*, II, xv ; Eng. tr., pp. 135–6.

[45] For Leukas see Strabo, 452 (ed. ut cit.) ; Aelian, *Nat. An.*, xi, 8 ; Photius, *Lexicon*, ed. S. A. Naber, Leyden, 1864–5, s.u. Λευκάτης. For Kourion in Cypus, Strabo, 683. See also Ovid, *Ibis*, 467–470, for a probable allusion to human sacrifices to Apollo at Abdera, " Urbs Thraciae initio anni hominem deuouet pro salute communi, obruitque lapidibus " ; *Ouidii Opera*, Oxonii, 1826, vol. v, p. 504.

[46] For the cult of Apollo Λύκειος, see Farnell, *Cults of the Greek States*, Oxford, 1907, vol. iv, chapter iv, pp. 112–124 and notes ; Ridgeway, *The Early Age of Greece*, vol. ii, pp. 475–7 ; Frazer, *Golden Bough*, Spirits of the Corn and of the Wild, vol. ii (ed. 1925), pp. 283–4, " Wolf Apollo " erroneously, or at least partially, explained as Apollo the " Wolf-slayer " ; also Frazer, *Pausanias*, vol. ii, pp. 195 sqq., for wolves in connection with Apollo ; Andrew Lang, *Myth, Ritual, and Religion*, 1887, vol. ii, pp. 199–201.

[47] Op. cit., vol. iv, p. 114.

[48] For Leto as a she-wolf see Aristotle, *Hist. An.*, vi, 35 ; Scholiast on Apollonius Rhodius, ii, 124, ἤματι χειμερίῳ πολιοὶ λύκου ὁρμηθευτες, who tells us that the wolf was honoured at Athens ; Aelian, *Nat. Anim.*, iv, 4, and x, 26 ; Antigonus, *Historiarium Mirabilium collectanea*, 56 (61) in *Scriptores rerum mirabilium Graeci* (p. 77). ed. A. Westermann, Brunswick, 1843. Servius on Vergil, *Æneid*, iv, 377, speaks of Apollo as a wolf.

[49] Aristotle, p. 580a, 17 : " ἐν τοσαύταις ἡμέραις τὴν Λητὼ παρεκόμισαν οἱ λύκοι ἐξ Ὑπερβορέων εἰς Δῆλον, λύκαιναν φαινομένην διὰ τὸν τῆς Ἥρας φόβον."

[50] Diodorus Siculus, v, 56 (from Xeno Rhodius) ; Antoninus Liberalis, *Transformationum congeries*, 35, in Westermann, *Scriptores* (ut sup.).

[51] iv, 101 and 119. The epithet is incorrectly explained by Autenrieth, *Homeric Dictionary* (English ed. by R. P. Keep, 1896), p. 198 : " λυκη-γενέϊ, (lux), *light-born*, epithet of Apollo as sun-god." Liddell and Scott are doubtful, for they say " commonly explained *Lycian-born*, i.e. at Patara ", ed. 1897, p. 906. Many of the older scholars were doubtless misled by Macrobius, *Saturnalia*, I, xvii, who derived Λυκηγενής from λύκη, dawn. He writes :

"Antipater Stoicus Lycium Apollinem nuncupatum scribit . . . Cleanthes Lycium Apollinem appellatum notat, quia ueluti lupi pecora rapiunt ita ipse quoque humorem eripit radiis," a striking example of far-fetched and much-mistaken ingenuity.

[52] *Iliad*, iv, 119.

[53] According to Servius on Vergil, *Æneid*, iv, 877 : " (Lycius Apollo) siue quod est λευκός a candore, idem enim et sol creditur, siue quod transfiguratus in lupum cum Cyrene concubuit : siue quod in lupi habiter Telchinas occiderit . . ." The Telchines are represented under different aspects, but the most general accounts speak of them as sorcerers of Rhodes or actual demons who had the power to assume any shape they pleased, and could bring on hail, storm, and snow. Ovid, *Metamorphoseon*, vii, 865–7, follows a tradition which says they were destroyed by Jupiter in a deluge on account of their malignancy, for they possessed the evil eye :—

> Telchinas,
> Quorum oculos ipso uitiantes omnia uisu
> Jupiter exosus, fraternis subdidit undis.

Uitiare, i.e. *fascinare*.   They were βάσκανοι.

[54] See Pindar, *Pythian*, ix, 5 ; Apollonius Rhodius, ii, 500–7 ; Diodorus Siculus, iv, 81. Apollo at Keos was himself called Aristaios (᾽Αρισταῖος). See also Pindar, *Pyth*., ix, 68 ; and Servius on Vergil, *Georgics*, i, 14.

[55] The Scholiast on Sophocles, *Electra*, 6.

[56] Farnell, op cit., vol. iv, p. 115.

[57] Aelian, lib. xiii, cap. 40 : " Τιμῶσι δὲ ἄρα Δελφοὶ μὲν λύκον." Clement of Alexandria, *Cohortatio ad Gentes*, 30 : Λυκοπολῖται δὲ λύκον [σέβουσι]. Migne, *P.G.*, vol. viii, 120.

[58] ii, 124.

[59] *Bulletin de Correspondance hellénique*, 1895, p. 12, an inscription of the fifth century B.C. Pausanias, x, 14, 7. Eusebius, iii, 14, 5 (from Porphyry, περὶ τῆς ἐκ λογίων φιλοσοφίας) :

> ἀνὰ δ᾽ ἐξέθορες, μάντι Λυκωρεῦ,
> τόξοτα Φοῖβε.

Also see Plutarch, *De Pythiae oraculis*, xii.

[60] Apollodorus, 1, 9, 15 ; Euripides, *Alcestis*, the opening of the play, Apollo's speech ; Tibullus, II, iii, 11–28 ; *Georgics*, iii, 2. Cf. Aeschylus, *Septem*, 145 :

> Λύκει᾽ ἄναξ, λύκειος γενοῦ στρατῷ δαΐῳ.

Cf. also *Iliad*, xxi, 488, and the Homeric Hymn to Hermes, 22, 70, etc.

[61] The Scholiast on Demosthenes, xxiv, 114.

[62] Pausanias, ii, 9, 6.

[63] 10, 1. τοὺς λύκους ὁ ᾽Απόλλων προοίμιον λοιμοῦ ποιεῖται . . . εὐχώμεθα οὖν ᾽Απόλλωνι Λυκίῳ τε καὶ Φυξίῳ.

[64] *Lex Salica*, 58 : "*wargus* sit—hoc est, *expulsus* . . ." Cf. the Old Norman Laws, Laws of Canute, Laws of Henry I, as quoted later in Chapter IV.

[65] " Circum quaque etiam in cultu daemonum luci succreuerant, in quibus ad huc eodem tempore infidelium insana multitudo sacrificiis sacrilegis insudabat." *Uita S. Benedicti*, auctore S. Gregorio Magno, cap. 11. Bollandists, *Acta SS.*, die xxi Martii. Tom. iii (Martii), Antverpiae, folio, 1668, p. 280 F.

[66] No. 196 : ed. Karl von Halm. Teubner, 1889, pp. 97–8.

[67] Fincel does not appear in Moréri's *Grand Dictionnaire Historique*, nor yet in the *Nouvelle Biographie Générale*. There is, however, a brief notice, which I have supplemented, in N. F. J. Eloy's *Dictionnaire Historique de la Médicine*, 4 tomes, Mons, 1778 ; vol. ii, p. 233. The *Wunderzeichen* is not even recorded by Graese or Caillet.

[68] Francofurti, 1612. Pars iii, pp. 153–7. Fincel's elegiaes are skilfully turned and not without poetic and personal feeling.

[69] 2 vols., 1869, vol. ii, ch. xxi, pp. 82–4.

[70] Curt Wachsmuth, *Das alte Griechenland im neuen*, Bonn, 1864, p. 117 : "Hier tritt also, wie es scheint, deutlich hervor die sonst bei den neugriechischen Wrukolaken nicht mehr erkennbare Natur des Werwolfes . . . S. Weleker kleine Schriften, iii, S. 187 ff. (*Lykanthropie ein Aberglaube*

und eine Krankheit) ; Otto Jahn, *über Lykoros* in den Berichten der sächs. Ges. der Wiss. ; 1847, S. 423 ff. ; vgl. im Allgemeiner Hannsel, *die Werwölfe* in der Zeitschr. f. deutsche Mythol., iv, S. 193 ff.

[71] Arthur und Albert Schott, *Walachische Märchen*, Stuttgart and Tübingen, 1845, p. 298.

[72] *Les Slaves de Turquie, Serbes, Monténégrins, Bosniaques, Albanais et Bulgares.* Édition de 1844, Paris, 2 vols. 1852, vol. i, p. 69.

[73] Ibid., pp. 68–70.

[74] Cambridge, 1903, pp. 215–17.

[75] J. G. von Hahn, *Albanesische Studien*, Jena, 1854 ; i, p. 16.

[76] Cambridge, 1910. For the Callicantzari see pp. 190–255.

[77] *De Graecorum hodie quorundam opinationibus* Cologne, 1645, cap. ix.

[78] Op. cit., p. 209.

[79] Παραδόσεις, i, p. 344, being part ii of the series Μελέται περὶ τοῦ βίόυ καὶ τῆς γλώσσης τοῦ 'Ελληνικοῦ λαοῦ.

[80] Lawson, op. cit., pp. 216–19.

[81] Ibid., p. 384.

[82] See for further details the chapter " Der Wolf " (pp. 158–177) in Otto Keller's *Thiere des Classischen Allerthums in Culturgeschichtlicher Beziehung*, Innsbruck, 1887.

[83] Festus, *De Uerborum Significatione*, lib. ix, Amstedolami, 1700, p. 193, has : " Irpini appellati nomine lupi, quem irpum dicunt Samnites."

[84] Pliny, *Nat. Hist.*, vii, 19 ; Vergil, *Æneid*, xi, 784 sqq., with the glosses of Servius who quotes from Varro ; Strabo, v, 2, 9 ; Dionysius Halicarnasensis, *Antiquit. Roman.*, iii, 32. See also Frazer, *The Golden Bough, Balder the Beautiful*, vol. ii, ed. 1923, pp. 14 sqq., and *The Dying God* (1923), p. 186. Festus tells us that the Samnites were guided by a wolf. L. Preller, *Römische Mythologie*, 3rd ed., Berlin, 1881–3 ; i, 268, follows G. Curtius (*Grundzüge der griechischen Etymologie*, 5th ed., Leipzig, 1879) in linking up the first syllable of Soranus and Soracte with the Latin *Sol* (sun), which is impossible.

[85] ll. 175–181. Andrew Lang mentions the Hirpi in his *Myth Ritual and Religion* (1887); vol. ii, p. 213. See further, W. Mannhardt, *Antike Wald- und Feldkulte*, Berlin, 1877, pp. 327 sqq. He compares the rites of the Soranian wolves with the ceremonies of the Norman fraternity of the Green Wolf at Jumièges. (In no part of France was werewolfism more prevalent of old than in Normandy.) Frazer (*Balder the Beautiful*, chapter vi, 2, " The Meaning of the Fire-Walk ") regards the fire-walk as a charm to dispel the incantations of malevolent witches and as a preservative from spectres. This may be true in some instances, but the Hirpi Sorani were themselves witches and wolves.

[86] *Petronii Satirae*, tertium ed. Franciscus Buecheler, Berolini, 1895 ; 61, 62, pp. 40–1.

[87] *pulcherrimum bacciballum.*

[88] *ut mecum ad quintum miliarium ueniat.*

[89] *fortis tanquam Orcus.*

[90] The Roman custom being to bury by the side of the roads. " The tombs were ranged on either side of the roads leading from the towns . . . The forms of the monuments are very varied." J. E. Sandys, *A Companion to Latin Studies*, Cambridge, 1910, p. 183.

[91] *intellexi eum uersipellem esse.* Baring Gould, *The Book of Were-Wolves* (1865), pp. 64–5, says that *uersipellis* " resembles the Norse *hamrammr* ", the idea being that the skin is reversed or turned inside out, for which he quotes the case of the countryman at Pavia as related by Job Fincel. This, however, is certainly incorrect, for the notion that the werewolf when in human form is merely wearing his wolf's pelt with the fur turned inside, and to change his shape he has but to uncase and reverse, is not contained in *uersipellis.*

[92] 57 ; ed. cit., p. 37.

[93] *Zu Petronius, Satirae* 62. No. vi in *Philologische Abhandlungen. Martin Hertz zum siebzigsten Geburtstage von ehemaligen Schülern dargebracht.* Berlin, 1888, pp. 69–80.

[94] Described by Captain J. G. Bourke in his *Compilation of Notes and Memoranda bearing upon the Use of Human Ordure and Human Urine in Rites of a Religious or Semi-Religious Character*, Washington, 1888, pp. 8–10.

[95] Schultze, *Fetichism*, New York, 1885, p. 52.

[96] J. Shortt, " Notes on the Hill Tribes of the Neilgherries," *Transactions of the Ethnological Society*, London, 1868, p. 268. See also Moor, *Hindu Pantheon*, London, 1810, p. 148.

[97] Bernard Picart, *Coûtumes et Cérémonies Réligieuses de Tous les Peuple der Monde*, Amsterdam, 1729, vol. vii, p. 28.

[98] Père Gabriel Sagard, *Histoire du Canada* (new edition), Paris, 1885, p. 107.

[99] Paris, 1741, tom. i, c. 5, p. 171.

[100] John Brand, *Popular Antiquities*, London, 1849, vol. ii, p. 86, " Christening Customs," also James Mooney (Bureau of American Ethnology), *Medical Mythology of Ireland*, Washington, 1887.

[101] J. G. Bourke, op. cit., p. 47.

[102] " La rociaba con sus orinos," J. de Torquemada, *Monarquia Indiana*, Madrid, 1723, lib. x, c. xxiii. See also lib. vi, cs. xiii and xvi.

[103] *De Ciuitate Dei*, xviii, 18.

[104] *The Geography of Witchcraft*, 1927, chapter i, pp. 27–31 ; *The Vampire in Europe*, 1929, chapter i, pp. 42–52. I have not hesitated to quote pretty freely from my two former books here.

[105] *The eleuen Bookes of the Golden Asse . . . Translated out of Latin into English by William Adlington*. London, 1596, chap. 17, p. 58.

[106] Ibid., chap. 47, p. 197.

[107] Father Cyril Martindale, S.J., article " Paganism ", *Catholic Encyclopœdia*, ed. New York, 1913, vol. xi, p. 393.

[108] Traube, Munich Academy, *Abhandlungen, Philosophisch-Philologische*, Classe, xix, 308, writes on the popularity of Apuleius in the middle ages.

[109] " quodam loci nostro monacho genere Aquitanico aetate prouecto arte medico in pueritia audisse me memini." Lib. ii, cap. 170 (ed. Stubbs, p. 198).

[110] *Gesta Regum Anglorum*, ed. W. W. Stubbs, Rolls Series, vol. i (1887), pp. 201–2.

[111] S. Peter Damian amongst other instances referred to the instances of Simon Magus and Faustinianus. S. Peter Damian, Doctor of the Church, Cardinal-Bishop of Ostia, 1007–1072.

[112] Amongst others, Matthew Paris, O.S.B., *Chronica Maiora*, ed. Luard (Rolls Series, 1872–1883), i, 518–19 ; *Flores Historiarum*, ed. H. R. Luard (Rolls Series, 1890), i, pp. 567–8 ; Roger of Wendover, O.S.B., *Flores Historiarum*, ed. H. O. Coxe (English Historical Society, five vols., 1841), i, pp. 485–6 ; John Brompton in Roger Twysden's *Historiae Anglicanae Scriptores X*, folio, 1652, column 940 ; Radulfus Niger, *Chronicon*, ed. Robert Anstruther, Caxton Soc., 1851, pp. 155–6 ; Vincent of Beauvais, *Speculum Naturale*, lib. ii, cap. cix, Venice, folio, 1591, tom. i, p. 26 ; Ulrich Molitor, *De lamiis et pythonicis mulieribus*, 1489, cap. iii ; Bodin, *Démonomanie*, ii, 6, 1580, p. 100 (verso), misprinted 80 ; Boguet, *Discours des Sorciers*, 1590, xlvii (Eng. tr. *Examen of Witches*, 1929, p. 142) ; Petrus Thyraeus, S.J., *De Spirituum Apparitionibus*, cap. xv, 222, ed. 1594, p. 114 ; *A Pleasant Treatise of Witches*, 1673, pp. 22–3.

[113] Ed. 1509 : sig. ll ii (pages not numbered).

[114] Thence by Simon Goulart, *Thrésor d'histoires admirables et memorables de nostre temps*, 2 vols., 12mo, Paris, 1600, and quoted by many other authors. By some untoward confusion of ideas John Webster, whose singularly futile *Displaying of Supposed Witchcraft*, London, 1677, quotes Fincel to disprove the possibility of werewolfism, p. 83. Webster has other allusions, pp. 68–9, p. 86, and pp. 91–106, which are not worth citing. Webster, of course, does not entirely deny the supernatural ; he is sufficiently sane to be cautious. Ed. 4 vols., 8vo, Genève, 1620, vol. ii, Lycanthropie, pp. 720–1. Simon Goulart of Senlis, a Lutheran minister and prolific compiler, was born 20th October, 1543, and died 3rd February, 1628. Goulart's work in question was translated into English by Edward Grimeston, *Admirable and Memorable*

Histories (there is an error, I. Goulart, on the title-page), 1607, and the account of the lycanthrope of Pavia is given on p. 387, where probably it was read by Webster. Burton, *Anatomy of Melancholy*, part i, sec. 1, mem. 1, subs. 4, refers to the lycanthrope of Pavia, but he derived the history from Weyer.

[115] *Curiosità Popolari Tradizionali*, Pitrè, Palermo, 1887 ; vol. iv, pp. 92–3, xlii, Lovò, Lupo.

[116] *Cur. Pop. Trad.*, Palermo, 1886, vol. iii, pp. 41–2, " Superstitioni Usi e Proverbi Monferrini," Giuseppe Ferraro.

[117] Otto Keller, *Thiere des Classischen Alterthums* . . ., 1887, ut cit. sup., p. 403, note 123.

[118] *Cur. Pop. Trad.*, Palermo, 1894, vol. xiii, p. 113, " Tradizioni Populari Abruzzesi," Gennaro Finamore. See also Finamore, *Credenze Usi e Costumi Abruzzesi*, Palermo 1890, vol. vii, pp. 141–6.

[119] Giuseppe Pitrè, " Usi e Costumi " ; *Biblioteca delle Tradizioni Popolari Siciliane*, xvi ; Palermo, 1889, vol. iii, pp. 463–470.

[120] Whence the proverb of anyone contorted with pain, *si torci* (or *fa*) *comu un lupunàriu.*

[121] Pitrè, op. cit., vol. iv (Palermo, 1889), pp. 224–231.

[122] Canto x.

[123] *Der Werwolf*, 1862, p. 89.

[124] I am confirmed in this opinion by what Mr. Elliott O'Donnell writes in his *Werwolves*, 1912, p. 194, chapter xii, The Werwolf in Spain : " Werwolves are, perhaps, rather less common in Spain than in any other part of Europe."

[125] Formerly in the Collection of the Duque d'Osuna.

[126] Op. cit. sup., p. 194.

[127] The chief authorities for werewolfism in Portugal are : Professor Z. Consiglieri-Pedroso, *Tradições populares portuguezas*, fasc. vii, *O lobis homem*, Porto, 1881 ; and Jose Leite de Vasconcellos, *Bibliotheca ethnographica portugueza*. I. *Tradições populares de Portugal*, xi. Porto, 1882. See also Coelho, *Revista d'ethnologia ; Entidades mythicas*, No. xviii, *Os lobis-homens*.

[128] *Portugal*, pp. 106–7. (*L'Univers.*) Paris, Firmin Didot, 1846. In a note M. Ferdinand Denis, who was Librarian of Ste-Geneviève, refers to his *Le monde enchanté ; Cosmographie et histoire naturelle et fantastique du moyen-âge*, Paris, 1843.

[129] *Travels in Portugal*, by John Latouche (i.e. Oswald Frederick Crawfurd, consul at Oporto), Ward, Lock and Co., 1875, pp. 28–36. These chapters were first published in consecutive numbers of the *New Quarterly Magazine* as " Notes of Travel in Portugal ". The book was extremely popular and a third edition appeared in 1879.

CHAPTER IV

ENGLAND AND WALES, SCOTLAND AND IRELAND

IT is undoubtedly far more difficult for those living to-day to imagine the old England of peace and prosperity, than it is for those of us who remember our country before the dawning of the twentieth century to trace in our minds a similar picture. And even fifty years since, when we travelled at leisure and in security through some of the wilder parts of the kingdom, we could scarce believe that such a journey as we were taking under so pleasant and easy conditions was once an enterprise fraught with considerable danger owing to the numbers of ferocious animals that infested the very woods and glens and moors we were thus serenely traversing.

To-day the risks are no less than in ancient times, the British and Anglo-Saxon periods, although truly the perils are of a different kind. From one end of our island to another the roads are packed and ploughed by mechanical conveyances of the ugliest and most vicious pattern, swift engines of death and destruction, goaded to a maniac speed amid stench unutterable and the din of devils.

When we see London, despoiled of all her beauty, her nakedness uncovered, throwing out hideous suburban tentacles for mile after mile on all sides, it is impossible to realize that between the tenth and twelfth centuries there came up wellnigh to her gates, but a few fair meadows and open pasture lands intervening, vast forests in whose depths dwelt the stag, and the wild-boar and the bull.

Even at a comparatively modern period nearly the whole of the county of Stafford was either moor or woodland. Cannock Chase alone measured no less an expanse than 36,000 acres. "The moorlands is the more northerly mountainous part of the county, lying betwixt Dove and Trent. . . . The woodlands are the more southerly, level part of the county, being from Draycote to Wichnor, Burton, etc. Between the aforesaid rivers, including Needwood-forest, with all its parks, are also the parks of Wichnor, Chartley, Horecross, Bagots, Loxley, Birchwood, and Paynesley (which anciently were all but as one wood, that gave it the name of woodlands)." [1] Maxwell forest, near Buxton, with the great forest of Macclesfield, the Peak forest, and the high Derbyshire moors united to make up "that mountainous and large featured district which in ancient times had been well timbered and formed part of the great midland forest of England ".[2] From Nottingham to Manchester, and thence far on into Yorkshire, was one continuous forest, and there came to meet it the even wilder and larger forest of Bowland.

In Scotland all the district between Chillingham and Hamilton, some eighty miles, was completely wooded, and further north lay the huge Caledonian forest itself.

Inadequate and readily to be supplemented as are these few haphazard details, they will perhaps suffice to show what magnificent tracts of unreclaimed forest-land once existed here, affording through centuries an impenetrable fastness for wild beasts, and especially for the wolves whom year after year it seemed wellnigh impossible to exterminate and dislodge.

The forests of Reedsdale in Northumberland; Blackburnshire and Bowland in Lancashire; Richmond Forest comitatu Ebur; Sherwood Forest, Nottinghamshire; Savernake Forest in Wilts; the New Forest; the forests of Bere and Irwell; and many more are recorded as being the strongholds of packs of the most swift and savage wolves.

Of all British animals that have become extinct within historic memory the wolf was the last to disappear.[3]

Wolf-hunting was a favourite pursuit of the ancient Britons, and legend tells how wicked Mempricius (or Memprys), one of the descendants of old King Brute, a monarch who may have ruled Albion about 980 B.C., in that year fell a prey to the wolves whom he delighted to hunt with his great hounds, as old Andrew of Wyntoun [4] sings :—

> His brother he slew and syne all thai
> That he trowit wald thaim ma
> For to succeid till him as king.
> It happinnit syne at a hunting
> With wolffis him weryit to be ;
> Sa endit his iniquite.

Verstegan (Richard Rowlands), in his *Restitution of Decayed Intelligence in antiquities*,[5] writes of the Saxons : " The moneth which wee now call *Ianuary* they called *Wolf-monat*, to wit *Wolf-moneth*, because people are wont alwayes in that moneth to bee in more danger to bee deuowred of wolues, then in any season els of the yeare ; for that through the extremitie of cold & snow, those rauenous creatures could not fynd of other beasts sufficient to feed vpon."

It is not without significance that in the *Poenitentiale* [6] of Egbert, Archbishop of York, who died 766, it is prescribed that " if a wolf shall attack cattle of any kind, and the animal so attacked shall thereof die, no Christian may eat of it ". It would appear as though the wolf imparted by his very bite some demoniac quality to the beeves he had torn and slain.

Speaking of Flixton near Filey in Yorkshire, Camden [7] records that here " in King Athelstanes time was built an *Hospitall, for the defense* (thus word for word it is recorded) *of way-faring people passing that way from Wolues, least they should bee devoured.* Whereby it appeereth for certaine, that in those daies Wolues made foule worke in this tract, which now are no where to be seene in England, no not in the very marches toward Scotland ; and yet within Scotland there be numbers of them in most places ".

When Athelstan in 938 won so signal a victory at Brunanbrugh over Constantine, King of Wales, he imposed upon the defeated a yearly tribute of money, cattle, hawks, and keen-scented dogs, which mulct of gold and silver his successor, King Edgar, permitted Ludwall (or Idwal), the heir of Constantine, to exchange for the pelts of 300 wolves. It is generally stated that Edgar did this " to the intent the whole Countrie might once be clensed and clerely ridde " of these ravenous creatures, " whose carcases being brought into Lloegres, were buried at Wolfpit, in Cambridgeshire, and by that meanes thereof within the compasse and terme of foure yeres, none of those noysome creatures were left within Wales and England. Since this tyme also we read not that anye Wolfe hath beene seene here that hath bene bredde within the bondes and limites of our country." [8] The legend certainly grew and stuck fast that in this way the wolves were utterly exterminated, as poets loved to repeat. Thus Michael Drayton, in his *Polyolbion*,[9] 1612, the ninth song, has :—

> Thrice famous *Saxon* King, on whom Time nere shall pray,
> O *Edgar !* who compeldst our *Ludwall* hence to pay
> Three hundred Wolues a yeere for trybute vnto thee :
> And for that tribute payd, as famous may'st thou bee,
> O conquer'd *British* King, by whom was first destroy'd
> The multitude of Wolues, that long this Land annoy'd.

In his note Selden is careful to remark : " But this was not an vtter destruction of them ; for, since that time, the Mannor of *Piddlesey* in *Leicester* shire was held by one *Henry* of *Augage*, per serjeantiam capiendi lupos, as the inquisition deliuers it." [10]

Edward Ravenscroft prefixed as a Preface to his tragi-comedy *King Edgar and Alfreda*,[11] acted at the Theatre Royal late in 1677, " *The* Life *of* Edgar, *King of the* West Saxons," in which the tribute he imposed upon the Princes of Wales " To clear the Land from Wolves " is duly recorded, but there is no reference to this in the play as we should perhaps have expected, and it is rather surprising that there is no mention of wolves in Thomas Rymer's unacted " Heroick Tragedy ", *Edgar, or The English Monarch.*[12]

William Somervile, in *The Chace* (1735),[13] has the following reference to " glorious Edgar " :—

> Wise, potent, gracious Prince !
> His Subjects from their cruel Foes he sav'd,
> And from rapacious Savages their Flocks.
> *Cambria's* proud Kings (tho' with Reluctance) paid
> Their tributary Wolves ; Head after Head,
> In full Account, 'till the Woods yield no more,
> And all the rav'nous Race extinct is lost.

Even so serious and careful an author such as Dr. John Caius, in his *De Canibus Britannicis*, 1570,[14] when treating of the Sheep-Dog *Canis Pastoralis*, and taking occasion to mention the tribute paid to Edgar, quite confidently wrote that our shepherd's dog " hath not to deal with the bloud thyrsty wolf, sythence there be none in England, which happy and fortunate benefite is to be ascribed to the puisaunt Prince *Edgar* . . . Synce which time we reede that no Wolfe hath bene seene in England, bred within the bounds and borders of this countrey ". He seems to have been little

aware that the wolf had not become entirely extinct in
England three-quarters of a century before, and did not
entirely vanish from the British Isles until 200 years after
his own day.

It is hardly necessary to review the ample evidence which
shows the abundance of wolves in England during the period
from the Norman Conquest until the beginning of the
sixteenth century.

Guido, Bishop of Amiens, in his *Carmen de Bello
Hastingensi*,[15] quite naturally relates that the Conqueror
left the dead bodies of the English on the battle-field to rot
and be devoured by beasts of prey :—

> uermibus, atque lupis, auibus canibusque uoranda,
> deserit Anglorum corpora strata solo.

The New Forest and the Forest of Bere, which, as we have
noted, both teemed with wolves, were favourite hunting-
grounds of the Red King and Henry I. It is chronicled in
the *Annales Cambriae* [16] that in 1166 a mad wolf bit two and
twenty persons, all of whom in a short space died.

In the reign of King John is said to have occurred the
well-known circumstance of faithful Gellert being rashly
slain by Prince Llewellyn, a story so familiar as it were
superfluous to relate.[17]

Henry III not infrequently made grants of lands to various
individuals upon the condition that these owners should
hunt down and destroy the menacing wolves. Similar
notices are found during the reigns of the three Edwards,
Richard II, and the three Henries.

In his *Boke of Saint Albans*,[18] written about 1480 and
printed at Saint Albans by the Schoolmaster-Printer in
1486, Dame Juliana Berners (or Barnes) includes the wolf
among the " Bestys of venery " :—

> Wheresoeuere ye fare by fryth or by fell
> My dere chylde take hede how Tristram dooth you tell
> How many maner beestys of venery ther were
> Lystyn to yowre dame and she shall yow lere
> Fowre maner beestys of venery there are
> The first of theym is the . hert . the secunde is the hare
> The boore is oon of tho . the Wolff and not oon moo.

There is hardly any hint afforded here that the wolf is
becoming a particularly scarce animal, although relentless

war had been waged against him from all sides for long enough. An old, but apparently unsupported, tradition says that the last wolf in England was killed at Wormhill Hall near Buxton in the county of Derby, and certainly it is probable that the royal Forest of the Peak, wild and of vast extent, would afford cover for the remnant of this savage tribe. Be that as it may, the reign of King Henry VII is certainly to be assigned as the term of the period to which the wolf lingered here. Seventy years or so later George Turbervile in his *Booke of huntynge* writes : " The Wolfe is a beaste sufficiently knowen in Fraunce and other Countries where he is bred : but here in Englād they be not to be foūd in any place. In Ireland (as I haue heard) there are great store of them." [19]

Long after he had been extirpated in England the wolf continued to be " rycht noysum to the tame bestiall in all partis of Scotland ".[20] Camden at the end of the sixteenth century remarks that Strath-Navern, " the utmost and farthest coast of all Britaine," is " sore haunted and annoied by most cruell wolues ", who not only set upon cattle but also " assaile men with great danger, and not in this tract onely, but in many other parts likewise of Scotland ".[21] But a hundred years after Sir Robert Sibbald avers that the animal had been wholly exterminated. Although their numbers were no doubt greatly diminished, especially after the great hunts arranged in the days of James V (born 1512, died 1542) and Queen Mary, his daughter, actually it was not until the year 1743 that the last of the species was destroyed at a remote spot between Fi-Giuthas and Pall-à-chrocain.

One winter day the Laird of MacIntosh was apprised that a large " black beast " supposed to be a wolf had been descried prowling in the glens, and less than twenty-four hours before had killed two children who were crossing the hills from Calder. A " Tainchel " or general drive was at once proclaimed, and amongst others summoned to the meet not the least important was a famous deer-stalker, MacQueen, who had the fleetest and strongest hounds in the country. All assembled at the tryst had waited long impatiently expecting MacQueen's arrival ere he appeared on the scene. MacIntosh began to upbraid his unusual

tardiness, when for answer the hunter lifted his plaid and
threw the bleeding head of the wolf at the laird's feet, to be
overwhelmed with congratulations and well feed in a generous
gift of land for his prowess.[22]

Even later did the wolf maintain his hold upon Ireland,
where formerly he existed in such numbers that a special
breed of dog, a tall rough greyhound of exceptional size
and power, and most highly esteemed, the Irish Wolf-hound,
was especially reared to hunt the fierce and fearful packs.
" They are not without woolues and grayhoundes to hunt
them, bigger of bone and limme then a colt," says Holinshed
in his description of Ireland,[23] and Camden writes, " much
noisance they have everywhere by Wolues." Thus in the
*Travels of Cosmo the Third, Grand Duke of Tuscany, through
England* [24] in 1669, wolves are spoken of as common in
Ireland, which indeed had acquired and long kept the nick-
name of " Wolf-land ".

" Wolves still abound too much in Ireland," Harting
quotes from *The Present State of Great Britain and Ireland,
1738* ; and in an article on the Irish Wolf-dog printed in
The Irish Penny Journal for 1841,[25] Mr. H. D. Richardson
says : " I am at present acquainted with an old gentleman
between eighty and ninety years of age, whose mother
remembered Wolves to have been killed in the county of
Wexford about the years 1730–1740, and it is asserted by
many persons of weight and veracity that a Wolf was killed
in the Wicklow Mountains so recently as 1770."

In his *Origins of English History* [26] Charles Isaac Elton
draws attention to the fact that there was no more usual
periapt among the ancient Britons than " crescents made of
the wolf's teeth and boars' tusks perforated and worn as
charms ". He also remarks, " We know that at one time
the wolves swarmed in Sherwood and Arden " ; and
emphasizes that " the wolf and wild boar lingered until the
end of the seventeenth century in the more remote recesses of
the island ", a generalization which is perhaps not strictly
accurate, since, as we have seen, the wolf in England was
extinct early in the sixteenth century, and in Scotland was
not finally destroyed until the fourth decade of the eighteenth.

That werewolfism was a sorcery not unpractised by Anglo-
Saxon warlocks is very certain, although the records are

neither numerous nor detailed. It is not surprising that many erroneous beliefs had grown up concerning these demoniac wolves which the Bishops and priests were at some pains to correct.

In an old *Poenitentiale Ecclesiarum Germaniae*,[27] 151, occurs the following : " Hast thou believed what some were once wont to hold, namely that those who are commonly called *Parcae* can effect what they are often supposed to effect, namely that when a man is born they can direct and achieve his destiny, and moreover by a magic spell whensoever certain men will they are able to transform themselves into wolves, and such a one of this kind is called (*teutonica*) ' Werewulff ',[28] or else they transform themselves into another animal shape as they list. If thou hast believed that Man made in God's Image and Likeness can be essentially changed into another species or form by any power save that of Almighty God alone, thou must fast therefor ten days on bread and water."

In England a precisely similar clause, xv — " whosoever shall believe that a man or woman may be changed into the shape of a wolf or other beast . . ."— occurs in the *Poenitentiale* [29] (1161–2) of Bartholomew Iscanus, Bishop of Exeter, who died 1184. It should be carefully remarked that no denial of werewolfism is implied, that was far too real and too terrible a sorcery, but it is insisted that there must be a right theological understanding of this dark matter. For many had been reduced into giving the Devil an almost unlimited power, and thus betrayed into the most horrid impiety.

Although it has already been quoted, we may not impertinently remind ourselves of the well-known passage in Gervase of Tilbury's *Otia Imperialia*, written during the years 1210–14, where he speaks of the English werewolves, men who are thus metamorphosed at the changes of the moon,[30] adding that such shape-shifting was then by no means uncommon in this island. He returns to the same subject a little later in his work, and chapter cxx [31] is sufficiently important to be quoted in full : " *Of men, who were wolves.* It is often debated among the learned whether Nabuchodonosor during the allotted time of his penance was indeed essentially metamorphosed into an ox, since all

theologians agree that 'twere easier to transform one shape
into another than to create out of nothing. Some authors
have written that he acted as an ox, and as a beast ate grass
and hay, being an ox in all things his shape excepted. One
thing I know that among us it is certain there are men who
at certain waxings of the moon are transformed into wolves.
In Auvergne—(the facts came under my personal observation)—a part of the diocese of Clermont, a certain great
noble, Ponce de Castres, outlawed and exiled Raimbaud de
Poinet, a valiant soldier, who had long carried arms. When
thus banished and become a wanderer on the face of the
earth, what time Raimbaud was wandering all alone, as if
he had been some wild animal, making his weary way through
trackless and untrodden paths, it happened that one night
there fell upon him a damp and sore amaze, and he grew
frantic being changed into a wolf, under which shape he
marauded his own native village, so that the farmers and
franklins in terror abandoned their cottages and manors,
leaving them empty and tenantless. This fearsome wolf
devoured children, and even older persons were attacked by
the beast, which tore their flesh grievously with its keen
and savage teeth. At last a certain carpenter was bold
enough to attack the aggressor, and with a swift blow of
his axe lopped off one of the beast's hind paws, whereupon
the werewolf at once resumed human shape. Raimbaud
publicly acknowledged that he was right glad thus to lose
his foot, since such dismembering had rid him for ever of
the accursed and damned form. For it is commonly reported
and held by grave and worthy doctors that if a werewolf
be shorn of one of his members he shall then surely recover
his original body.

 " In the neighbourhood of Chalus, in the diocese of Mende
and the department of Ardèche, there lived a man, Calce-
vayra by name, who was a werewolf. Now he at the plenilune was wont to go apart to a distant spot and there stripping
himself mother-naked he · would lay all his clothes under
some sheltered rock or thornbush. Next, nude as he was,
he rolled to and fro in the sand until he rose up in the form
of a wolf, raging with a wolf's fierce appetites. With gaping
jaws and lolling tongue he rushed violently upon his prey,
and he used to explain that wolves always run with open

mouths because this helps them to sustain their fleetness of foot. If they close their mouths they cannot easily unclench their teeth, wherefore they are more likely to be captured if by any chance they are pursued."

It were to be wished that, deeply interesting as are the histories he relates, Gervase of Tilbury had given us examples of werewolfism—and he must have known plenty of such instances—from England rather than from the south of France. It should be remarked that there exists from very ancient times a certain connection between the wolf and outlawry, the ritual of this procedure being essentially religious in character, as was clear enough from the ceremonial employed. In the *Lex Salica* of the old Franks we have the phrase : " wargus sit," " propie est, *eiectus, exue* " as Dom Bouquet glosses.[32] An early Norman Law prescribes as the punishment of certain crimes " wargus esto ", which is to say " Become a wolf ", so that anyone may pursue and slay the criminal, cutting him down as if he were a wolf, a savage beast.[33] The Laws of S. Edward the Confessor (about 1050), " De Hiis qui Pacem Ecclesie fregerint," concerning fugitives from justice have : " Et si postea repertus fuerit et teneri possit, uiuus regi reddatur, uel caput ipsius si se defenderit ; lupinum enim caput geret a die ut lagacionis sue, quod ab Anglis wluesheued nominatur. Et hec sententia communis est de omnibus ut lagis." [34] A statute of Henry I runs : " Et si quis corpus in terra, uel noffo, uel petra, sub pyramide uel structura qualibet positum, sceleratus infamacionibus effodere uel exspoliare presumpserit, wargus habeatur." [35] In *The Tale of Gamelyn*,[36] a spurious poem which Urry added to the list of Chaucer's works and Tyrwhitt removed, these lines occur in reference to Gamelyn being outlawed :—

Tho were his bonde-men . Sory and nothing glad,
When Gamelyn her lord . wolves-heed was cryed and maad.

A later instance of this word occurs in one of the Towneley plays, *The Buffeting* [37] (*c.* 1460), where raging Caiaphas cries :—

Now wols-hede and out-horne on the be tane !

During the autumn of 1216 King John Lackland was ravaging the eastern counties of England. On 3rd October

he sacrilegiously pillaged the church of good S. Guthlac at
Croyland, after which, having lost all his baggage and many
of his men in crossing the Welland, he pushed on in a black
rage to the Cistercian abbey of Swineshead, near Bolton,
where he surfeited himself by supping to excess on peaches
and a kind of March ale. An attack of dysentery followed
with fever. None the less he had himself conveyed to
Newark, where he arrived on the sixteenth, by which time
it became evident that the end was rapidly approaching.
His physician, the Abbot of Croxton, shrived and houselled
the dying king, who expired on the nineteenth of the month.
As his will directed, he was buried in Worcester Cathedral,
before the high altar.

At once strange legends began to fly abroad. In *The Brut,
or The Chronicles of England*,[38] chapter clv, we already have
the fully developed story of a monk at Swineshead, who
appalled at the king's wickedness and the famine he swore
to bring on England, went forth into the garden, where he
found a toad which he pierced with a pin through and
through till the venom had wholly infected a cup of lordly
make. This he took and filled with humming ale, which he
brought to John before whom he bent the knee lowlily,
saying, " Sir, Wassail ! for never days of your life drank you
of such a cup." " Begin, monk," quoth the king. So the
monk drank a draught, and the king drained the goblet
after him. Then the monk incontinently repaired to the
infirmary, and presently breathed his last. On whose soul
God have mercy. Amen ! And dirige with requiem shall
be sung for him so long as the Abbey stands. But the bad
king died within a few days, on the morrow after S. Luke.

Other chroniclers tell a different tale. Walter of Hemingburgh, the Austin Canon of Our Lady of Gisburn, writes how
the lewd king, hearing that the Abbot of Swineshead had an
exceedingly fair and virtuous sister, dispatched his pandars
to bring her to him, being determined to enjoy her. Whereupon a monk of the house poisoned certain goodly pears of
which the monarch ate, but not without first requiring the
donor to eat of them also.[39]

The story that King John was poisoned by a monk of
Swineshead has passed into the great body of Protestant
tradition and even to-day is sometimes repeated. That

half-crazed furious fanatic John Bale did not neglect to use
it in his clouterly play *King Johan*,[40] the original draft of
which was probably penned about 1538–1540 and considerably revised some two and twenty years later. Bale has the
effrontery to hold up King John as a great and good monarch,
a very father of his country. The legend of the poison
furnishes a dramatic episode in *The Troublesome Raigne of
King John*,[41] a foul and odious polemic, but the genius of
Shakespeare utterly rejected the thing, even at the expense
of losing what might well have been some powerful and not
ineffective scenes.[42]

The story, however, which concerns us is that the evil
monarch could not sleep in his tomb betwixt the shrines of
S. Oswald and S. Wulstan,[43] those two blessed prelates, to
the latter of whom in dying he had particularly recom-
mended his soul.[44] Walter of Hemingburgh tells us, however, that he might not rest in his buriels.[45] Terrible noises,
shrieks, howling, and other nocturnal disturbances were
heard about the haunted grave,[46] until at last the Canons
of Worcester disinterred his accursed body and flung the
vile carcass, which had been embalmed by the Abbot of
Croxton, out of the sanctuary on to a tract of unconsecrated
ground, and he was verily Lackland whose rotting corse,
the blackened features distorted in a hideous grin, had not
even six foot of earth for a grave. But after death he became
a werewolf,[47] and was seen abroad in this horrid shape, so
that all men were greatly afraid. It is very curious that
King John should become a werewolf after death, and one
suspects there may be some confusion here, and that he
became a vampire. For, as we know, in Germany, Serbia,
and modern Greece it is believed that a werewolf is doomed
to be a vampire after death.

Actually very few accounts of werewolfism in England
and Scotland have survived. Mr. Elliott O'Donnell [48] gives
an instance of a werewolf haunting in Cumberland, where in
a newly-built house far from any town a phantom " nude and
grey, something like a man with the head of a wolf—a wolf
with white pointed teeth and horrid, light eyes ", was seen.
There had previously been disturbances and howlings heard
in the vicinity of the house. In a cave among the hills
hard by were discovered a number of bones, among which

was a wolf's skull and a human skeleton lacking the head. These were burned, and the hauntings ceased.

The same author mentions " the tall grey figure of a man with a wolf's head ", a ghost seen in the Valley of the Doones, Exmoor. He records a similar phantom as having appeared in a lonely district of Merionethshire, and speaks of two particular spots in Wales, " one near Iremadac and the other on the Epynt Hills, where, local tradition still has it, werewolves once flourished."

There has been related to me the story of a werewolf incident [49] which occurred in the late eighties of the last century. An Oxford professor, being an ardent fisherman, had taken a small cottage for the summer on the shores of one of the remoter lakes in Merionethshire, among the hills, and here he and his wife were entertaining a guest. Whilst wading one day a few yards into the lake he stumbled over an object which seemed upon examination to be the skull of a dog belonging to an uncommonly large breed. Desirous of investigating further he carried it back to the house, where it was temporarily placed on a kitchen shelf. That evening his wife had been left alone awhile, and to her surprise not unmixed with fear she heard a snuffling and scratching at the kitchen door which led into the yard. Hesitant lest she should be confronted with a fierce dog, she went into the room to make sure the door was barred. As she moved something drew her attention to the window, and there she saw glaring at her through the diamond panes the head of a huge creature, half animal, half human. The cruel panting jaws were gaping wide and showed keen white teeth ; the great furry paws clasped the sill like hands ; the red eyes gleamed hideously ; it was the gaze of a man, horribly intensive, horribly intelligent. Half-fainting with fear she ran through to the front door and shot the bolt. A moment after she heard heavy breathing outside and the latch rattled menacingly. The minutes that followed were full of acutest suspense, and now and again a low snarl would be heard at the door or window, and a sound as though the creature were endeavouring to force its entrance. At last the voices of her husband and his friend, come back from their ramble, sounded in the little garden ; and as they knocked, finding the door fast, she was but able to open ere she fell in a swoon at their feet. When her senses returned, to find herself laid on the sofa and her husband anxiously bending over her, she told in halting accents what had happened. That night, having made all secure and extinguished the lamps, the two men sat up quietly, armed with stout sticks and a gun. The hours passed slowly, until when all was darkest and most lonely the soft thud of cushioned paws was heard on the gravel outside, and nails scratched at the kitchen window. To their horror in a stale phosphorescent light they saw the hideous mask of a wolf with the eyes of a man glaring through the glass, eyes that were red with hellish rage. Snatching the gun they rushed to the door, but it had seen their movement and was away in a moment. As they issued from the house a shadowy undefined shape slipped through the open gate, and in the stars they could just see a huge animal making towards the lake into which it disappeared silently, nor did a ruffle cross the surface of the water. Early the next morning the professor took the skull, and rowing a little way out from the shore flung it as far as possible into the deeper part of the tarn. The were-wolf was never seen again.

Here we have a phantom werewolf whose power for evil and ability to materialize in some degree were seemingly energized by the recovery of the skull.

There is a story of a werewolf which was seen by certain shepherds on lonelier hill-sides at night about the middle of the eighteenth century, and there is a tale of a woman who was terribly scared one evening owing to the appearance of a great furry dog with the eyes of a man, which, so far as I can learn, must have been about a hundred years ago, but both of these grow faint with the passing of time. It would not be at all extraordinary if werewolfism survived in the lonelier districts of Wales even at the present day.

It is doubtful whether Holinshed is referring to a werewolf in his *Historie of Scotland*,[50] " Straunge Sightes seene," when he writes : " Also a sort of Woolues in the night season set upon suche as were keeping cattayle abroade in the fieldes and carried away one of them to the woodes, & in the morning suffred him to escape from amongst them againe."   In any case he is speaking of a misty and legendary period.

Mr. Elliott O'Donnell gives two examples of werewolfism

in Scotland of comparatively recent years. The one occurred
in the Hebrides, and in its details resembles the Merionethshire
incident I have just told. The other, which is in some sense
more interesting, as relating to a live werewolf and not a
phantom, concerns " a mon with evil leerie eyes and eyebrows
that met in a point over his nose ", named Saunderson, who
dwelled in a cave of Ben MacDhui and who was a known
werewolf. His forefathers, too, who had also inhabited the
cave, were in their day more than suspect of lupine shape-
shifting. As I read, Saunderson would have lived towards
the end of the eighteenth century.

To come to an even later date, namely, some ten or at most
fifteen years ago, a shepherd who was then occupying a lonely
hut in a remoter tract of Inverness-shire, a man described
to me as possessing unusually piercing eyes and heavy brows
which met so as almost to form an arched bar across the forehead, was commonly reputed to be a werewolf, and certainly
the evidence seemed conclusive on this point.

Such cases, however, are rare, and it is clear that even
King James, a far more sceptical mind than is vulgarly
supposed, had never investigated a case of lycanthropy
at first hand, inasmuch as in his *Daemonologie* [51] (1597), the
following passage occurs, the interlocutors being Philomathes
and Epistemon : " *Phi.* And are not our war-woolfes one
sorte of these spirits also, that hauntes and troubles some
houses or dwelling-places ?

" *Epi.* There hath indeede bene an old opinion of such like
thinges ; For by the *Greekes* they were called λυκανθρωποι,
which signifieth men-woolfes. But to tell you simplie my
opinion in this, if anie such thing hath bene, I take it to haue
proceeded but of a naturall super-abundance of Melancholie,
which as wee reade, that it hath made some thinke themselues Pitchers, and some horses, and some one kinde of
beast or other. So suppose I that it hath so viciat the
imagination and memorie of some, as *per lucida interualla*,
it hath so highlie occupyed them, that they haue thought
themselues verrie Woolfes indeede at these times ; and so
haue counterfeited their actiones in goeing on their handes
and feete, preassing to deuoure women and barnes, fighting
and snatching with all the towne dogges, and in vsing such
like other bruitish actiones, and so to become beastes by a

stronge apprehension, as *Nebuchad-netzar* was seuen yeares ; but as to their hauing and hyding of their hard & schellie sloughes, I take that to be but eiked, by vncertaine report, the author of all lyes."

Nevertheless it was dangerous to accuse anyone of werewolfism. In the Records of the Presbytery of Kelso, 6th November, 1660, a memorial is noted that " Michell Usher, or Wishart, at Sproustoun, and Mausie Ker his wife, complean of John Broun, weaver ther, for calling him a warwoof, and her a witch ".

There is no mention of the metamorphosis into a wolf in such authorities as George Sinclar, *Satans Invisible World Discovered*,[52] Edinburgh, 1685 ; *A History of the Witches of Renfrewshire*, Paisley, 1809 ; Dr. Samuel Hibbert-Ware, *A Description of the Shetland Islands*,[53] 1822 ; Charles Kirkpatrick Sharpe, *A Historical Account of the Belief in Witchcraft in Scotland*,[54] 1820 (1884) ; Sir Walter Scott, *Letters on Demonology and Witchcraft* (Murray's Family Library), 1830 ; Sir John Graham Dalyell, *The Darker Superstitions of Scotland*,[55] 1834 ; the Rev. John Gregorson Campbell,[56] *Superstitions of the Highlands & Islands of Scotland*, Glasgow, 1900, and *Witchcraft & Second Sight in the Highlands & Islands of Scotland*, Glasgow, 1902 ; H. Drummond Gauld, F.S.A. Scot., *Ghost Tales and Legends*, 1929 ; Alexander Polson, F.S.A. Scot., *Our Highland Folklore Heritage*, Inverness, 1926, and *Scottish Witchcraft Lore*, Inverness, 1932.[57]

With regard to Wales also, neither William Howells, *Cambrian Superstitions*,[58] 1831 ; nor Wirt Sikes, *British Goblins*, 1880 ; nor even the Rev. Elias Owen in his exhaustive study, *Welsh Folk-Lore*,[59] 1896 ; nor Professor John Rhŷs, *Celtic Folklore, Welsh and Manx*,[60] 1901 ; has any mention of werwolfery.

On the other hand, most, if not indeed all, of these writers afford very detailed and considerable evidence concerning the shape-shifting of witches, especially to cats or hares.

Although strictly speaking this metamorphosis, which is generally accomplished by glamour, lies a little outside our province (however nearly akin to it), it cannot be entirely ignored in this connection. I am very well aware that it requires more chapters than I am able to afford pages for a consideration of so important a shape-shifting which should be in any sense deemed adequate or more than a mere touching upon it most lightly in passing.

Gervase of Tilbury writes [61] : " I know from mine own experience that certain women when prowling about at night in the form of cats have been espied by those who were quietly watching in silence and in secret. When these animals have been wounded, upon the very next day the women bear on their bodies in the numerical place the wounds inflicted upon the cat, and if so be a limb has been lopped off the animal, they have lost a corresponsive member." This author, accordingly, fully recognizes the phenomenon of repercussion.

In the *Malleus Maleficarum*,[62] part ii, question i, chapter 9, is related how a workman, living in a certain town of the diocese of Strasburg, was one day chopping wood when he was attacked by three great cats, biting and scratching him. He drove them off with great difficulty, bruising and beating them. To his surprise he was an hour later arrested, and brought before the judge. Nor could he for some days learn the charge since the judge was angry, supposing him to be obstinate in denying the truth. At length he was told he had on such a day at such an hour assaulted three ladies and batooned them so severely they were lying sick abed. Now he knew that was the very time he had driven off the cats, and he revealed the whole matter to the magistrates. Amazed at the event, yet convinced of the sincerity of the man, they realized it was the work of the Devil and dismissed him privily enjoining silence.

Sprenger and Kramer point out that this appearance of the three witches could have happened in two ways. Either the women were converted by glamour into the shape of cats ; or else their three familiars in the likeness of cats attacked the man. In this latter case the blows received by the demons would be instantaneously transferred to the women. Our authors are of opinion that the first method is most likely.

This incident is recorded by several writers as worthy of remark. I find it, for example, in Bodin, *Démonomanie*, livre II, vi ; and in Boguet, *Discours*, c. xlvii.

Bartolomeo Spina in his *Quaestio de Strigibus* [63] holds

PLATE VI

LES LUPINS
By Maurice Sand (See p. 237)

[face p. 194

it as certain and proven that by the exercise of black magic and evil glamour witches can and do appear in the shape of cats.

In the year 1566, during the witch-trials of the Evreux district, some terrible and extraordinary evidence was forthcoming. In an old and ancient castle at Vernon [64] a number of sorcerers were wont to assemble for their Sabbat. Four or five rash investigators resolved to watch the proceedings, only to find themselves assailed by a multitude of fierce cats. One of the company was killed by the bites and scratchings of these demoniacal animals, whilst the flesh of the others was shockingly ploughed and torn by their talons. None the less they succeeded in maiming and wounding some of the rout. The next day certain persons long suspect of witchcraft were found to be strangely injured and hurt. [65]

Boguet supplies many instances of this metamorphosis which came under his own experience. [66] One such adventure happened to a man named Charcot of the bailiwick of Gez. Another took place at the Château de Joux, when a traveller wounded a wild cat with his carbine. On arriving at the next inn he found the hostess had just been hurt in the hip by a shot from a carbine.

Paul Sébillot speaks of a sabbat of witches under the glamorous form of cats held in the haunted forest of Bonlieu, and also of two notorious sorceresses, la Dame de Florimont, who lived in the Rossberg (Hautes Vosges) district, and was eventually burned as a witch ; and Madame de Badon, of the Château de Marçay, near Chinon, both of whom were adepts in the foul craft of shape-shifting. [67]

In 1875–6 the Rev. Wentworth Webster learned the following in the district of the Labourd : " Witches still appear in the shape of cats, but generally black ones. About two years ago we were told of a man who, at midnight, chopped off the ear of a black cat, who was thus bewitching his cattle, and lo ! in the morning it was a woman's ear, with an earring in it. He deposited it in the Mairie, and we might see it there; but we did not go to look, as it was some distance off." [68]

In English trials for witchcraft the metamorphosis of the accused into a hare or a cat is often brought forward in evidence. [69] One example of each, which shall be chosen from later cases, may be adduced.

At the Summer Assizes held at Taunton before Justice Archer in 1663, Julian Cox, aged about seventy years, was indicted for practising witchcraft. The evidence upon which she was found guilty was overwhelming, but the point that concerns us here is " The first Witness was an Huntsman, who swore that he went out with a pack of Hounds to hunt a Hare, and not far off from *Julian Cox* her house, he at last started a Hare. The *Dogs* hunted her very close, and the third ring hunted her in view, till at last the Huntsman perceiving the Hare almost spent, and making towards a great Bush, he ran on the other side of the Bush to take her up, and preserve her from the Dogs. But as soon as he laid hands on her, it proved to be *Julian Cox*, who had her head groveling on the ground, and her globes (as he exprest it) · upward. He knowing her, was affrighted, that his Hair on his Head stood on end ; and yet spake to her, and askt her what brought her there. But she was so far out of Breath, that she could not make him any answer. His Dogs also came up with full cry to recover the game, and smelt at her, and so left off hunting any further. And the Huntsman with his Dogs went home presently, sadly affrighted ".

This account is given by Joseph Glanvil in his *Saducismus Triumphatus*,[70] a work which even so complete an agnostic as W. E. H. Lecky [71] was compelled to acknowledge as— in his own phrase—" probably the ablest book ever published in defence of the superstition," a belief in the supernatural, whilst Glanvil himself, he candidly wrote as philosopher, scholar, and thinker, " has been surpassed in genius by few of his successors."

It does not seem possible that any reasoning and un-prejudiced mind should cavil at the evidence of this witness in the trial. It is a plain, straightforward, and essentially veracious statement of fact. Yet, Glanvil remarks, some half-witted people thought he swore false, which " *I suppose was because they imagined that what he told implied that* Julian Cox *was turned into an Hare. Which she was not, nor did his report imply any such real Metamorphosis of her body, but that these ludicrous Dæmons exhibited to the sight of this Hunts-man and his Doggs the shape of an Hare, one of them turning himself into such a form, and others hurrying on the body of* Julian *near the same place, and at the same swiftness, but*

interposing betwixt that Hare-like Spectre and her body,
modifying the Air so that the scene there to the beholders sight,
was as if nothing but Air were there, and a shew of Earth
perpetually suited to that where the Hare passed. As I have
heard of some Painters that have drawn the Sky in a huge large
Landskip, so lively that the Birds have flown against it, thinking
it free Air, and so have fallen down. And if Painters and
Juglers by the tricks of Legerdemain can do such strange feats
to the deceiving of the sight, it is no wonder that these Airy
invisible Spirits as far surpass them in all such præstigious
doings as the Air surpasses the Earth for subtilty ".[72]

Glanvil's explanation is interesting and quite admissible.
Indeed, it differs only in an unessential detail from the
traditional and accepted explanation of glamour, which
myself I might perhaps be rather disposed to prefer in this
case of the witch Julian Cox.

There is an interesting allusion to the hare-metamorphosis
of witches in Matthew Morgan's *Poem Upon the Late Victory*
over the French Fleet at Sea (1692) [73] :—

> So Huntsmen think they have a Hare in view,
> And do with eager Cries her Flight pursue.
> But when Sagacious *Jouler* comes so near,
> To seize her hinder Legs and pluck to tear,
> *Comidia* is Couchant in the Thorn,
> And by their half-spent Mouths a Witch is Torn.

One of the latest—although perhaps quite strictly speaking
not the very last—of witch-trials in England was the case
of Jane Wenham,[74] the " Wise Woman of Walkerne ", who
on 4th March, 1711–12, was brought before Mr. Justice Powell
at Hertford Assizes. Extraordinary interest had been roused,
not only throughout the district but even in London, where
the accused became " the discourse of the town ". The
evidence proved overwhelming, and in spite of the efforts of
Justice Powell, whose attitude showed him to be entirely
sceptical, Jane Wenham was formally condemned, only to be
reprieved forthwith and soon pardoned.

There were many witnesses, and Anne Thorn, who had been
bewitched by Jane Wenham, " saw Things like Cats appear
to her " and " always before a Fit she saw a Cat, which
would not only appear to her, but speak, and tell her several
Things, tempting her to go out of Doors. It was also taken

notice of that a dismal Noise of Cats was at that Time, and
several Times after, heard about the House, sometimes
their Cry resembling that of Young Children, at other Times
they made a Hellish Noise, to which nothing can be resembled;
this was accompany'd by Scratchings, heard by all that were
in the House, under the Windows, and at the Doors, which
startled and affrighted them all to a great degree ; and
several People, particularly *James Burvile, Thomas Ireland,*
and others, saw these Cats, sometime Three or Four in a
Company, which would run to *Jane Wenham*'s House whenever any Body came up to them." Anne Thorn also deposed
that " *in the Morning of the 26th of* February, *as she was lying
in bed, she saw a Cat sitting in the Window, which spoke to her* ".
Naturally in a great fear " *she hid her Head in the Bed-cloathes* ",
and presently the cat vanished.

Thomas Ireland was sworn, and deposed " That he hearing
a Noise of Cats crying and screaming about the House
several Times, went out, and saw several of them, which
made towards *Jane Wenham*'s House ; that he saw a Cat
with a Face like *Jane Wenham* ".

" *James Burvile* was also sworn, who said, That hearing
the Scratchings and Noises of Cats, he went out, and saw
several of them ; that one of them had a Face like *Jane
Wenham.*" [75]

Various   sceptical   and   agnostic   pamphleteers   with
" plentiful Scatterings of *Billingsgate* Language " soon began
to assert " The Impossibility of Witchcraft ", but they were
very ably and convincingly answered by Dr. Francis Bragge,
who had impartially inquired into the case.   As might be
expected, Grub Street made a mighty jest of the apparition
of a cat which spoke as something " very ridiculous and
incredible ", but Dr. Bragge fairly clinches the matter by
his answer : " Is it more ridiculous and incredible, that an
evil Spirit should assume the Shape of a Cat, and in such a
Shape speak so as to be heard and understood, than that
the Devil should speak to *Eve* in the Shape of a Serpent ?
Which we are oblig'd to believe upon the Credit of Divine
Revelation." [76]

I myself have known in my own experience an instance of
a witch who assumed the shape of a cat (Oxfordshire), and also
a similar metamorphosis into a hare (Devonshire).   In both

cases I make no doubt there was glamour induced by the black art.

In *Memories of Hurstwood, Burnley, Lancashire*,[77] by Tattersall Wilkinson and J. F. Tattersall, is given an interesting account of an old woman, by name Sally Walton, who lived at Cloughfoot Bridge in that district, some forty or fifty years before, and who was reputed a witch. A farmer, who dwelt near, awaking one night saw a large black cat sitting at his feet and watching him intently. Laying hold of a knife which was close at hand the farmer hurled it at the cat, striking one of its fore-legs. The animal vanished, leaving no trace anywhere. The very morning after it was noticed that old Sally had her corresponding arm wrapped in a kerchief, and there was not a neighbour but believed that she had assumed feline shape and visited the farmer's cottage, being wounded by him.

Some cat and hare incidents are recorded by the Rev. W. Henry Jones, of Mumby Vicarage, Alford, in *Lincolnshire Notes and Queries*,[78] October, 1889. A parishioner once told this gentleman that she saw a white rabbit in the church-yard, which being chased into the south porch vanished. At Hogsthorpe there was a hare no dogs could ever catch. One day, passing the house where a reputed witch lived, they heard a great noise, and entering found the old woman being chased about by dogs. The Rev. W. H. Jones' servant from Kirton Lindsey said : " One night my father and brother saw a cat in front of them. Father knew it was a witch and hammered it. Next day the witch had her face all tied up, and shortly afterwards died." " A story of a wizard taking the form of a hare and being slain was told to me a few miles west of Alford." At Grasby a witch who entered a house as a cat was attacked and beaten only to disappear. A little later a woman died, and those who laid out the body saw it was marked just in the same places where the cat had been struck.

Mr. W. Self Weeks, writing in the *Transactions of the Lancashire and Cheshire Antiquarian Society*, vol. xxxiv (1916),[79] relates that he was told by a farmer of Grindleton, near Clitheroe, that a weaver once found a cat near his loom which he in vain tried to drive away. At last in a rage he took a piece of rope and strangled the animal. The next day

an old woman long held to be a witch was found dead in
her bed. A farmer at Milton related that a few years ago
a good house belonging to the Duke of Devonshire, near
Bolton Abbey, fell vacant.   There were many applicants,
and it was eventually let to a man whose family were old
tenants of His Grace.   He took possession, but was not
allowed a moment's peace.   When he went to bed he was
troubled by bad attacks of nightmare, which he seemed to
hear enter his room in spectral form and wellnigh throttle
him in a violent grasp.   He consulted several doctors who
were unable to afford relief, and at last he visited a well-
known " wise man " at Leeds.   The wise man told him
that a certain woman, a neighbour, was at the bottom of
the mischief.   He was bidden lay a scythe by his bed ready
to hand, and when the nightmare seemed to be upon him,
to start up and slash at it through the air several times.
He followed the instructions implicitly, and was never
troubled again.   The next morning, however, he heard that
a woman who lived near had been taken suddenly and
mysteriously ill.   She was confined to her bed, and although
she lingered many months before she died, she could never
walk again.   Her name was Hannah H——, an elderly
woman, a regular chapel-goer, and esteemed a highly
respectable person.

   Mrs. Ella Mary Leather, in *The Folk-Lore of Herefordshire,*[80]
writes : " Witches can change themselves into the form of
animals, usually bats or black cats.   A man from Eardisley,
going one night to see a neighbour on the Kington Road,
whose wife was a reputed witch, met a large black cat at the
garden gate.   Entering, he asked the man how his wife
was. ' Didn't you meet her,' was the answer. ' She has
only this minute gone out through the door there ! ' ' So
it was certain after that,' my informant added, ' she was a
witch, right enough.' . . . At Much Marle (near Ledbury)
it was believed that witches became hares in order to lead
the foxhounds off the right scent."

   The famous Mrs. Anna Eliza Bray, in that most interesting
work, *The Tamar and the Tavy,*[81] recounts the story of an
old witch, living near Tavistock, who when she needed
money would assume the shape of a hare and bid her grandson inform a certain ardent Nimrod who resided hard by

that a hare was to be found in a given place. The lad was thus always sure to receive a good vail. At length, as the hare could never be caught, suspicion was aroused, and on one occasion when the old woman and her grandson were seen to leave their cottage the hounds were held in readiness to prevent them. The chase was speedier then than the witch cared, and she had only got within her cottage and resumed her shape when the huntsman accompanied by a justice and the parson of the parish were at the door which upon her refusal to open they forced. They found the old hag bleeding, covered with wounds, and still panting, hard breathed. She denied she had cozened them in the shape of a hare, but when they threatened to call in the pack she confessed her sorceries.

With regard to Scotland, I have collected a not inconsiderable amount of evidence, some from oral sources, but this must be reserved for a special study of the subject. At the present it will suffice to refer to the instances given by the Rev. J. G. Campbell in his *Witchcraft & Second Sight in the Highlands & Islands of Scotland*, to which study attention has already been drawn. He mentions the various forms in which the warlock may be disguised—ravens, rats, mice, black sheep, " and very frequently cats and hares." " The stories of witches assuming the shape of hares are numberless.
. . . When a witch assumes this shape it is dangerous to fire at her without putting silver, a sixpence or a button of that metal, in the gun. If the hare fired at was, as indeed it often was, a witch in disguise, the gun burst, and the shot came back and killed the party firing, or some mischance followed. Old women used, therefore, to recommend that a sixpence be put in the gun when firing at a hare." [82]

A very remarkable account is given in Charles St. John's *Wild Sports and Natural History of the Highlands* [83] of the tranvection of a witch " possessed of more than mortal power ". After having long plagued the countryside with her sorceries she is said to have been brought down one night as she skirled through the air by a pot-valiant old soldier who loaded his gun with a double charge of powder and in place of shot a crooked sixpence and some silver buttons. Well-lined with whisky he fired when he saw her " just coming like a muckle bird right towards him ". In the morning he was found lying half-asleep and half in a swoon, his gun burst beside him, and a fine large heron shot through and through on the ground, " which heron as everyone felt assured was the cailleach herself ". The place where this happened is a bleak cold-looking piece of water known as Lochan-na-cailleaich (the witch's tarn), and Donald the beater who told the story added : " her ghaist is still to the fore, and the loch side is no canny after the gloaming." Allowing for natural exaggeration there is certainly a true story here.

W. N. Neil, in a study *Witch-Cats in Scotland,*[84] remarks : " The murderous ferocity of these Highland witch-cats compared to the milder nature of their sisters in the Low-lands almost leads one to think that it was not the common domestic cat that was the therianthropic shape chosen by the northern witches, but that of the spitting, swearing, untameable wild-cat which is a prominent representative of the Highland fauna to this day. The same conjecture may also explain the absence of the true werwolf from Scottish story, although the actual wolves persisted in its mountains and its moors till the eve of the Battle of Culloden. The wild-cat being comparatively common and noted for its cruelty and ferocity would be a far more suitable disguise for a witch than a sporadic and possibly timid wolf." The timidity of the wolf may be questioned.

The Rev. Elias Owen, in his *Welsh Folk-Lore,* to which reference has already been made, gives a large number of instances of witches transforming themselves into cats or hares. One example of each must briefly suffice. On the road between Cerrigydrudion and Bettws-y-Coed stood an inn kept by two women, sisters, of prepossessing manners and appearance, which, however, acquired an ill-name owing to the mysterious robberies that occurred in the house, although travellers confessed that the doors of their rooms always remained locked in the morning just as they had fastened them the night before. The parson of Llan Festiniog [85] resolved to unravel the business. Accordingly he obtained a lodging at the hostelry, but on going to bed kept a candle burning in the room. As he feigned sleep two cats stealthily crept through a narrow partition, and approaching his clothes seemed to fumble them with their paws as though feeling for his purse. Like lightning he struck with his sword and amid terrible screams the animals disappeared. Next morning only one of the sisters waited on him, and he was informed the other sister was indisposed. However, he forced his way to her presence and found that her right hand was bandaged just where he had wounded the cat. He then revealed who he was, and solemnly exhorted them to abandon their shape-shifting and sorceries.

The following incident happened to the Rector of Llanycil a few years before *Welsh Folk-Lore* was written, and is therefore an entirely modern example. When his servant was churning milk it was found that in spite of her efforts the milk would not churn. Upon removing the lid, however, out leaped a huge hare and ran off at full speed, whereupon the milk came easily enough. A wise man in Wales said that a witch in the shape of a hare could only be caught by a black greyhound. Mr. Owen also notes the unlucky omen of a hare crossing the path, and gives an interesting example.

C. I. Elton, in his *Origins of English History*,[86] writes that " The oldest Welsh laws contain several allusions to the magical character of the hare which was thought to change its sex every month or year, and to be the companion of witches who often assumed its shape ". In Western Brittany hares are much feared. Essex Smith, in his *Fairies and Witches in Old Radnorshire*,[87] has several examples of hare and cat transformations. " Witches in the form of hares were numerous in Radnorshire. One huge hare, grey with extreme age, lived on Clyro Hill for many years ; she could neither be shot nor caught with harriers or greyhounds ; and was believed by all the countryside to be a witch. She had her regular rounds, and every morning early she came and sat under a bush near Tynessa."

The Manx witches are known as *butches*, which is probably nothing more than a variant of the English word. They are credited with the power of shape-shifting and their especial metamorphosis is that of the hare, when they are so fleet that only a black greyhound can catch them, and no shot save it be silver can hurt them. In Wales, generally speaking, only women can appear as hares, but in the Manx tradition both men and women assume this shape. This property is also said to run in certain families, and Professor

Rhŷs in his *Celtic Folklore* [88] mentions a smith in the
neighbourhood of Ramsey who was known as *gaaue mwaagh*
"the hare smith". A witch if wounded as a hare resumes
the human shape and the spell is broken, but the hurt
always remains.

The cat-transformation is known in the Channel Islands,
and here also werewolfery was once rife, but the tradition
wanes. Sir Edgar MacCulloch in his *Guernsey Folk Lore,* [89]
a book of the deepest interest, says : " The ' Varou ', now
almost entirely forgotten, seems to have belonged to the
family of nocturnal goblins. He is allied to the ' Loup-
Garou ' of the French, and the ' Were-Wolf ' of the English,
if, indeed, he is not absolutely identical with them. He is
believed to be endowed with a marvellous appetite, and it
is still proverbially said of a great eater ' Il mange comme
un varou '.

" ' Aller en varouverie ' was an expression used in former
times in speaking of those persons who met together in
unfrequented places for the purposes of debauchery or other
illicit practices. Thus one night such a one was heard
saying that the time was propitious ' pour aller en varouverie
sous l'épine '. *Varou* was originally from the Breton *Varw*—
' the dead '—and was identified with the ' Heroes ' or beatified
warriors who were, by Homer and Hesiod, supposed to be
in attendance on Saturn. Guernsey, in the days of Demetrius,
was known by the name of the Isle of Heroes, or of Demons,
and Saturn was said to be confined there in a ' golden rock '
bound by ' golden chains '."

In Guernsey the word *varou* still lingers in place-names.
The " Creux des Varous " is a subterranean cavern, which
extends, folk say, from Houmet to L'Erée ; a plot of ground
near the cromlech of L'Erée (" Le Creux des Fées ") is still
known as " Le Camp du Varou ", and an estate in the parish
of S. Saviour is called " Le Mont-Varou ". " Old people
still remember that it used to be said in their youth that ' Le
Char des Varous ' was to be heard rolling over the cliffs and
rocks on silver-tyred wheels, between Houmet and the Castle
of Albecq, before the death of any of the great ones of the
earth ; and how this supernatural warning was sure to be
followed almost immediately by violent storms and tempests."

" Sorcerers have the power of taking the forms of different

animals, but when thus disguised cannot be wounded but by silver.

" A Mr. Le Marchant, ' des grent mesons,' had often fired at a white rabbit which frequented his warren, but without success. One day, however, beginning to suspect how the case really stood, he detached his silver sleeve-button from his wrist-band, loaded his gun with it, took a steady aim, and fired. The rabbit immediately disappeared behind the hedge. He ran up, and, hearing some person groaning as if in great pain on the other side, looked over and recognized a neighbour of his, a lady of the Vale, who was lying with her leg broken and bleeding profusely from a fresh wound."

The evidence for werewolfism in Ireland is of immemorial antiquity and persists through the centuries. Lycanthropy was believed for the most part to run in families, and an early tradition in the *Cóir Anmann* (*Fitness of Names*) has : " Laignech *Fáelad*, that is, he was the man that used to shift into *fáelad*, i.e. wolf-shapes. He and his offspring after him used to go, whenever they pleased, into the shapes of the wolves, and, after the custom of wolves, kill the herds. Wherefore he was called Laignech *Fáelad*, for he was the first of them (the group composed of Laignech and his descendants) to go into a wolf-shape." [90] This was in Ossory. [91]

From the *Leabhar Na H-Uidhri* (*The Book of the dun Cow*), [92] the oldest volume now known entirely in the Irish language, we learn that the Druids practised the magic art of shape-shifting.

An old Irish legend, which is given in *Kongs Skuggsjo* (*Speculum Regale*), a Norse book compiled about 1250, runs as follows : " There is also in that land (Ireland) one wonderful thing, which will seem very untruthful to men. Yet the people who inhabit that land say that it is certainly true. And that befell on account of the wrath of a holy man. It is said that when the holy Patricius was preaching Christianity in that land, there was one great race more hostile to him than the other people that were in the land. And these men tried to do him many kinds of injury. And when he preached Christianity to them as to other men, and came to meet them when they were holding their assembly, then they took this counsel, to howl at him like wolves.

But when he saw that his message would succeed little with
these people, then he became very wroth, and prayed God
that He might avenge it on them by some judgement, that
their descendants might for ever remember their disobedience.
And great punishment and fit and very wonderful has since
befallen their descendants ; for it is said that all men who
come from that race are always wolves at a certain time,
and run into the woods and take food like wolves ; and they
are worse in this that they have human reason, for all their
cunning, and such desire and greed for men as for other
creatures.   And it is said that some become so every seventh
year, and are men during the interval.   And some have
it so long that they have seven years at once, and are never
so afterwards." [93]

I do not find this in the life of S. Patrick and the account
of this Saint given by the Bollandists, under 17th March, [94]
although one might have expected to meet with it in
chapter xiii of the *Vita S. Patricii* by the Cistercian Jocelyn
of Furness (*fl.* 1200), which has rubric *Patricio resistentes
seuere castigantur*.   Neither is the incident mentioned in the
Tripartite Life of S. Patrick, but among the miracles of the
Saint is recorded " Coroticus King of the Britons [changed]
into the shape of a fox in his country ". [95]

In the *Book of Ballymote*, [96] a miscellaneous collection
embracing historical, legendary, genealogical, and other
matter, some of which is very ancient, compiled about the
beginning of the fifteenth century, a passage says that " the
children of the wolf " in Ossory could transform themselves
and go abroad to devour people.

A Latin hexameter poem of the thirteenth century on the
Wonders of Ireland, printed by Thomas Wright and J. O.
Halliwell in their *Reliquiae Antiquae*, [97] has fourteen lines
De hominibus qui se uertunt in lupos, which run : " There are
certain men of the Celtic race who have a marvellous power
which comes to them from their forbears.   For by an evil
craft they can at will change themselves into the shape of
wolves with sharp tearing teeth, and often thus transformed
will they fall upon poor defenceless sheep, but when folk
armed with clubs and weapons run to attack them shouting
lustily then do they flee and scour away apace.   Now when
they are minded to transform themselves they leave their

own bodies, straitly charging their friends neither to move or touch them at all, however lightly, for if this be done never will they be able to return to their human shape again. If whilst they are wolves anyone hurts or wounds them, then upon their own bodies the exact wound or mark can plainly be seen. And with much amaze have they been espied in human form with great gobbets of raw bleeding flesh champed in their jaws." The same account, commencing "The descendants of the Wolf are in Ossory", is given in the Irish version (MS. D) of the *Historia Britonum* of Nennius of Bangor.[98]

Giraldus Cambrensis, in his *Topographia Hibernica*,[99] Distinctio ii, cap. 19, has the following account of were-wolfery: "About three years before the arrival of Prince John in Ireland,[100] it chanced that a certain priest, who was journeying from Ulster towards Meath, was benighted in a wood that lies on the boundures of Meath. Whilst he, and the young lad his companion, were watching by a fire they had kindled under the leafy branches of a large tree, there came up to them a wolf who immediately addressed them in the following words: 'Do not alarm yourselves and do not be in any way afraid. You need not fear, I say, where there is no reason for fear.' The travellers none the less were thrown in a great damp and were astonied. But the wolf reverently called upon the Name of God. The priest then adjured him, straitly charging him by Almighty God and in the might of the Most Holy Trinity that he should do them no sort of harm, but rather tell them what sort of creature he was who spake with a human voice. The wolf replied with seemly speech, and said: 'In number we are two, to wit a man and a woman, natives of Ossory, and every seven years on account of the curse laid upon our folk by the blessed Abbot S. Natalis,[101] a brace of us are compelled to throw off the human form and appear in the shape of wolves. At the end of seven years, if perchance these two survive they are able to return again to their homes, reassuming the bodies of men, and another two must needs take their place. Howbeit my wife, who labours with me under this sore visitation, lies not far from hence, grievously sick. Wherefore I beseech you of your good charity to comfort her with the aid of your priestly office.'

When he had so said, the wolf led the way to a tree at no great distance, and the priest followed him trembling at the strangeness of the thing. In the hollow of the tree he beheld a wolfen,[102] and she was groaning piteously mingled with sad human sighs. Now when she saw the priest she thanked him very courteously and gave praise to God Who had vouchsafed her such consolation in her hour of utmost need.

" The priest then shrived her and gave her all the last rites of Holy Church so far as the houselling. Most earnestly did she entreat him that she might receive her God, and that he would administer to her the crown of all, the Body of the Lord.

" The priest, however, declared that he was not provided with the holy viaticum, when the man-wolf, who had withdrawn apart for a while, came forward and pointed to the wallet, containing a mass-book and some consecrated Hosts which, according to the use of his country, the good priest was carrying suspended from his neck under his clothing. The man-wolf entreated him not to deny them any longer the Gift of God, which it was not to be questioned, Divine Providence had sent to them. Moreover to remove all doubt, using his claw as a hand, he drew off the pelt from the head of the wolfen and folded it back even as far down as the navel, whereupon there was plainly to be seen the body of an old woman. Upon this the priest, since she so instantly besought him, urged though it may be more by fear than by reasoning, hesitated no longer but gave her Holy Communion, which she received most devoutly from his hands. Immediately after this the man-wolf rolled back the skin again, fitting it to its former place.

" These holy rites having been duly rather than regularly performed, the man-wolf joined their company by the fire they had kindled under the tree and showed himself a human being not a four-footed beast. In the early morning, at cock-light he led them safely out of the wood, and when he left them to pursue their journey he pointed out to them the best and shortest road, giving them directions for a long way. In taking leave also, he thanked the priest most gratefully and in good set phrase for the surpassing kindness he had shown, promising moreover that if it were God's will he should return home (and already two parts of the period during which he was under the malediction had passed) he would take occasion to give further proofs of his gratitude.

"As they were parting the priest inquired of the man-wolf whether the enemy (the English invader) who had now landed on their shores would continue long to possess the land. The wolf replied : ' On account of the sins of our nation and their enormous wickedness the anger of God, falling upon an evil generation, hath delivered them into the hands of their enemies. Therefore so long as this foreign people shall walk in the way of the Lord and keep His commandments, they shall be safe and not to be subdued ; but if—and easy is the downward path to iniquity and nature prone to evil—it come to pass that through dwelling among us they turn to our whoredoms, then assuredly will they provoke the wrath of the Lord upon themselves also.'

"It so happened that about two years later when I was passing through Meath, the Bishop of that diocese had summoned a synod, and had requested the honourable attendance of the Bishops of neighbouring sees and my Lords the Abbots, in order that they might take counsel together concerning this incident which the priest had related to him. The Bishop, learning that I was travelling in those parts, sent two of his priests to me, asking me if it were possible to attend the synod at which a matter of such grave importance was to be deliberated, and, if indeed I could not assist in person, he begged me at least to give them my opinion and judgement in writing. When I had heard the whole circumstance in detail from the two priests (although indeed I had been told of it before by many others), inasmuch as I was prevented by many weighty affairs from attending the synod, I was fain amend for my absence by giving my advice in a letter. The Bishop and the full synod so far approved of my counsel, that they followed it forthwith, commanding the priest to travel to Rome, and there to lay the whole thing before the Holy Father,[103] delivering to him letters containing the priest's own account, which was certified by the seals of all the Bishops and Abbots who had been present at the conclave.

"It is not to be disputed, but must be most certainly believed that for our salvation the Divine Nature assumed human nature. Now in the present case we find that at God's bidding

in order to manifest His supreme power and righteousness
by a very miracle human nature assumed the form of a wolf.

"The point arises : Was this creature man or beast ? A
rational animal is far above the level of a brute beast. Are
we to class in the species man a four-footed animal, whose
face is bent to the earth, and who cannot indulge in the
visible faculty ? Would he who slew this animal be a
murderer ? We reply that the miracles of God are not to
be made the subjects of argument and human disputation,
but are to be wondered at in all humility."

Giraldus, having come to this very admirable and sane
conclusion, then discusses the famous passages in S. Augustine,
De Ciuitate Dei, xvi, 8, and xviii, 17 and 18.

He sums up : " In our own day also we have seen persons,
who deeply skilled in magic arts, turned any substance which
was of sufficient quantity into fat porkers as they seemed
(but curiously they were always of a reddish hue), and these
they sold in the markets. None the less the glamour vanished
as soon as they crossed any water and the substance returned
to its true material form. However carefully they were
kept, they could not retain their spurious appearance more
than three days.

" It is commonly known, and has been bitterly complained
of in former days as well as now, that certain foul hags in
Wales, as well as in Ireland and Scotland, change themselves
into the shape of hares, and under this counterfeit form
sucking the teats of cows they secretly rob other persons of
their milk.

" We hold then with S. Augustine that neither demons nor
sorcerers can either create or essentially change their natures ;
but those, whom God has created are able by His permission to
metamorphize themselves so far as mere outward appearance
is concerned, so that they appear to be what truly they are
not, and the senses of men beholding them are fascinated
and deceived by glamour, so that things are not seen as they
really exist, but by some phantom power or magic spell
the human vision is deluded and mocked inasmuch as it
rests upon unreal and fictitious forms."

Camden,[104] writing of Wolf-men in Tipperary, says :
" Whereas some of the Irish and such as would be thought
worthy of credit, doe affirme, that certaine men in this

tract are yeerely turned into Wolves ; surely I suppose it be a meere fable : unlesse happly through that malicious humour of predominant unkind Melancholie, they be possessed with the malady that the Phisitians call Λυκανθρωπία, which raiseth and engendreth such like phantasies, as that they imagine themselves to be transformed into Wolves. Neither dare I otherwise affirme of these metamorphised *Lycaones* in *Liveland*, concerning whom many writers deliver many and meruailous reports."

Sir William Temple, in his essay *Of Poetry*,[105] commenting upon "those Trophies of Enchantment . . . Productions of the *Gothick Wit* . . . all the visionary Tribe of *Fairies*, *Elves*, and *Goblins*, of *Sprites* and *Bulbeggars* ", continues : " How much of this Kind, and of this Credulity remained even to our own Age, may be observed by any Man that reflects so far as thirty or forty Years ; how often avouched, and how generally credited, were the Stories of *Fairies*, *Sprites*, *Witchcrafts*, and *Enchantments*? In some Parts of *France*, and not longer ago, the common People believed certainly there were *Lougaroos*, or Men turned into Wolves ; and I remember several *Irish* of the same Mind."

NOTES TO CHAPTER IV

[1] A note by Sir Simon Degge, who was born in 1612 and lived to the age of 92. This note is printed in the Rev. Thomas Harwood's edition (1820) of Sampson Eredeswick's *Survey of Staffordshire*, pp. 2 and 3.

[2] Robertson, *Buxton and the Peak*, p. 41, quoted by Harting.

[3] The authoritative study is *British Animals Extinct within Historic Times*, by James Edmund Harting, F.L.S., F.Z.S., London, Trübner, 1880, an admirable work from which I have not hesitated to draw freely for details of the wolf in Great Britain and Ireland. Harting emphasizes (p. 204) that " in order to confine the subject within reasonable limits " he carefully abstains from any mention of the werewolf or wolf-legends. If I give any quotation from Harting, and not from the original source, I have been careful to mention this in the corresponsive note.

[4] *The Original Chronicle of Andrew of Wyntoun*, ed. F. J. Amours, The Scottish Text Society, vol. ii, p. 312 (Wemyss MS.), ch. xxxix, ll. 617–622.

[5] Antwerp, 1605, p. 59.

[6] Migne, *Patres Latini*, lxxxix, column 426, D. The *Poenitentiale* is now generally considered to be a Frankish compilation of the ninth century and largely drawn from Halitgar. See H. J. Schmitz, *Die Bussbücher und die Bussdisciplin der Kirche*, Mainz, 1883, Theil iii, Kapitel 4, " Poenitentiale Egberti," pp. 565–587.

[7] *Britannia. Britain* . . . " Written first in Latine by *William Camden*, Clarenceux K. of A. Translated newly into English by *Philemon Holland* . . . Finally revised . . . by the said Author." Folio, Londini, 1610, Yorke-shire, p. 715.

⁸ Raphael Holinshed, *The Firste volume of the Chronicles of England, Scotlande, and Irelande*, 1577; The Thirde Booke, cap. 7, "Of sauuage beastes and vermines," p. 108. Holinshed claims that England is "void of noysome beasts, as Lions, Beares, Tygers, Wolfes, and such like : by meanes whereof our countrymen may trauaile in safetie". Which cannot be said to-day.

⁹ Folio, 1612, p. 185.

¹⁰ Ibid., p. 144. Selden quotes as his authority : *Itin. Leicest.* 27. *Hen.* 8. *in Archiu. Turr.* Londin.

¹¹ 4to, 1677. Term Catalogues, Hilary, 28th February, 1678.

¹² 4to, 1678. Term Catalogues, Michaelmas, 26th November, 1677.

¹³ 4to, 1735. Book the Third, ll. 13–19 ; pp. 50–1.

¹⁴ Joannis Caii Britanni *de Canibus Britannis*. Liber Unus. Londini, per Gulielmum Seresium. 8vo, 1570. I have used the edition in *The Works of John Caius, M.D.*, ed. John Venn and E. S. Roberts, Cambridge, 1912, p. 10 (*De Canibus*), and quote the English version *Of Englishe Dogges*, by Abraham Fleming, 1576, as there reprinted, pp. 21 and 22 of the *Treatise*. Thomas Pennant, *Tours in Wales*, 1778–1781 (new edition, by Professor Rhŷs, 3 vols., 1883), remarks that "the report of *Edgar*'s having extirpated the race of wolves out of the principality, is erroneous," vol. i (1883), p. 113.

¹⁵ *Monumenta Historica Britannica*, vol. i, pp. 856–872, *De Bello Hastingensi Carmen*, ll. 571–2 ; p. 867. Guy was Bishop of Amiens 1059 to 1075.

¹⁶ Harl. MSS., No. 3859, ed. Williams, Rolls Series, pp. 50–1. "Apud Kermerden lupus rabiosus duo de uiginti homines momordit qui omnes fere protinus perierunt." The MS. is believed to be a translation from the original Welsh.

¹⁷ It is said that the story of Gellert is found in many literatures. It certainly resembles the tale of the Knight and his Greyhound in *The Seven Wise Masters*. See further, Heinrich Adelbert von Keller, *Li romans des sept sages*, Tübingen, 1830, p. clxxviii. William Robert Spencer's poem, *Beth-Gêlert, or The Grave of the Greyhound*, signed Dôlymelynllyn, 11th August, 1800, was privately printed (4 pp.) by Collingwood, Oxford, but not published. *Beth-Gêlert* was first published in *Poems* (pp. 78–86) by William Robert Spencer, London, Cadell and Davies, 1811.

¹⁸ I have used the facsimile edition with introduction by William Blades, London, Elliot Stock, 1881. The allusion to Tristram is to Sir Tristram of the Table Round, who was a mighty hunter and a great authority on all matters of venery. He was popularly supposed to have been the author of many (if not all) hunting terms, and his name was constantly invoked to clench a statement, as it were.

¹⁹ *The Noble Arte of Venerie or Hunting*, 4to, 1575, chapters 75 and 76. The pages are wrongly numbered, 863 and 862 ; followed by p. 205 to p. 214. Turbervile gives two chapters to hunting the wolf.

²⁰ *Heir beginnis the hystory and croniklis of Scotland*. John Bellenden's translation of Boece. Edinburgh, 1541. Ca. xi, "of the gret plente of haris, hartis, and vthir vvild bestiall in Scotland." Sig. C. ii.

²¹ Trans. Philemon Holland, ut cit. sup., *Scotia, Scotland*, p. 54.

²² There are, of course, various stories concerning the killing of the last wolf who infested a certain district in Scotland, as for example the last wolf killed at Lochaber by Sir Ewen Cameron in 1680, which Pennant misunderstood to be the last wolf killed in Scotland : *British Zoology*, vol. i, p. 88, and *Tour in Scotland*, vol. i, p. 206. Surtees, *History and Antiquities of the County of Durham*, vol. ii, p. 172, gives 1682 as the date of the killing of the last wolf in Scotland. Sir Thomas Dick Lauder in his *Account of the Moray Floods of August, 1829*, relates how MacQueen of Pall-à-chrocain slew the last wolf, but says that the scene of this exploit was in the parish of Moy, county Inverness. He also has another story of two old wolves and their cubs being killed at Knoch of Braemory, near the source of the Burn of Newton.

²³ Holinshed, op. cit., p. 9 ; Camden, op. cit., *Ireland*, p. 63. Cf. from MS. Rawl. B. 512 : "As Paradise is without beasts, without a snake, without a lion, without a dragon, without a scorpion, without a mouse, without a

frog, so is Ireland in the same manner without any harmful animal, save only the wolf, as sages say." *Tripartite Life of S. Patrick*, ed. W. Stokes, Rolls Series, part i (1887), p. xxx.

[24] "Translated from the Italian Manuscript in the Laurentian Library at Florence," London, 1821, p. 103.

[25] p. 354. This article was afterwards incorporated by the author in his *The Dog: its Origin, Natural History, and Varieties*, 1848. My reference to *The Irish Penny Journal* is from Harting, p. 202. In *A Brief Character of Ireland*, 12mo, 1692 (Licensed 16th Nov., 1691), a stupid enough squib, the peasants of remoter districts are described as " like their Native Wolves ", p. 47.

[26] London, 1882 : p. 149, p. 228, and p. 3.

[27] Herm. Jos. Schmitz, *Die Bussbücher und das Kanonische Bussverfahren*, ii Band, " Die Bussbücher und die Bussdisciplin der Kirche," Düsseldorf, 1898, p. 442.

[28] Variants are : weruvolff, Werewolf, werwolf, Werewl., and wertvoos.

[29] " Liber poenitentialis . . . per magistrum Bartholomaeum Exoniensem episcopum collectus . . ." British Museum, Cotton MSS., Faust. A. viii ; 1.

[30] See Chapter I, n. 18.

[31] *Otia Imperialia*, ed. Felix Liebrecht, Hanover, 1856, pp. 51–2.

[32] Titulus, LVIII, i. *Recueil des Historiens des Gaules et de la France*, Paris, 1741, ed. Dom Martin Bouquet, O.S.B. (Maurist). Tom. iv, p. 154.

[33] Frédéric Pluquet, *Contes Populaires*, Rouen, 1834, 2me édition, " Le Loup-garou," p. 15.

[34] Benjamin Thorpe, *Ancient Laws and Institutes of England*, 1840, vol. i, p. 445.

[35] Ibid., p. 591. Henrici Primi, lxxxiii, 5. The Laws of Henry I are now generally regarded as a twelfth-century compilation with a generic title.

[36] To be dated *c.* 1400. *Gamelyn*, 700–1. Chaucer, ed. W. W. Skeat, Oxford, 1894 ; vol. iv, *Canterbury Tales*, text. Appendix to Group A, p. 662. John Urry died 1715, and his edition of Chaucer was published posthumously in 1721. Tyrwhitt's *Canterbury Tales* was issued 4 vols., 1775 ; a fifth volume followed in 1778.

[37] No. xxi, ed. England and Pollard, *Early English Text Society*, 1897, p. 282, l. 139. See also Lydgate, *Bochas*, vii, 1261.

[38] Ed. F. W. D. Brie, *E. E. Text Soc.*, 1906, part i, pp. 169–170.

[39] Walter of Hemingburgh, *Chronicon*, ed. H. C. Hamilton, London, 1848 ; vol. i, pp. 252–4.

[40] *The Dramatic Writings of John Bale*, edited by J. S. Farmer. Early English Dramatists, 1907. *King Johan* has been edited separately by J. H. P. Pafford, 1931.

[41] In two parts, 4to, 1591.

[42] It is, of course, true that in *King John*, Act V, scene 6, Hubert cries :—

> The King I fear is poyson'd by a Monke, . . .
> A Monke I tell you, a resolued villaine
> Whose Bowels sodainly burst out :

and in the following scene the "fell poison" is spoken of, whilst the King himself exclaims : " Poyson'd, ill fare." But previous to all this on the battle-field, v, 3, King John had groaned :—

> Aye me, this tyrant Feauer burnes mee vp, . . .
> Weaknesse possesseth me, and I am faint.

The Troublesome Raigne of King John is gutter Protestantism, and as such of no account. Bowden in his *Religion of Shakespeare* (p. 120) acutely observes : " Shakespeare, in adapting it, had only to leave untouched its virulent bigotry and its ribald stories of friars and nuns to secure its popularity, yet as a fact he carefully excludes the anti-catholic passages and allusions, and acts throughout as a rigid censor on behalf of the Church." J. P. Chesney, *Shakespeare as a Physician*, 1884, comments on the cry " Poyson'd, ill fare " that " the case of King John bears a much closer analogy to a case wherein the hand of nature has been instrumental in saturating the system with poison, than it does to one in which a ' villainous Monk ' had been the instrument. Miasmatic exhalations had no doubt wrought the evil in this case ".

⁴³ " Coram altari magno in medio inter sacrosancta corpora Oswaldi et Vulfstani, pontificum beatorum."   Nicolas Trivet O.P., *Annales*, ed. T. Hog, London, 1845, p. 197.

⁴⁴ Roger of Wendover, iii, 385.

⁴⁵ " Sepultus, dico, est, sed non cum honore regio, quia terra quae in operibus suis pessimis turbata extitit nondum ad plenum pacificata quieuit."   Ed. cit., p. 254.   Walter of Hemingburgh has a story of King John appearing " in uestibus quasi deauratis " and all fulgent with light to a certain priest, but he obviously doubts the tale, and indeed the vision may have been a diabolic illusion, although, as we hope, he was saved by the intercession of S. Wulstan.

⁴⁶ See Gabriel de Moulin, Curé de Maneual, *Histoire générale de Normandie*, livre xiv, xxxiii, Rouen, folio, 1631, p. 559.

⁴⁷ Amélie Bosquet, *La Normandie romanesque et merveilleuse*, Paris, 1845, chap. xii, p. 238.

⁴⁸ *Werwolves*, London, 1912, chapter vi, pp. 92–109.

⁴⁹ This is, I think, the same incident as was told by Mr. J. Wentworth Day in *The Passing Show*, 9th July, 1932, " Exploring the Uncanny—No. 4. The Terror on the Mountain," pp. 24–5.   Mr. Day also mentions the werewolf seen by the shepherds, and the incident of the woman scared by the great dog with the eyes of a man.

⁵⁰ Ed. cit., pp. 40–1.

⁵¹ Third Booke, chap. i, edited by G. B. Harrison, " The Bodley Head Quartos," 1924, pp. 61–2.

⁵² I have used the reprint by Thomas George Stevenson, Edinburgh, 1871.

⁵³ " Witchcraft of Shetland," pp. 572–584, and notes, pp. 592–601.

⁵⁴ For which see Bibliography.

⁵⁵ It should perhaps be mentioned that the same author's *Rare and Remarkable Animals of Scotland*, 2 vols., London, 1848, deals with animal products resembling flowers, or shrubs, or trees, and " with other foliaceous products " (vol. ii, chapter i, p. 1) and various zoophytes, but does not treat of any quadrupeds.

⁵⁶ The Rev. John Gregorson Campbell was minister of Tiree 1861–1891, and the collections in his two books are especially valuable in that they were " Collected entirely from Oral Sources ".   In his *Witchcraft and Second Sight*, pp. 30–44, he deals with witches as sheep, hares, cats, rats, gulls, cormorants, whales.

⁵⁷ The Scotch and Welsh folklore contained in Κρυπτάδια, " Recueil de documents pour servir à l'étude des Traditions populaires," vol. ii, Heilbronn, 1884, although valuable, is almost entirely of an erotic nature and has no mention of werewolfery.   This is also the case with the French, Polish, and Russian collections given in vol. v (Paris, 1898) of the same series.

⁵⁸ William Howells, the son of the Rev. J. Howells, vicar of Tipton, was only eighteen at the time he wrote this book.

⁵⁹ *Welsh Folk-Lore*, by the Rev. Elias Owen, M.A., F.S.A., of Llanyblodwel. Oswestry and Wrexham, 1906, pp. 224–233.

⁶⁰ 2 vols., Oxford, 1901 ; vol. i, pp. 293–6.

⁶¹ *Otia Imperialia*, Tertia Decisio, xciii, ed. cit., p. 45.

⁶² Eng. tr., ut cit. sup., pp. 126–7.

⁶³ 4to, Romae, 1576, cap. xix :   " Experientiae apparentis conuersionis strigum in catos."

⁶⁴ Vernon on the Eure is some 25 kilometres from Evreux.   The castle is of the thirteenth century.   See Th. Michel, *Histoire de la ville et du canton de Vernon*, 1851 ; and E. Mayer, *Histoire de la ville de Vernon*, 2 vols., 1875–7.

⁶⁵ Bodin, *Demonomanie*, Liv. ii, ch. vi.   See a note by M. F. Bourquelot, *Recherches sur la Lycanthropie : Mémoires de la Soc. des Antiquaires de France*, tome xix (N. Série, tom. ix), Paris, 1849, pp. 246–7.   Also Paul Sébillot, *Le Folk-Lore de France*, tom. iv, Paris, 1907, p. 195.

⁶⁶ *Discours des Sorciers*, 1590, ch. xlvii. Eng. tr. *Examen of Witches*, 1929, p. 142.

[67] Sébillot, op. cit., tom. i, p. 281, and tom. iv, pp. 304–5.

[68] *Basque Legends*, second ed., 1879, p. 70 n. The first edition is 1877.

[69] The shape-shifting of a witch is, of course, an entirely different thing from the appearance of a familiar in animal guise. None the less, Mr. G. L. Kittredge has persistently confused the two, and in consequence his chapter " Metamorphosis " (*Witchcraft in Old and New England*, 1928, pp. 174–184) presents an entanglement not a little difficult to unravel.

[70] London, 1681, the Second Part, Relation viii, pp. 190–1.

[71] *History of the Rise and Influence of the Spirit of Rationalism in Europe*, 2 vols., 1865 ; vol. i, p. 126, and p. 120.

[72] Ed. cit., Relation viii, p. 200.

[73] 4to, 1692, p. 18. For *Comidia* we should surely read *Canidia*.

[74] See Montague Summers, *The Geography of Witchcraft*, 1927, ch. ii, pp. 158–160.

[75] *A Full and Impartial Account of the Discovery of Sorcery and Witchcraft Practis'd by Jane Wenham of Walkerne in Hertfordshire . . . Also Her Tryal . . .* London, 1712, pp. 17, 23, 29.

[76] *Witchcraft Farther Display'd*, London, 1712, p. 38. Introduction signed F[rancis] B[ragge], *Ardely-Bury, April* the 8d, 1712. He remarks that even " while she is in Prison " the " wicked old Witch " Mother Wenham, " has found out a Way to get plenty of Money."

[77] 1889, pp. 57–8.

[78] Vol. i, part 8, pp. 244–9.

[79] Manchester, 1917, pp. 104–6.

[80] Hereford, 1912 ; " Witchcraft," p. 52.

[81] *A Description of the Part of Devonshire bordering on the Tamar and the Tavy*, 3 vols., London, 1836, vol. ii, pp. 277–9. For parallels to this story see Rev. Elias Owen, *Welsh Folk-Lore*, 1896, pp. 230–3, and Mrs. Ella Mary Leather, *The Folk-Lore of Herefordshire*, 1912, p. 52.

[82] Op. cit., pp. 6–8.

[83] Edited by the Rt. Hon. Sir Herbert Maxwell, Bt., London and Edinburgh, 1919, pp. 37–9. Charles St. John died in July, 1856.

[84] *The Occult Review*, August, 1924 ; vol. xl, No. 2, pp. 102–8.

[85] Huw Lloyd, 1533–1620, who was apparently regarded as possessed of extraordinary powers of exorcism. Parson Richard Dodge, who was vicar of Talland in Cornwall from 1718 until his death, aged 98, in January, 1746, enjoyed the same reputation. See Thomas Bond, *Historical Sketches of the Boroughs of East and West Looe*, 1823, pp. 154–5: " About a century since the Rev. Richard Dodge . . . had the reputation of being deeply skilled in the black art, and could raise ghosts, or send them into the Red Sea, at the nod of his head."

[86] London, 1882, p. 297.

[87] *The Occult Review*, June, 1921 ; vol. xxxiii, No. 6, pp. 352–9.

[88] Vol. i, p. 294.

[89] Edited by Edith F. Carey, London and Guernsey, 1903, pp. 230–2. For a witch as a white rabbit, pp. 360–1 ; sorcerers as hares, pp. 361–5. See also pp. 315–337, witchcraft trials.

[90] *Irische Texte*, ed. Whitley Stokes and Ernst Windisch, iii serie, 2 heft. Leipzig, 1897, p. 377 (No. 215).

[91] *The Irish Version of the Historia Britonum of Nennius*, ed. with a translation by James Henthorn Todd. Irish Archæological Society, 1848, pp. 204–5, and note.

[92] A collection of pieces in prose and verse compiled and transcribed about 1100 by Moelmuiri Mac Ceileachair. A facsimile of the MS. (sixty-seven large quarto pages) was published Dublin, 1870. See 54*b* and 36 sqq.

For the heathenism of these transformations see *Irische Texte*, Stokes and Windisch, iii serie, 1 heft, Leipzig, 1881. [Do chuphur in da muccado] : suithi n-genntlecta la cectar-de in da mucuith 7 nus delbdais in cech riet . . . the learning of gentilism which enabled them to shift into any shape (p. 235).

The Rev. Edward Davies, *Mythology and Rites of the British Druids*, 1809, does not mention this art of shape-shifting. Mr. Lewis Spence, *The Mysteries of Britain*, 1928, also has no remark upon metamorphosis, but he refers to Sir J. G. Frazer's *The Golden Bough* (*Balder the Beautiful*, vol. ii, 1928, pp. 41–3— Mr. Lewis does not give the exact reference, which is this), where it is suggested that the men and animals burned to death at certain Celtic festivals were warlocks, and sorcerers disguised in brute form. This is, to say the least, extremely hypothetical, and in view of the evidence from the *Leabhar Na H-Uidhri* inadmissible.

[93] *Folk-Lore*, vol. v, No. 4, pp. 310–11. Kuno Meyer, The Irish Mirabilia.

[94] *Acta Sanctorum*, Martii tom. ii, Antwerpiae, 1668, pp. 517–592.

[95] *Tripartite Life*, ed. Whitley Stokes, Rolls Series, 1887 ; part i, p. 249 and note ; part ii, p. 271 and note.

[96] Ed. Robert Atkinson, Dublin, 1887, 140*b* : "The Conarian Race of Ireland and Scotland."

[97] London, 1843, vol. ii, pp. 103–7. The poem is from MS. Cotton. Titus, D. xxiv, fol. 74, vo.

[98] Ed. Todd, 1848, ut cit. sup., pp. 204–5.

[99] Ed. by the Rev. James F. Dimock, *Works*, vol. v, 1867, pp. 101–7, Rolls Series. The book of Giraldus appeared in 1188, and was dedicated to Henry II.

[100] The adventure with the wolf-man took place in 1182 or 1183.

[101] S. Natalis, Abbot, is honoured as the founder of monasticism in North Ireland. The son of Aengus, he was of the royal family of Munster, and lived in the sixth century. He is the Patron of Invernaile, Donegal, and Kinnawly. Feast 27th January.

[102] "A female werewolf (*ben tét i cuanricht*) was called *conel*." *Irische Texte*, Stokes and Windisch, iii serie, 2 heft. Leipzig, 1897, p. 421.

[103] Lucius III (Ubaldo Allucingoli), elected to the Chair of Peter, 1st September, 1181 ; died at Verona, 25th November, 1185.

[104] Camden, op. cit., *Ireland*, p. 83.

[105] Temple, *Works*, 2 vols., folio, London, 1720. Volume the First, part ii, *Miscellanea*, p. 244. There is an interesting allusion to werewolfery in Giles Rose's *The Theatre of the World : or, A Prospect of Humane Misery*, 1679, being a translation of Pierre Boaistuau's *de Théâtre du Monde*, Paris, 8vo, 1558 (and many subsequent editions). The passage (pp. 204–5) runs : " Others have fancied themselves to be transformed into a Wolf, and ceased not from running at Nights with the Wolves over the Mountains and desart places, following their howlings and gestures through all places in the Country, so greatly were they tormented with their Distempers, till the Sun had cast her Beams and Rayes upon the Earth : The *French* call this Distemper the *Loupos Garoux* ; but the Greeks call this sort of Sickness *Lycanthropeia* : A thing that need not seem strange, nor fabulous to any that has read the holy Scriptures, and in it the pitiful estate of *Nebuchadnezzar*, who was transformed into an Oxe, for the space of seven Years, to reduce him to the knowledge of his God, *Dan.* 4."

CHAPTER V

FRANCE

SIR WILLIAM TEMPLE'S observation is in one respect at least just, for in France the belief in werewolfism has certainly survived, and the tradition descends unbroken from the very dawn of history. Shape-shifting (as has already been remarked) was part and parcel of the wizard lore of the Druids, of whose sacred shrines none was more secret and more evil than the little isle of Sain, off Finistère, near " le Ras de Fontenay ", so infamous for shipwrecks, an eyot dedicated to He'ro Dias, the mistress of witches. There dwelt nine fearful beldames, ministers of the demon oracle of " Sena ", the Hag ; " Gallizenas uocant," says Pomponius Mela, who attributes to them evil powers of brewing storms and peering into futurity, but above all, " seque in quae uelint animalia uertere," and they ken full subtily to change themselves into the shapes of whatsoever animals they list.[1]

As of old upon Mount Carmel the sorcerer bishops of Baal withstood the prophet Elias, so the devotees of dark heathen rites battled in Britain and in Gaul against the holy evangel, and very many are the existing records of the contests between the Druid colleges or devilish covens and the Saints of God.[2] As may be supposed, the warlock host set in motion the whole thaumaturgy and sleeveless machinery of hell to prevent and eclipse the miracles of the Saints, and of course contended frustrate and in vain.

" This man casteth not out devils but by Beelzebub the prince of the devils," quoth the Pharisees. " If they have called the goodman of the house Beelzebub, how much more them of his household ? "[3] That charges should be brought against the enemies of the demon was but to be expected. Thus Saint Ronan was maligned by certain evil men, professing Christians but in their hearts ethnic and profane. This great Saint was a native of Ireland, and a disciple of S. Senan in Scatling Island. He followed his

preceptor to Cornwall and thence to Brittany, where settling
in the vicinity of Leon, about the year 510 he founded
Locronan. He died near Hillian on the Anse d'Iffignac,
Domnonia, in 540. At Locronan his Feast is on the Second
Sunday in July ; at Tavistock in Devon on 30th August.
A Feast of the Translation of his Relics is observed on
5th January.[4] Now the evil and envious eyes of certain
unrighteous, amongst whom was a sinful woman named
Keban, could not bear but were dazzled by the splendour
of the virtues and piety of S. Ronan, wherefore they most
wickedly and lyingly made plaint to King Grallon, who
then with all his following held high court at Kemper, that
S. Ronan was a varlet and a warlock foul, and that, even as
the dreaded werewolves of old, by art, magic, and black
cantrips not a few, he would often change himself into a
brute beast, ay, into a raging wolf, and so guised he was
wont to prowl abroad and raven through the countryside.
Moreover, in the malice of her heart Keban averred that her
child had been devoured by a wolf, the same savage beast
who marauded the flocks and herds, and that S. Ronan was
this very wolf. The Saint, however, easily cleared himself
of the foul charge, and in his charity not only forgave, but
(it is said) converted his enemies.

Werewolfism was a very terrible and real thing, a sorcery
which, as we have already seen from Gervase of Tilbury,
persisted through the centuries. In his *Origines Gauloises*,[5]
La Tour-D'Auvergne-Corret, writing of the period following
the introduction of Christianity into Gaul, says that from
pagan times a certain occultism and witchcrafts were
maintained for many generations. Although the Bretons
are truly enlightened by the Catholic Faith and very devout,
there yet endure in dark corners goetic practices and
necromancies. There are, and there have always been,
impious men so lost and abandoned that they do not hesitate
to make pacts with the prince of evil in order to acquire
temporal advantage and supernatural powers. Many of
these warlocks, the Bretons relate, either dress themselves
at night in wolf-skins, or assume the shape of wolves in
order to repair to these assemblies over which Satan (it is
averred) presides in person. These masqueradings or shape-
shifting of the men-wolves, a craft descending from the

PLATE VII

LE MENEU' DE LOUPS
By Maurice Sand (See p. 237)

[face p. 218

earliest days of ancient Armonica, may be fitly compared
with what history tells us of the Irish lycanthropes as also
with the werewolfery recorded by Herodotus, Pliny, and
other classical authors.

In 1131, Hugues de Camp-d'Avesnes, Comte de Saint-Pol,
attacked and burned to the ground the Abbey of Saint-
Riquier, where two of his enemies, the Comte d'Auxi and
the Comte de Beaurain-sur-Canche, had taken refuge with
their followers. In the pillage and the fire on 28th July
nearly three thousand persons perished. Some few, including
the Abbot, hardly escaped to Abbeville. Hugues de Saint-
Pol, in spite of the Abbot's complaint, continued to ravage
Ponthieu, but he reckoned without Louis-le-Gros, who soon
let him learn that he intended to take the field and avenge
the massacre. In terror Hugues threw himself at the feet
of Innocent II, but the Pontiff, aghast at the sacrilege,
held out litle hope of pardon, at least the culprit must expect
to dree a long a weary weird. The Count, however, founded
the Abbey of Cercamp, richly endowing it as a reparation.
Nevertheless after his death he was doomed for many
centuries to haunt the district he had so cruelly ravaged.
He was seen nightly prowling near the Abbey of Saint-
Riquier, a horrible phantom, black and loaded with chains,
in the form of a wolf, howling most piteously. Sometimes
this terrible spectre even invaded the streets of Abbeville,
where it was known as *la bête Canteraine.*[7]

The famous lay *Bisclavret*,[8] by that sweet and gracious
poetess Marie de France, who dedicated her collected work
to our King Henry II, shows that she had very considerable
knowledge of the traditional craft of werewolfery, and affords
so many interesting details that it must certainly be briefly
mentioned here. *Bisclavret* is the Breton term for the
Norman *Garulf*, werewolf.

> Bisclavret a nun en Bretan,
> Garulf l'apelent li Norman.
> Jadis le poeit hum oïr
> e sovent suleit avenir,
> hume plusur garulf devindrent
> e es boscages maisun tindrent.
> Garulf, ceo est beste salvage ;
> tant cum il est en cele rage,
> humes devure, grant mal fait,
> es granz forez converse e vait.

Bisclavret tells of a great lord of Brittany, wealthy and much honoured, who dearly loved and was loved by his wife. One thing, however, troubled her. For three days each week he privily leaves his home and never explains these absences. By much cajolery his wife persuades him to confess that during these three days he becomes a werewolf, and roves in the depths of the forest living by violence and blood, " de preie et de ravine." He is stark naked at the time of the metamorphosis. He even confides to her where he closets his clothes, under a stone in an ancient hermitage, but this secret he only tells after much coaxing, since if he cannot recover this same attire upon his return to the spot he will be doomed always to remain a wolf. The lady, filled with fear, dissembles, but soon persuades a certain knight, who has long loved her, to search out the clothes and steal them away, so that her lord can never recover human shape. This done, she marries her lover and they enjoy the werewolf's riches and estates. Eventually the plot is discovered, and the Bisclavret is enabled to transform himself into a man, since the apparel has been fortunately preserved.

Passing mention may here perhaps not impertinently be made of the *Roman de Guillaume de Palerne*, which was translated from the French by the command of Sir Humphrey de Bohun about 1350 as *The Romance of William of Palerne*, otherwise known as *William and the Werwolf.*[9] The original tale was in its day immensely popular, although apparently only one MS. has been preserved. Skeat dates the composition as between 1178 and 1200. At the beginning of the sixteenth century the poem was turned into French prose. The story is one of long and complicated incident. Embrons, King of Apulia, and his wife Felice, daughter of the Emperor of Greece, have a fair son named William, who whilst he is at play (at Palermo) is caught by a wolf, with wide, gaping jaws, " un grans leus, goule baee." This animal swims the sea with him to Italy and carries him to a forest near Rome, where it tends and feeds him. This wolf was actually a werewolf, Alphonsus, heir to the crown of Spain, who had been thus ensorcelled by his stepmother Braunde, so that her son Braundinis might succeed.

la nuit le couche joste soi ;
li leus-garous le fil le roi
lacole de ses iiii pies.
si est de lui aprivoisies,
li fix le roi, que tot li plaist
ce que la beste de lui fait.[10]

However, whilst the werewolf is away seeking food, a
cowherd finds the child and adopts him. The Emperor of
Rome one day whilst hunting meets William, who so pleases
him that he appoints the boy as page to his daughter Melior.
Presently the young couple are in love, and as the Emperor
of Greece sends to ask the hand of Melior for Prince Partendon,
his son, they escape, sewn up in the skins of two white bears.
Thus disguised they wander in the forest, and are found by
the werewolf who succours the truant pair. They reach
Benevento, and only elude capture by the werewolf's aid.
Next they dress up as a hart and hind, and with the werewolf
reach Sicily. Palermo is besieged by the Spaniards, since the
King of Spain seeks the hand of Florence (William's sister)
for Prince Braundinis and has been refused. At the request
of Queen Felice, his mother, William joins battle against
the Spaniards, and when she asks what cognizance he will
have on his shield, he demands a werewolf shall be painted
there :—

" i coueyte nought elles
but that I haue a god schel[d] · of gold graithed clene,
& wel & faire with-inne · a werwolf depeynted,
that be hidous & huge · to haue alle his rightes,
of the couenablest colour · to knowe in the feld ;
other armes al my lif · atteli neuer haue." [11]

Thus armed William performs doughty deeds, takes the
King of Spain and his son prisoners, and routs the foe.
Wicked Queen Braunde is sent for and forced to dissolve the
charm, so Prince Alphonsus recovers his human shape. It
appears that the good werewolf stole William to save him
from the plots of King Embrons' brother, who coveted the
sceptre of Sicily. William marries Melior ; Alphonsus,
soon to be King of Spain, weds Florence. A little while,
and the Emperor of Rome dying, William is crowned Emperor
with great pomp and ceremony.

The narrative is most excellently told, but it will be
understood that I have only been able to touch upon a few

of the crowding incidents, and many characters and episodes I have necessarily omitted.

In the Middle Ages it was often believed that if any person had been denounced from the altar and remained impenitent, refusing to make restitution and confess, the curse of the werewolf fell upon him. In Normandy any man who was excommunicate became a werewolf for a term of three or seven years. In Basse-Bretagne any person who had not been shriven for ten years nor used holy water could become a werewolf. This belief was still current in the middle of the eighteenth century. In La Vendée the man who was excommunicate became a werewolf for seven years, during which he was obliged to haunt certain ill-omened and accursed spots.[12]

William of Auvergne, Bishop of Paris, who died in 1249, in his *De Universo*,[13] pars. II, iii, cap. 13 : *Qualiter maligni spiritus uexant, et decipiunt homines*, treats of diabolical werewolfism at some length, and tells of a demoniac, possessed by an evil spirit, who drove him out into some secret and privy place, there leaving him as dead. Meanwhile the demon entered into a wolf, or it may be assumed the form of a ravening wolf, and rushed abroad into the village street and lanes, howling fearfully, snapping and rending with his teeth, so that all were horribly afraid and amazed at this monster of hell. The story soon went forth that this man was a werewolf. Moreover, the man himself believed that he was changed into a very wolf, that wolf which filled the whole countryside with panic and alarm. It happened that a holy religious heard the rumour, and presently he came to the village where these things were wrought, and calling together the good folk he told them plainly that this man was not essentially metamorphosed into a wolf, as all believed. By divine inspiration he even led them to the spot where the man lay entranced, as one dead, and showed him thus to the people. The religious then awoke him, and even commanded the wolf to show himself, which the beast did howling. He then exorcized the man and forever freed him from this ensorcellment of Satan.

Wherefore, says the good bishop, we find that in this instance at least the Devil impressed the imaginative faculty of the men with the idea that he was a wolf. Nevertheless, his essential part, his soul, never entered nor could enter into the body of a wolf, although deluded by the demon he steadfastly conceived such to have been the case. In chapter 28 of the same work he discusses the glamour caused by the Devil and magic crafts—*ludificationes daemonum.*

" It is like the sin of witchcraft, to rebel," and it can surprise nobody that throughout the sixteenth century, when all hell stirred to its depth to lash to fury the hoaming sea of infidelity and schisms that surged and roared round the Rock of Peter, there was an almost unprecedented eagre of sorcery and evil. To-day, as of old, in many a European country, rebellion and revolt against God and the ordinances of God are being crutched by Satanism. Four hundred years ago England was ravaged by the dissolution of her religious houses ; France was rent and torn by the horrors of intestine war.

It is during the sixteenth century that in France especially the rank foul weeds of werewolfery flourished exceedingly.

In December, 1521, at Poligny, Pierre Burgot, known as " Gros Pierre ", and Michel Verdun were tried before Maître Jean Boin, O.P., S.T.D., Prior of the Dominican convent at Poligny and Inquisitor General for the diocese of Besançon. Day after day the Court was thronged. Pierre Burgot confessed that nineteen years before, on the day of Poligny Fair, whilst owing to a great storm of thunder and hail he was collecting his flocks, there met him in a lonely place three horsemen clothed in black, riding black steeds. Of these one accosted him asking what ailed him. He replied his flocks were lost and he feared lest they should fall a prey to wild beasts. The man—or rather demon—then said that if he would acknowledge and serve him as his lord and master not one sheep should be missing. He accepted the proposal and agreed to meet him a sennight after to seal the bond. This he did, and kneeling before the demon in homage, vowed to obey him, renouncing God, Our Lady, all the Company of Heaven, his Baptism and Chrism. He swore also never to assist at Holy Mass, nor yet to use Holy Water. He then kissed the demon's left hand, which was black, and cold as the hand of a corpse. The demon promised Pierre money, and bade the shepherd call upon him by the name of Moyset. Howbeit as the years went by he grew weary of

his allegiance, to which he was recalled by Michel Verdun
of Plane, a village near Poligny, and he attended a sabbat
of warlocks in a wood near Château Charlou. Michel bade
him strip naked and then anointed him from head to foot
with a certain unguent, after which he seemed to himself
to be changed into a wolf, his limbs were hairy, his hands
and feet the paws of a beast. In running his speed was that
of the wind. Michel, who also shifted his shape, accompanied
him with surpassing fleetness. The unguent was given to
Pierre by Moyset ; and to Michel Verdun by his familiar,
Guillemin. After these courses Pierre felt an intense
weariness.

In the shape of wolves Pierre and Michel attacked and
tore to pieces a boy of seven years old. An outcry was raised
and they fled. On another occasion they killed a woman who
was gathering peas. They also seized a little girl of four years
old and ate the palpitating flesh, all save one arm. Several other
persons were murdered by them in this way, for they loved
to lap up the warm flowing blood. On one occasion Pierre
with his keen white teeth tore out the throat of a girl aged
about nine, whom they assaulted in a vineyard. Another
time they killed and ate raw a goat belonging to Maître
Pierre Bongré.

Other hideous crimes did they confess, and especially that
they had frequently covered she-wolves, taking more pleasure
in this coupling than in the natural entering of women.

Turbervile, in his *Booke of huntynge*, chapter 75, 1575,[14] tells
us : " The Wolfe (sayeth he) goeth on clicketing in February,
in such sort as a Dogge lineth a bitch whē she goeth saulte,
wherein they abide ten or twelue dayes : many Wolues
(where store be) do follow one she Wolfe, euē as Dogges
follow a Bitche : but she will neuer be lined but onely with
one. She will suffer many to follow hir, and will carrie them
after hir sometime eight or tenne dayes without meate, drinke,
or rest : and when they are ouerwearied, then she suffreth
them all to take their ease, untill they route and be fast on
sleepe : & then will she awake yᵉ Wolfe which seemeth most
to haue folowed hir, and that oftentimes is the foulest and
worst fauourd, bycause he is ouerwearied and lankest : him
will she awake and tyce him away with her farre frō the
rest, and suffer him to line hir. There is a common Prouerbe,

which saith that : *Neuer Wolfe yet sawe his Syre* : for indeed
it hapneth most comonly that whē all the rest of the Wolues
do awake and misse the female, they follow them by the
sent, and finding them oftentimes togyther, they fall upon
that Wolfe and kill him for despite."

Michel Verdun was discovered upon his attacking, whilst
in the shape of a wolf, a traveller who wounded the animal
which fled into the thicket. Following the trail the gentleman
came to a hut where he found Verdun, who had resumed his
human form, and his wife was bathing the wound.

Associated with Pierre Burgot and Verdun was a third
werewolf named Philibert Montot. All three were duly
executed for their hideous crimes and sorceries, and pictures
of this leash of witches were hung in the Jacobin Church at
Poligny.[15]

A story is related of an incident which occurred about the
year 1580 concerning an old chateau near Poitiers, which
was very ill reputed as the rendezvous of sorcerers and
demons. Three young men, more rash than cautelous,
resolved out of a great curiosity to investigate the matter.
One Friday at midnight they very secretly repaired to the
place, and through the chink of a shuttered window they
were witnesses of the abominations of the sabbat. When
they sought to fly they were beset by three huge wolves.
With difficulty they escaped, and one of them in the fray
Malchused the beast who was biting him. On the following
day it came to his knowledge that a lewd woman of the
town, long suspect of witchcraft, was ill in bed, her ear having
been recently sliced off by a sword.[16]

One of the most famous of all werewolf trials was that of
the loup-garou Gilles Garnier, a native of Lyons, " the hermit
of Dole," as he was called, who was executed at Dole on
18th January, 1573, having been found guilty of the most
hideous sorceries. A contemporary letter, addressed by
Daniel d'Auge to the learned Matthieu de Challemaison,
Dean of the Chapter of Sens,[17] says : " This Gilles Garnier,
the werewolf (*lycophile*), was a solitary who took to himself
a wife, and then unable to find food to support his family
fell upon such evil and impious courses that whilst wandering
about one evening through the woods he made a pact with
a phantom or spectral man, whom he encountered in some

remote and haunted spot. This phantom deluded him with fine promises, and among other gauds eke taught him how to become a wolf, a lion, an ounce, just as he would list, only advising that since the wolf was the least remarkable of savage beasts this shape would be the more conformable. To this he agreed, and received an unguent or salve wherewith he anointed himself when he went about to shift his shape. He died very penitent, having made full confession of his crimes."

The *Arrest memorable de la Cour de parlement de Dole, du dixhuictiesme iour de Ianuier, 1573, contre Gilles Garnier, Lyonnois, pour auoir en forme de loup-garou deuoré plusieurs enfans, et commis autres crimes* was printed at Sens in 1574.[18] This is a document of the first importance.

Anno 1573, on the one part, Henry Camus, Doctor of Laws, Councillor of our Lord the King, in the Supreme Court of the Parliament of Dole, in this case Procurer-General and Public Prosecutor touching the murders committed on the persons of several children and the eating of their flesh in the shape of a werewolf and other crimes and offences committed by Gilles Garnier, a native of Lyons, now held prisoner in the conciergerie of this town, defendant, on the other part.

It is proven that on a certain day, shortly after the Feast of S. Michael last, Gilles Garnier, being in the form of a wolf, seized upon in a vineyard a young girl, aged about ten or twelve years, she being in the place commonly called és Gorges, the vineyard de Chastenoy, hard by the Bois de la Serre, about a quarter of a league from Dole, and there he slew and killed her both with his hands, seemingly paws, as with his teeth, and having dragged the body with his hands and teeth into the aforesaid Bois de la Serre, he stripped her naked and not content with eating heartily of the flesh of her thighs and arms, he carried some of her flesh to Apolline his wife at the hermitage of Saint-Bonnot, near Amanges, where he and his aforesaid wife had their dwelling.

Moreover, eight days after the Feast of All Saints last, again being in the form of a wolf, Gilles Garnier attacked another girl in or about the same place, to wit near the meadow called la Ruppe, in the vicinity of Authume, a spot lying between the aforesaid Authume and Chastenoy, and a little before noon of the aforesaid day, he slew her, tearing her body and wounding her in five places of her body with his hands and teeth, with the intention of eating her flesh, had he not been hindered, let and prevented by three persons. This he has several times freely acknowledged and confessed.

Moreover, some fifteen days after the aforesaid Feast of All Saints, again being in the form of a wolf, having seized yet another child, a boy of ten years old, in a vineyard called Gredisans, at a spot about a league from the aforesaid Dole, situate between the aforesaid Gredisans and Menoté, and having in the same manner as before strangled and killed the aforesaid boy, he ate the flesh of the thighs, legs, and belly of the aforesaid boy, and tore off from the body a leg, dismembering it.

Moreover, upon the Friday before the Feast of S. Bartholomew last he seized a young boy aged twelve or thirteen years under a large pear-tree near the wood which marches with the village of Perrouze in the parish of Cromany, and this young boy he dragged into the said wood, where he strangled him in the same manner as before, with the intention of eating him, which he would have done, had he not been seen and prevented by certain persons who came to the help of the young boy, who was however already dead. The said Gilles Garnier was then and at that time in the form of a man and not of a wolf, yet had not he been let, hindered and prevented he would have eaten the flesh of the aforesaid young boy, notwithstanding that it was a Friday. This hath he freely confessed.

Wherefore this Most High and Honourable Court having carefully considered the plea of the Prosecutor, and having made full inquisition into all depositions and interrogatories touching this present case as well as duly weighing the full and free confessions of the accused, not affirmed and deposed once only but many times unambiguously reiterated, acknowledged and avowed, doth now proceed to deliver sentence, requiring the person of the accused to be handed over to the Master Executioner of High Justice, and directing that he, the said Gilles Garnier, shall be drawn upon a hurdle from this very place unto the customary place of execution, and that there by the aforesaid Master Executioner he shall be burned quick and his body reduced to ashes. He is moreover mulcted in the expenses and costs of this suit.

Given and confirmed at the aforesaid Dole, in the said

Court, upon the eighteenth day of the month of January, in the present Year of Grace fifteen hundred and seventy-three.

The Parliament of Franche-Comté, appalled at the prevalence of lycanthropy in that district, on 3rd December, 1578, issued a special proclamation dealing with the punishment and apprehension of werewolves.[19]

In 1558 occurred a case of werewolfism to which reference is often (but for the most part somewhat incorrectly) made. One evening a landed gentleman, whose château was near a village about two leagues from Apchon in the highlands of Auvergne, met a huntsman whom he knew well and whom he asked to bring him some of the bag on his return. As the huntsman went along a valley he was attacked by a large wolf. Since his arquebus missed aim he was obliged to grapple with the beast which he caught by the ears. By a dexterous feat, however, he managed to draw his keen knife and severed one of the wolf's paws, which he put in his pouch as the beast fled howling. He then took his way back, passing near the gentleman's château, which was actually in sight of the spot where he encountered the wolf. As he told his friend the tale he drew the paw from his pouch, and found therein no paw but a woman's hand with a gold ring upon one of the fingers, a jewel the gentleman immediately recognized as belonging to his wife. With deadly fear in his heart he entered the house to find his wife ill nursing a bandaged arm. When compelled to show her wound it was seen that she had lost a hand, upon which she confessed that in the form of a wolf she had attacked the hunter. Not long after she was burned at Ryon. This was told to Boguet by one who had stayed in that very place a fortnight after the thing had happened, so there can be question as to the actual truth of the occurrence.[20]

There are, indeed, few names more celebrated in the history of witchcraft than that of Henry Boguet of Saint-Claude, Supreme Judge of this district in Burgundy, who in his *Discours des Sorciers* [21] has left us so plain and concise a record of the trials over which he presided, during the epidemic of sorcery—as it may not unfairly be termed—which so grievously infected Burgundy towards the end of the sixteenth century. The bibliography of the *Discours* is extremely complicated, but the issue of the First Edition, which cannot be absolutely determined, is now generally assigned to 1590, and there were at least twelve reprints between that year and 1611. Boguet, honoured and respected by all as the most fearless enemy of the Satanists, died in 1619.

Many of the accused who came before him were guilty of werewolfery, and he devotes chapter xlvii of his *Discours* to an impartial and admirably reasoned discussion *of the Metamorphosis of Men into Beasts, and Especially of Lycanthropes or Loups-garoux*. Since an English translation of his work is readily accessible it will not be necessary here to do more than indicate one or two of the most remarkable cases he was called upon to investigate.

It was in 1584 that Benoist Bidel of Naizan, a lad some sixteen years old, and his younger sister were attacked, whilst plucking wild fruit, by a huge wolf without a tail. Some peasants hastened to their assistance, but the boy had already received his death from the claws and teeth of the animal, which in its turn was killed by those who ran up, and in its last throes crawled behind a thicket, where when it was followed they discovered no wolf but the dead body of Perrenette Gandillon. Soon after, this woman's brother, Pierre Gandillon, and his son George were accused of witchcraft, and it presently came out that they were in the habit of anointing themselves with the Devil's unguent and assuming the form and fierceness of wolves, under which shape they had murdered and eaten many young children. Boguet describes this pair as horrible to look upon, having lost wellnigh any resemblance to humanity, loping on all fours rather than walking upright, creatures with foul horny nails, unpared and sharp as talons, keen white teeth, matted hair, and red gleaming eyes. In the guise of wolves they had frequently attended the sabbat and adored the demon. Both reaped the full reward of their crimes and perished at the stake.

Clauda Jamprost, a wicked old witch, was one of the Orcieres coven, to which crew also belonged Thievenne Paget and Clauda Jamguillaume. All three confessed that by the Devil's aid they had shifted their shape to wolves and haunted the wood of Froidecombe. They used the magic salve, as also did Jacques Bocquet, a werewolf, who was sentenced with them. Clauda Gaillard, a witch of Ebouchoux, likewise guilty of werewolfism, was executed at the same time. Actually Clauda Jamprost was the first to be sent to the stake. She died very penitent. Another witch who was guilty of the same foul offences and suffered the same fate was la Micholette. Françoise Secretain, a notorious witch, who confessed to having attended the sabbat on numberless midnights, to having slain women and children by her craft and killed cattle, to having given herself carnally to the demon who knew her in the shape of a tall black man, was accused of werewolfery by the warlock Jacques Bocquet, but this she did not acknowledge. She was executed in July, 1598.

On the 14th December of the same year at Paris, a tailor of Châlons was sentenced to be burned quick for his horrible crimes. This wretch was wont to decoy children of both sexes into his shop, and having abused them he would slice their throats and then powder and dress their bodies, jointing them as a butcher cuts up meat. In the twilight, under the shape of a wolf, he roamed the woods to leap out on stray passers-by and tear their throats to shreds. Barrels of bleaching bones were found concealed in his cellars as well as other foul and hideous things. He died (it is said) unrepentant and blaspheming. So scabrous were the details of the case that the Court ordered the documents to be burned.

In the same year, again, a werewolf trial took place at Angers. In a remote and wild spot near Caude, Symphorien Damon, an archer of the Provost's company, and some rustics came across the nude body of a boy aged about fifteen, shockingly mutilated and torn. The limbs, drenched in blood, were yet warm and palpitating, and as the companions approached two wolves were seen to bound away into the boscage. Being armed and a goodly number to boot, the men gave chase, and to their amaze came upon a fearful figure, a tall gaunt creature of human aspect with long matted hair and beard, half-clothed in filthy rags, his hands dyed in fresh blood, his long nails clotted with garbage of red human flesh. So loathly was he and verminous they scarce could seize and bind him, but when haled before the magistrate he proved to be an abram-cove named Jacques Roulet, who with his brother Jean and a cousin Julien vagabonded from village to village in a state of abject poverty. On 8th August, 1598, he confessed to Maître Pierre Hérault, the lieutenant général et criminel, that his parents, who were of the hamlet of Gressière, had devoted him to the Devil, and that by the use of an unguent they had given him he could assume the form of a wolf with bestial appetite. The two wolves who were seen to flee into the forest, leaving the body of the slain boy whose name was Cornier, he declared were his fellow padders, Jean and Julien. He confessed to having attacked and devoured with his teeth and nails many children in various parts of the country whither he had roamed. As to his guilt there could be no question, since he gave precise details, the exact time and place, where a few days before, near Bournaut, had been found the mutilated body of a child, whom he swore he had throttled and then eaten in part as a wolf. He also confessed to attendance at the sabbat. This varlet was justly condemned to death, but for some inexplicable reason the Parliament of Paris decided that he should be rather confined in the hospital of Saint Germain-des-Prés, where at any rate he would be instructed in the faith and fear of God. It would seem that the wretched creature was a mere dommerer who could hardly speak plain, but uttered for the most part animal sounds. The full details of the case are not clear.[22]

During the early spring of the year 1603 there spread through the St. Sever districts of Gascony in the extreme south-west of France, the department Landes, a veritable reign of terror. From a number of little hamlets and smaller villages young children had begun mysteriously to disappear off the fields and roads, and of these no trace could be discovered. In one instance even a babe was stolen from its cradle in a cottage whilst the mother had left it for a short space safe asleep, as she thought. People talked of wolves; others shook their heads and whispered of something worse than wolves. The consternation was at its height when the local magistrate advised the puisné Judge of the Barony de la Roche Chalais and de la Châtellenie that information had been laid before him by three witnesses, of whom one, a young girl named Marguerite Poirier, aged thirteen, of the outlying hamlet of Saint-Paul, in the Parish of Espérons, swore that in full moon she had been attacked by a savage

beast, much resembling a wolf. (Espérons is now known as
Eugénie-les-Bains, owing to the visits of the Empress Eugénie
to the warm sulphur baths here. This small spa has about
610 inhabitants.) The girl stated that one midday whilst
she was watching cattle, a wild beast with rufulous fur, not
unlike a huge dog, rushed from the thicket and tore her
kirtle with its sharp teeth. She only managed to save herself
from being bitten owing to the fact she was armed with a
stout iron-pointed staff with which she hardly warded
herself. Moreover, a lad of some thirteen or fourteen years
old, Jean Grenier, was boasting that it was he who attacked
Marguerite as a wolf, and that but for her stick he would have
torn her limb from limb as he had already eaten three or
four children.

Jeanne Gaboriaut, aged eighteen, deposed that one day
when she was tending cattle with Jean Grenier in her company
(both being servants of a well-to-do farmer of Saint-Paul,
Pierre Combaut), he coarsely complimented her as a bonny
lass and vowed he would marry her. When she asked who
his father was, he said : " I am a priest's bastard." [23] She
remarked that he was sallow and dirty, to which he replied :
" Ah, that is because of the wolf's-skin I wear." He added
that a man named Pierre Labourat had given him this pelt,
and that when he donned it he coursed the woods and fields
as a wolf. There were nine werewolves of his coven who went
to the chase at the waning of the moon on Mondays, Fridays,
and Saturdays, and who were wont to hunt during the
twilight and just before the dawn. He lusted for the flesh of
small children, which was tender, plump, and rare. When
hungry, in wolf's shape he had often killed dogs and lapped
their hot blood, which was not so delicious to his taste as
that of young boys, from whose thighs he would bite great
collops of fat luscious brawn.

These informations were lodged on 29th May, 1603. Jean
Grenier was arrested and brought before the Higher Court
on the following 2nd June, when he freely made a confession
of the most abominable and hideous werewolfery, crimes
which were in every particular proved to be only too true.
He acknowledged that when he had called himself the
by-blow of a priest he had lied. His father was Pierre Grenier,
nicknamed " le Croquant ", a day-labourer of the hamlet

Saint-Antoine de Pizon, which is situate toward Coutras.
He had run away from his father, who beat him and whom
he hated, and he got his living as best he could by mendicity
and cowherding. A youth named Pierre de la Tilhaire, who
lived at Saint-Antoine, one evening took him into the depths
of a wood and brought him into the presence of the Lord of
the Forest. This Lord was a tall dark man, dressed all in
black, riding a black charger. He saluted the two lads, and
dismounting he kissed Jean, but his mouth was colder than
ice. Presently he rode away down a distant glade. This was
about three years ago, and on a second meeting he had
given himself to the Lord of the Forest as his bond-slave.
The Lord had marked both boys on each thigh with a kind
of misericorde, or small stiletto. He had treated them well,
and all swigged off a bumper of rich wine. The Lord had
presented them each with a wolf-skin, which when they
donned, they seemed to have been transformed into wolves,
and in this shape they scoured the countryside. The Lord
accompanied them, but in a much larger shape, (as he thought)
as an ounce or leopard. Before donning the skin they
anointed themselves with an unguent. The Lord of the
Forest retained the unguent and the wolf's pelt, but gave
them to Jean whenever he asked for their use. He was
bidden never to pare the nail of his left thumb, and it had
grown thick and crooked like a claw. On more than one
occasion he had seen several men, of whom he recognized
some four or five, with the Lord of the Forest, adoring him.
Jean Grenier then related with great exactitude his tale of
infanticide. On the first Friday of March, 1603, he had
killed and eaten a little girl, aged about three, named
Guyonne. He had attacked the child of Jean Roullier, but
there came to the rescue the boy's elder brother, who was
armed and beat him away. Young Roullier was called as a
witness and remembered the exact place, hour, and day when
a wolf had flown out from a thicket at his little brother,
and he had driven the animal off, being well weaponed. It
would be superfluous and even wearisome to chronicle the
cases, one after another, in which the parents of children
who had been attacked by the wolf, boys and girls wounded
and in many cases killed, came forward and exactly
corroborated the confession of Jean Grenier.

The Court ordered Pierre Grenier, the father, who Jean accused of sorcery and werewolfism, to be laid by the heels, and hue and cry was made for Pierre de la Tilhaire. The latter fled, and could not be caught, but Pierre Grenier on being closely interrogated proved to be a simple rustic, one who clearly knew nothing of his son's crimes. He was released.

The inquiry was relegated to the Parliament of Bordeaux, and on 6th September, 1608, President Dassis pronounced sentence upon the loup-garou. The utmost clemency was shown. Taking into consideration his youth and extreme ignorance Jean Grenier was ordered to be straitly enclosed in the Franciscan friary of S. Michael the Archangel, a house of the stricter Observance, at Bordeaux,[24] being warned that any attempt to escape would be punished by the gallows without hope of remission or stay.

Pierre de Lancre, who has left us a very ample account of the whole case,[25] visited the loup-garou at S. Michael's in the year 1610, and found that he was a lean and gaunt lad, with small deep-set black eyes that glared fiercely. He had long sharp teeth, some of which were white like fangs, others black and broken, whilst his hands were almost like claws with horrid crooked nails. He loved to hear and talk of wolves, often fell upon all fours, moving with extraordinary agility and seemingly with greater ease than when he walked upright as a man. The Fathers remarked that at first, at least, he rejected simple plain food for foulest offal. De Lancre calls attention to the fact that Grenier or Garnier seems for some reason to be a name not infrequently borne by werewolves.

Jean Grenier told de Lancre that the Lord of the Forest, who was certes none other than the demon, had twice entered his room at the Friary, tempting him, but that he had warded off the evil one by the Sign of the Cross. The hapless youth, tended to the last by the good religious, died in November, 1611.

Nynauld, *De La Lycanthropie*, relates a history of five sorcerers, werewolves, of Cressi, a village not far from Lausanne, who under the forms of wolves stole a child whom they carried to the sabbat, offering the little boy to the demon. They killed this child, quaffed the blood, and cutting the body to pieces, boiled and ate it, using the fat for their ointments. All five confessed, and were burned quick at Lausanne in 1604.

In the same year a peasant of a hamlet near Lucerne, encountering a fierce wolf on a lonely road was attacked, howbeit he defended himself so well that he struck off the animal's front leg. The beast crawled away, but on being followed a woman was discovered bleeding profusely with her arm severed. She was brought to justice and burned.[26]

During the years 1764 and 1765 a fearful monster, commonly known as the Wild Beast of Gévaudan, spread terror throughout France. The *London Magazine*, January, 1765 [27] (21st December, 1764), notes that the wild beast had ravaged several districts, and " a detachment of dragoons has been out six weeks after him. The province has offered a thousand crowns to any persons that will kill him ". He was supposed by some to be a panther or hyena ; others said he was the offspring of a tiger and a lioness. For months this animal panic-struck the whole region of Languedoc, and is said to have devoured more than a hundred persons. Not merely solitary wayfarers were attacked by it, but even larger companies travelling in coaches and armed. Its teeth were most formidable. With its immense tail it could deal swindging blows. It vaulted to tremendous heights, and ran with supernatural speed. The stench of the brute was beyond description. In vain a Royal Proclamation was issued and large rewards offered for its destruction. During one week of June, 1765, it devoured a woman, a child of eight, a girl of fifteen, and a fourth person. With mysterious skill the beast baffled and even spurned its pursuers.

Writing on 1st April, 1765,[28] Grimm remarks : " For several months now the *Gazette de France* has been chronicling exploits of a new kind, for it never misses to give us an extraordinary recital of this ferocious beast in the Gévaudan, and loudly praises the heroic and memorable feats of those who take the field against this monster." In one particular instance a boy named Portefaix—" l'illustre Portefaix " Grimm salutes him with a smile—although only eleven years old, defended four children from the beast. Mr. Anon at once burst forth into a pæan of poetical praise, and gave

the world an Epic Poem in two cantos entitled *Portefaix*.[29]
This panegyric occupied five and a half pages.

The countryfolk in the Gévaudan district were well assured
that the monster was a warlock, who had shifted his shape,
and that it was useless to attempt to catch him. One farmer,
a well-to-do and much respected man, deposed before a
magistrate that on one occasion when he had encountered
the beast, which made a prodigious bound through the air,
he heard it murmur in human accents : " Convenez que, pour
un viellard de quatre-vingt-dix ans, ce n'est pas mal sauter."

Sutherland Menzies [30] quotes the MS. authority " of a
learned but anonymous writer " as remarking, " I remember
to have seen an engraving in which that animal was
represented devouring a girl, and subscribed Lycopardus
Parthenophagus, vulgò *La Bête de Gévaudan*. Parthenophagy,
or a peculiar delight in the flesh of girls, is an enormity of
the lycanthropes and not of wolves ; from which we may
infer in what light the people of the Gévaudan regarded that
famous beast." After being in vain pursued by thousands of
the people, the monster was at last killed by a Monsieur
Antoine, porte-arquebuse du Roi.

A belief in the connection between the werewolf and the
vampire lingered in Normandy until at least the beginning
of the ninenteenth century. If it was seen that any grave
in the churchyard was disturbed the peasants thought a werewolf was buried there. Secretly they exhumed the body, cut
off the head with a clean hatchet which must never have
been used before, and threw the body into a river or into
the sea.[31]

In many parts of France, but more especially perhaps in
Britanny, *le Meneur des Loups* is a well-known figure. He is
generally considered to be a wizard, who when the werewolves of the district have met and sit in a hideous circle
round a fire kindled in the heart of some forest, leads forth
the howling pack and looes them on to their horrid chase.
Sometimes he himself assumes the form of a wolf, but speaks
with human voice. Gathering his flock around him he gives
them directions, telling them what farm-towns are ill-guarded
that night, what flocks, what herds, are negligently kept,
which path the lonely wayfarer setting out from the inn is
taking.

" I know," says George Sand, writing in 1858, " several persons who at the first faint rising of the new moon have met near the carfax of the Croix-Blanche old Soupison, nicknamed *Démmonet*, walking swiftly along with great giant strides followed in silence by more than thirty wolves."

One night in the Forest of Châteauroux two wayfarers heard at no small distance the howl of a wolf. They lost no time in climbing a tree for safety sake, and from between the foliage of a high branch they beheld to their amaze a clearing before a woodman's hut, where in the plenilune had gathered a countless pack of wolves. The animals uttered a raucous howl when the door opened, the rustic came out and walked among them, patting their heads and speaking to them, after which they dispersed with every sign of content.

Two gentlemen who were crossing a forest glade after dark suddenly came upon an open space where an old verderer was standing, a man well-known to them, who was making passes in the air, weaving strange signs and sigils. The two friends concealed themselves behind a tree, whence they saw thirteen wolves come trotting along. The leader was a huge grey wolf who went up to the old man fawning upon him and being caressed. Presently the verderer uttering a sing-song chant plunged into the wood followed by the wolves. The two gentlemen who witnessed this themselves related the incident to George Sand, and most solemnly swore that they could not possibly have been mistaken.[32]

At the beginning of the nineteenth century " le grand Julien " of Saint-Août, a skilled player on the *musette*, was a well-known " meneu' de Loups ".

In Normandy tradition tells of certain fantastic beings known as *lupins* or *lubins*. They pass the night chattering together and twattling in an unknown tongue. They take their stand by the walls of country cemeteries, and howl dismally at the moon. Timorous and fearful of man they will flee away scared at a footstep or distant voice. In some districts, however, they are fierce and of the werewolf race, since they are said to scratch up the graves with their hands, and gnaw the poor dead bones.[33]

Adolphe D'Assier in his *Posthumous Humanity* [34] has two instances which he terms lycanthropy, although perhaps the

term is loosely enough used. About the year 1868 at Saint-
Lizier an animal like a calf suddenly appeared in a room
where two brothers were sleeping. Adjured in the name of
God it seemed to pass through the door and could be heard
on the staircase. The house-door was found fast locked in
the morning, and the elder boy always maintained that the
appearance was that of a man living in the town who was
under no light suspicion of werewolfery.

At Serisols, in the Canton Sainte-Croix, lived a miller
named Bigot, a reputed warlock. One morning his wife rose
early leaving him asleep in bed, and proceeded to the yard to
busy herself with some washing. In a corner of the yard
she presently espied an animal something larger than a dog.
Seizing the wooden beetle she flung it with all her force,
hitting the beast in the eye. At the same moment Bigot
awoke in his bed, shrieking out, " Wretch, you have blinded
me." Since then he always wore a shade over one eye.
This incident was attested by his own children as happening
in the year 1879.

Baring-Gould, in 1863, found that after dark nobody dared
to cross the plain near Champigni (Vienne), because of a
loup-garou who infested that spot, "His tongue hanging out,
and his eyes glaring like marsh-fires ! " [35]

In November, 1925, a curious case of werewolfery occurred
in Alsace, where the *garde-champêtre*, or village policeman, of
Uttenheim, near Strasburg, was tried for shooting dead a
boy, who had mischievously worked upon his belief that he
was haunted by animals with human faces. He knew that
on many occasions the boy had played tricks upon him, but
he declared his conviction that, by means of sorcery, the
lad had acquired the power of turning himself into the
forms of other animals. This was firmly credited by the
whole village, and I for one am not prepared to deny that
by some glamour, just as Jean Grenier of old, this young
lad owing to an impious pact may have been initiated into
the dark and horrid secrets of werewolfery.

NOTES TO CHAPTER V

[1] Pomponius Mela, *Chorographia*, iii, 48, ed. Frick, Teubner, 1880, p. 67. See also MacCulloch, *Guernsey Folk Lore*, 1903, pp. 282–3.

[2] For the expression " druid colleges or devilish covens " see the *Uita Sancti Geraldi*, ix : " In eadem quoque regione erat quidam famosus magus, qui multos sue artis habebat discipulos. Hic quoque in monticulo quodam iuxtu monasterium Sanctorum cum suis habitabet, uendicans sibi uis hereditarium in eadem terra. Unde usque in hodiernum diem Collis magorum nominatur." Plummer, *Uitae Sanctorum Hiberniae*, 2 vols., Oxford, 1910, vol. ii, p. 111.

[3] S. Matthew, xii, 24, and x, 25.

[4] Bollandists, *Acta Sanctorum*, 1st June, folio, Antwerp, 1695, pp. 83–4. Certain of the Relics of S. Ronan were translated to Tavistock Abbey, Devon, by Earl Ordgar of Devon in 990. The Bollandists relate that on more than one occasion S. Ronan compelled a wolf who had carried off a lamb to return the prey safe and sound. It is this perhaps which is represented in a very ancient sculpture in the church of S. Thomas at Strasburg. (Or it may be S. Blaise who is thus portrayed.) The deliverance of a lamb from a wolf is a miracle which has been wrought by many Saints, as, for example, by S. Norbert, S. Gudwal, the Vallombrosan Blessed Torello, of whom mention has already been made, and see the Bollandists, *Acta Sanctorum*, Martii, tom. ii, die xvi, folio, Antverpiae, 1668, pp. 499–505. S. Simpert of Augsberg and S. Robert of Molème recovered children who had been carried off by wolves, and returned them unharmed to their homes. The wolf enters into the histories of S. Vat of Arras, S. Arnoul of Soissons, S. Austreberte of Pavilly, S. Malo, S. Poppo of Stavelo (who raised to life a shepherd killed by a wolf), S. Laumer, S. Mark the Hermit. S. Fillan, S. Solas of Solenhofen, S. Bernard of Tiron, S. William of Monte-Vergine, S. Silvestro Gozzolini, S. Odilo of Cluny, S. Eustorgius, S. Gens the Solitary, Blessed Christina of Stommeln, and many more. S. Houarniaule, who leads a wolf, is one of the Saints Guérisseurs of Notre-Dame du Haut, near Moncontour. He is invoked as a protector against fear and panics. A wolf acted as guide to S. Hervé, who was blind (hence the Breton expression *le barbet de saint Hervé*), and two wolves guided S. Trivier when he had lost his way in a forest. Wolves protected the body of S. Vincent as also the relics of S. Carpophorus. A wolf protected the severed head of S. Edmund, King and Martyr. Baronius relates that in the year 617 large packs of wolves attacked and devoured a number of heretics. Wolves guarded the Most Holy House of Loreto against the profane assault of Duke Francesco Maria of Urbino who would have spoiled the Sanctuary.

S. Remacle of Maestricht is depicted with a wolf to symbolize his dominion over evil spirits. S. Andrea Corsini the Carmelite is painted with a wolf and a lamb to show that after a thoughtless youth he became a great saint. (His mother dreamed she had borne a fierce wolf who changed into a gentle lamb.) The history of S. Francis and the Wolf of Gubbio is known to all. S. Radiana (or Radigunde) of Wellenburg is said to have been devoured by demon wolves.

S. Julius (Novara and the Italian Alps), S. Defendente (Lombardy and especially at San-Martino-di-Lupari), and S. Ignatius Loyola (Lanzo) are invoked as protectors against wolves. I have only been able to touch in this note the fringe of a very extensive field of hagiographical research.

[5] See the *Revue Celtique*, xi (1890), pp. 242–8, where quotations are given from ancient lives of S. Ronan. The details slightly differ. Thus in one version Keban complains that her only daughter has been eaten by the wolf, " sa fille unique que cet homme abominable avait dévorée " (*Vie des Saints de Bretagne*, by Dom Lobineau, Rennes, 1725, p. 42), which is derived from the Latin account edited by Perè de Smedt from a MS. in the Bibliothèque nationale. *La vie, gestes, mort et miracles des saints de la Bretagne Armorique* of Albert le Grand (1st ed. 1637, p. 131), speaks of the child as a boy. But these details actually are insignificant.

[6] Troisième Édition, A Hambourg, 1801, pp. 36–8.

[7] F. C. Lonandre, *Histoire Ancienne et Moderne d'Abbeville*, Abbeville, 1834, pp. 74–5. For an account of the Abbey of Saint-Riquier, destroyed at the Revolution, see pp. 554–6.

[8] *Die Lais der Marie de France*, ed. Karl Warnke, 2nd ed., Halle, 1900 (*Bibliotheca Normannica*, iii). *Bisclavret*, pp. 75–85. See also the Introduction, pp. xcviii–cvii.

The *Histoire de Biclarel, Roman du Renard Contrefait*, printed by P. Tarbé in his *Poètes de Champagne antérieurs au siècle de François Ier*, pp. 138–151, is nearly identical with and was obviously derived from the *Bisclavret* of Marie de France. The *Lai de Mélion* of the fourteenth century, printed by W. Horak in the *Zeitschrift für romanische Philologie*, vi, pp. 94 sqq., presents analogous features.

[9] *The Romance of William of Palerne*, ed. W. W. Skeat, Early English Text Society, 1867.

[10] ll. 181–6. The English text is incomplete and does not commence until line 187. Skeat, p. 6.

[11] ll. 3215–3220. Skeat, p. 105.

[12] Paul Sébillot, *Le Folk-Lore de France*, 1906, iii, pp. 54–7.

[13] *Opera Omnia*, folio, Venetiis, 1591, pp. 983–4. See also cap. xxiv, pp. 1000–1004.

[14] pp. 363–362 (in this order). The pages are incorrectly numbered, p. 202 is followed by 359, 358, 363, 362, 205 . . .

S. Albertus Magnus, *De Animalibus*, lib. ii, trac. i, cap. iii, says : " Quorumdam autem uirgae sunt ex ossea substantia, sicut lupi et uulpis et huiusmodi." *De Animalibus Libri XXVI*, ed. Hermann Stadler, p. 241. 15 Band. *Beiträge zur Geschichte der Philosophie des Mittelalters*, Münster, 1916. Of the wolf Ulisse Aldrovandi writes : " Ei genitale osseum quale in canibus et uulpibus obseruatur, Aristoteles, Plinius, et Albertus assignarunt." *De Quadrupedibus Digitatis Uiuiparis*. Bononiae, folio, 1637, lib. i, cap. vi, p. 146.

[15] The chief authorities are Weyer, *De Magorum Infamium Poenis*, caps. xiii and xiv, *Opera Omnia*, 1660, pp. 494–502 ; Boguet, *Discours*, xlvii (Eng. tr. *Examen*, pp. 140 and 153–4). This important case is cited by many writers, as for example Leonard Vair, *De Fascino*, lib. ii, cap. 12, Paris, 1583, p. 168, to whom it was related by his patron, the famous Cardinal de Granvelle, French ed., *Des Charmes*, Paris, 1583, p. 334 : by Claude Prieur, *Lycanthropie*, Louvain, 1596, pp. 36–7, and many more.

[16] *Réalité de la Magie et des Apparitions*, Paris, 1819, pp. 86–7.

[17]   Qui fuit eximia clarus uirtute Matthaeus,
                          Insignis Callae gloria celsa domus.

Matthieu de Challemaison was admitted Dean of the Chapter 15th November, 1555. He died 17th March, 1577. See *Gallia Christiana*, tom. xii, Paris, 1770, pp. 114–15.

[18] There is a reprint in *Archives Curieuses de l'Histoire de France*, edited by Louis Cimber (Louis Lafaist) and François Danjou, 1re Série, tome 8, Paris, 1836, pp. 7–11. Le Loyer, *Discours des Sorciers*, ii, 7, ed. 1608, p. 140, remarks : " Le procès faict à l'Hermite de Dole tant couru par tous les cantons de la France, Allemagne, & Flandre, que ce seroit presque peine perduë d'en dire quelquechose.

[19] Bourquelot, *Recherches sur la Lycanthropie*, Mémoires . . . *sur les Antiquités* . . . *de France*, nouvelle série, tome ix (1849), p. 245.

[20] Boguet, *Discours*, xlvii. Eng. tr. *Examen*, pp. 140–1. This story is very frequently repeated. Heywood and Brome use it in *The Late Lancashire Witches*, produced at the Globe in 1634 ; 4to, 1634 ; Act V, where the soldier who watches a night in the haunted mill is beset by cats and in routing them slices off a tabby's paw. The next morning it is discovered to be a hand which by the ring Master Generous recognizes as that of his wife, who lies at home sick in bed. Shadwell copies the incident in Act V of his *The Lancashire Witches*, acted in the autumn of 1681 ; 4to, 1680. He remarks : " The cutting off the hand is an old story." See my edition of Shadwell's *Works*, 1927, vol. iv, pp. 182–3 and notes.

[21] English translation, *An Examen of Witches*, 1929. For the life of Boguet and a bibliographical account of the *Discours*, see my introduction and notes to this edition. Chapter xlvii occupies pp. 186–155.

[22] De Lancre, *L'incredulité et mécréance du sortilège*, 4to, 1622, p. 785 sqq.

[23] " Certains hommes, notamment des fils de prêtres, sont forcés, à chaque pleine lune, de se transformer en loups-garous." This is the common belief in Périgord. Sébillot, *Le Folk-Lore de France*, tom. ii, p. 205.

It is interesting to meet with the following allusion in Zola's *La Faute de l'Abbé Mouret* (1874), livre premier, xii, when Frère Archangias and la Teuse are discussing Albine : " —Jamais elle n'a fait sa première communion, dit la Teuse, à demi-voix, avec un léger frisson.—Non, jamais, reprit Frère Archangias. Elle doit avoir seize ans. Elle grandit comme une bête. Je l'ai vue courir à quatre pattes, dans un fourré, du côté de la Palud.—A quatre pattes, murmura la servante, qui se tourna vers la fenêtre, prise d'inquiètude."

[24] The Franciscans founded their first house at Bordeaux during the episcopate of Guillaume II, 1207–1227. *Gallia Christiana*, tom ii, Parisiis, 1720, pp. 820–2.

[25] *Tableau de l'Inconstance des Mauvais Anges et Demons*, Paris, 1613 ; livre iv, discours ii, iii, iv, pp. 252–326. Baring-Gould, *The Book of Were-Wolves*, chapter vii, pp. 85–99, has told the story of Jean Grenier most interestingly, but he has (unless I mistake) permitted himself something of the licence of the novelist in his details.

[26] Paris, 1615, pp. 52–3.

[27] *The London Magazine, or Gentleman's Monthly Intelligencer*, vol. xxxiv, 1765, pp. 56, 140–1, 160, 214, 380.

[28] *Correspondance Littéraire . . . de Grimm et de Diderot*, Paris, 15 vols., 1829. Tom. iv, pp. 238–9.

[29] *Portefaix*, poème héroïque, Amsterdam et Paris, 8vo, 1765.

[30] The Wer-Wolf. *Court Magazine* (United Series), vol. xiii (1838), pp. 262–3.

[31] Sébillot, *Folk-Lore en France*, tome iv, p. 240.

[32] George Sand, *Légendes Rustiques*, Paris, 1858, pp. 29–32 ; viii, Le Meneu' de Loups.

[33] Ibid., pp. 45–8 ; xii, Lubins et Lupins.

[34] Translated by Henry S. Olcott, London, Redway, 1887, with the authorization of Adolphe D'Assier from the *Essai sur l'Humanité Posthume et le Spiritisme par un Positiviste*. Chapter xi, pp. 258–262 ; Lycanthropy.

[35] *The Book of Were-Wolves*, London, 1865, chapter i, pp. 1–5.

CHAPTER VI

The North, Russia, and Germany

SO immense is the wealth of tradition concerning shape-shifting contained in the ancient Sagas of the North that it becomes difficult in a strictly limited space even to indicate some of the better-known and most striking of these histories, whose legendary lore, if it is at all adequately to be examined, demands a concentrated study of no inconsiderable extension.

In Norway and Iceland those men who could assume another shape were said to be *eigi einhamir* " not of one form ". The adopted shape was called by the same name as the original shape, *hamr*, and the process of transformation they called *skipta hömum* or *at hamaz*. *Hamremmi* signifies the supernatural strength thus acquired ; the going about in that form was *hamför*, or *hamfarir*. A man who thus became possessed of more than human might was *hamrammr* ; a man who travelled with surpassing speed therefore was *hamhleypa*.

The man borrowed the animal, with whose force he was invigorated, with whose fleetness he was endowed. He follows the instincts of the beast whose body he has made his own, but his own intelligence is neither clouded nor snuffed. The soul remains unchanged, and hence the mirror of the soul, the eye, can by no art be altered. Frigg and Freyja had their *valshamr* " falcon-mantles ", attired in which they could cleave the air with the swiftness and surety of that bird. Loki, the tale went, donned one of these, and so exactly resembled a falcon that none could have discovered him save for the malicious glint of his eyes.[1]

The name for a wolf-shirt which effected the metamorphosis to a wolf was *úlfahamr*,[2] and the werewolf himself was commonly known as *vargr*.[3] In modern Scandinavia the term is *varúlf*, which has been extended to include the shape-shifting to a bear, for of all the *hamrammir* none were more famous than the *berserkir* or *berserkr*,[4] the bear-sark men.[5] Twelve berserkers were the chief followers of several kings of old, as for example the Danish King Rolf Krake, King Adils, and Harald Hárfagri. In battle the berserkers were subject to fits of frenzy (*furor bersericus*) [6] termed *berserksgangr*, when they howled like wild beasts, foamed at the mouth, and bit through the iron rim of their shields. During these fits they were, according to popular belief, proof against steel and fire, and made terrible havoc in the ranks of the foe. When the fever abated they were weak and tame. In the *Icelandia Jus Ecclesiastica* the *berserksgangr* is regarded as diabolic possession, and can only be cured by religious vows. [7]

William of Auvergne, Bishop of Paris, in his *De Uniuerso*, ii, pars. iii, [8] tells of a bear in Saxony who carried off a soldier's wife, and kept her for years in a cave and knew her so that she bore him children, and when she escaped these children accompanied her in her flight. They lived for many years, and were exceedingly fierce and good soldiers. They had bear in their faces, and were called Orsini (*Ursini* from *ursus* their sire). Bishop William says that the semen ursinum so resembles the semen humanum that a child may be born of a woman.

In his *Bekerung der Norwegischen Stammes zum Christenthume* [9] Konrad Maurer relates the history of Ulfr Bjalfason, the Evening-Wolf, from the Aigla. Folk said that Ulfr was much given to shifting his shape (*hamrammr*) and he was called *kveldúlfr*, Evening-Wolf. When the werewolf fit came over him and his companions their exploits were bloody with the most ferocious savagery. Whilst the passion endured none could withstand their might, but once it had passed they were weak as water for a while.

Here it should be remarked that the Norwegian berserker were often none other than professional gangs of marauding mohocks who roamed the countryside plundering and terrorizing wherever they went. It was their wont that some bully of gigantic strength among them should challenge a landowner to " holmgang ", the duello, and if the berserk conquered he would carry off his dead opponent's wife and daughters, extorting ransom, or possessing himself of the property entire. Often the titan brigand is slain by the gallant Icelandic hero.

Famous among ancient Norse stories is the legend of

Sigmund the Volsung and his son Sinfjötli. It so befell
that on a day in summer-tide these twain went forth through
the forest, seeking spoil. And they lighted upon a certain
house in the which were two men with great gold rings deeply
fallen upon sleep. These were two king's sons, spell-bound
skin-changers, and above them on the wall hung two wolf-
shirts. Now it was the tenth day, and on that day alone
were they released from the spell, and might come out of
the skins. Sigmund and Sinfjötli don the shirts, but can
by no means put them off, for upon them the ensorcellment
had taken hold, and the weird of the king's sons must they
dree, for they howled as wolves, and they understood one
another as afore when they had spoken in the voice of men.
So they go forth into the forest depths, adventuring, and
slay many, being full weary after the slaughter. At the last
they repair to the hidden house, and on the tenth day they
doff the wolf-shirts, burning this gear in the fire.

Another story in the *Volsunga saga* tells how an old bitch-
wolf, huge and grim, came out of the forest and night after
night ate a man alive. This wolfen, it was thought, was the
mother of King Siggeir, and she had shifted her shape by
troll's lore and devilry.[10]

To come to a later day, Arvad August Afzelius in his
Svenska Folk-Visor Fran Forntiden has an important note
upon the " *Varulf*, eller *Man-ulf* ", and also relates that a
Swedish soldier from Calmar, during the last war with
Russia in 1808–9, was homesick and came back in the shape
of a wolf. Unluckily he was shot by a hunter just outside
his native village. When the dead wolf, a huge beast, was
skinned, a man's shirt was found next to the body. A woman
identified it as one she had stitched for her husband before
he left for the field.[11]

Albert Krantz, in his *Chronica Regnorum Aquilonarium
Daniae, Suetiae, Noruagiae*, liber i, caput xxxii,[12] tells a
tradition of the death of King Froto III of Denmark, before
whom a witch turned her son into a calf and by glamour herself appeared as an ox. The monarch, wondering at such
ensorcellment, approached too near, whereupon the ox,
bellowing fiercely, charged and pierced his side with two
great branching horns, of which wound the old King died
presently.

The learned Joannes Tritheim, Abbot of Sponheim, in his *Annales Hirsaugienses*,[13] relates that in the year 970 there ruled over Bulgaria two brothers, Peter and Baianus, the sons of King Simeon, who had erstwhile been a monk. Now Prince Baianus was the most skilful magician of his day and wrought many a marvel which set all men agape. For by the aid of the Devil he would change himself into a wolf, or into a bird, or take whatever form of beast he list. By his evil craft and ensorcellments not unseldom did he mock and beguile the folk with these devil's delusions.

This is from the *Speculum Historiale* of Vincent of Beauvais,[14] liber xxiv, cap. 87, which concludes : " Hoc tempore [Othonis Imperatoris] Bulgaribus dominabantur filii Symeonis Petrus et Bayanus, quorum Bayanus in arte magica adeo ualebat, ut quotiens uellet Lupus, uel quaelibet fera fieri uideretur."

Olaus Magnus, in his *Historia de Gentibus Septentrionalibus*,[15] Rome, 1555, has much to say of wolves in general and devotes the last three chapters of his Eighteenth Book to werewolfery, emphasizing the hellish ferocity of the werewolf, and discussing these transformations with examples of such metamorphosis both from old days and in his own time. " In the Feast of Christs Nativity, in the night, at a certain place, that they are resolved upon among themselves, there is gathered together such a huge multitude of Wolves changed from men that dwell in divers places, which afterwards the same night doth so rage with wonderfull fiercenesse, both against mankind and other creatures, that are not fierce by nature, that the Inhabitants of that Country suffer more hurt from them, than ever they do from true naturall Wolves. For as it is proved they set upon the houses of men that are in the Woods with wonderful fierceness, and labour to break down the doors, whereby they may destroy both men and other creatures that remain there. They go into Beer-Cellars, and there they drink out some Tuns of Beer or Mede . . . wherein they differ from natural and true Wolves. . . . Between *Lituania, Samogetia,* and *Curonia,* there is a certain wall left, of a Castle that was thrown down ; to this at a set time some thousands of them come together, that each of them may try his nimblenesse in leaping ; he that cannot leap over this wall, as commonly the fat ones cannot, are beaten with whips by their Captains. And it is constantly affirmed that amongst that multitude are the great men & chiefest Nobility of the Land."

Olaus Magnus relates how when a certain Nobleman was travelling through the woods who had many servile Country-fellows in his company that were acquainted with this witchcraft of shape-shifting, and they were not only benighted but withal sore pinched with hunger and want, when a flock of sheep was spied at a distance one of the company promised they should have a lamb to roast for supper. Presently he goes into a thicket that no man might see him, and then he changed his human shape like to a Wolf. After this he fell upon the flock with all his might, and in the form of a Wolf brought back a sheep to the Chariot. His companions being conscious how he stole it, receive it with grateful mind, and hide it close in the Chariot : but he that had changed himself into a Wolf, went into the wood again, and became a man.

Also in Livonia not many years since, continues our author, it fell out that the wife of a great Lord openly said that men could not be turned into Wolves. Whereupon one of the servants standing by declared that he would presently show her an example of that business, so he might do it with her permission. He goes alone into the cellar, and anon he comes out in the form of a wolf. The dogs ran after him through the fields to the wood, and they bit out one of his eyes though he defended himself stoutly enough. The next day he came with one eye to his Lady.

It is fresh in memory how the Duke of Prussia giving small credit to such a Witchcraft, compelled one who was cunning in this Sorcery, whom he held in chains to change himself into a Wolf ; and he did so. Yet that he might not go unpunished for this Idolatry, he afterwards caused him to be burnt. For such heinous offences are severely punished both by Divine and Human Laws.

Caspar Peucer [16] says that although he long deemed the histories of werewolfery impossible and absurd, he was at last wholly convinced of their truth. In Livonia during the Christmas octave a boy who is lame in one foot goes round the countryside and summons in mysterious fashion all the warlocks, of whom there are very many. These varlets are compelled to follow the Devil's messenger, and if they delay another man soon visits them, armed with a huge whip knotted with iron, and they are eke compelled to hurry to the appointed station else he does not hesitate to flog them unmercifully tearing their flesh with his scourge. How bitter is the bondage of Satan! The wizards then all assemble at a certain rendezvous, and by their horrid art they change themselves into wolves. The man goes first with his huge whip, and the lupine train follow, evil folk who deceived by the Devil are persuaded that they are wolves. When they come to a river the leader strikes the water with his whip, and they seem to pass through by a dry path in horrid mockery of the miracle of the Red Sea, when Pharaoh's host were drowned. These wretches remain as wolves for a space of twelve days, during which they attack and devour cattle and sheep, but are not allowed to kill men. At the end of this period the glamour is dispersed and they return each to his home.

Simone Maiolo, Bishop of Volterra, in his *Dies Caniculares*,[17] has much to say of werewolfism and lycanthropy. He gathers instances and examples from many authorities when " *Rustici* illi ἀρκτολύκοι, quos nominamus *Bärwolff*, ambiguos lupos " come under discussion. He writes of a case of werewolfery which came under his notice not many years before, when a countryman was brought before a Duke of Muscovy, whose cattle he was said to have attacked and devoured in bestial form. This wretch was deformed and hideous to see, more like a beast than a man. His face and legs were covered with wounds, where he said he had been bitten by dogs when he was in the shape of a wolf. The Duke interrogated him straitly, and he confessed that twice a year, at Christmastide and about the Feast of S. John Baptist, Midsummer Day, there fell upon him a lupine ecstasy so that he rushed into the woods howling, and his shape was changed, hair covering his whole body. After the access he was weary to death and sick. In order to test the truth of the matter he was kept in hold for a year and more, but although the Lord's Birthday and S. John came round he was not metamorphosed. Clearly the man was a lycanthrope, not a werewolf.

Antonio de Torquemada, in his *Jardin de las Flores curiosas*,[18] jornada vi, tells of a Russian prince, who learning there was a shape-shifting warlock in his territory, ordered the varlet to be brought before him in chains, and then bade him give a sample of his skill. The man retired to a small room and presently came forth as a wolf, but the Prince let loose two fierce bandogs which he had in readiness, and these tore the wretched creature to pieces.

There are many werewolves in Russia, says Bishop Maiolo, haunting above all the Caucasus and Ural Mountains. The Yakuts of Siberia believe that every shaman is a past-master in shape-shifting, and moreover he keeps his soul or one of his souls incarnate in some animal mysteriously concealed where none may find it. The most powerful wizards are they whose souls are confined in elks, black bears, boars, fierce wolves, or eagles. The Samoyeds of the Turukhinsk say that every wizard leads a familiar about with him in the shape of a boar, guided by a magic belt. When the boar dies the shaman dies also, so closely knit is his soul to the familiar.[19] The Kamtchatkans fear the whale, the bear, and the wolf, whose names must never be mentioned when they are seen, for they understand human speech, they are warlocks in disguise.[20] The Siberians are loth to name the bear, who is termed of them " the little old man ", " the master of the forest ", " the sage ", all phrases of utmost significance.[21]

Among the latest Soviet propaganda [22] is the utilization of fantastic legends about Lenin. In Siberia, among the aborigines, the story runs that Lenin was originally a bear, for the bear is the Siberian totem. " The bear Lenin lived for a long time in the virgin forest. There came a Russian general to the forest and tried to trap the bear. He placed a barrel of vodka in the forest, and Lenin having drunk it became intoxicated. Thus he fell into the hands of the Russian general who compelled him to wander about all over the world and to dance for him. Finally he escaped, became a man, and now he is revenging himself on all generals."

In Russia itself Lenin has been subtly introduced to the peasantry as a saint, and on the 1st May thousands of peasants light a candle in front of Lenin's picture just as they honour a real Saint upon his festa.

According to an article in *The Tablet*, 1st October, 1932,

these abominations—amazing and incredible as it may seem—
are even to be found in our midst, and we have " Anti-God
Bolshevism on English soil ". Thus the church at Sneyd,
near Burslem, which is run on extremely ritualistic lines, is
a centre of " The League of Militant Youth " which claims
as its patrons " John Ball, the Communist leader of the
English peasants, and Lenin, the Liberator " ! A large red
flag is suspended at the chancel arch, and Soviet emblems—
the Sickle and the Hammer—are prominent. " In the vestry
hangs a framed portrait of Lenin, before which, according
to our Anglican informant, candles are sometimes lighted." [23]
There is nothing new in all this. It is the heresy of the Cainites,
so called from Cain, the first murderer, whom they praised
and honoured most religiously, hailing him as their father.[24]
The Cainites venerated and worshipped evil men, their father
Cain ; the rebels Core, Dathan, and Abiron, who went down
alive into hell; the traitor Judas Iscariot. To-day they
venerate Lenin. It is indeed nothing more nor less than
Satanism, the worship of the Devil. It is of these that—as
S. Epiphanius tells us—Our Lord said : " You are of your
father the Devil, and the desires of your father you will
do." [25] Origen, too, is justly scandalized that such heretics
and worse than heretics should dare to claim that they
are Christians.[26] So Satanism and socialism walk hand in
hand, as was ever their wont, for Satan was the first socialist.

In an important study, " The Witches of the Gypsies,"
contributed by Dr. Heinrich von Wlislocki to the *Journal
of the Gypsy Lore Society*,[27] in July, 1891, it is explained that
these witches in order to preserve their health suck the blood
of such men who are born at the waxing of the moon. The
gypsies of Hungary and the Balkans term their victims
pañikotordimako (literally *water-casks*). This belief prevails
in Russia, Poland, and Hungary. The men who are thus
vampirized fall into a kind of lycanthropy. They are
characterized by a pale sunken countenance, hollow mournful
eyes, swollen lips, and flabby inert arms. They are parched
by a burning thirst, and soon can only utter bestial sounds,
for the most part howling like wolves, and many at night
are transformed into fierce wolves. Being larger and stronger
than the natural wolf, these creatures become " wolf-kings ",
and their subjects must supply them with the finest meat.

At dawn they recover the human shape, but they can eat nothing save raw flesh and they lap blood. In Romani they are termed *ruvanush* " wolf-man ", from *ruv* " wolf " and *manush* " man ".

Dr. Wlislocki further relates a story which was told him in reference to the murder of a Gypsy musician ten years before, that is to say in 1881. At Tórész, in the north of Hungary, there lived a Gypsy fiddler, named Kropan, who was very poor, and who in spite of his music could only get from the peasants a few coppers enough to buy a morsel of bread for himself and his wife. Remarking his wife's absences from home at night, he suspected an intrigue and watched her privily. When she deemed him asleep she slipped out of their hut, and in the dawn to his deadly fear the door opened and there slipped in a huge grey wolf carrying a mangled lamb in its mouth. The next thing he knew was that his wife was roasting him a dish of savoury meat. He said nothing, but from that day the woman provided him with the beast meats, sheep, calves, cows, and pigs. Kropan, indeed, used to sell quantities of meat in the nearest town, so that the villagers knew nothing of his transactions. He grew rich, and opened a fine inn where one could obtain dishes dirt cheap, so the whole neighbourhood flocked to him. The day arrived when suspicion was aroused, for the wolf had ravaged the countryside. The villagers bound Kropan and his wife, and the priest exorcized them, sprinkling them with holy water. As the drops touched her the woman shrieked as though she had been plunged into boiling oil, and this witch who nightly became a *ruvanush* disappeared. The peasants in a rage slew Kropan. The two ringleaders were imprisoned for six years in the jail at Ilova, but in 1881 they had been released and were living in Tórész.

It has been said, but quite incorrectly, that in Germany the werewolf was confined almost entirely to the Hartz Mountains. This region was indeed a centre of all known sorceries, but the depredations of the werewolf unhappily covered a far wider range.

Johannes Janssen, in his *History of the German People*,[28] part iii, chapter iii, is of opinion that the traditions of sorcery and shape-shifting which developed so grimly among the Germanic peoples to a large extent grew out of the old

Teutonic system of supernatural beings, so that the gods
and demi-gods came to be regarded as magicians, an idea
embodied by Snorri Sturluson, who died in 1241, in the
Ynglinga Saga. Like Wotan and Freyja, the warlock and
sorcerers could change themselves into wolves and cats, the
sacred animals of those deities. It was furthermore believed
that such a metamorphosis was essential, at any rate the
common folk either did not or could not distinguish correctly,
and the most erroneous ideas began to prevail, inasmuch as
Pope S. Gregory VII on 19th April, 1080, admonished
King Harold of Denmark that he must no longer tolerate
but root out the gruesome superstitions which filled people's
lives with terror and dishonoured God by attributing almost
unlimited power to the devils of darkness. This state of
affairs was aggravated by the appearance of certain gnostic
Manichaean sects who taught duality, that there were two
conflicting, equally balanced principles, coexisting from
eternity, the good and the bad.

An old German Penetential " Corrector ",[29] 151, has :
" Credidisti quod quidam credere solent, ut illae quae a
uulgo parcae uocantur, ipsae, uel sint, uel possint hoc facere
quod creduntur ; id est dum aliquis homo nascitur, et tunc
ualeant illum designare ad hoc quod uelint ut quandocunque
ille homo uoluerit, in lupum transformari possit quod
teutonica Werewulff uocatur, aut in aliam aliquam figuram ?
Si credidisti, quod unquam fieret aut esse possit, ut diuina
imago in aliam formam aut in speciem transmutari possit
ab aliquo, nisi ab omnipotente Deo, decem dies in pane et
aqua debes poenitere."

Stephan Lanzkranna, Provost of S. Dorothy's in Vienna,
did not hesitate in his *Himmelstrasse*, 1484, to class a heathen
notion of werewolfery as a deception, more heathen than
Christian, and a very great sin.

A Lübeck confession book, *Das Licht der Seele*, of the
same year asks the penitent : " Have you done harm to
anyone with the devilish art ? Have you practised magic
or witchcraft with the Holy Sacraments ? Have you believed
that people can become werewolves ? . . . Let each one
search his own conscience and make a clean breast to his
Father Confessor."

In yet another confession book, widely circulated in the

fifteenth century, the penitent is asked if he believes that
" women can change themselves into cats, monkeys, and
other animals, fly up through the air, and suck the blood
of children ? "

It was a false and pagan tradition that was thus denounced,
but not the true and Christian belief in the reality of the
forces of evil.   The famous Augustinian preacher Gottschalk
Hollen, who died in 1481, relates in his *Praeceptorium* how
a woman who had been seemingly transformed by a witch
into a mare was sprinkled with holy water and the glamour
dispersed. Matthias   von   Kemnat,   court   chaplain   to
Frederick the Victorious of the Upper Palatinate, in his
Chronicle of this Prince relates many similar instances of
diabolical sorcery.[30]

During a Lenten course preached at Strassburg in 1508
by a famous pulpiteer, Dr. Johann Geiler von Kaisersberg,
stirring discourses taken down by the Guardian of the
Fransicans of the Strict Observance in that city, Father
Johann Paul, who first published the collection in 1517 as
Die Emeis,[31] is a sermon delivered on the third Sunday in
Lent, with rubric, " Am dritten sontag den fasten, Occuli,
predigt den doctor vor den Werwölffen."   The good doctor
discusses lycanthropy, apparently regarding werewolves as
wolves of uncommon ferocity, who having tasted human
flesh find it far more delicate than any other and desire it
always. Hence they lie in wait to devour men.   He certainly
says that the Demon often appears in the shape of a wolf,
and in his sermon on wild men of the woods he speaks of
lycanthropes in Spain.

Guazzo in the *Compendium Maleficarum*,[32] book i, chapter
13, speaks of a shepherd named Petronius who was tried at
Dalheim in 1581.   " Whenever he felt moved with hatred
or envy against the shepherds of neighbouring flocks (as is
the way of such men) he used to change himself into a wolf
by the use of certain incantations, and so for a long time
escaped all suspicion as being the cause of the mutilation
and death of his neighbours' sheep."

On 2nd September, 1663, at a meeting of the Royal Society,
Sir Kenelm Digby " read a letter, sent to him out of the
Palatinate, concerning some children snatched away in those
parts by beasts, that had the appearance of wolves ; but

found killed after so strange a manner, that all people there-
about surmised, that they were not wolves, but *lycanthropi*,
seeing, that nothing of the bodies of those children were
devoured, but the heads, arms, and legs, severed from their-
bodies, the skulls opened, and the brains taken out and
scattered about the carcases, and the heart and bowels, in
like manner, pulled out, but not devoured." [33]

One of the most famous of all German werewolf trials was
that of Peter Stump (or Stumpf, Stube, Stubbe, Stub, as
the name is indifferently spelled—and there are other
variants), who was executed for his horrid crimes at Bedburg,[34]
near Cologne, on 31st March, 1590. The case caused an
immense sensation,[35] and was long remembered and quoted.
Thus we have the following allusion by Samuel Rowlands
in *The Knave of Harts* [36] :—

> A *German* (called *Peter Stumpe*) by charme,
> Of an inchanted Girdle, did much harme,
> Transform'd himselfe into a Wolfeish shape,
> And in a wood did many yeeres escape
> The hand of Iustice, till the Hang-man met him,
> And from a Wolfe, did with an halter set him :
> Thus counterfaiting shapes haue had ill lucke,
> Witnesse *Acteon* when he plaid the Bucke . . .

The contemporary pamphlet which gives an account of
this werewolf is of the last rarity,[37] beyond which it has
indeed such intrinsic interest that I have thought it well
to reproduce it here in full.

> *A true Discourse.*
> Declaring the damnable life
> and   death   of   one   Stubbe   Peeter,   a   most
> wicked   Sorcerer,   who   in   the   likenes   of   ᵽ
> *Woolfe, committed many murders, continuing this*
> diuelish practise 25. yeeres, killing and de-
> *uouring Men, Woomen, and*
> Children.
> *Who for the same fact was ta-*
> ken   and   executed   the   31.   of   October
> *last past in the Towne of* Bedbur
> neer the Cittie of *Collin*
> in *Germany.*

Trulye translated out of the high Duch, according to the Copie printed
 in Collin, brought ouer into England by George Bores ordinary
 Poste, the xj. daye of this present Moneth of Iune 1590. who
 did both see and heare the same.

AT LONDON
Printed for Edward Venge, and are to be
solde in Fleet-street *at the signe of the*
Vine.

¶ A most true Discourse,
declaring the life and death of one
Stubbe Peeter, being a most
wicked Sorcerer.

THose whome the Lord dooth leaue to followe the Imagination of their own hartes, dispising his proffered grace, in the end through the hardnes of hart and contempt of his fatherly mercy, they enter the right path to perdicion and destruction of body and soule for euer : as in this present historie in perfect sorte may be seene, the strangenes whereof, together with the cruelties committed, and the long time therein continued, may driue many in doubt whether the same be truth or no, and the ratherfore that sundry falce & fabulous matters haue heertofore passed in print, which hath wrought much incredulitie in yͤ harts of all men generally, insomuch that now a daies fewe thinges doo escape be it neuer so certain, but that it is embased by the tearm of a lye or falce reporte. In the reading of this story, therfore I doo first request reformation of opinion, next patience to peruse it, because it is published for examples sake, and lastly to censure thereof as reason and wisdome dooth think conueniet, considering the subtilty that Sathan vseth to work the soules destruction, and the great matters which the accursed practise of Sorcery dooth effect, the fruites whereof is death and destruction for euer, and yet in all ages practised by the reprobate and wicked of the earth, some in one sort and some in another euen as the Deuill giueth promise to perfourme. But of all other that euer liued, none was comparable vnto this helhound, whose tiranny and cruelty did well declare he was of his Father the deuill, who was a murderer from the beginning, whose life and death and most bloody practises the discourse following dooth make iust reporte. In the townes of Cperadt and Bedbur neer vnto Collin in high Germany, there was continually brought vp and nourished one Stubbe Peeter, who from his youth was greatly inclined to euill, and the practising of wicked Artes euen from twelue yeers of age till twentye, and so forwardes till his dying daye, insomuch that surfeiting in the Damnable desire of magick, negromancye, and sorcery, acquainting him selfe with many infernall spirites and feendes, insomuch that forgetting yͤ God that made him, and that Sauiour that shed his blood for mans redemption : In the end, careles of saluation gaue both soule and body to the deuil for euer, for small carnall pleasure in this life, that he might be famous and spoken of on earth, though he lost heauen thereby. The Deuill who hath a readye eare to listen to the lewde motions of cursed men, promised to giue vnto him whatsoeuer his hart desired during his mortall life : wherupon this vilde wretch neither desired riches nor promotion, nor was his fancy satisfied with any externall or outward pleasure, but hauing a tirannous hart, and a most cruell bloody minde, he only requested that at his plesure he might woork his mallice on men, Women, and children, in the shape of some beast, wherby he might liue without dread or danger of life, and vnknowen to be the executor of any bloody enterprise, which he meant to commit : The

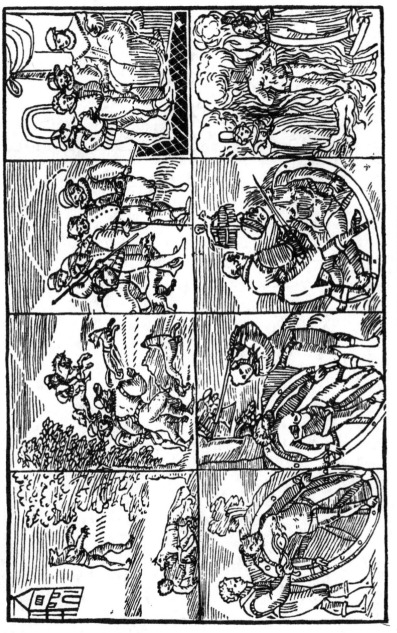

PLATE VIII

THE LIFE AND DEATH OF PETER STUMP

[face p. 254]

Deuill who sawe him a fit instrumēt to perfourm mischeefe as a wicked feend pleased with the desire of wrong and destruction, gaue vnto him a girdle which being put about him, he was straight transfourmed into the likenes of a greedy deuouring Woolf, strong and mighty, with eyes great and large, which in the night sparkeled like vnto brandes of fire, a mouth great and wide, with most sharpe and cruell teeth, A huge body, and mightye pawes : And no sooner should he put off the same girdle, but presently he should appeere in his former shape, according to the proportion of a man, as if he had neuer beene changed.

Stubbe Peeter heerwith was exceedingly well pleased, and the shape fitted his fancye and agreed best with his nature, being inclined to blood and crueltye, therfore satisfied with this strange and diuelish gifte, for that it was not troublesome nor great in cariage, but that it might be hidden in a small room, he proceeded to the execution of sundry most hainous and vilde murders, for if any person displeased him, he would incontinent thirst for reuenge, and no sooner should they or any of theirs walke abroad in the feeldes or about the Cittie, but in the shape of a Woolfe he would presentlye incounter them, and neuer rest till he had pluckt out their throates and teare their ioyntes a sunder : And after he had gotten a taste heerof, he tooke such pleasure and delight in shedding of blood, that he would night and day walke the Feelds, and work extreame cruelties. And sundry times he would goe through the Streetes of Collin, Bedbur, and Cperadt, in comely habit, and very ciuilly as one well knowen to all the inhabitants therabout, & oftentimes was he saluted of those whose freendes and children he had buchered, though nothing suspected for the same. In these places, I say, he would walke vp & down, and if he could spye either Maide, Wife or childe, that his eyes liked or his hart lusted after, he would waite their issuing out of yᵉ Cittie or town, if he could by any meanes get them alone, he would in the feeldes rauishe them, and after in his Wooluishe likenes cruelly murder them : yea often it came to passe that as he walked abroad in the feeldes, if he chaunste to spye a companye of maydens playing together, or else a milking of their Kine, in his Wooluishe shape he would incontinent runne among them, and while the rest escaped by flight, he would be sure to laye holde of one, and after his filthy lust fulfilled, he would murder her presentlye, beside, if he had liked or knowne any of them, look who he had a minde vnto, her he would pursue, whether she were before or behinde, and take her from the rest, for such was his swiftnes of foot while he continued a woolf : that he would outrunne the swiftest greyhound in that Countrye : and so muche he had practised this wickednes, that yᵉ whole Prouince was feared by the cruelty of this bloody and deuouring Woolfe. Thus continuing his diuelishe and damnable deedes within the compas of fewe yeeres, he had murdered thirteene yong Children, and two goodly yong women bigge with Child, tearing the Children out of their wombes, in most bloody and sauedge sorte, and after eate their hartes panting hotte and rawe, which he accounted dainty morsells & best agreeing to his Appetite.

Moreouer he vsed many times to kill Lambes and Kiddes and such like beastes, feeding on the same most vsually raw and bloody, as if he had beene a naturall Woolfe indeed, so that all men mistrusted nothing lesse then this his diuelish Sorcerie.

He had at that time liuing a faire yong Damosell to his Daughter, after whom he also lusted most vnnaturallye, and cruellye committed most wicked inceste with her, a most groce and vilde sinne, far surmounting Adultrye or Fornication, though the least of the three dooth driue the soule into hell fier, except hartye repentance, and the great mercy of God. This Daughter of his he begot when he was not altogither so wickedlye giuen, who was called by the name of Stubbe Beell, whose beautye and good grace was such as deserued commendacions of all those that knewe her: And such was his inordinate lust and filthye desire toward her, that he begat a Childe by her, dayly vsing her as his Concubine, but as an insaciate and filthy beast, giuen ouer to woork euil, with greedines he also lay by his owne Sister, frequenting her company long time euen according as the wickednes of his hart lead him : Moreouer being on a time sent for to a Gossip of his there to make merry and good cheere, ere he thence departed he so wunne the woman by his faire and flattering speech, and so much preuailed, y^t ere he departed the house : he lay by her, and euer after had her companye at his commaund, this woman had to name Katherine Trompin, a woman of tall and comely stature of exceeding good fauour and one that was well esteemed among her neighbours. But his lewde and inordinat lust being not satisfied with the company of many Concubines, nor his wicked fancye contented with the beauty of any woman, at length the deuill sent vnto him a wicked spirit in the similitude and likenes of a woman, so faire of face and comelye of personage, that she resembled rather some heauenly Helfin then any mortall creature, so farre her beauty exceeded the choisest sorte of women, and with her as with his harts delight, he kept company the space of seuen yeeres, though in the end she proued and was found indeed no other then a she Deuil, notwithstanding, this lewd sinne of lecherye did not any thing asswage his cruell and bloody minde, but continuing an insatiable bloodsucker, so great was the ioye he took therin, that he accoūted no day spent in pleasure wherin he had not shed some blood not respecting so much who he did murder, as how to murder and destroy them, as the matter ensuing dooth manifest, which may stand for a speciall note of a cruell and hard hart. For hauing a proper youth to his sonne, begotten in the flower and strength of his age, the firste fruite of his bodye, in whome he took such ioye, that he did commonly call him his Hartes ease, yet so farre his delight in murder exceeded the ioye he took in his only Sonne, that thirsting after his blood, on a time he inticed him into the feeldes, and from thence into a Forrest hard by, where making excuse to stay about the necessaries of nature, while the yong man went on forward, incontinent in the shape and likenes of a Woolfe he encountred his owne Sonne, and there most cruelly slewe him, which doon, he presently eat the brains out of his head as a most sauerie and dainty delycious meane to staunch his greedye apetite : the most monstrous act that euer man heard off, for neuer was knowen a wretch from nature so far degenerate.

Long time he continued this vilde and villanous life, sometime in the likenes of a Woolfe, sometime in the habit of a man, sometime in the Townes and Citties, and sometimes in the Woods and thickettes to them adioyning, whereas the duche coppye maketh mention, he on a time mette with two men and one woman, whom he greatly desired to murder, and the better to bring his diuelish purpose to effect, doubting by them to be ouermatched and knowing one of them by name, he vsed this pollicie to bring them to their end. In subtill sorte he conuayed himselfe far before them in their way and craftely couched out of their sight, but as soone as they approched neere the place where he lay, he called one of them by his name, the pàrtye hearing him selfe called once or twice by his name, supposing it was some familiar freend that in iesting sorte stood out of his sight, went from his companye towarde the place from whence the voice proceeded, of purpose to see who it was, but he was no sooner entred within the danger of this transformed man, but incontinent he was murdered ín yᵉ place, the rest of his company staying for him, expecting still his returne, but finding his stay ouer long : the other man lefte the woman, and went to looke him, by which means the second man was also murdered, the woman then seeing neither of both returne againe, in hart suspected that some euill had fan vpon them, and therfore with all the power she had, she sought to saue her selfe by flight, though it nothing preuailed, for good soule she was also soone ouertaken by this light footed Woolfe, whom when he had first deflowred, he after most cruelly murdered, the men were after found mangled in the wood, but the womans body was neuer after seene, for she the caitife had most rauenouslye deuoured, whose fleshe he esteemed both sweet and dainty in taste.

Thus this damnable Stubbe Peeter liued the tearme of fiue and twenty yeeres, unsuspected to be Author of so many cruell and vnnaturall murders, in which time he had destroyed and spoyled an vnknowen number of Men, Women, and Children, sheepe, Lambes, and Goates : and other Catttell, for when he could not through the warines of people drawe men, Women, or Children in his danger, then like a cruell and tirannous beast he would woorke his cruelty on brut beasts in most sauadge sort, and did act more mischeefe and cruelty then would be credible, although high Germany hath been forced to taste the trueth thereof.

By which meanes the inhabitantes of Collin, Bedbur and Cperadt, seeing themselues so greeuously endaungered, plagued, and molested by this greedy & cruel Woolfe, who wrought continuall harme and mischeefe, insomuch that few or none durst trauell to or from those places without good prouision of defence, and all for feare of this deuouring and fierce woolf, for oftentimes the Inhabitants found the Armes & legges of dead Men, Women, and Children, scattered vp and down the feelds to their great greefe and vexation of hart, knowing the same to be doone by that strange and cruell Woolfe, whome by no meanes they could take or ouercome, so that if any man or woman mist their Childe, they were out of hope euer to see it again aliue, mistrusting straight that the Woolfe had destroyed it.

And heere is to be noted a most strange thing which setteth foorth the great power and mercifull prouidence of God to yᵉ comfort of eache Christian hart. There were not long agoe certain small Children playing in a Medowe together hard by yᵉ town, where also some store of kine were feeding, many of them hauing yong calues sucking upon thē : and sodainly among these Children comes this vilde Woolfe running and caught a prittie fine Girle by the choller, with intent to pull out her throat, but such was yᵉ will of God, that he could not pearce the choller of the Childes coate, being high and very well stiffened & close claspt about her neck, and therwithall the sodaine great crye of the rest of the childrē which escaped, so amazed the cattell feeding by, that being fearfull to be robbed of their young, they altogether came running against the Woolfe with such force that he was presently compelled to let goe his holde and to run away to escape yᵉ danger of their hornes, by which meanes the Childe was preserued from death, and God be thanked remains liuing at this day.

And that this thing is true, Maister Tice Artine a Brewer dwelling at Puddlewharfe, in London, beeing a man of that Country borne, and one of good reputation and account, is able to iustifie, who is neere Kinsman to this Childe, and hath from thence twice receiued Letters conserning the same, and for that the firste Letter did rather driue him into wondering at the act then yeelding credit therunto, he had shortlye after at request of his writing another letter sent him, wherby he was more fully satisfied, and diuers other persons of great credit in London hath in like sorte receiued letters from their freends to the like effect.

Likewise in the townes of Germany aforesaid continuall praier was vsed vnto god that it would please him to deliuer thē from the danger of this greedy Woolfe.

And although they had practised all the meanes that men could deuise to take this rauenous beast, yet vntill the Lord had determined his fall, they could not in any wise preuaile : notwithstanding they daylye continued their purpose, and daylye sought to intrap him, and for that intent continually maintained great mastyes and Dogges of muche strength to hunt & chase the beast whersoeuer they could finde him. In the end it pleased God as they were in readines and prouided to meete with him, that they should espye him in his wooluishe likenes, at what time they beset him round about, and moste circumspectlye set their Dogges vpon him, in such sort that there was no means to escape, at which aduantage they neuer could get him before, but as the Lord deliuered Goliah into yᵉ handes of Dauid, so was this Woolfe brought in danger of these men, who seeing as I saide before no way to escape the imminent danger, being hardly pursued at the heeles presently he slipt his girdle from about him, wherby the shape of a Woolfe cleane auoided, and he appeered presently in his true shape & likenes, hauing in his hand a staffe as one walking toward the Cittie, but the hunters whose eyes was stedfastly bent vpon the beast, and seeing him in the same place metamorphosed contrary to their expectation : it wrought a wonderfull amazement in their mindes, and had it not beene that they knewe the man so soone as they sawe him, they had surely taken the same to haue beene some Deuill in a mans likenes, but for as much as they knewe him to be an auncient dweller in the Towne, they came vnto him, and talking with him they brought him by communication home to his owne house, and finding him to be the man indeede, and no delusion or phantasticall motion, they had him incontinent before the Maiestrates to be examined.

Thus being apprehended, he was shortly after put to the racke in the Towne of Bedbur, but fearing the torture, he volluntarilye confessed his whole life, and made knowen the villanies which he had committed for the space of xxv. yeeres, also he cōfessed how by Sorcery he procured of the Deuill a Girdle, which beeing put on, he forthwith became a Woolfe, which Girdle at his apprehension he confest he cast it off in a certain Vallye and there left it, which when the Maiestrates heard, they sent to the Vallye for it, but at their comming found nothing at al, for it may be supposed that it was gone to the deuil from whence it came, so that it was not to be found. For the Deuil hauing brought the wretch to al the shame he could, left him to indure the torments which his deedes deserued.

After he had some space beene imprisoned, the maiestrates found out through due examination of the matter, that his daughter Stubbe Beell and his Gossip Katherine Trompin, were both accessarye to diuers murders committed, who for the same as also for their leaud life otherwise committed, was arraigned, and with Stubbe Peeter condempned, and their seuerall Iudgementes pronounced the 28 of October 1589, in this manor, that is to saye : Stubbe Peeter as principall mallefactor, was iudged first to haue his body laide on a wheele, and with red hotte burning pincers in ten seuerall places to haue the flesh puld off from the bones, after that, his legges and Armes to be broken with a woodden Axe or Hatchet, afterward to haue his head strook from his body, then to haue his carkasse burnde to Ashes.

Also his Daughter and his Gossip were iudged to be burned quicke to Ashes, the same time and day with the carkasse of the aforesaid Stubbe Peeter. And on the 31. of the same moneth, they suffered death accordingly in the town of Bedbur in the presence of many peeres & princes of Germany.

Thus Gentle Reader haue I set down the true discourse of this wicked man Stub Peeter, which I desire to be a warning to all Sorcerers and Witches, which vnlawfully followe their owne diuelish imagination to the vtter ruine and destruction of their soules eternally, from which wicked and damnable practice, I beseech God keepe all good men, and from the crueltye of their wicked hartes. Amen.

AFter the execution, there was by the aduice of the Maiestrates of the town of Bedbur a high pole set vp and stronglye framed, which first went through ye wheele wheron he was broken, whereunto also it was fastened, after that a little aboue the Wheele the likenes of a Woolfe was framed in wood, to shewe unto all men the shape wherein he executed those crueltis. Ouer that on the top of the stake the sorcerers head it selfe was set vp, and round about the Wheele there hung as it were sixteen peeces of wood about a yarde in length which represented the sixteene persons that was perfectly knowen to be murdered by him. And the same ordained to stand there for a continuall monument to all insu-
ing ages, what murders by Stub Pee-
ter was committed, with the order of his Iudgement, as
this picture doth more
plainelye ex-
presse.

Witnesses that this is
true.
Tyse Artyne.
William Brewar.
Adolf Staedt.
George Bores.
With diuers others that haue seen the same.

NOTES TO CHAPTER VI

[1] Konrad Maurer, *Die Bekerung des Norwegischen Stammes zum Christenthume*, 2 vols., Munich, 1856 ; vol. ii, p. 101 sqq. with the notes.

[2] In the Icelandic Poem of Hornklofi, beginning of the tenth century, a dialogue between a Valkyrie and a raven, the Valkyrie says : at berserkja reiðu vil bek ik spyrja, to which the raven replies : Ulfhéðnar vóru, *they are called Wolfcoats.*

[3] See also Hertz, *Der Werwolf*, Stuttgart, 1861, p. 61 with the notes.

[4] Now generally considered to be derived from " bear-sark " (berr-serkr, *ursus* and shirt).

[5] Bear-men and bear-women are, of course, quite common in folk-lore and fable. Thus in Basile's *Pentamerone* (*Lo Cunto de li Cunti*), the Sixth Diversion of the Second Day, we have Antonella's tale of *The She-Bear : Le'Orza*, trattenemiento 6, jornata ii, ed. Napoli, 1788, tom. i, pp. 202–211 ; translated by Sir Richard Burton, 2 vols., London, 1893 ; vol. i, pp. 181–190. See also *The Pentamerone of Giambattista Basile* (Benedetto Croce), translated by N. M. Penzer, 2 vols., 1932 ; vol. i, pp. 170–7, " The She-Bear."

[6] *Furor athleticus*, of which a description is found in several Sagas, e.g. Snorri Sturluson's *Ynglinga Saga*, 6 ; *Hervaser Saga* ; *Egils Saga*, 27 ; *Grettis Saga*, 42 ; *Eyrlyggia Saga*, 25 ; and others. For these see the collection, 3 vols., Rafn, Copenhagen, 1829–1830. See also the essay *De furore Bersercico* at the end of the *Kristni Saga*, in the edition *Biskupa Sögur*, vol. i, Copenhagen, 1858.

[7] See *Icelandic-English Dictionary*, Cleasby and Vigfusson, Oxford, 1874, under *ber-serkr*, p. 61.

[8] *Opera Omnia*, folio, Venetiis, 1591, p. 1009.

[9] Vol. ii, p. 108 sqq.

[10] *Volsunga saga ; Det Norske old skriftselskabs samlinger viii* : ed. S. Bugge, 8vo, Christiana, 1865. *Volsunga Saga*, translated from the Icelandic by Eiríkr Magnússon and William Morris, ed. by H. H. Sparling, London, 1888, chapters viii and (for King Siggeir's mother) v.

[11] *Svenska Folk-Visor . . . af* Er. Gust. Geijer och Arv. Aug. Afzelius, 3 vols., Stockholm, 1814–16. Tredje delen (1816), pp. 119–120. The line annotated runs : " Och som'a skapte hon till *ulfvar* grä."

[12] Albert Krantz of Hamburg, died in December, 1517. *Chronica*, folio, 1546, pp. 35–6.

[13] Typis Monasterii S. Galli. Folio, 1690, " Nunc primum . . . publicae luci datum," pp. 112 and 120.

[14] *Speculum Maius : Speculum Historiale*, tom. iv, p. 342, verso ; ed. folio, Venetiis, 1591.

[15] There is an English version and abridgement, *A Compendious History of the Goths, Swedes, & Vandals*, folio, 1658. In this the reference is Book xviii, chapters 32 and 33. I have adopted a phrase here and there from this old version, but it must be used cautiously as there are many important omissions.

[16] *Commentarius de Præcipuis Generibus Diuinationum*, Witebergae, 1572, pp. 130–4.

[17] Folio, Offenbaci ad Moenum, 1691 : Colloquium ii, pp. 28–9 ; Coll. iii, pp. 432–6. The good Bishop does not neglect the " *Sagae in feles conuersae* ". He also mentions the water-ordeal. Indeed, the whole Colloquium iii, *De Sagis*, should be read. It should perhaps be mentioned that some ascribe this section to George Draud of Davernheim (1573–1635).

[18] Salamanca, 1570. This book ran into several French editions as the *Hexameron*, " Fait en Hespagnol et mis en françois par Gabriel Chappuys, Tourangeau," Lyons, 16mo, 1579.

[19] *Journal of the Anthropological Institute*, vol. xxiv, 1895, pp. 133–4 ; Professor V. M. Mikhailoviskij, " Shamanism in Siberia and European Russia."

[20] G. W. Steller, *Beschreibung von dem Lande Kamtschatka*, Frankfort and Leipzig, 1774, p. 276.

[21] P. Labbé, *Un Bagne russe, l'île de Sakhaline*, Paris, 1903, p. 231. Cf. the

name given to a bear in the *Pentamerone*, tratteniemento vi, jornata ii, *Le'Orza*, ed. Napoli, 1788, tom. i, pp. 202–211, " Ma lo Prencepe decenno all'Orza, Chiappino mio, non me vuoje cocenare ? " (p. 210). " But the Prince said to the Bear, Teddy dear, won't you cook me something ? " Porta has a comedy *La Chiappinaria*.

[22] *Anglo-Russian News*, No. 188, 18th January, 1929. " Legends of Lenin as Propaganda."

[23] Apparently in the vestry of All Saints, Manchester, is enshrined the portrait of a dramatist, George Bernard Shaw. Can folly go further ? I do not know whether tapers are lighted before this new Beato or Saint or whatever he is esteemed to be. See *The Tablet*, vol. 160, No. 4821, pp. 425–6, " Comprehensive Indeed ! " Also, *Tablet*, 8th Oct., pp. 457–8 ; 15th Oct., p. 495 ; 22nd Oct., pp. 525–6 ; 29th Oct., p. 559 ; 5th Nov., p. 592.

[24] " ἀπὸ τοῦ Κάϊν εἰληφότες . . . Οὗτοι γὰρ τὸν Κάϊν ἐπανοῦσι, καὶ πατέρα ἑαυτῶν τοῦτον τάττουσι." And a little later : " 'Επαινοῦσι γὰρ τὸν Κάϊν καὶ τὸν 'Ιούδαν." S. Epiphanius Aduersus Haereses, lib. i, tom. iii. Migne, *Patr. Gr.*, vol. xli, 653–666. See also S. Irenaeus, *Contra Haereses*, lib. i, cap. xxxi. Migne, *P.G.*, vol. vii, 704–6, " De Caianis."

[25] S. John's Gospel, viii, 44.

[26] *Contra Celsum*, vi, 28. Origen is speaking directly of the Ophites who were Satanists even as the Cainites. " τοσοῦτον ἀποδέουσι τοῦ εἶναι Χριστιανοί, ὥστε οὐκ ἔλαττον Κέλσου κατηγυρεῖν αὐτοὺς τοῦ Ἰησοῦ."

[27] Vol. iii, No. 1, pp. 38–45.

[28] *Geschichte des deutschen Volkes seit dem Aufgang der Mittelalter*, 6 vols., Freiburg, 1878–9 ; new ed. Ergänzt und herausg. von Ludwig Pastor, 8 vols., Freiburg, 1897. Eng. tr. *History of the German People after the Close of the Middle Ages*, 16 vols., by M. A. Mitchell and A. M. Christie. Vol. xvi (1910), tr. A. M. Christie, pp. 216–526.

[29] Hermann Joseph Schmitz, *Die Bussbücher und die Bussdisciplin der Kirche*, Band ii. Düsseldorf, 1892, p. 442.

[30] For these details the authority is Dr. Heinrich Geffeken, who is quoted by Janssen, Eng. tr., vol. xvi, pp. 230–2 and notes.

[31] " Die Emeis. Dis ist das büch von der Omeissen, und dauch Herr der Künnig ich diente gern. Und sacht von Eichtenschafft der Omeissen. Und gibt underweisung von den Unholden oder Hexen, und von gespenst der geist, und von dem Wütenden heer wunderbarlich." Folio, 1517. (Bodley, fol. Θ. 583.) p. xxxxi. See also the Sermon " Von wilden Mannen," p. xxxxi (recto). Johann Geiler was born in 1445 at Schaffhausen and lived at Strassburg in 1508. For further details see Joseph Hansen, *Quellen und Untersuchungen zur Geschichte des Hexenwahns*, Bonn, 1901, pp. 284–291.

[32] Eng. tr., 1929, p. 52.

[33] Thomas Bird, *History of the Royal Society of London*, 4 vols., 1756–7, vol. i, p. 300.

[34] Bedburg to-day is a little town of 2,925 inhabitants. It is situated on the Erit, an affluent of the left of the Rhine. The railway station (the second after Düsen) is on the Aix-la-Chapelle to Neuss line.

[35] There is a reference by Delrio, *Disquisitionum Magicarum*, liber ii, q. xviii, ed. Moguntiae, 1603, pp. 165–6, who mentions the sensation caused by the trial. Verstegan (Rowlands), *Restitution of Decayed Intelligence*, 1605, p. 287, mentions that " One *Peeter Stump* for beeing a were-wolf, had hauing killed thirteen children, two women, and one man was at *Bedbur* not far from *Cullen* in the yeare 1589 put vnto a very terrible death ". See also Edward Fairfax, *Daemonologia*, ed. Grainge, 1882, p. 97.

[36] *The Knave of Harts. Haile Fellow well met.* 4to, 1612. *Epigram* preceeding Epilogue, p. 47.

[37] The only two copies of which I have any knowledge, and I believe none others have been traced, are those in the British Museum and in the Lambeth Library respectively. The original is black letter. I have corrected one misprint ; p. 258, l. 45, where I read " no delusion " for " no selusion ".

A NOTE UPON THE WEREWOLF IN
LITERATURE

Homo homini lupus.—Old Saw.

IT has been said, but with something more than exaggeration, that *L'Histoire des Imaginations Extravagantes de
Monsieur Oufle (Le Fou)* is the *Don Quixote* of occultism.
Laurent Bordelon, however, was far from being a Cervantes,
although he has confessedly, and indeed wisely, taken that
great master as his model. Born at Bourges in 1653, l'Abbé
Bordelon died at Paris, 6th April, 1730. Of his many works
Monsieur Oufle, first published in 1710, is (I think) unquestionably the best. In chapter ii we have a list of the principal
books in Monsieur Oufle's library, and it is indeed a collection
which both Mr. Hazilrigge and myself might envy. Chapter iii
tells how Monsieur Oufle was convinced that there are werewolves—the English translator turns *Loups-garoux* as *Hob-
goblins* and rather misses the point here—" qu'on appelle
en Poitou, *la bête bigourne qui court la galipode*," and in
chapter iv we have a good Carnival adventure, briskly enough
related. Having drunk pretty freely at supper, where there
was company, Monsieur Oufle finding by chance a masking
dress in his son's room, proceeds to don it. This habit was
made of bear-skins, and very soon after he is clothed in it
he imagines himself a wolf, and that it is incumbent on him
to run out into the streets and howl. This he forthwith
proceeds to do most successfully. A number of pleasant
incidents ensue, and the town is for some while after terrified
by the rumours of the Loup-garou, " ce Sorcier de Loup."

Bordelon had certainly read widely, and the ample notes
he has furnished to his chapters are in themselves valuable.
As badinage *Monsieur Oufle* is amusing enough and harmless,
although occasionally open to the charge of ill-manners, but
it does not and indeed could not seriously touch upon and
speer the dark problems of the supernatural and unseen.

In lighter mood also is written Dudley Costello's
*Lycanthropy in London; or, The Wehr-Wolf of Wilton-
Crescent*, which appeared in *Bentley's Miscellany*, 1855,

vol. xxxviii, the famous periodical having just come under the editorship of Harrison Ainsworth. This comical little tale is told with a sense of humour and a brio that seem to be a particular Victorian quality for which we may look in vain to-day. Another lost virtue is evident in this droll mournival of chapters. Costello was clearly well read in his subject. Moreover, although he may banter he is always in good taste.

At the same time it might justly be argued that so terrible a thing as werewolfery is not suited for whimsical fiction.

That the subject could not fail to attract the sombre and sullen genius of Maturin we should have expected, and the figure of the lycanthrope in his last romance *The Albigenses*, 1824, is drawn with remarkable and remorseless power. The novel itself has, it must be confessed, in its 1,400 pages a few passages that are long drawn-out, whilst historically it is far to seek, but it is never uninteresting, and it is frequently energized by episodes that are at once terrible and stirring. In the dungeons of l'Aigle sur la Roche Sir Paladour is confronted with a shapeless form howling and yelling with hideous grimace : " I am a mad wolf . . . The hairs grow inward—the wolfish coat is within—the wolfish heart is within—the wolfish fangs are within ! " The loathly horrors of the wolf's den lurk below.

It is a little surprising that " wonder-working Lewis " did not include the werewolf among his " wild yagers and what-not ", but actually he only has a slight reference to shape-shifting in his *Journal of a West India Proprietor*, published posthumously in 1834, under 19th April, 1817 (p. 295), in connection with a " Nancy-story " of obeahism, wherein a familiar appears as a monstrous black dog named Tiger, which gives occasion to mention the celebrated Zingha, Queen of Angola, who was believed by her whilom subjects to have transmigrated after death into the body of a hyena which was ravaging the land.

There are few better told stories of their kind than the narratives of Hermann Krantz in Marryat's *The Phantom Ship* (1839), which was reprinted by Mr. V. H. Collins in his *Ghosts and Marvels* (1924) as " The Werewolf ", and by myself in *The Supernatural Omnibus* (1931) as " The White Wolf of the Hartz Mountains ". A little old-fashioned, so I have heard

it called. Maybe, and none the worse for that. Who to-day
can spin a yarn thus well ?

Mrs. Catharine Crowe, who might not altogether
impertinently have devoted a paragraph or even a half-page
to the werewolf in her *Night Side of Nature*, 1848, wrote
A Story of a Weir-Wolf which appeared in *Hogg's Weekly
Instructor*, Saturday, 16th May, 1846. The locale is a village
of Auvergne, anno 1596. Out of a great jealousy Manon
Thierry, by working upon her admirer Pierre Bloui, contrives
that Francoise Thilouze together with her father, a physician,
Michael Thilouze, shall be accused of witchcraft. Owing to
various circumstances Francoise is believed to be guilty of
werewolfery, and both father and daughter are condemned
to be burned at Loques. They are, however, saved at the last
moment, and Francoise weds the young Count Victor de
Vardes, who has long loved her, and who secures her pardon
from Henri IV. Manon, who has repented of her malice,
endeavours—not unsuccessfully—to atone. This is a well-told
and interesting narrative.

In chapter 5, vol. iii, of *Light and Darkness ; or, Mysteries
of Life* (1850), under the title " The Lycanthropist ",
Mrs. Crowe discusses " wolfomania " and vampires, describing
the cases of Jean Grenier and Sergeant Bertrand. She wisely
concludes : " I have said enough to prove that, beyond a
doubt, there has been some good foundation for the ancient
belief in ghoulism and lycanthropy ; and that the books of
Dr. Weir and others, in which the existence of this malady
is contemptuously denied, have been put forth without due
investigation of the subject."

" The Lycanthropist " was reprinted in *Reynolds's
Miscellany*, 30th November, 1850, volume v (new series),
No. 125, pp. 293–4, as " Extracted from Mrs. Crowe's *Light
and Darkness* ".

From Mrs. Crowe's *A Story of a Weir-Wolf* was taken *The
Weirwolf*, a Tragedy by William Forster, 1876. This poetic
drama not being intended for the stage has many speeches
of considerable length and intermingles descriptive passages
with the slow-moving dialogue. It possesses very considerable merit, and is not without passages of real beauty. The
Trial Scene in Act III is vigorously written, and the characters
throughout are nervous and alive.

Actually the werewolf is not a theme for the theatre, as indeed must be plain from mere practical considerations. What a skilful producer might be able to achieve upon the films I am not prepared to say, although I am bound to acknowledge that such attempts at the supernatural as I have witnessed upon the screen were almost uniformly banal or ridiculous.

Old Thomas Heywood and Dick Brome did not hesitate, it is true, to introduce into their " well-received Comedy " *The Late Lancashire Witches*, produced at the Globe, Bankside, 1634 (4to, 1634), the scene of the haunted mill in the Fifth Act, where the witches, or rather their familiars in the shape of cats, beset the soldier, and are worsted. The stage directions are : " *Enter* Mrs. Generous, Mal, *all the* Witches *and their* Spirits (*at severall dores*)." Mrs. Generous looes on Nab, Jug, and Peg to scratch the sleeping soldier, " *The* Witches *retire ; the* Spirits *come about him with a dreadfull noise : he starts.*"

clawes I feele
But can see nothing,

he cries ; " Have at you then," " *Beates them off, followes them in and enters againe.*" (I quote from the Halliwell reprint, 1853, p. 222.)

Shadwell, in his *The Lancashire Witches, and Tegue o Divelly The Irish Priest*, acted at Dorset Garden in September, 1681 ; 4to, 1682 ; Act V, has a similar episode. " Enter *Tom Shacklehead* with a Candle, and *Tegue O'Devilly* " to Sir Timothy and young Harfort. Then " Enter *M. Hargrave, M. Madge*, and two Witches more ; they mew, and spit like Cats, and fly at 'em, and scratch 'em ". Young Harfort bawls out : " We are set upon by Cats." " They are Witches in the shape of Cats," cries Sir Timothy in a sad plight. " *They Scratch all their Faces till the Bloud runs about 'em.*" Tom Shacklehead cuts at them with a great sword, " *The Witches screek and run away.*"

When Reginald St. Leon in Godwin's romance *St. Leon* (1799) is brought before the tribunal of the Holy Office at Madrid, the Inquisitor asked : " Whether I had never assumed a form different from my real one, either a different age and appearance, or a different species of animal ?

Whether I had never been wounded in my absence, by a blow aimed at my astral spirit or apparition ? " Chapter viii.

In *The Witch of Edmonton*, by Rowley, Dekker, and Ford, produced at the Cockpit, Drury Lane, in 1621 ; 4to, 1658 ; the Dog, a Familiar, companies with Mother Sawyer, and extremely effective were these two rôles as acted by Russell and Sybil Thorndike in the Phœnix production of this tragedy, April, 1921.

Shirley, in his fine drama *St. Patrick for Ireland*, acted in Dublin 1639–40 ; 4to, 1640 ; makes but passing allusion to Irish wolves ; as when in the forest scene, Act V, Ferochus says :—

> our fear to die i' the sight
> Of men hath brought us hither with our blood,
> To quench the thirst of wolves ;

and shuns the cave, crying : " It may be a lion or fierce wolf's den." In the last scene S. Patrick rebukes the magicians who seek to kill him :—

> Like wolves, you undertake
> A quarrel with the moon, and waste your anger.

Murtough Murphy, in Lover's *Handy Andy* (1842), chapter xxiii, tells a eerie and rather frightening story, something in the Ingoldsby vein, " Ye Marvellous Legend of Tom Connor's Cat," concerning the cat metamorphosis of a witch. The severing of a wolfen's hand is the subject of a grim little *Ballad of the Were-Wolf* by Graham R. Tomson in *Macmillan's Magazine* for September, 1890 (vol. lxii, p. 368), of which I quote eight stanzas, so excellent a ballad have we here :—

> The gudewife sits i' the chimney-neuk,
>   An' looks at the louping flame ;
> The rain fa's chill, and the win' ca's shrill,
>   Ere the auld gudeman comes hame.
>
> " Oh why is your cheek so wan, gudewife ?
>   An' why do ye glower on me ?
> Sae dour ye luik i' the chimney-neuk,
>   Wi' the red licht in your e'e !
>
> " Yet this nicht should ye welcome me,
>   This ae nicht mair than a',
> For I hae scotched yon great grey wolf
>   That took our bairnies twa . . .

" An' 'twas ae sharp stroke o' my bonny knife
 That gar'd her hand awa' ;
Fu' fast she went out owre the bent
 Wi'outen her right fore-paw . . ."

He's flung his pouch on the gudewife's lap,
 I' the firelicht shinin' fair,
Yet naught they saw o' the grey wolf's paw,
 For a bluidy hand lay there.

O hooly, hooly, rose she up,
 Wi' the red licht in her e'e,
Till she stude but a span frae the auld gudeman,
 Whiles never a word spak' she.

But she stripped the claiths frae her lang right arm,
 That were wrappit roun' and roun' ;
The first was white, an' the last was red,
 And the fresh bluid dreeped adown.

She stretchit him out her lang right arm,
 An' cauld as the deid stude he.
The flames louped bricht i' the gloamin' licht—
 There was nae hand there to see !

In *The Court Magazine and Monthly Critic* (United Series)
for 1838 (vol. xiii, pp. 259–274), Sutherland Menzies tells
with quite unusual power *Hugues, The Wer-Wolf*, a Kentish
Legend of the Middle Ages. The episode in which Hugues
breaks open the lid of the old chest, laid aside in a forgotten
corner, is admirably described. " This chest, which had
evidently long remained unopened, contained the complete
disguise of a wer-wolf :—a dyed skeepskin, with gloves in
the form of paws, a tail, a mask with an elongated muzzle,
and furnished with formidable rows of yellow horse-teeth."
The haunting of the severed hand reminds one of The
Narrative of the Ghost of a Hand in Sheridan Le Fanu's
The House by the Churchyard (1863). There is not a little
of Le Fanu's sombre power in Sutherland Menzies, than
which I can pay him no greater compliment.

The essay prefixed to *The Wer-Wolf* is scholarly and
valuable.

The incidents of *Wagner : The Wehr-Wolf*, a romance by
the prolific George W. M. Reynolds, which ran as a serial
of no less than seventy-seven chapters in *Reynolds's Miscellany*
from 7th November, 1846, to 24th July, 1847, and was further
issued in twenty-four weekly penny numbers commencing
on 18th November of the same year, with woodcuts by Henry
Anelay, are so many, so swift, and so complicated that it is

wellnigh impossible to give any idea of the thread of the
adventures which range from the Black Forest to Florence,
from Florence to the Island of Snakes off the African coast
of the Mediterranean Sea, thence to Syracuse ; and in the
werewolf course, which is excellently described in chapter xii,
we scour with lightning speed over hill and vale of Tuscany.

In vol. iv, No. ii, 6th June, 1893, of *The Spirit Lamp*, an
Oxford Magazine edited by Lord Alfred Douglas, was printed
a story by Count Eric Stenbok, *The Other Side*, which has
always seemed to me a piece of quite uncommon beauty.
In this " Breton Legend " the boy Gabriel by crossing the
lycanthropous brook and plucking the strange blue flower
falls under the dominion of darkness, " and through the
darkness he heard wolves howling and shrieking in the hideous
ardour of the chase, and there passed before him a terrible
procession of wolves (black wolves with red fiery eyes) and
with them men that had the heads of wolves and wolves that
had the heads of men, . . . and last of all seated on an
enormous black ram with hideous human faces the wolf-
keeper, on whose face was eternal shadow."   And so the
morrow morn when he went to the grey old church to serve
Mass, as the Abbé Félicien said, " Introibo ad altare Dei,"
he made response : " Qui nequiquam laetificauit iuuentutem
meam."   But at the last he was saved.

Clemence Housman's exquisite prose poem, *The Were-Wolf*,
1896, reprinted from *Atalanta*, is told with feeling that is as
rare as it is beautiful.   Without a harrowing detail we are
brought fully to realize the terror of " the dreadful Thing
in their midst ", White Fell, the foul wolfen in woman's
shape.   Very poignant is the end of Christian, who out of his
great love for Sweyn lays down his life amid the pathless ice
and snows in order that his brother might be saved from
the caress of the were-wolf.   By Christian's death the Thing
dies.   " The great grim jaws had a savage grin, though dead-
stiff."   And Sweyn's reason totters upon its seat when he
thinks of the kiss he had so fondly printed there.

In Guarini's *Pastor Fido*, Act IV, scene 2, Dorinda disguises
herself as a she-wolf—un'effeto d'amore—and so skilfully
that Linco warns her :—

> Chi ti conoscerebbe
> Sotto queste si rozze horride spoglie
> Per Dorinda gentile ?

S'io fosse un fiero can, come son Linco,
Mal grado tuo t'avrei
Troppo ben conosciuta.

This is derived from the stratagem of Dorco, who " be-
wolfed " himself (ἐκθηριώσας δ'αὐτὸν) in *Daphnis and Chloe*,
i, 20, and Dunlop tells us that the troubadour Vidal was
hunted down in consequence of a similar experiment.

John Cameron Grant's *The Ethiopian* (1900) quite strictly
can hardly claim a place here. It is " A Narrative of the
Society of Human Leopards ", yet I mention it as to my
mind it certainly contains a wholesome doctrine, and necessary
for these times.

To those who can enjoy a rattling boy's yarn, and he must
be a grum old put who cannot, I heartily recommend *The
Wolf Demon ; or, Buffalo Bill and the Barge Mystery* (1907),
by the author of *Buffalo Bill*. The Demon of Wolf River
Canyon is quite well done ; Quincy and Ernest Redmond are
first-rate villains ; whilst the fighting of which there is good
store is quite in the most approved T. P. Cooke fashion.

Gabriel-Ernest by Saki, which originally appeared in the
Westminster Gazette and was included in *Reginald in Russia*
(1910), is a mordant sketch. H. H. Munro always showed
himself particularly interested in lycanthropes, and he has
often said to me : " Now let us talk werewolfism" *Gabriel-
Ernest* has something more than a touch of cruel genius.
(I hope " genius " is not too great a word.)

Algernon Blackwood, in his *John Silence*, 1908 (to whose
return I am greatly looking forward), has a cat story, *Ancient
Sorceries*, of which I can never tire. I think I betray no
secret if I identify the town therein as Laon. Almost equally
good is Case V, *The Camp of the Dog*, where the etheric double
of Sangree is seen to leave his body in the shape of a huge
wolfish hound. These two tales are certainly both of the first
order. The same author's *Strange Adventures* in *The Empty
House* (1906) deals with the lycanthropic appetites of two
bestial men, semi-animal in their lust, whilst repercussion is
the theme of *The Empty Sleeve* in *The Wolves of God and
Other Fey Stories* (1921) by Algernon Blackwood and Wilfred
Wilson. Here " the desire-body of a violent man " assumes
animal shape, and when the front leg of an enormous cat is
wellnigh severed by a swashing blow from a scimitar it is
later discovered that the horrible Isidore Hyman has lost an

arm. In the same volume we have a fine story *Running Wolf*.
A young Indian brave who has killed a wolf, the totem
animal of his tribe, is doomed after death to appear in lupine
form until at last he drees his weird in satisfaction complete
and full atonement.

In February, 1899, was published, London, Sands and Co.,
Loup-Garou ! by Eden Phillpotts. The scene of *Loup-Garou !*,
the first of these ten stories of West Indian life, is laid at
Dominica. In the West Indies " Loups-garou and jumbies,
it must be explained, are horrid monsters akin to the vampire
and were-wolf. They are held to be particularly active at
times of death. A corpse will drag them out of their secret
hiding-places, and any dead person not sung or prayed for
prior to burial will most surely be practically devoured or
mutilated by these creatures. Singing, however, keeps them
away, but nothing can kill them save a bullet consecrated
in some place of worship. Weird and frightful tales are told
of these demons ; and the legends concerning them, while
French in origin, have been greatly added to and improved
upon by the mystery-loving negroes ". The power of these
horrible demons endures from sunset to dawn.

Mrs. Mallion, the widow of a Dominican coffee-planter,
has two nephews, Noel and Roger Warne. The elder brother
is a Moravian, " a burning and a shining light." Roger, who
is a Catholic, is careless and somewhat reckless in his ways.
The younger is his aunt's favourite, but Noel cunningly
contrives to gain an ascendency over her, and practically
banishes Roger from her house, the Villa St. Joseph. When
Mrs. Mallion dies and is laid out the negroes are full of stories
of creepy-crawly spectres. " Loo-garoo, him terr'ble busy
jus' now. An de jumbies, dey busy too." Roger determines
to watch a last vigil by his aunt, whom he loved, and he
takes the precaution to arm himself with a revolver, the
bullets of which he has dipped in holy-water.

As he kneels there and prays in the moonlight, " a silent,
black and hairy hand clasps the sill." He turns, and " shook
at what he saw. Framed there stood an inky silhouette—
a misshapen, living thing, half-man, half-ape. The moonlight
showed its hairy body, outlined its shaggy ears, and played
like white fire in its round eyes as it turned to listen ". Silent
as a spider it crawls to the foot of the bed. Roger is paralyzed

with fear, but his courage returns amain when the thing walked over to Ruth Mallion's bureau. "Man or demon, it wants money, not blood." He fires, and it falls. When the servants crowd into the room and tear off the grinning carnival demon-mask they see the dead face of Noel Warne.

Roger is duly acquitted. It appeared that Noel attempted to possess himself of the money he feared would come to his brother, perhaps he had wished to destroy the will. And yet had he but known it, a later will than the one which he had accidentally seen left him all.

It only remains to add that the tale is admirably told. It should be remarked that there is mention of the " loo-garoo " " him terr'ble bad fellow " in *The Obi Man*, a story in the same volume.

In *The Black Douglas*, a stirring romance by Samuel Rutherford Crockett, first published in April, 1899, Gilles de Rais plays an important part. Astarte, " a huge and shaggy she-wolf," whose eyes gleam with yellow treachery, is his constant companion. Now Astarte is La Meffraye, who procures lads and children for the Black Mass and the sacrifices to Barran-Sattanas in the Castle of Machecoul. In the form of a huge wolf, who rushes out of a forest glade, she thus snatches away Jean Verger, a woodman's son, aged five. When Caesar, her husband, a half-natural, is minded to betray her he meets a fearful end and is found with his throat wellnigh bitten away by a wolf. Legions of wolves come at her call. One noon La Meffraye brings a child hidden under her long black cloak by the private postern of the Castle of Machecoul. At the moment of the last sacrifice when Gilles de Rais is taken the she-wolf springs on Laurence McKim and ploughs her teeth in his shoulder whilst he buries his dagger in the beast's hairy chest. The body of La Meffraye is found with two gaping wounds in her breast. "But Astarte, woman-witch or were-wolf, was never seen again, neither by starlight, moonlight, nor yet in eyes of day."

The Were-Wolf, a Russian story by Fred Whishaw, appeared in *Temple Bar*, November, 1902; vol. cxxvi, No. 504. The tale turns upon the belief that if a man " has insulted the Liéshui " he is condemned by them to inhabit the body of a wolf, which thenceforward becomes a werewolf, a terror and a pest to all who dwell within the area of its pernicious hunting-ground.   The Liéshui are spirits of the forest, and Timothy Harkof, a cowherd upon the country estate at Ryábova of Johnnie Baxter, an English merchant of S. Petersburg, is supposed to be under the curse, since he has offended the spirits by dancing at midnight in an open glade which is sacred to them.   Ivan the keeper and Spiridion his assistant urgently summon Baxter to the scene.   Actually the dread werewolf is a wolf of uncommon size and ferocity who is marauding the district.   Harkof, a knave not a fool, is making capital of the panic to cover up his own rogueries and thefts. Baxter shoots the wolf, and Harkof feigns to be cured and in his right wits.   The rustics believe, but Baxter has scented the trick and compels Harkof to confess privately to him, when he puts a stop to the knavery, but allows the villagers to continue disillusioned yet happier in their gullibility than had he exposed the chouse.

Mr. E. F. Benson has an admirably told Scotch story of hare metamorphosis, *The Shootings of Achnaleish*, in his collection *The Room in the Tower*, 1912.

The Were-Wolf, by Arthur L. Salmon, in *The Ferry of Souls* (1927) is brief but good.   In *The Master of the House* (*The Painted Face*, 1929), by Oliver Onions, a varlet who has learned Oriental magic, is able to shift his shape to that of an Alsatian dog.   Charles Swem in his *Were Wolf* (1929) describes a bedridden old man who in sudden paroxysms of frenzied strength, rises, dons a wolf's head and skin to run amok in frantic lycanthropy.   *The Wolf's Bride*, by Madame Aino Kallas, translated by Alex Matson and Bryan Rhys (1930), tells of a woman who is by day a gentle and loving wife, but who at night ranges the fields and the forests, a wolfen marauding blood.

In *All Souls' Night*, A Book of Stories by Hugh Walpole, 1933, is a tale entitled *Tarnhelm ; or, The Death of my Uncle Robert*, which relates how an old man is able to transform himself into " the evillest-looking yellow mongrel of a dog that you can fancy ".   The dog is shot, and the warlock is found dead, " shot through the throat.   On the floor by his side, was a grey skull-cap."

If I now speak of a few stories very cursorily it must not (I would emphasize) be taken as any lack of appreciation of their merits, but because limitations of space compel and constrain me. Kipling's *The Mark of the Beast*, when the curse of a leper priest puts a beast's soul into a man, whose companions are sickened by the stench thereof, " such a horrid doggy smell in the air," will, of course, be familiar to all. Another Indian story is *A Vendetta of the Jungle*, by Arthur Applier and H. Sidney Warwick. A tiger devours a woman, assimilating not only her body but her soul, which looks forth from the animal's eyes. This tiger kills the second wife who marries the bereaved husband. When he hunts the beast down and levels his gun to fire the eyes that look at him are those of his lost love. In Eugene Field's *The Werewolf*, this metamorphosis comes upon young Harold as a curse from an evil grandsire. Ambrose Bierce, in *The Eyes of the Panther*, takes the theme of a prenatal weird. A young girl is doomed to be a panther at night. When her eyes are espied glaring through a window they fire, and following the tracks of blood come upon the dying girl. Frank Norris, in his posthumous novel *Vandover and the Brute*, studies the moral degeneration of the soul. The youth, of whom he tells, falls to such utter degradation that he imagines his body turned into the beast his soul symbolizes, and runs naked on all fours about the room howling " Wolf, wolf ! " The doctors term his madness " lycanthropy-mathesis ".

An adventure—the wolf-man of Opcina—in Mr. James Strachey Barnes' *Half a Life* (1988), is so eerie and significant that it must assuredly be quoted here : " There was a full moon ; and at midnight I was awakened by such a barking of the dogs in the village as never I had heard in all my born days. They were yelping and snapping and growling themselves hoarse, tugging at their chains, furious or terrified, in a chorus that gradually grew closer and closer. . . . And then I realized that in the midst of it all, some Thing was howling, closer and closer, advancing up the street. ' Woo-hoo-hoo-hoo-hoo—Woo-hoo-hoo-hoo-hoo.' Was it another dog, or a wolf ? . . . I crept out of bed and shuffled to the window.

" There in the glare of the moonlight, stood what appeared to be a tramp. Anyhow, it was a man, hesitating—one would say—at the cross-roads, lifting up his chin towards the moon, with far-away staring eyes. ' Woo-hoo-hoo-hoo-hoo.' After a while he decided to turn to the left ; and away he padded, literally padded, stopping every now and then to lift his chin and bay to the moon, while the accompanying chorus of outraged canine sensibility gradually subsided into the stillness of the night."

The Werewolf's Helmet, a novel by Edgar L. Cooper (published John Long, Ltd., September, 1931), is the story of the hunt for the lost treasure of the Barbarossa Chalice— an heirloom of fabulous value. Actually there is no lycanthropy in the tale. The helmet is merely " a commonplace Boche's officer's tin hat " in which various clues are concealed. It belonged to Hermann Karl Stendahl, *alias* Gröner the Phantom Werewolf, " a Continental Jekyll and Hyde." Why " Werewolf " is never made plain, save that it gives a fillip to the title.

Mr. G. Willoughby-Meade, in his *Chinese Ghouls and Goblins*, 1928, relates a number of werewolf legends and stories to which I may be pardoned for drawing attention, although these actually lie outside my present scope.

Demetrios Bikelas (1885–1908), one of the best known of modern Greek authors, has given us a short story of a peasant who, being bitten by a mad bitch-wolf, exhibits signs of a lycanthropy the fearful villagers deem uncanny if not frankly demoniacal. " Fear fills the heart of the ignorant with the passions of wild beasts." This story, which is told with a very real and rather ghastly power, has been translated into English as " The Priest's Tale ".

It has already been remarked that the tradition of werewolfism is comparatively rare in Spain, but it has been utilized by Cervantes in *Los trabajos de Persiles y Sigismunda, Historia sententrional*, first edition, Madrid, 1617 (I have used the Barcelona edition, same date, of this Northern History), " Libro. primero, capitulo diezyocho." Mention is made of "una enfermedad, a quiē llaman los Medicos, Mania lupina, que es de calidad, que al que la padece, le parece, que se ha conuertido en lobo, y ahulla como lobo, y se juntan con otros heridos del mismo mal, y andan en manadas por los cāpos, y por los montes, ladrando ya como perros, ò ya ahullando como lobos, despedaçan los arboles, matan a quien encuentran, y comen la carne cruda de los muertos . . ." (pp. 61–2).

Mention must not be omitted here—more perhaps on

account of his extraordinary personality rather than with reference to his writings—of Pétrus Borel " le lycanthrope ", Pierre-Joseph Borel d'Hauterive. Born at Lyons, 30th June, 1809, he died at Mostaganem in Algeria 14th July, 1859. " Pétrus Borel, on Champavert le Lycanthrope, auteur de *Rhapsodies*, de *Contes immoraux* et de *Madame Putiphar*, fut une des étoiles du sombre ciel romantique," wrote Baudelaire in his *L'Art Romantique, Oeuvres*, iii, 1868 (p. 350). " Lycanthrope bien nommé ! Homme-loup on loup-garou, quelle fée on quel démon le jeta dans les forêts lugubres de la mélancolic ! . . . Sa specialité fut la *Lycanthropie*." Gautier frequently speaks of Pétrus Borel in his *Histoire du Romantisme*, " le plus parfait spécimen de l'idéal romantique," a veritable " héros de Byron ", whose first book was eagerly awaited, for " il n'en était pas encore aux hurlements à la lune du lycanthrope, et ne montait pas trop à la gorge du genre humain " (ed. 1874, p. 22).

Rhapsodies first appeared in 1832 ; *Contes immoraux* (Champavert) in the following year ; and *Madame Putiphar* in 1839. For further details of these and his other works see Talvert et Place, *Bibliographie des Auteurs Modernes*, tom. ii (1930), pp. 118–20.

In many native quarters it seems the fashion to-day— and a very bad and petty fashion it is—to disparage the romances of Erckmann-Chatrian. Be it granted that their output was unequal, at the same time it must be allowed they were very prolific, and it is hardly to be expected that all their work should reach the same standard. When they are at their best, which is not unseldom, I find them of an excellent quality. The man who cannot relish a tale admirably told is not to be envied, and niggling indeed must be the literary judgement of those who so affectedly disdain our twin brethren of Alsace.

Hugues-le-Loup (*Contes de la Montagne*, 1869) is certainly to be ranked high, very high, among their stories. I know few writers who can convey as well as Erckmann-Chatrian the sense of winter cold and Arctic loneliness. As we read their pages we draw near the fire and long to wrap ourselves in pelts and furs. The dark night lowering over the frozen landscape, the snow-burthened trees of the forest, the awful silence of great open spaces under a December sky, the

distant castle on the hillside to which we are making our
way through drifts and frozen roads, all occur again and
again as their theme. In *Hugues-le-Loup*, the sojourn of the
young doctor at the château du Nideck, his strange patient,
the almost feudal manners of the retainers, the mystery that
lurks in the background, are described with graphic and
most telling touches. I could wish perhaps that the solution
were frankly supernatural. Yet it is ill to complain of such
appetizing fare.

Le Meneur des Loups was written by Alexandre Dumas
during his sojourn at Brussels 1852–4, although actually he
did not sign the introductory chapters until 31st May, 1856.
It was published in three volumes, Paris, Cadot, 1857.

It has been well said that " In *The Wolf-Leader* Dumas
allows his imagination and fancy full play. Using a legend
told to him nearly half a century before, conjuring up the
scenes of his boyhood, and calling into requisition his
wonderful gift of improvisation, he contrives in the happiest
way to weave a romance in which are combined a weird
tale of *diablerie* and continual delightful glimpses of forest
life. Terror, wood-craft, and humour could not be more
felicitously intermingled." The scene lies in the great forest
of Villers-Cotterets. *Le Meneur des Loups* for some reason
does not appear to be well known in England, but those who
have not read it are to be congratulated, for they have in
store a rare treat.

Prosper Merimée, in his *Lokis* (*Manuscrit du Professeur
Wittembach*), 1868, which is published among the *Dernières
Nouvelles*, deals with the theme of the werebear. " On
appelle *lokis*, en lithuanien, l'animal que les Grecs ont
nommé ἄρκτος, les Latins *ursus* et les Allemands *bär*."
There is no real transformation, although the count is
possessed of the ferocity and strength of a bear and kills
by his bite.

In Maupassant's *Le Loup*, again, we meet with savage
beasts and men more savage yet than they. At a " diner de
Saint-Hubert " the Marquis d'Arville relates why none of
his house have ever since the year 1764 joined in the chase.
Two of his forbears, brothers, Jean and François, once
hunted down a fierce bitch-wolf. She killed the younger, but
Jean tracked her and slew her very horribly. The legend

is terrible and cruel. Significant indeed is the following conversation between the brothers as they ride :—

L'aîné disait :
— Cette bête-là n'est point ordinaire. On dirait qu'elle pense comme un homme.

Le cadet répondit :
— On devrait peut-être faire bénir une balle par notre, cousin l'évêque, ou prier quelque prêtre de prononcer les paroles qu'il faut.

Puis ils se turent.

Le Loup is contained in the volume *Clair de Lune*, Oeuvres complètes illustrées de Guy de Maupassant ; Librairie Paul Ollendorff, Paris.

Maurice Barrès has touched lightly upon the loup-garou in *La Colline inspirée*, 1913.

Le Loup-garou, a little play by Maurice Ourry and Francis, 8vo, 1807, is a trifle which merits no more than passing notice. The theme is not serious. Of the same kind, although rather better, is *Le Loup-garou* of Eugène Scribe and Mazères, which was acted (and published) in 1827, a tuneful opéra-comique, for which the music was composed by Mlle. Bertin.

As I conclude these few brief notes upon the werewolf in literature, I am only too well aware that I have omitted much that is of interest, and in my defence I can but plead severe limitations of space. There are, moreover, many stories not only of England and France, but German and Italian, which I have read in the course of years, short stories in magazines both old and new, feuilletons, zauberromanen and novelle, which now escape my memory, not to mention the legends of oral tradition I have heard long ago, whereof my recollection is fainter still.

I lay down my pen, and there come into my mind those lines of Byron, *Don Juan*, canto ix, 20 :—

> Oh ! ye immortal Gods ! what is Theogony ?
> Oh ! thou, too, mortal man ! what is Philosophy ?
> Oh ! World, which was and is, what is Cosmogony ?
>   Some people have accused me of Misanthropy ;
> And yet I know no more than the mahogany
>   That forms this desk, of what they mean ;—*Lykanthropy*
> I comprehend, for without transformation
> Men become wolves on any slight occasion.

BIBLIOGRAPHY

ABBOTT, GEORGE FREDERICK. *Macedonian Folklore*. Cambridge, 1903.

ADAMS, FRANCIS. *The Seven Books of Paulus Ægineta*. Sydenham Society, 3 vols. 1844. Vol. i, pp. 389-390.

AFANASIEFF, ALEXANDER NIKOLAEVICH. *Poeticheskija Vozzrienija Slavjan na Prirodu*. Moskwa, 1865-9. 3 vols. Vol. iii, pp. 549-553.

AFZELIUS, ARVARD AUGUST. *Svenska Folk-Visor*. Stockholm, 1814-16. 3 vols. Vol. iii, pp. 119-120.

ALBY, ERNEST. *Les trois loups-garoux*. In *Le magasin littéraire*. Paris, 1845. Vol. ix, No. 54, pp. 49-53.

ANDREE, RICHARD. *Ethnographische Parallelen und Vergleiche*. Stuttgart, 1878. Werwolf, pp. 62-80.

APULEIUS, LUCIUS. *Metamorphoseon Libri XI*. Editio princeps, 1469. I have used the edition by J. Van der Vleit, Teubner, 1887. There are many English translations, none perhaps entirely satisfactory. William Adlington's version first appeared in 1566. (I quote from the ed. 1596, *The eleuen Bookes of the Golden Asse*.) This has been frequently reprinted, for example in the Tudor Translations, 1893 ; and, revised by G. S. Gaselee, in the Loeb Classical Library, vol. xliv, 1915. Thomas Taylor's translation first appeared in 1823, a private and limited impression. The translation in Bohn's Library, 1853, is useful and well done. There are, of course, very numerous dissertations on the *Metamorphoses*. *Apuleius and his Influence* (1927), by E. H. Haight, is extremely slight, but might serve as introductory.

Arrest memorable de la Cour de parlement de Dole, du dixhuictiesme iour de Ianuier, 1573, contre Gilles Garnier, Lyonnois, pour auoir en forme de loup-garou deuoré plusiers enfans, et commis autres crimes : enrichy d'aucuns poincts recueillis de diuers authheurs pour esclairir la matiere de telle transformation. Imprimé a Sens, par Iean Sauine, 1574. Reprinted in Archives Curieuses de l'Histoire de France, par Louis Cimber (i.e. Lafaist) et F. Danjou. Paris, 1836. 1ʳᵉ Serie, Tome 8, pp. 7-11.

AUGE, DANIEL D'. *Discours sur l'arrêt donné au parlement de Dole en Bourgogne, touchant un homme accusé & convaincu d'être loup-garou*. Not in the Bibliothèque Nationale. I only know this book from a reference in La Croix du Maine, *Les Bibliothèques Françoises*. Paris, 1772. Tom. i, p. 162. No place and no date given.

AUGUSTINE, S. (Of Hippo.) *De Ciuitate Dei*. Ed. J. E. C. Welldon, D.D. 2 vols. 1924.

B., H. G. *Lycanthropy*. In: *The Occult Review* (London). April, 1917. Vol. xxv, No. 4, pp. 214-17.

BAISSAC, JULES. *Les Grands Jours de la Sorcellerie*. Paris, 1890. Chapitre xiii, pp. 307-338 ; Chapitres xv et xvi, pp. 366-418.

—— *Le Folk-Lore de l'Île Maurice*. 1888. pp. 146-179.

BARING-GOULD, SABINE. *The Book of Were-Wolves : Being an Account of a Terrible Superstition*. London, 1865.

BARNES, JAMES STRACHEY. *Half a Life.* 1933.

BARRÈS, MAURICE. *La Colline Inspirée.* Paris, 1913. (Fiction.)

BEAUGRAND, H. *The Werwolves.* (Fiction.) *Century Illustrated Magazine.* New York, 1898. Vol. lvi, pp. 814–823.

BEAUVOYS DE CHAUVINCOURT, Le Sieur de. *Discours de la Lycantropie ou de la transformation des hommes en loups.* Paris, 1599.

BEELE, SLOET VAN DER. *De Diesen in het Germansche Volksgeloof en Volksgebruik.* 1887. pp. 42–72.

—— *Le Loup Garou.* (Extrait de la *Revue Internationale*, vii.) 1885.

BENSON, EDWARD FREDERIC. *The Shootings of Achnaleish* in *The Room in the Tower.* London, 1912. (Fiction.)

BERNOU, J. *La chasse aux sorcières dans le Labourd* (1609). Étude historique, Agen, 1897. From De Lancre.

BINSFELD, PETER. (Suffragan Bishop of Trèves.) *Tractatus de confessionibus maleficorum.* Trèves, 1589.

BIRCH, THOMAS. *The History of the Royal Society of London.* London, 1756–7. 4 vols. Vol. i, p. 300.

BLACK, GEORGE F. *A List of Works relating to Lycanthropy.* New York, 1920.

BLACKWOOD, ALGERNON. *The Empty House, and other Ghost Stories.* 1906. (Fiction.)

—— *John Silence, Physician Extraordinary*, 1908. (Fiction.)

—— (with WILFRID WILSON). *The Wolves of God, and other Fey Stories*, 1921. (Fiction.)

BODIN, JEAN. *De la Démonomanie des Sorciers.* Paris, 1580.

BOETTIGER, CARL AUGUST. *Aelteste Spuren der Wolfswuth in der griechischen Mythologie. Mit einem Zusatz von K. Sprengel.* In K. P. J. Sprengel, *Beyträge zur Geschichte der Medicin.* Halle, 1795. Bd. i, St. 2, pp. 3–72.

BOGUET, HENRY. *Discours des Sorciers.* 3º édition. Lyon, 1590. Some editions have *Discours exécrable des Sorciers.* Eng. tr. *An Examen of Witches.* London, 1929.

BOISSARD, J. J. *Tractatus postumus de diuinatione.* Oppenheim, n.d. [1610].

BON, ANTOINETTE. *Le seigneur Loup-garou. Legende de l'Auvergne.* In the *Revue des traditions populaires.* Paris, 1890. Vol. v, pp. 216–18.

BORDELON, L'ABBÉ LAURENT. *L'Histoire des Imaginations Extravagantes de Monsieur Oufle causées par la Lecture des Livres qui traitent de la Magie, du Grimoire, des Démoniaques, Sorciers, Loups-garoux, Incubes, Succubes & du Sabbat.* 2 vols. 1710. Eng. tr., *A History of the Ridiculous Extravagancies of Monsieur Oufle.* London, 1711.

BOREL, PÉTRUS. (Pierre-Joseph Borel d'Hauterive.) *Rhapsodies.* 1832. (Poems.)

—— *Champavert Contes Immoraux*, par Pétrus Borel le Lycanthrope. Bruxelles, 1872. (Fiction.)

BOSQUET, AMÉLIE. *Normandie romanesque et merveilleuse, traditions, legendes, et superstitions populaires de cette province.* Paris, 1845. Chap. xii.

BOURQUELOT, FÉLIX. *Recherches sur la lycanthropie.* In the *Société des antiquaires de France. Mémoires et dissertations sur les antiquités.* Paris, 1849. Vol. xix (nouvelle série, vol. ix), pp. 193–262. A separate issue of this valuable study was published in Paris, E. Duverger, 1848. 8vo, 70 pp.

BURTON, ROBERT. *The Anatomy of Melancholy.* First ed. 1621. Pt. i, Sect. i, Mem. i, Subs. 4.

CALMEIL, LOUIS FRANÇOIS. *De la folie considérée sous le point de vue pathologique, philosophique, historique, et judicaire.* Paris, 1845. 2 vols.

—— *Lycanthropie.* Article in the *Dictionnaire encyclopédique des sciences médicales.* Paris, 1870. Série ii, T. 3, pp. 359–371.

CAMERARIUS, PHILIPPUS. *Operae Horarum Subcisiuarum,* 1591. Centuria Prima, cap. lxxii ; centuria altera, cap. xc.

CAUZONS, THEODORE DE. *La Magie et la Sorcellerie en France.* Paris, 1900, etc. 4 vols.

CERVANTES, MIGUEL DE. *Los trabajos de Persiles y Sigismunda. Historia sententrional.* Madrid, 1617. Lib. i, cap. 18.

CHAPISEAU, FELIX. *Le Folk-Lore de la Beauce et de la Perche.* Paris, 1902. T. i, pp. 217–220, 239–240 ; ii, 206–9.

CLARÉTIE, JULES. *Pétrus Borel le lycanthrope, sa vie, ses écrits, sa correspondance, poésies et documents inédits.* Paris, 1865.

COELHO, J. ADOLPHO. *Revista d'ethnologia. Entidades mythicas.* No. xviii, *Os lobis-homens.* Porto, 1881.

CONSIGLIERI-PEDROSO, Z. *Tradicções populares portuguezas.* (*Materias para a ethnographia di Portugal: mythologia, cantos, usos, superstições, proverbios, jogos infantis, contos lendas e tradicções locaes de nosso paizi.*) Porto, Imprensa Commercial, 1881. Fasc. vii : *O lobis homem.*

COSTELLO, DUDLEY. *Lycanthropy in London; or, the Wehr-Wolf of Wilton-Crescent. Bentley's Miscellany,* vol. xxxviii, 1855, pp. 361–379. (Fiction.)

CROCKETT, S. R. *The Black Douglas.* London, 1899. (Fiction.)

CROWE, CATHERINE. *A Story of a Weir-Wolf.* In *Hogg's Weekly Instructor.* Edinburgh, Saturday, 16th May, 1846. Vol. iii, No. 64, pp. 184–9. (Fiction.)

—— *Light and Darkness; or, Mysteries of Life.* London, 1850. 3 vols. Vol. iii, chap. v, " The Lycanthropist." Reprinted in *Reynolds's Miscellany,* 30th November, 1850.

CUMMING, C. F. GORDON. *Wolves and were-wolves. Temple Bar.* London, 1890. Vol. xc, pp. 351–368.

DALYELL, JOHN GRAHAM. *The Darker Superstitions of Scotland, Illustrated from History and Practice.* Edinburgh, 1834.

DAMBIELLE, ABBÉ. *La sorcellerie en Gascogne.* In the *Société archéologique du Gers,* année 7. Auch, 1906. pp. 330–1.

Danmarks Folke Saga. Vol. ii, p. 279.

DANNHAUER, JOANNES CONRADUS. *Theologia Conscientiaria.* P. ii, fol. 462.

DASENT, GEORGE WEBBE, SIR. *Popular Tales from the Norse.* Edinburgh, 1859. Introductory essay, pp. lviii–lxii.

D'ASSIER, ADOLPHE. *Posthumous Humanity : A Study of Phantoms.* Tr. by Henry S. Olcott. London, 1887. Chapter xi, pp. 258–262. Translation authorized by M. D'Assier from his *Essai sur l'Humanité Posthume et le Spiritisme,* " par un Positiviste."

D'AUTUN, JACQUES. Capuchin. *L'Incredulite Scavante et la Credulite Ignorante.* Lyon, 1678. Discours xxix and xxx, pp. 890–908.

DEACON and WALKER. *Dialogicall Discourses of Spirits and Devils.* London, 1601. pp. 158–163.

DELRIO, S.J., MARTIN. *Disquisitionum Magicarum Libri Sex.* Ed. Moguntiae, 1608. Lib. ii, Qu. xviii, pp. 163–6.

DENIS, JEAN FERDINAND. *Portugal.* (*L'Univers.*) Paris, 1846. pp. 106–7.

—— *Le monde enchanté; Cosmographie et histoire naturelle et fantastique du moyen-âge.* Paris, 1843.

DROUET, DR. *Le loup-garou en Limousin.* In the *Revue d'ethnographie et de sociologie.* T. ii, pp. 146–157. Paris, 1911.

DUMAS, ALEXANDRE (père). *Le Meneur des Loups.* Paris, 1857. 3 vols. (Reprinted by Dumas in his journal *Le Monte-Cristo*, 1860.) English tr. by Alfred Allinson, *The Wolf-Leader.* London, 1904.

DUMAS, GEORGES. *Les loups-garous.* In the *Journal de psychologie normale et pathologique.* Paris, 1907. Année 4. pp. 225–239.

—— *Les loups-garous.* In the *Revue du mois.* Paris, 1910. T. iii, pp. 402–432.

DUPONY, EDMOND. *Psychologie morbide.* Paris, 1907. Chap. v, pp. 62–101.

ENCAUSSE, GERARD. *La Magie et l'hypnose.* Paris, 1897. pp. 243–256. " La sorcellerie—la lycanthropie."

ERCKMANN-CHATRIAN, MM. (EMILE ERCKMANN and LOUIS GRATIEN CHARLES ALEXANDRE CHATRIAN.) *Hugues-le-Loup; Contes de la Montagne.* Paris, 1860. English tr. by F. A. M., *The Man-Wolf and Other Tales.* London, n.d. (1872–8, English Catalogue).

ERNAULT, EMILE. *Une prétendue inscription contre les loups-garous.* In *Mélusine.* Tom. iii, col. 92–3.

FABRICIUS, WOLFG. AMBROS. *Die von Wolfg. Ambros: Fabricius am 26. Februar 1649 in der Aula zu Strassburg vertheidigten Thesen von der ΛΥΚΑΝΘΡΩΠΙΑ.* Argentorati [Strassburg], 1649.

FIELD, EUGENE. *The Werewolf* in *Works* (Collected ed.). New York, 1911. Vol. x, pp. 243–256. (Fiction.)

FINCEL, JOB. *Wunderzeichen, Warhafftige Beschreibung und gründlich verzeicnus schrecklicher Wunderzeichen und Geschichten, die von . . . MDXVII bis auff . . . MDLVI geschechen und ergangen sind, noch der Jarzal . . .* Jhena, 1556.

FISCHER, WILHELM. *Dämonische Mittelwersen Vampir und Werwolf in Geschichte und Sage.* Stuttgart, [1906]. *Aberglaube aller Zeiten.* Bd. 3.

FISKE, JOHN. *Werewolves and swan-maidens.* In *The Atlantic Monthly.* Boston, 1871. Vol. xxviii, pp. 129–144. Reprinted in *Myths and Myth-makers.* Boston, [1914]. pp. 69–103.

FOIX, V. *Folklore. Glossaire de la sorcellerie landaise.* In the *Revue de Gascogne.* Auch, 1903–4. Nouv. série, t. iii, pp. 450–2. " Lou loup-garous."

FORSTER, WILLIAM. *The Weirwolf.* A Tragedy. London and Edinburgh, 1876.

FRANCESCO, DE. *Il Lupo mannaro* in *La Provincia di Molise.* Campobasso, 1885. An. v, No. 33.

FRANCISCI, ERASMUS. *Der Höllische Proteus.* Nürnberg, 1695. 2nd ed. pp. 334–364, 378–386.

FREGOSO GIANBATISTA. *Baptistae Fulgosi de dictis factisque memorabilibus.* Milan, 1509.

FRISON, J. *Contes et legendes de la Basse-Bretagne.* In the *Revue des traditions populaires.* Paris, 1914. Tom. xxix, p. 22. " Le domestique loup-garou."

FROMANN, JOHANN CHRISTIAN. *De Fascinatione . . . magica.* Norimbergae, 1675. Fol. 752.

GARINET, JULES. *Histoire de la Magie en France.* Paris, 1818.

BIBLIOGRAPHY 283

GARNETT, DAVID. *Lady into Fox.* London, 1922. (Fiction.)

GEIBEL, FRANZ EMANUEL AUGUST. *Romanze vom Werwolf.* A poem in his *Gesammelte Werke.* Stuttgart, 1883. Bd. iv, pp. 136–8.

GEILER, JOHANN VON KAISERBERG. *Die Emeis.* Strassburg, 1516.

GELIN, H. *Legendes de sorcellerie, personnes changées en bêtés, feés et sorciers, re tour des galipotes à la forme humaine, cas de dédoublement de la personnalité.* Ligugé, 1898.

GERVASE OF TILBURY. *Otia Imperialia.* Ed. Felix Liebrecht. Hanover, 1856.

GODELMANN, JOHANN GEORG. *De magis, ueneficis, et lamiis tractatus.* Frankfort, 1601.

GOECKEL, EBHARD. *Tractatus polyhistoricus magicus medicus curiosus.* Frankfort, 1717.

—— *Vom Beschreien und Bezaubern.* Nürnberg, 1699.

GOULART, SIMON. *Histories admirables et Memorables de notre temps.* Paris, 1607. pp. 239–244.

GRANT, JOHN CAMERON. *The Ethiopian.* " A Narrative of the Society of Human Leopards." Paris, 1900. (Fiction.)

GRIMM, FRIEDRICH MELCHIOR, BARON VON. *Correspondance littéraire.* Paris, 1829–1831. 15 vols.

GRIMM, JAKOB LUDWIG CARL. *Deutsche Mythologie.* Göttingen, 1835. Eng. tr. (J. S. Stallybrass), 4 vols., London, 1880–8.

GROHMANN, JOSEF VIRGIL. *Sagen aus Böhmen.* Prag, 1863. *Sagen-Buch aus Böhmen und Mähren.* Theil i, pp. 120–1, " Der Wahr-wolf," and note on " Vlkodlaci ", pp. 119–120.

GUAZZO, FRANCESCO MARIA. *Compendium Maleficarum.* Milan, 1608 ; 2nd ed., 1626. Eng. tr., London, 1929. Book i, chaps. x, xiii, and xiv.

GUBERNATIS, CONTE ANGELO DE. *Zoological Mythology.* Eng. tr. 2 vols. London, 1872. Vol. ii, pp. 144–8. See also Cesare Antonio di Cara, *Errori mitologici del prof. A. de Gubernatis.* Prato, 1883.

Guillaume de Palerme. Publié d'après le manuscrit de la Bibliothèque de l'Arsenal à Paris, par H. Michelant. Paris, 1876. *Société des anciens textes français.*

The Romance of William of Palerne. Ed. W. W. Skeat. London, 1867. Early English Text Society.

Gypsy Lore Society, Journal of the. Vol. iii, No. 1, July, 1891, Heinrich von Wlislocki, " The Witches of the Gypsies," pp. 38–45.

HAHN, J. G. VON. *Albanesische Studien.* Jena, 1854. *Griechische und albanesische Mänchen.* Leipzig, 1864. Vol. ii, pp. 189–190.

HAKEWILL, GEORGE. *An Apologie of the Power and Providence of God in the Government of the World.* Oxford, 1627. Lib. i, cap. i, sect. 5.

HAMEL, FRANK. *Human Animals.* London, 1915.

HANUŠ, IGNÁC JAN. *Die Wer-wölfe oder vlko-dlaci.* In *Zeitschrift für deutsche Mythologie und Sittenkunde.* Gottingen, 1859. Bd. iv, pp. 193–8.

—— *Der Werwolf (vlkolak).* " Ein slovakisches Märchen." Ibid., Bd. iv, pp. 224–8. Translated by Baring-Gould, *Book of Were-wolves,* pp. 124–8.

HARDWICK, CHARLES. *Traditions, superstitions and folklore* . . . Manchester, 1872. " Werewolves and the transmigration of souls," pp. 224–241.

HAUBER, EVERHARD DAVID. *Bibliotheca Acta et Scripta Magica.* Lemgo, 1739–1745. 3 vols. Stück 29 (anno 1742), ccxliii, *Curiose Erzählung von der Währ-Wolffen,* pp. 284–9.

HAXTHAUSEN, AUGUST VON, BARON. *Transcaucasia. Sketches of the Nations and Races between the Black Sea and the Caspian.* London, 1854. Chapter xi, p. 359. "Story of the Werewolves." An Armenian legend.

HERODOTUS. *Historiarum Libri IX.* Lib. iv, cap. 105. Ed. H. R. Dietsch, curauit H. Kallenberg. Teubner, Lipsiae, 2 vols., 1894–8. Vol. i, p. 369.

HERTZ, WILHELM. *Der Werwolf. Beitrag zur Sagengeschichte.* Stuttgart, 1862.

HEUSINGER, CARL FRIEDRICH. *Ein Beitrag zur Geschichte der Lykanthropie nach Scheik Mohammed el Tounsy.* In *Janus.* Breslau, 1847. Bd. ii, pp. 364–370.

HEWIN, JAN VAN. *Heurnii Opera Omnia.* Lugduni, 1658. 2 vols. Vol. i, p. 877.

HOUSMAN, CLEMENCE. *The Were-wolf.* London, 1896. (Fiction.) This story first appeared in *Atalanta.*

HYLTEN-CAVALLIUS, GUNNAR OLAF, and GEORGE STEPHENS. *Svenska folk-sagor och äfventyr.* Stockholm, 1844–9. 2 vols. "Varulfen," pp. 312–322.

JAHN, ULRICH. *Volkssagen aus Pommern und Rügen.* Stettin, 1886. pp. 879–887.

JAMES I, KING (of England). *Daemonologie, In Forme of a Dialogue.* Edinburgh, 1597. Reprint, ed. G. B. Harrison, Bodley Head Quartos, London, 1924.

KALLAS, AINO, Madame. *The Wolf's Bride.* Tr. Alex Matson and Bryan Rhys. London, 1930. (Fiction.)

KELLER, OTTO. *Thiese des Classischen Alterthums in Culturgeschichtlicher Beziehung.* Innsbruck, 1887. "Der Wolf," pp. 158–177, and important notes, pp. 398–406.

KELLY, WALTER KEATING. *Curiosities of Indo-European tradition and folk-lore.* London, 1863. pp. 242–265.

KITTREDGE, GEORGE LYMAN. *Witchcraft in Old and New England.* Harvard Univ. Press, Cambridge, Mass., 1928. Chap. x, "Metamorphosis," pp. 174–184.

KNOOP, OTTO. *Sagen und Erzählungen aus der Provinz Posen.* Posen, 1893. *Historiche Gesellschaft für die Provinz Posin.* ("Der Bürger Ridt wird in einen Werwolf verwandelt," p. 162.)

KORNMANN, CONRADUS. *De miraculis uiuorum.* Francofurtae, 1614. p. 212.

KRAMER, O.P., HENRY. See under *Malleus Maleficarum.*

KRAUSE, MICHAEL HENRICUS. *Theranthropismus fictus.* Wittebergae, 1673.

KRAUSS, FRIEDRICH SALOMON. *Slavische Volkforschungen.* Leipzig, 1908. "Der Werwolf," pp. 137–144.

KRUIJT, ALB. C. *De weerwolf bij de Toradjas van Midden-Celebes.* In *Tijdschrift voor Indische taal-, land-, en volkenkunde.* Batavia, 1899. Vol. xli, pp. 548–567.

KUHN, FRANZ FELIX ADALBERT. *Märkische Sagen und Märken.* Berlin, 1843. "Der Werwolf," No. 243, pp. 259–260.

KUHN, F. F. A., and SCHWARTZ, WILHELM. *Norddeutsche Sagen, Märchen und Gebräuche* . . . Leipzig, 1848. Sagen xxii and cclviii, and notes.

LANCRE, PIERRE DE. *Tableav de l'Inconstance des Mavvais Anges et Demons.* Paris, 1613. Livre iv, Discours 11, pp. 252–326. "De la Lycanthropie et Changement de l'Homme en Loup et autre sorte d'animaux." The Jean Grenier case.

LANCRE, PIERRE DE. *L'incredulité et mescréance du sortilège plainement convaincue.* Paris, 1622.

LAUBEN, THEOPHILUS. *Dialogi und Gespräche von der lycanthropia oder der Menschen in Wölff Verwandlung.* Frankfurt, 1686.

LAWSON, JOHN CUTHBERT. *Modern Greek Folklore.* Cambridge, 1910.

LEMBAY, M. DE. *The Werewolf of the Africans.* In *Goldthwaite's Geographical Magazine.* New York, 1892. Vol. iii, pp. 303–4.

LEUBUSCHER, RUDOLPH. *Ueber die Wehrwölfe und Thierverwandlungen im Mittelalter. Ein Beitrag zum Geschichte der Psychologie.* Berlin, 1850.

LICETUS, FORTUNIUS. *Ulisses apud Circen. Dialogus de quadruplici transformatione, hominum.* Utini [Eutin], 1636.

The London Magazine or, Gentleman's Monthly Intelligencer. Vol. xxxiv. For the year 1765. pp. 56, 140, 160, 215 (with plate), 380. (Beast of Gévaudan.)

Loup garou, Procès fait à un. The case of Gilles Garnier of Dol. Nicolas Toursaint Moyne (Des Essarts), *Supplément à l'essai sur l'histoire générale des tribunaux des peuples tant anciens que modernes.* Paris, 1782. Tom. vii, pp. 177–9.

LOVER, SAMUEL. *Handy Andy.* London, 1842. A Serial in *Bentley's Miscellany,* vols. v and vi, 1839 and 1840. Chap. xxiii. (Fiction.)

LOYER, PIERRE LE. *Discours des Spectres, ou Visions et Apparitions d'Esprits, comme Anges, Demons, et Ames, se monstrans visibles aux hommes.* Paris, 1608. (Seconde Edition, reveve et avgmentee.) Liure ii, ch. vii. "De l'extase des Sorciers, de la transmutation des Sorciers & Sorcieres." pp. 188–145.

Lycanthropy. Article in *The Anglo-American.* New York, 1843. Vol. i, pp. 173–5.

Lycanthropy. In *Chambers's Edinburgh Journal.* Edinburgh, 1850. New Series, vol. xii, pp. 124–5. Reprinted in *The Eclectic Magazine of Foreign Literature, Science, and Art.* New York, 1850. Vol. xix, pp. 190–2.

MacCULLOCH, EDGAR, SIR. *Guernsey Folk Lore.* Edited by Edith F. Carey. London and Guernsey, 1903.

MacCULLOCH, J. A. *Lycanthropy.* Article in *Encyclopædia of Religion and Ethics.* Ed. Rev. James Hastings, vol. viii, 216.

—— *Medieval Faith and Fable.* London, 1923. Chap. v, "Shape-Shifting."

MACKAY, CHARLES. *Memoirs of Extraordinary Popular Delusions.* London, 1852. 2 vols. (Very frequently reprinted.)

M'LENNAN, JOHN FERGUSON. *Lycanthropy. Encyclopædia Britannica.* 9th ed., 1888. Vol. xv, pp. 89–92.

MADDEN, SIR FREDERICK. *Note on the word "werwolf".* In *The Romance of William of Palerne.* London, 1867. E.E.T.S. pp. xxv–xxix.

MADDEN, RICHARD ROBERT. *Phantasmata, or illusions and fanaticisms of protean forms.* London, 1857. 2 vols.

MAGNUS, OLAUS. *Historia de Gentibus Septentrionalibus.* Romae, 1555. Liber xviii, caps. xlv–xlvii, pp. 642–4. See also pp. 611–18. The Eng. tr., folio, 1658, *A Compendious History of the Goths, Swedes, & Vandals,* is abridged and must not be used without reference to the original. The corresponding chapters on werewolfery are Book xviii, xxxii, and xxxiii, pp. 193–4.

MAIOLO D'ASTI, SIMONE (Bishop of Valterna). *Dies caniculares*. Folio. Offenbaci ad Moenum, 1691. (Bishop Simone born about 1520, died *c.* 1597. This edition of 1691 is one of the most esteemed of a work frequently printed.)

Malleus Maleficarum. (James Sprenger, O.P., and Henry Kramer, O.P.) Eng. tr. by Montague Summers, London, 1928. Part i, qn. ix (pp. 61–5) ; pt. ii, qn. i, chap. viii (pp. 122–8). For Bibliography see the Note to this ed., xli–xlii.

MARCELLUS SIDETA. Περὶ λυκανθρώπου. In : "Πλουτάρχου περὶ τῆς τῶν ἐλευθέρων παιδῶν ἀγωγῆς. Accedunt bina ejusdem Plutarchi et Marcelli Sidetae medici fragmenta recensuit Joh. G. Schneider." Argentorati [Strassburg], 1775. p. 109.

MARIE DE FRANCE. *Bisclavret*. In: *Die Lais der Marie de France, herausgegeben von Karl Warnke.* Halle, 1885. pp. 75–88. See also Introduction, pp. lxxiv–lxxxi.

—— *The lay of Bisclavret.* In : L. S. Costello, *Specimens of the Early Poetry of France.* London, 1835. Whence reprinted in Longfellow's *The Poets and Poetry of Europe.* Philadelphia, 1845.

—— *The lay of Bisclavret; or, The wehr-wolf.* In : J. W. Thoms, *Lays and Legends of various nations. Lays and Legends of France.* London, 1834. pp. 57–68.

MARRYAT, FREDERICK. *The Phantom Ship.* 3 vols., 1839. (Fiction.) This romance appeared serially in the " New Monthly Magazine " during 1837.

MATHER, INCREASE. *Illustrious Providences.* Boston, 1684. Reprint London, 1855 ; re-issue, 1890.

MATURIN, CHARLES ROBERT. *The Albigenses.* 4 vols., 1824. (Fiction.)

MAUPASSANT, GUY DE. *Le Loup.* (Fiction. A short story.)

MAURER, KONRAD. *Die Bekehrung des Norwegischen Stammes zum Christenthume.* München, 1856. 2 vols. Vol. ii, pp. 101–110.

MEI, MICHAEL. *De Lycanthropia.* Witteburgae, 1654.

MELANDER, OTHO. *Jocorum atque Seriorum Libri II.* Smalcaldiae [Schmalkalden], ex officina Kezeliana, 1611. Nos. 776, " De puella in equam uersa," and 777, " De quodam Lycaone rustico " ; pp. 819–821.

MENABRÉA, LÉON. *De l'origine, de la forme et de l'esprit des jugements rendus au moyen âge contre les animaux.* Chambéry, 1846. " Lycanthropie," p. 71. Reprinted in *Memoires de la Société académique de Chambéry,* t. xii.

MUELLER, WILHELM. *Der Werwolf.* See under *Schambach,* Georg.

MÜLLER, JACOBUS FRIDERICUS. *De transmutatione hominum in lupos.* Lipsiae, 1673.

MUNRO, HECTOR HUGH. *Gabriel Ernest.* In *Reginald in Russia.* 1911. (Fiction.)

MUSAEUS, JOHANN-CARL-AUGUST. *Volksmärcher der Deutschen.* Gotha, 1782–6. (I have used the Leipzig ed., 1842.)

NAAKÉ, JOHN THEOPHILUS. *Slavonic Fairy Tales.* Collected and translated from the Russian, Polish, Servian, and Bohemian. London, 1874. " Men wolves," from the Polish, pp. 135–140.

NAPIER, ARTHUR SAMPSON. *Werwolf.* In *Beiträge zur Geschichte der deutschen Sprache und Literatur.* Bd. xxiii, pp. 571–3. Halle, 1898.

NIPHANIUS, CONRAD. *De Lycanthropia.* Witteburgae, 1654.

Die Nixe des Brunnens. " Der Wæhrwolf." pp. 153–168.

NYNAULD, JEAN DE. *De La Lycanthropie, Transformation, et Extase des Sorciers.* Paris, 1615. Jean Millot, who transferred some copies to Nicolas Rousset.

O'DONNELL, ELLIOTT. *Werwolves.* London, [1912].

ONIONS, OLIVER. *The Master of the House.* In *The Painted Face.* London, 1929. Three Tales : pp. 229–294. (Fiction.)

OURRY, E. T. MAURICE (and FRANCIS). *Le Loup-garou.* 8vo. 1807. A farcical play.

OVID. *Metamorphoses.* Lib. i, ll. 177–243. The story of Lycaon, king of Arcadia.

PAULUS ÆGINETA. See under ADAMS, FRANCIS.

PERTY, MAXIMILIEN. *Die mystischen Erscheinungen der menschlichen Natur.* Leipzig, 1872. 2 vols. (2. ed.)

PETRONIUS ARBITER. *Satyricon.* (*Satirae.*) Tert. Ed. Franciscus Buecheler. Berolini, 1895.

PEUCER, CASPAR. *Commentarius de praecipius generibus diuinationum.* Witerbergae, 1572. Excudebat Iohannes Lufft. pp. 130–4.

PHILLPOTTS, EDEN. *Loup-Garou!* 1899. (Fiction.)

Philosophische Abhandlung von dem Entstehen, der Natur und dem Aushören der Waarwölfe. Danzig, 1746.

Physici Medici Graeci Minores, ed. Julius Ludwig Idaler. Berlin, 1841. 2 vols.

PINEAU, LÉON. *Le folk-lore du Poitou.* Paris, 1892. Tom. xviii, of the *Collection de contes et de chansons populaires.* ("Loups-garous et sorciers," pp. 107–115.)

PISCHEL, RICHARD. *Zu Petronius, Satirae 62.* No. vi (pp. 69–80) in *Philologische Abhandlungen. Martin Hertz zum siebzigsten Geburt-stage von ehemaligen Schülern dargebracht.* Berlin, 1888.

PITRÈ, GIUSEPPE. (General Editor.) *Curiosità Popolari Tradizionali.* Palermo, vol. i (1885)—vol. xiii (1894).

PLINIUS SECUNDUS, CAIUS. *Historia Naturalis* : viii, 22, *De lupis.* Apud Hackios. Lugd. Bat., 1669. i, pp. 515–17. Editions by Sillig, Gotha, 1853 ; Jan, Leipzig, 1870 ; Detlessen, 1873.

PLUQUET, FRÉDÉRIC. *Contes Populaires, Préjugés, Patois, Proverbes, Noms de Lieux de l'Arrondissement de Bayeux.* (Deuxième ed.) Rouen, 1834. Le Loup-garou, pp. 15–16.

POQUEVILLE, FRANÇOIS CHARLES HUGUES LAURENT. *Voyage de la Grèce.* Paris, 1826–7. 2ᵉ éd., 6 vol. Tom. vi, liv. xix, ch. 3 (p. 186).

PRAETORIUS. *Gründlicher Bericht von zauberen und zauberern.* Frankfort, 1629. p. 74.

—— *Anthropodemus Plutonicus.* Magdeburg, 1666. p. 255.

PRIEUR, CLAUDE, DE LAVAL. *Dialogue de la Lycanthropie, ou trans-formation d'hommes en loups, vulgairement dit loups-garous, et si telle se peut faire.* Louvain, 1596.

RALSTON, WILLIAM RALSTON SHEDDEN. *The Songs of the Russian People.* London, 1872. pp. 403–9, 432.

Réalité de la Magie et des Apparitions, ou Contre-Poison du Dictionnaire Infernal. Paris, 1819. Loups-garous, pp. 84–7.

REINHARD, JOHANN. *Therantropismus.* Wittebergae, 1673.

REMY, NICOLAS. *Daemonolatria.* Lyons, 1595. Lib. ii, cap. 5. Eng. tr. *Demonolatry.* London, 1930. pp. 108–114.

REYNOLDS, GEORGE WILLIAM McARTHUR. *Wagner: The Wehr-Wolf.* In *Reynolds's Miscellany,* serial from 7th November, 1846, to

24th July, 1847. Published weekly in 24 penny numbers commencing 13th November, 1847, and afterwards in book form, one volume.

RHANÆUS. *Sammlung von Natur- und Medicin.* . . . Supplement iii. Breslau, 1728. On Courland werewolves.

RIEZLER. *Geschichte der Hexenprozesse in Bayun.* 1896. pp. 293–4.

ROLLAND, EUGÈNE. *Faune populaire de la France.* Paris, 1877–1883. Tom. i, pp. 153–9.

SALGUES, JEAN-BAPTIST. *Des Erreurs et Préjugés.* 2 tom., 2e ed. Paris, 1811. Tom. i, pp. 314–333 : " Sabbat, Possédés, Loups-Garous, Incubes et Succubes, Lutins, Farfardets, etc."

SALMON, ARTHUR L. *The Were-wolf* (p. 87) in *The Ferry of Souls.* London, 1927. (Fiction.)

SAND, GEORGE. *Légendes Rustiques.* Paris, 1858. *Le Meneu' de Loups*, p. 29 ; *Le Lupeux*, p. 33 ; *Lubins et Lupins*, p. 45.

SCHAMBACH, GEORG, and WILHELM MUELLER. *Der Werwolf.* In *Niedersächsische Sagen und Märchen.* Gottingen, 1854. pp. 182–5.

SCHELWIG, SAMUEL. *De Lycanthropia.* Gedani [Danzig], 1679.

SCHMIDT, BERNHARD. *Das Volksleben der Neugriechen.* Leipzig, 1871. pp. 159–160.

SCHWANOLD, H. *Lippische Werwolf-Sagen. Verein für rheinische und westfälische Volkskunde. Zeitschrift.* Elbenfeld, 1918. Jahrg. 10, pp. 123–7.

SCHWARTZ, FRIEDRICH LEBERECHT WILHELM. *Der Ursprung der Mythologie.* Berlin, 1860.

SCOT, REGINALD. *The Discoverie of Witchcraft.* London, 1584. (Recent reprints, Brinsley Nicholson, London, 1886 ; Montague Summers, London, 1930.) Book v, chapters i–vi.

SCRIBE, EUGÈNE (and MAZÈRES). *Le Loup-garou.* Opéra-comique. Paris, 1827. Music by Mlle Bertin.

SÉBILLOT, PAUL. *Le Folk-Lore de France.* Paris. 4 tom. : Tom. i (1904), pp. 284–7 ; Tom. ii (1905), pp. 205–6, 373, 437 ; Tom. iii (1906), pp. 54–7 ; Tom. iv (1907), pp. 209–210, 240, 304.

SELIGMANN, GOTTLIEB FRID. *De dubiis hominibus, inquibus forma humana et bruta mista fertur.* Lipsiae, 1679.

SENNERT, DANIEL. *Opera Omnia.* Parisiis, 1641.

SHINKICKI, TAKAHASHI. " *Is lycanthropy confined to the province of Shikohu?* " Tokei, Ijishenshi, 1879. No. 86, 15th November. Text in Japanese.

SIMROCK, KARL JOSEPH. *Deutsche Sagen.* Stuttgart, 1869. p. 467.

SMITH, KIRBY FLOWER. *An Historical Study of the Werwolf in Literature.* Publications of the Modern Language Association of America. Vol. ix, 1 (New Series, vol. ii, 1). Baltimore, 1894. An abstract of this paper under the title *The were-wolf in Latin literature* appeared in the *John Hopkins University Circular*, vol. xii, p. 21, January, 1893 (Baltimore).

SOLDAN-HEPPE. *Geschichte der Hexenprozesse.* München. 2 vols. New ed., n.d.

SPENCE, LEWIS. *The Cult of the Werwolf in Europe.* In : *The Occult Review*, vol. xxxiv, No. 4. October, 1921. pp. 221–6.

SPONDE, JEAN DE. *Homeri Quae Extant Omnia* . . . *Perpetuis item iustisque in Iliade simul et Odysseam Io. Spondani Mauleonensis Commentariis.* Basileæ, folio, 1583. Odyssey, Lib. x, pp. 137–140.

SPRENGEL, K. P. J. See Boettiger, Carl August.

SPRENGER, O.P., JAMES. See under *Malleus Maleficarum.*

STENBOK, COUNT ERIC. *The Other Side. A Breton Legend.* (Fiction.) In : *The Spirit Lamp*, iv, 2nd June, 1893. Oxford. pp. 52–68.

STEPHENS, GEORGE. See Hylten-Cavallius, Gunnar Olaf.

STEWART, CAROLINE TAYLOR. *The Origin of the Werewolf Superstition.* The University of Missouri Studies, vol. ii, No. 3. Social Science Series. Univ. of Missouri, April, 1909.

STOLBERG, GRAFZU, FRIEDRICH LEOPOLD. *Der Wehrwolf.* In the *Deutsches Museum.* Leipzig, 1783. Vol. ii, pp. 155–6.

Stubbe Peeter. A true Discourse Declaring the damnable life and death of one Stubbe Peeter, a most wicked Sorcerer, who in the likenes of a *Woolfe, committed many murders, continuing this* diuelish practise 25. yeeres, killing and de*uouring Men, Woomen, and* Children, *who for the same fact was* taken and executed the 31. of October *last past in the Towne of* Bedbur neer the Cittie of *Collin in Germany.* Trulye translated out of the high Duch. London, [1590].

SULLIVAN, J. M. *The Trial of Gilles Garnier.* In the *Green Bag.* Boston, 1903. Vol. xv, p. 86.

SUMMERS, MONTAGUE. *The Geography of Witchcraft.* London, 1927. pp. 22–6, 396–7, 399–400, 401, 447–8.

—— *The Vampire: His Kith and Kin.* London, 1928. pp. 21, 165–7.

—— *The Vampire in Europe.* London, 1929. pp. 19–20, 41–2.

SWEM, CHARLES. *Were Wolf.* London, n.d. [1929]. (Fiction.)

THOMAS, NORTHCOTE WHITRIDGE. *Werwolf.* In the *Encyclopœdia Britannica*, 11th ed., vol. xxviii, Cambridge, 1911.

—— *Lycanthropy.* Ibid., vol. xvii.

THOMASIUS, JOANNES. *De transformatione hominum in bruta.* Lipsiae, 1673.

THYRAEUS, S.J., PETRUS. *De Uariis tam Spirituum quam Uiuorum Hominum Prodigiosis Apparitionibus* . . . Coloniae Agrippinae, 1594. Lib. ii, cap. xv—cap. xxv, pp. 111–186.

TOMSON, GRAHAM R. *A Ballad of the Were-wolf.* In *Macmillan's Magazine.* London, 1890. Vol. lxii, p. 368.

TOZER, HENRY FANSHAWE. *Researches in the Highlands of Turkey.* London, 1869. 2 vols. Vol. ii, chap. xxi, pp. 80–98.

TYLOR, SIR EDWARD BURNETT. *Primitive Culture.* 2nd ed. London, 1873. 2 vols.

VAIR, LEONARD. *De Fascino Libri Tres* . . . Leonardo Vairo, Beneuentano, Ordinis S. Benedicti Canonico regulari, ac sacrae Theologiae Doctore sapientissimo, auctore. Parisiis, 1583. Liber ii, cap. xii, pp. 160–172. See also pp. 5, 14, 41, 115–16.

Varulven. Dansk Folkeblad. Kjøbenhavn, 1842. Aargang 7, p. 235.

VASCONCELLOS, JOSE LEITE DE. *Bibliotheca ethnographica portugueza.* I. *Tradiçóes populares de Portugal.* XI. *Entidades sobrenaturales.* Porto, 1882.

VECKENSTEDT, EDMOND. *Wendische Sagen, Märchen und abergläubische Gebräuchte.* Graz, 1880. No. xli, Der Werwolf, p. 395.

VERSTEGAN, RICHARD. (Richard Rowlands.) *A Restitution of Decayed Intelligence.* Antwerp, 1605. pp. 286–7.

VINCENT OF BEAUVAIS. *Speculum Naturale.* Lib. ii, cap. xix. *Opera*, Venice, 1591. Tom. i, p. 26.

Volsunga Saga: The Story of the Volsungs and Niblungs. Translated from the Icelandic by Eiríkir Magnússon and William Morris. Ed. by H. Halliday Sparling. London, 1888. "The Camelot Series." Chapters v and viii.

WALPOLE, HUGH. *All Souls' Night: A Book of Stories.* 1933. (Fiction.)

WANTSCHERUS, CHRISTOPHERUS. *De lupo et lycanthropia.* Wittebergae, 1666.

WEBSTER, JOHN. *The Displaying of Supposed Witchcraft.* London, 1677. pp. 33, 68–9, 86, 91–7.

Der Weerwolf. In *Taschenbuch für die vaterländische Geschichte. Herausgegeben durch die Freyherren von Hormayr und von Mednyansky.* Wien, 1828. Jahrg. ix, pp. 299–312.

The Wehr Wolf. In *The Story-Teller, or Journal of Fiction.* London, 1833. Vol. ii. (Fiction.)

Wehrwolves. In *Household Words.* London, 1857. Vol. xv, pp. 405–8.

A Were-buffalo. In *Saturday Review.* London, 1894. Vol. lxxviii, pp. 288–9.

Were-wolves. In *The Anglo-American.* New York, 1846. Vol. vi, pp. 423–4.

Werewolves. In *All the Year Round.* London, 1883. Vol. lii, pp. 399–403. Reprinted in *The Eclectic Magazine of Foreign Literature, Science, and Art.* New York, 1884. Vol. xxxix, pp. 59–63.

WEYER, JOHANN. *Ioannis Wieri. Opera Omnia.* Amstedolami, 1660. *De Lamiis,* iii, cap. x, pp. 189–190.

—— *De Magorum Infamium Poena,* vi, cap. xiii and cap. xiv, pp. 494–502.

—— *De Lamiis,* cap. xiv, pp. 710–12.

WHISHAW, FRED. *The Were-wolf.* In *Temple Bar.* London, 1902. Vol. cxxvi, pp. 568–579. (Fiction.) Reprinted in *The Living Age,* vol. ccxxxv, pp. 204–211. Boston, 1902.

WILLIAM OF AUVERGNE. *De Uniuerso.* ii, iii, 13. *Opera Omnia,* 1674. Tom. i, pp. 1048–4.

William of Palerme. See *Guillaume de Palerme.*

Witches and their Craft. Cornhill Magazine. London, 1868. Vol. xviii, pp. 54–72. (Lycanthropy, pp. 69–72.)

WOJEICKI, KAZIMIERZ WLADUSLAW. *Klechdy, Starozytne podania i powiesci ludowe.* Warszawa. i, 101–113, 152–8.

WOLF, JOHANN WILHELM. *Niederländische Sagen.* Leipzig, 1843. No. 242, "Wärwölfin"; No. 243, "Warwolf"; No. 501, "Wärwolf ertrappt"; No. 502, "Der verschwundene Wärwolf"; No. 503, "Wärwolf erlöst."

The Wolf Demon; or, Buffalo Bill and the Barge Mystery. By the Author of Buffalo Bill. "The Penny Serial Story Book." No. 583. 9th March, 1907. London. (Fiction.)

WOLFESHUSIUS, JOANNES FRIDERICUS. *De Lycanthropis: an verè illi, ut fama est, luporum & aliarum bestiarum formis induantur, Problema Philosophicum. Pro sententia Joan. Bodini Iurecos. Galli . . . adversus dissentaneas aliquorum opiniones noviter assertum.* Lipsiae, 1591.

WYNTER, ANDREW. *Were-wolves and lycanthropy.* In *Fruit between the leaves.* London, 1875. pp. 106–122.

YOUNG, ALEXANDER. *A terrible superstition.* In *Appleton's Journal.* New York, 1872. Vol. ix, pp. 168–171.

Zeitschrift für deutsche Mythologie. Bd. i, pp. 241, 344.

ZIEGRAE, CONRAD. *Disputatio contra Opliantriam, Lycanthropiam, et Metempsychosim.* Witteburgae, 1650.

WITCH OINTMENTS

By Dr. H. J. Norman

IT is not an easy matter to decide what the effects of these, frequently complicated, concoctions may have been. That the effects alleged—transformation of human beings into animals, enabling witches to fly through the air, and so on—could have been produced, may with assurance be denied : but that they could assist in bringing about such illusions of the senses may as readily be maintained. Some of the ingredients were evidently incorporated in the mess merely because of their fantastic nature and their picturesque suggestiveness. The multifariousness of the constituents is reminiscent of the contemporary medical prescriptions in which it was probably hoped that something would hit the mark and produce the desired effect.

Some of the drugs used were very potent—especially if taken internally : but there also seems to be no doubt that absorption would take place through the skin, for it was the custom to mix them with some fatty substance, for example, the fat of children, as mentioned by Wier, by Porta, and by Shadwell in *The Lancashire Witches*, where Mother Demdike refers to the fat of an " unchristen'd brat ". Even so it is unlikely that any considerable amount of the drug could be absorbed in this way : for it was not probable that it could be in any degree of concentration. The chief effect was brought about as the result of the high degree of suggestibility of the individuals, who were undoubtedly in numerous instances psychopathic and mentally deranged.

An example of a common drug and one easily obtained is belladonna (*Atropa Belladonna* with its active principle Atropine), the Deadly Nightshade. It is a powerful poison, acting locally on the sensory nerve-endings and also on the central nervous system. According to Professor Dixon, " in man, after a large dose, there are general excitement, restlessness, vertigo, talkativeness, laughter, and disturbance of vision giving rise to illusions generally of a pleasing character." [1]   The well-known effect of dilatation of the pupils of the eyes might assist in the production of the illusions of sight—the " seeing of visions ".   Henbane (*Hyoscyamus Niger*) also contains potent alkaloids, or active substances.   It is possibly what Shakespeare meant when he spoke of ". . . the insane root that takes the reason prisoner ".   With it there is the tendency to the production of illusions of sight.   Aconite root (from *Aconitum Napellus*), or Monks-hood, contains aconitine and other alkaloids : acts on the sensory nerve-endings, producing tingling, numbness, and anæsthesia : and when absorbed has a definite effect on the heart and on respiration.   Hemlock (*Conium Maculatum*) tends to produce loss of muscular power and eventually paralysis : it is presumed to be the drug taken by Socrates, with the results described by Plato.

The list of potent drugs employed might easily be extended : but it will be gathered from what has already been mentioned that the witches' armamentarium was by no means an ineffective one.   It is a subject which seems to have received much less scientific attention than it deserves : but there was an interesting article written by Dr. Robert Fletcher in 1896 and entitled *The Witches' Pharmacopœia.*[2]

[1] *Manual of Pharmacology*, by Walter E. Dixon, M.D.,etc. Sixth edition : London, 1925.

[2] *Bulletin of The John Hopkins Hospital*, vol. vii, No. 65.

INDEX

Abbeville, 219, 240
Abbott, G. F., 56, 171
Abruzzi, 162
Abyssinia, 21
Acolastus, 69, 124
Acosta, S.J., José de, 56
Actuarius, Joannes, 39, 40
Adagia (Erasmus), 125
Adams, Francis, 38-9
Adelphi, 124
Adils, King, 243
Admirable Histories (Grimeston), 176
Admirable victoire du corps du Dieu (Boulæse), 129
Adone, L', 127
Ady, T., 57
Ælian, 125, 144, 173, 174
Æthelstan, 4, 61
Aëtius, 38-9, 42
Afzelius, Arvad August, 244
Agriopas (Apollas, Copas, Scopas), 139-140
Ainsworth, W. Harrison, 263
Albanesische Studien, 175
Albertus, Magnus, O. P., S., 31, 60, 117, 128, 240
Albigenses, 5
Alcestis, 174
Alcock, Bishop John, 66, 124
Aldrovandi, Ulisse, 64, 105, 124, 126, 240
Alessandri, Alessandro, 126
Alexander of Hales, 87, 96
Alexandra (Lycophron), 136-7
Allacci, Leone, 150
Allridge, T. J., 56
All Souls' Night, 272
Aloisia Sigæa (Meursii *Elegantiae*), 68-9, 126
Alsaharavius, 39, 40
Altdeutsches Wörterbuch, 9
Alte Griecheland im neuen, Das, 174
Altjüdische Zauberwesen, Das, 131
Altomari, Donato Antonio, 42, 45-6
Ambrose, S., 66, 127
Aminta, 127
Amphitruo, 18
Anania, Lorenzo, 84, 92
Anatomy of Melancholy, The, 61, 177
Ancient Laws . . . of England, 52
Ancyra, Synod of, 84
Andrea Corsini, S., 239
Andrew of Wyntoun, 179, 211
Angelo, Bl., di Chivasso, 28, 31-2, 58, 60
Angles, José, O. F. M., 31, 60

Animal Kingdom (Cuvier), 124
Annales Cambriæ, 182
Annales Hirsaugienses, 245
Annales (Zonaras), 126
Anthologia Græca, 125
Antigonus of Carystus, 126, 173
Antiquitates Septentrionales, 129
Antiquitatum Libri (Varro), 140
Antiquités de Vésone, 131
Antoninus, O.P., S., 89
Antoninus Liberalis, 173
Apchon, the wolf-witch of, 228
Apocryphes Ethiopiens, Les, 56
Apollodorus, 186
Apollo Lykaios, Legend and cult of, 143-4, 173-4
Apollonius Rhodius, 144, 173
Apuleius, 19, 27, 55, 75, 80, 83, 156-8, 176
Aquila, Richard Petrus de, 96
Aratus, 126
Arcadia, 184-148, 172
Arcadian wolves, 82
Archives Cosmologiques, 124
Archives Curieuses de France, 240
Arculanus, Joannes, 42-3, 49
Argentine, Richard, 43-4
Aristaenetus, 66, 125
Aristaios, 143
Aristogeiton, 68, 125
Aristophanes of Byzantium, 71, 125
Aristotle, 27, 58, 173, 240
Arkadischen Kulte, Die, 172
Arnoul of Soissons, S., 239
Arrest . . . contre Gilles Garnier, 226-8
Art of Rhetorique, 124
Artemidorus, 71
Asser, 4, 52
Astral Plane, The, 102
Athenæus, 125
Aubrey, John, 71
Aubry, Nicole, 97
Augustine of Hippo, S., 32, 60, 66, 75, 80, 81, 82, 91, 92, 96, 98, 120, 140, 156, 173, 210
Aulnoy, Madame d', 156
Aulus Gellius, 57, 58
Aureoli, Pietro, 31
Ausonius, 68, 125, 126, 172
Austreberte of Pavilly, S., 239
Avicenna, 39, 40, 45

Baal-cults, 136, 141-2
Babiole, 156
Bacon, Lord, 28

falcon-mantles, 242
Farnell, Lewis, 140–1, 143, 144, 178, 174
Fasti (Mantuan), 101, 129
Faust, 101
Faustinianus, 81, 176
Faute de l'Abbé Mouret, La, 241
Fernel, Jean, 79, 127
Feronia, Festival of, 152
Ferry of Souls, The, 272
Field, Eugene, 278
Fillan, S., 239
Fincel, Job, 41, 42, 74, 146, 160, 174
Finnbogi saga, 20
Flagellum Haereticorum, 85
Flagellum Maleficorum (Mamor), 19, 80
Flores Caluinistici, 19
Flores Historiarum (Luard), 176
Flores Theologicarum Quaestionum (Angles), 31
Florimont, La Dame de, 195
Flyting of Dunbar and Kennedie, The, 7
Flyting of Montgomerie and Polwart, The, 8
Folk-lore de France, Le, 181, 241
Folk-lore of Herefordshire, The, 200
Folklore of the Santal Parganas, 56
Forcellini, Egidio, 20
Foreest, Pierre van, 44–5, 49
Forests, Old, in England, Scotland, Ireland, France, Germany, 22
Forster, William, 264
Forgemont, le Docteur, 98
Formulae Ueteres Exorcismorum, 116
Fort, John, 161–2, 266
Fourgères, G., 141
Franche-Comté, werewolves in, 228
Francis of Assissi, S., 239
Franciscans at Bordeaux, 241
Francken, Franz, 104
Frazer, Sir J. G., 171, 178, 175, 215
Freyja, 21, 242, 251
Frigg, 21, 242
Froto III, 244
Fulgosi, Baptista, 160
Fuller, Thomas, 61
Fur-bearing Animals, 124

Gaboriaut, Jeanne, 232
Gaillard, Clauda, 122–8, 280
Galen, 13, 27, 127
Gallia Christiana, 127, 240, 241
Gandillon, Perrenette, 122, 229
Gandillon, Pierre and George, 112, 116, 229
Garassus, S.J., François, 128
Garnier, Gilles, 62, 76, 78, 98, 128, 225–8
Gaston III de Foix, 11

Gauld, H. Drummond, 198
Gautier, A.-J.-M., 131
Gellert, 182, 212
Gemma, Cornelius, 27
Genesis, 124
Gens the Solitary, S., 239
Geographica (Strabo), 142, 178
Geography of Witchcraft, The, 59, 62, 176, 215
Geoponika, 127
George I, Elector of Saxony, 24
Georgics, 124
George, S., 110
Gervase of Tilbury, 6, 16–17, 112, 118, 185, 187, 194, 218
Geschichte des Hexenwahns (Hansen), 127
Geschichte der Lustseuche im Alterhume, 178
Gesetze der Angelsachen, Die, 52
Gesner, K., 124
Gesta Regum Anglorum, 159, 176
Gévaudan, the Wild Beast of, 235–6
Ghosts and Marvels (Collins), 263
Ghost Tales and Legends (Gauld), 198
Giffard, George, 59, 60
Giles, Herbert A., 56
Giraldus Cambrensis, 207–210, 216
Giustiniani, S. Lorenzo, 118
Glaber, Raoul, 5
Glanvil, Joseph, 196–7
Glossarium Germanicum, 9, 129
Godefroy, Frédéric, 10, 58
Godelmann, Johann Georg, 49, 62, 90
Godfrey of Fontaines, 80
Godwin, William, 265
Golding, Arthur, 171
Golden Bough, The, 175, 215
Gordonius, Bernard, 22, 48, 57
Goulart, Simon, 176
Graecorum hodie quorundam opinationibus, De, 175
Graese, Johann Georg Theodor, 174
Grant, John Cameron, 56, 269
Gratian the canonist, 84
Greek Lexicon (Sophocles), 18
Gregory Nanzianzen, S., 19
Gregory the Great, Pope S., 174
Gregory VII, Pope S., 251
Grenier, Jean, 105, 112, 117–18, 123, 231–4, 238
Grenier, Pierre, 232, 234
Griechische und albanesische Märchen, 13, 53
Grillandus, Paulus, 24, 49, 57, 62
Grimeston, Edward, 176
Grimm, Baron, 235–6, 241
Grimm, Jacob, 181
Groot, J. J. M. de, 56
Grundriss der Germanischen Philologie, 9